Introduction to the Old Testament

Biblical Hermeneutics Rediscovered

The Series as the name suggests will focus on Biblical Hermeneutics, i.e., literary works concerned with methods of interpreting the Old and New Testaments of Bible via different stream of topics like Literature & Poetry, Indigenous Philosophizing, Ethical response towards Ecology, Health & Healing, Science & Technology, Feminist Theology, Sociological approach towards Human Rights, Law & Politics, Arts, History of Ideas, Ancient Civilizations, Cultural Contiguity, Religious Cosmologies & Mysticism, Appraisal of various Theologians, World Peace & Harmony, Global Capitalism, Network Marketing, Cybertheology, Population & Demographics, Epigraphic Studies, Contextualized Education, and many others. We welcome a Mss. on any topic/s mentioned, whether they are original works, scholarly monographs, collections of conference papers, revised dissertations, or translations of historical documents. Through the Series we, the Publishers, are striving to put forward published works that may help Institutions, Academic Bodies, Researchers, Scholars and the World at large in furthering their respective knowledge and understanding on the concerned subject. We welcome your comments on our efforts and further suggestions on how we can enshrine new ray of analysing & explaining the written Texts through our upcoming books.

Biblical Hermeneutics Rediscovered - 18

Introduction to the Old Testament

Tracing the History, Culture & Scripture of Ancient Israel

Kondasingu Jesurathnam

Christian World Imprints

Edition: 2022

Christian World Imprints
Christian Publishing & Books from India
C-3, Wazirpur Industrial Area
Delhi-110052
cwidelhi2017@gmail.com
www.ChristianWorldImprints.com
Phone: +91 11 41526079

ISBN: 978-93-5148-295-6 (HB)
ISBN: 978-93-5148-296-3 (PB)

Cover design: Rev. Paul Karunakar Nalla

Printed in India.

This work is dedicated to the loving memory
of my beloved brother late Kondasingu Suresh Babu,
whose love and contribution in my life
cannot be forgotten.

Contents

Preface

Writing an introduction to any part of the Holy Bible is not an easy task. I realized it only after the beginning of my writing. I realized this more and more by the time I completed my writing. It has been a challenging as well as exhilarating task to begin and complete writing an introductory volume to the history and content of the Old Testament. It has been my desire to work on a project like this since I began my teaching of the Old Testament introduction in late 1990s to my BD and MDiv students. I realized the passion and dedication of several authors who wanted to communicate God's revelation and message to this world. I also realized that I am privileged to study and teach, and also appropriate the content of the Hebrew Bible to my students and fellow travellers in my theological journey. More I teach and study the Hebrew Bible more I come to realize that one cannot exhaust the vast amount of knowledge to be pursued in the study of Hebrew Bible. Keeping this limitation in mind, the objectives of this book can be stated as follows:

- To trace the history and culture of Ancient Israel from the beginning to the Greek Period.
- To make a general survey on the historical background, content, style, composition, structure and theological focus of different books in the Old Testament.
- To know the nature and the canonical status of different Old Testament books.
- To be aquainted with some important post-biblical Jewish writings and their significance.

In the Indian context, many theological schools both the mainline as well as small denominational ones make the teaching of the Hebrew Bible mandatory. Some would even think that the study of the Hebrew Bible is indispensable and mandatory to the study of the New Testament. While such an attitude is not really encouraging I want the readers to see the worth of the Old Testament in its own right and study it as a part of the Holy Scripture and

God's revelation. With that focus in mind if the readers look at the content of this book it will be of immense value for their knowledge and understanding of the entire Bible. I have not presented any implications of the discussed topics in the present socio-ecclesial context. It is up to the readers to do so in their own socio-cultural and ecclesial contexts.

In the light of above discussion, I would like to briefly explain the structure of the material presented in this book as follows:

The book contains three main sections: the first section deals with the material on the nature, inspiration and authority of the Bible. Some amount of background information is provided on the people and lands in so far as they are directly and indirectly related to Ancient Israel. The second section deals with the topics and issues related to the history of ancient Israel from her beginnings till the Greek period and briefly in the post-biblical period. The third section gives a brief survey on different sections and books of the Old Testament. This section also briefly introduces post-biblical Jewish writings and a brief discussion on the Canonization of the Hebrew Bible. Before coming to the discussion of the various books a brief process of the formation of the books of the Old Testament is discussed. Where possible some books are elaborately discussed. This section concludes with the two major issues of formation of the Old Testament and the issue of canonization of the books of the Old Testament. In all these sections very minimum foot notes is added. It is upto the readers to supplement the material in this book with additional reading material and bibliographic sources supplied at the end of this book. This book deliberately skipped the matters concerning the biblical and exegetical tools for the want of space. Perhaps, those issues would be covered in another separate volume. The readers are encouraged to consult other books and materials for the area of biblical exegetical and interpretive tools.

Several people must be thanked at this juncture for making my task easier and memorable. First of all, I thank God Almighty for giving me strength and grace to begin and complete this project. I thank all my students in the past and the present at various levels like undergraduate, postgraduate and doctoral. But for my interaction with them at various points I would not have got such a clarity on many topics and complex issues of this subject. I thank all of them for making my knowledge clear and progressive by their pointed and perceptive questions. I express my sincere thanks to Mr. A. Sam Thomas a special Old Testament student at UTC for his work in formatting this book. I thank Mr. Sudhanshu Kanda and the entire staff of Christian World Imprints, New Delhi, for accepting this work and doing an excellent job in its publication within a short span of time. I thank many libraries and staff in those places whose assistance has immensely helped me to search and find what I am looking for. Above all, I thank the staff at UTC library who are always willing to help me with their smiling approach. I thank the Biblical department and all my colleagues at UTC for their kind help and encouragement. I thank Rev. Paul Karunakar Nalla, Postgraduate student of Theology for his beautiful cover design painting. I express my gratitude to my maternal uncle Rev. T. Punnaiah and aunty Grace for their prayers and support. I thank my wife Beatrice Veena and son David Sunil Wesley Raju for their love and support. Above all, I thank my younger brother late Mr. K. Suresh Babu, who loved me so much and in whose name I dedicate this work.

I hope and pray that this critical Introduction to the Old Testament will inspire many young and old scholars to read and appropriate God's word for their daily living.

Bangalore, 46
May 2018.

List of Abbreviations

ANE	Ancient Near East
ANET	Ancient Near Eastern Texts edited by J. B. Pritchard
Ant.	Josephus' Antiquities
AWA	Ancient West Asia
BCE	Before Common Era
BJ	Josephus' Jewish War (Bellum judaicum)
CE	Common Era
Cf.	Compare
Ft.	Feet
Kms	Kilometers
LXX	The Sepuagint
MT	The Masoretic Text
OT	Old Testament
TANAK	Torah, Nebiim and Ketuvim
UTC	United Theological College, Bangalore

Biblical/Extra-biblical Abbreviations

Old Testament (OT)

Gen
Exod
Lev
Numb
Deut
Josh
Judg
Ruth
1-2 Sam
1-2 Kgs
1-2 Chron
Ezra
Neh
Esther
Job
Ps/Pss
Prov
Eccl
S. Song
Isa
Jer
Lam
Ezek
Dan
Hos
Joel
Amos
Obad
Jonah
Micah
Nah
Hab
Zeph
Hag
Zech
Mal

New Testament (NT)

Matt
I Cor
Eph
Col
Rev
Extra Biblical Books

1 QS: Community Rule/Manual of Discpline

1 QM: War Scroll
1 Q Gen AP: Genesis Apocryphon

Section I

Introduction

Chapter 1

Introduction

1. NATURE OF THE BIBLE: INSPIRATION AND AUTHORITY

The word "Bible" is derived from the Old French word *bible* based on Latin *biblia* and in Greek *biblia* means "books". This word refers to the scriptures of the Christian Church, and it may also denote "the Canon of the Jewish scriptures."

The Church of England is perfectly clear in its formularies as to the nature of the Bible. The Bible is the Word of God (e.g. Articles 19 & 20). This is not just a title. It recognizes that the Bible is what God has spoken. Therefore, in the Homily entitled "An Information for them which take offence at certain places of the Holy Scripture" it is plainly stated that 'the whole Scriptures, says St. Paul, were given by the **inspiration of God (2 Timothy 3:16).** Inspiration in the 16th Century was not a slippery term as it is today but was much closer to the actual bible meaning – "God breathed." This fact is spelt out in homily. "The Scriptures were not brought unto us by the will of man; but holy men of God, as witnessed by St. Peter, whospoke as they were moved by the Holy Spirit of God." The fact that the Bible is the Word of God has a very important consequence - it is without error. The homily speaks of the "infallible word." Prior to the 20th century this word was perfectly well understood as meaning without error. Unfortunately, it is often now necessary to use the word inerrant because some have hijacked 'infallible' to mean true in spiritual matters but not in matters of fact. The character of the Word of God as infallible or inerrant derives from the very character of God Himself. No-one can claim to have proved that the Bible is true, such a claim would be ludicrous since much of what it says concerns events still in the future. Rather, the Bible is accepted as utterly true and utterly trustworthy because that is the character of its author. There are solid grounds for asserting that the Bible has been shown to be reliable when it has been tested. But, ultimately, it is a matter of faith that God and Father of our Lord Jesus Christ, the God of Abraham, Isaac and Jacob is true in his very character and therefore His Word is Truth. Because the Bible is God's Word and is without error it is the supreme authority for the Church. The Thirty-Nine Articles are very plain on this point. The Church can err (Articles 19) and therefore it is not lawful for it to ordain anything that is contrary to God's Word written (Article 20). Indeed, because of the supremacy of the Word the Church must ensure that it doesn't set one part of scripture against another (Article 20).

There were many heretics in the early church who would not accept the teaching of the Bible. Some accepted certain books but would not accept the rest. Others, such as Marcion took particular books and cut out from them all the bits they didn't like. This has been a common practice amongst some academics and many church leaders for the last century and a half. More difficult to comprehend are the now widespread open evangelicals. Since, there is no agreed definition of this term some care is needed. Many call themselves open simply because they wish to be more open to new ways of doing things and more open to people of other backgrounds than their forbears were. However, some open evangelicals consciously define themselves in relation to biblical inerrancy. They are not prepared to accept that the Bible is true in all its detail. They may accept that the fundamental spiritual truths are true, but not the detail. There is no shortage of variations on this theme but all boil down to the same thing. The Bible is not reliable in all that it says. Surely, the inference of this is that either the Bible is not the Word of God in its entirety, or God is not reliable. Either way this is a significant departure from historic evangelicalism and from historic Anglicanism.

Is the Bible the Word of God in its entirety or is it not? This is the issue that confronts us today. Until it is clear what the nature of the Bible is there is no point in arguing about methods of interpretation. If someone thinks that the Bible simply contains the Word of God then presumably they will make it their utmost priority to determine what exactly God's Word is and what is not. Their approach to interpretation will depend upon the extent to which the extent a particular passage is God's Word and to what extent they think it is something else. We will approach the Bible with a great deal of reverence and humility knowing that we are handling the oracles of the living God. As **Justin Martyr** commented when dealing with difficult passages:

> Since I am entirely convinced that no Scripture contradicts another, I will rather acknowledge that I do not understand what is written. We will also believe that God has spoken and presumably wished therefore that we should hear and has spoken in ways that are at

> least intelligible to us. On the whole we should not expect the Bible to be difficult or to require immense expertise to understand it. We will believe that because God has spoken then what matters supremely in interpreting the Bible is not how we read the Bible, but what God its author intends to teach us through it. This will make us particularly eager to test our understanding today against that of Christians through the ages.[1]

Finally, we will want to ensure that if God has spoken, we are eager to listen. As the Homily says:

> the Holy Scriptures are God's treasure-house; wherein are found all things needful for us to see, to hear, to learn, and to believe, necessary for the attaining of eternal life. God therefore, for his mercies' sake, vouchsafe to purify our minds through faith in his Son Jesus Christ, and to instil the heavenly drops of his grace into our hard stony hearts, to supple the same, that we be not deriders of his infallible word; but that with all humbleness of mind and Christian reverence, we may endeavour ourselves, to hear and to read his sacred Scriptures, and inwardly so to digest them, as shall be to the comfort of our souls, and sanctification of his holy Name: to whom, with the Son and the Holy Ghost, three persons and one living God, be all laud, honour, and praise, for ever and ever. Amen.[2]

In the above light, we can conclude that by all means the Holy Scripture was well and strongly defended as a rule and canon of Christian faith both by the early church and in the subsequent eras and of course the idea of sola scriptural during reformation period has reclaimed the diminished value of scripture over against the traditions of the church.

1.1. Formation of the Bible

The Hebrew Bible (or the Old Testament) occupies a unique place in our contemporary society. Subtle allusions to these ancient texts find their way into films, public debates, and even political speeches. References to what "the Bible says" in contemporary culture often give the impression that these ancient texts appeared without any human assistance; but in fact the writing, editing, and collecting of these texts were the result of human activity over the centuries.

Prior to modern times, readers assumed that the texts of the Hebrew Bible were composed by important figures from Israel's history—individuals

---

1 Justyn Martyr and his apologetic speech on the Holy Scripture and its inspiration.

2 Ibid.

like Moses, Joshua, or Samuel, who took it upon themselves to record their experiences. This traditional understanding of biblical authorship originated in the texts themselves. For example, several passages refer to Moses writing God's commands (Exod 17:14, Exod 24:4, Exod 34:28, Numb 33:2, Deut 31:9, Deut 31:22), and many others make mention of the "law(s) of Moses" (for example, Josh 8:30-31, 2Kgs 14:6, Ezra 3:2). Clues like these led readers to identify Moses as the author of the Pentateuch.

Similarly, because Solomon often appears in the Wisdom literature and is remembered as an exceptionally wise individual (1Kgs 4:29-34), premodern readers credited Solomon with writing books such as the Song of Songs (Song 1:1), Ecclesiastes (Eccl 1:1, Eccl 1:12), and major portions of Proverbs (Prov 1:1, Prov 10:1). Associations like these not only provided a straightforward explanation of how the Hebrew Bible came into being, they also lent the collection a special authority. As faithful accounts from biblical heroes, these texts were believed to be trustworthy representations of Israel's experience and God's character. According to this traditional perspective, the Hebrew Bible was simply a collection of individually authored texts composed and collected over several centuries (from about the 13th century through the fifth century B.C.E.).

With the dawn of the modern era, however, scholars began to propose other models for the Hebrew Bible's formation in light of newer reading methods and the textual details they revealed. Scholars in classical studies had developed particular ways of analysing ancient Greek and Roman literature in order to determine how those texts were composed, when they were written, how they were edited, and what situations brought them about. As early as the 17th century, biblical scholars began to adopt these methods and apply them to the Hebrew Bible. Their analyses first took note of obvious issues in the flow of Pentateuchal stories—things like the repetition of a story, multiple introductions or changes in writing style and grammar within a story, or interruptions in plot.

Instead of attempting to resolve these narrative problems by maintaining Mosaic authorship, modern scholars saw these hurdles as clues to a different model for the Hebrew Bible's composition. This newer model understood the Bible to be the result of an extended writing, editing, and compiling process that brought individual traditions together into larger books over a period of time. These insights were further confirmed by the increase of archaeological data and a growing understanding of how other cultures recorded, edited, and preserved their important texts. Like these other texts, the Bible is likely not the work of prominent individuals. Rather, the Bible is the product of generations of authors and editors who wrote, edited, and supplemented these books across Israelite, Judean, and Jewish history.

Although, the last two centuries have witnessed a variety of theories about how the Hebrew Bible came into being, most scholars today conclude that the first major period of literary production was not during the time of Moses (13th century B.C.E.) but instead during the political peak of the southern kingdom of Judah (eighth–sixth centuries B.C.E.). This is not to say that biblical texts were not written earlier than this time. Northern traditions (for example, Jacob stories that take place in northern locations such as Bethel) were likely written prior to the northern kingdom of Israel's destruction in 722 B.C.E., and texts like the earliest portions of Proverbs, some of the royal psalms, or even the Covenant Code (Exod 20:19-23:33) may date as early as the 9th century B.C.E. However, most scholars no longer attribute large blocks of written material to the time of the "united monarchy." On the contrary, archaeology has shown that Judah developed a writing culture quite late in its history, with the 8th and 7th centuries marking the zenith.

This does not mean, however, that the *majority* of the biblical corpus was composed during the later period of the Judean monarchy, nor does it suggest that exilic and postexilic Judeans had only a slight editorial role in the formation of the Hebrew Bible. In fact, critical scholars understand much of the Hebrew Bible (especially the Pentateuch) to be a product of the Persian period (sixth–third centuries B.C.E.). Many texts composed during the exile (for example, Ezekiel and Deutero-Isaiah) and after (for example, the Priestly source of the Pentateuch, Ezra-Nehemiah, and Daniel). Scribes from these periods continually edited and supplemented whatever written traditions they inherited from pre-exilic times. The biblical texts as they now stand (from Pentateuch to Prophets) are either the written by or the editorial product of Persian and Hellenistic Jews.

Although, "editing" may imply tampering with or misrepresenting "authentic" or "original" writings of older generations, scholars now understand that the scribal revision of texts was intended not to deceive new readers but rather to make sense of the previous materials for their present circumstances. Thus, editing, adding, and combining were ways of faithfully receiving and interpreting Israel's stories and writings for the readers who lived after the exile. Within the Hebrew Bible itself, we can witness the fascinating history of how generations of readers appropriated the stories of those who preceded them.

1.2. Formation of TANAK (The Hebrew Bible or The Old Testament)

The Hebrew Bible is often called MT (The Masoretic Text) is a collection of twenty-four books written in Hebrew (except few passages in Aramaic). The Texts receptus (received text) is from the 10th century MSS esp. from Codex Leningradensis, out of this text the present Hebrew text is printed.Originally the text was with only consonants, but later supplied with vowels by Masorates.

This is the basic text from which several English translations are rendered. The division of the Hebrew Bible based on the above codex is as follows:

The Law: (The Torah): It is the basic core of Jewish and Hebrew Scriptures containing five books often called the Pentateuch, the five volumed work. The books include in this section are: Genesis, Exodus, Leviticus Numbers and Deuteronomy.

The Prophets: (Heb. Nebi'im): It is furtherdivided into two sections:

Former Prophets: Joshua, Judges, Samuel, Kings.

Latter Prophets: Isaiah, Jeremiah, Ezekiel (Major Prophets), and 12 minor Prophets: Hosea, Joel, Amos, Obadiah, Jonah, Micah, Nahum, Habakkuk, Zephaniah, Haggai, Zachariah, Malachi.

The Writings: (Heb. Ketubim): These are books lately composed and added to the Hebrew Bible. They include Psalms, Job, Proverbs, Ruth, Song of Solomon, Ecclesiastes, Lamentations, Esther Daniel, Ezra-Nehemiah, Chronicles.

The **Tanakh** Hebrew: תַּנַ״ךְ, Pronounced as *Tenakh*, *Tenak*, *Tanach*) or ***Mikra*** is the canon of the Hebrew Bible. The traditional Hebrew text is known as the Masoretic Text. *Tanakh* is an acronym of the first Hebrew letter of each of the Masoretic Text's three traditional subdivisions: Torah ("Teaching", also known as the Five Books of Moses), Nevi'im ("Prophets") and Ketuvim ("Writings")—hence ***TaNaKh***. The name "*Mikra"* (מקרא), meaning "that which is read", is another Hebrew word for the *Tanakh*. The books of the Tanakh were passed on by each generation, and according to rabbinic tradition were accompanied by an oral tradition, called the Oral Torah.

1.3. Development of the Hebrew Bible Canon

There is no scholarly consensus as to when the Hebrew Bible canon was fixed. Some scholars argue that it was fixed by the Hasmonean dynasty, while others argue it was not fixed until the second century CE or even later. According to the Talmud much of the contents of the Tanakh was compiled by the men of the Great Assembly (*Anshei K'nesset HaGedolah*), a task completed in 450 BCE, and has remained unchanged since that date. Formal closure of the canon has often been ascribed to Rabbinic Judaism after the destruction of the First Temple in 587 BCE. The twenty-four book canon is mentioned in the Midrash Koheleth 12:12.

Language and pronunciation: The original writing system of the Hebrew text was an abjad: consonants written with some applied vowel letters ("*matres lectionis*"). During the early Middle Ages scholars known as the Masoretes created a single formalized system of vocalization. This was chiefly done by Aaron ben Moses ben Asher, in the Tiberias school, based on the oral tradition for reading the Tanakh, hence the name Tiberian vocalization. It also included some innovations of Ben Naftali and the Babylonian exiles. Despite the comparatively late process of codification, some traditional sources and some Orthodox Jews hold the pronunciation and cantillation to derive from the revelation at Sinai, since it is impossible to read the original text without pronunciations and cantillation pauses. The combination of a text (מקרא *mikra*), pronunciation (ניקוד *niqqud*) and cantillation (טעמים *te`amim*) enable the reader to understand both the simple meaning and the nuances in sentence flow of the text.

Books of the Tanakh with more details: As was noted above the Tanakh consists of twenty-four books: it counts as one book each Samuel, Kings, Chronicles and Ezra-Nehemiah and counts *Trei Asar* (תרי עשר, the Twelve Prophets; literally "twelve") as a single book.

a) Torah: its books (תּוֹרָה, literally "teaching") consists of five books, commonly referred to as the "Five Books of Moses". Printed versions of the Torah are often called *Chamisha Chumshei Torah* (חמישה חומשי הורת, literally the "five-sections of the Torah"), and informally a *Chumash.*

In Hebrew, the five books of the Torah are identified by the first prominent word in each book.

- Bereshit (בְּרֵאשִׁית, literally "In the beginning") - Genesis
- Shemot (שְׁמוֹת, literally "Names") - Exodus
- Vayikra (ויקרא, literally "And He called") - Leviticus
- Bəmidbar (במדבר, literally "In the desert [of]") - Numbers
- Devarim (דברים, literally "Things" or "Words") - Deuteronomy

b) Nevi'im: its books

- Former Prophets Joshua, Judges, Samuel, Kings
- Latter Prophets (major): Isaiah, Jeremiah and Ezekiel
- Latter Prophets (Twelve minor): Hosea, Joel, Amos, Obadiah, Jonah, Micah, Nahum, Habakkuk, Zephaniah, Haggai, Zechariah and Malachi.

c) Ketuvim: its books

Three Poetic Books: Psalms, Proverbs and Job in some manuscripts (and some printed editions), Psalms, Proverbs and Job are presented in a special two-column form emphasizing the parallel stichs in the verses, which are a function of their poetry. Collectively, these three books are known as *Sifrei Emet* (an acronym of the titles in Hebrew, איוב, משלי, תהלים yields *Emet* אמ"ת, which is also the Hebrew for "truth"). These three books are also the only ones in Tanakh with a special system of cantillation notes that are designed to emphasize parallel stichs within verses. However, the beginning and end of the book of Job are in the normal prose system.

d) **Five Megilloth (Scrolls)**: Song of Songs, Ruth, Lamentations, Ecclesiastes, and Esther - The five relatively short books of the Song of Songs, the Book of Ruth, the Book of Lamentations, Ecclesiastes and the Book of Estherare collectively known as the *Hamesh Megillot* (Five Megillot). These are the latest books collected and designated as "authoritative" in the Jewish canon even though they were not complete until the 2nd century CE. These scrolls are traditionally read over the course of the year in many Jewish communities. The list below presents them in the order they are read in the synagogue on holidays, beginning with the Song of Solomon on Passover.

e) **Other Books:** Daniel, Ezra-Nehemiah and Chronicles - Besides the three poetic books and the five scrolls, the remaining books in Ketuvim are Daniel, Ezra–Nehemiah and Chronicles. Although, there is no formal grouping for these books in the Jewish tradition, they nevertheless share a number of distinguishing characteristics.

- Their narratives all openly describe relatively late events (i.e. the Babylonian captivity and the subsequent restoration of Zion).
- The Talmudic tradition ascribes late authorship to all of them.
- Two of them (Daniel and Ezra) are the only books in Tanakh with significant portions in Aramaic.

The following list presents the books of Ketuvim in the order they appear in most printed editions. It also divides them into three subgroups based on the distinctiveness of *Sifrei Emet* and *Hamesh Megillot*.

The three poetic books (*Sifrei Emet*)

- Tehillim (Psalms) תְהִלִּים
- Mishlei (Book of Proverbs) מִשְׁלֵי
- Iyyôbh (Book of Job) אִיּוֹב

The Five Megillot (*Hamesh Megillot*)

- Shīr Hashīrīm (Song of Songs) or (Song of Solomon) שִׁיר הַשִּׁירִים (Passover)
- Rūth (Book of Ruth) רוּת (Shavuot)
- Eikhah (Lamentations) איכה (Ninth of Av or Tisha B'Av) [Also called *Kinnot* in Hebrew.]
- Qōheleth (Ecclesiastes) קהלת (Sukkot)
- Estēr (Book of Esther) אֶסְתֵר (Purim)

Other books

- Dānî'ēl (Book of Daniel) דָּנִיֵּאל

- ‘Ezrā (Book of Ezra-Book of Nehemiah) עזרא
- Divrei ha-Yamim (Chronicles) דברי הימים

The Jewish textual tradition never finalized the order of the books in Ketuvim. The Babylonian Talmud (Baba Batra 14b-15a) gives their order as Ruth, Psalms, Job, Proverbs, Ecclesiastes, Song of Solomon, Lamentations of Jeremiah, Daniel, Scroll of Esther, Ezra, Chronicles.

In Tiberian Masoretic codices, including the Aleppo Codex and the Leningrad Codex, and often in old Spanish manuscripts as well, the order is Chronicles, Psalms, Job, Proverbs, Ruth, Song of Solomon, Ecclesiastes, Lamentations of Jeremiah, Esther, Daniel, Ezra.

Translations

- *The Holy Scriptures According to the Masoretic Text: A New Translation with the aid of Previous Versions & with the Constant Consultation of Jewish Authorities* was published in 1917 by the Jewish Publication Society. It was replaced by their *Tanakh* in 1985
- *Tanakh*, Jewish Publication Society, 1985, ISBN 0-8276-0252-9
- *Tanach: The Stone Edition*, Hebrew with English translation, Mesorah Publications, 1996, ISBN 0-89906-269-5, named after benefactor Irving I. Stone.
- Tanakh Ram, an ongoing translation to Modern Hebrew (2010-) by Avraham Ahuvya (RAM Publishing House Ltd. and Miskal Ltd.)

Jewish Commentaries:

There are two major approaches towards study of, and commentary on, the Tanakh. In the Jewish community, the classical approach is religious study of the Bible, where it is assumed that the Bible is divinely inspired. Another approach is to study the Bible as a human creation. In this approach, Biblical studies can be considered as a sub-field of religious studies. The later practice, when applied to the Torah, is considered heresy by the Orthodox Jewish community. As such, much modern day Bible commentary written by non-Orthodox authors is considered forbidden by rabbis teaching in Orthodox yeshivas. Some classical rabbinic commentators, such as Abraham Ibn Ezra, Gersonides, and Maimonides, used many elements of contemporary biblical criticism, including their knowledge of history, science, and philology. Their use of historical and scientific analysis of the Bible was considered acceptable by historic Judaism due to the author’s faith commitment to the idea that God revealed the Torah to Moses on Mount Sinai.

The Modern Orthodox Jewish community allows for a wider array of biblical criticism to be used for biblical books outside of the Torah, and a few Orthodox commentaries now incorporate many of the techniques previously found in the academic world, e.g. the *Da’at Miqra* series. Non-Orthodox Jews, including those affiliated with Conservative Judaism and Reform Judaism, accept both traditional and secular approaches to Bible studies. "Jewish commentaries on the Bible", discusses Jewish Tanakh commentaries from the Targums to classical rabbinic literature, the midrash literature, the classical medieval commentators, and modern day commentaries.

The above mentioned Hebrew Bible had its earliest form of translation (The Pentateuch Part) in the 3rd century B.C.E in Greek. This collection of translation is called The Septuagint (LXX), containing not only the books of Hebrew Bible but also other books. Although there are variations in different MSS the following are the most commonly found books in addition to what is in the Hebrew Bible. They include 1 Esdras, The Wisdom of Solomon, the wisdom of Ben Sirach (Ecclesiasticus), Judith, Tobit, Baruch, the letter of Jeremiah, 4 books of Maccabees, plus additions to the books in the MT, notably additions to Daniel (Susanna, Bel and the Dragon, the Prayer of Azariah and the Song of the three youngmen) and additions to the book of Esther. Christian Bible contains both the Old and the New Testament. For the Roman Catholic, and the Eastern Church the OT is based on Lxx. While most Protestant churches accept books of the Hebrew Bible (MT) as their canon, the apocryphal books are not accepted for public reading in the Protestant churches but they recognize them as useful for private meditation and devotion.

2. GEOGRAPHY OF PALESTINE, THE FERTILE CRESCENT

Before entering into the proper historical details of the people of the Old Testament and also their surroundings, it would be appropriate to look into the area and its significance in terms of its vitality and rich resources available. By all means we are only presenting a brief and quick survey of the region in order to show its significance in the ancient world.

2.1. Limitation of the Region

Palestine is insignificant in area; in the OT it is often elliptically referred to by the expression "from Dan to Beer-Sheba". In other words, it includes the territory stretching from Dan, at the sources of the Jordan to the north down to Beer-Sheba in the northern part of the Negab desert in the South, a distance of only about 250 to 300 kms. From the western boundary, i.e., the Mediterranean, to the traditional eastern one the river Jordan, the distance is about 50 km in the northern part of the country and about 120 km in the southern part. Under ordinary conditions one would expect this area to be politically organized under some central authority. But it has not been done so because of: the lack of natural boundaries against the surrounding countries.

2.2. Physical Structure

The physical structure of the region also serves to explain the historical lack of political unity, as it aided fragmentation into innumerable small or merely moderate regional enclaves. The land by nature is divided by its largely mountainous character into small units, often existing independent of one another. Moreover, Palestine was continually exposed to attacks from outside either from the greater powers of Egypt, Mesopotamia or Asia Minor, or from the invasion of those who lived on the fringe of the more fertile area and to whom the rich life of Canaan (Palestine) made a strong appeal (cf: Deut 26:9, 8:7-10).

The land is divided into four main regions:

a) The highlands west of Jordan, the Galilean hills rising at Mt. Tabor to over 1,900 ft, south of the plain of Jezreel (Esdraelon), the central and southern highlands rise in places to over 3,000 ft.
b) To the west, the hills slope more gently towards the coastal plain and these lower hills the shephelah – had valleys rich in grain, with vineyards and olive groves on the hill sides.
c) To the east, there is a more rapid descent by steep valleys to the Jordan, nearly 700 ft. below sea level at the Sea of Galilee and over 1,200 ft. below the Dead Sea. This valley is deep and hot, but perpetual springs as at Jericho provide useful areas of fertile land.
d) Beyond Jordan lies a high plateau, run through by deep valleys and stretching out into the desert.

2.3. Climate and Fertility

a) *Water supply*: The climate is subtropical, with completely dry summers and vital period of rain in the winter months. The rainy season begins with some light precipitation in September or October (the so called 'early rain'), and diminishes in March or April (the 'later rain') The actual rainy season extends from the months of November to February. In large parts of the country this winter rain is sufficient to enable the growth of vegetation, and thus permits agriculture. From May to September the weather is dry, and the annual vegetation dies away, leaving only trees and shrubs except where perpetual springs or artificial irrigation provide water supply. The heat during this period is somewhat tempered in places by west winds, and dew provides a valuable extra water supply. In the years when rains do not come the agriculture is based on the existence of artificially collected rain water (Via. cisterns) or on the water derived from natural springs or rivers.

b) *Flora and Fauna and Human's encroachments on them*: With the intervention of human beings resulted in the fact woody growth was seriously deforested in order to make room for cultivable fields. This has happened in the regions of Palestine in historical times. The consequences of this process result in erosion of the soil in the forest during the rainy season. Moreover, due tothe deforestation carnivores animals such as lion and leopards are disturbed resulted in the extinction of the species.

2.4. Demography and Economy

Regions susceptible to cultivation, such as the mountainous areas were also capable of supplying the needs of its peasant population, but hardly the same relative numbers of individuals are in the valleys or plains. For reasons of health, and possibly with a view to defence, the inhabitants appear to have lived in the hinterlands where they farmed the ridges of valleys.

In all parts of the country in which agriculture was feasible, the most important in crops were cereals. Particularly barley and wheat. However, there was also a considerable production of wine, and olives which are more profitable cultivated at mountain slopes Dates are known to some extent. Barley and wheat are grown in the valleys. Especially in Jezreel and the coastal plains. Outside the cultivated areas around each village settlement lay the pasturage for the flocks and herds. A special variety of animal husbandry, i.e., nomadism was practised, to pinch more families and family groups (i.e. clans or tribes) concentrate on the herding of animals to such an extent that other occupations become either wholly or partially excluded.

2.5. The Differentiated Society and its Way of Life

One would expect the fundamental agriculture structure in Palestine to produce a society which is broadly speaking homogenous that is, without significant class distinctions. Therefore, scholars envisaged an agricultural society in which peasants own their own land, dwell in villages, and have no contact with urban culture, tends to develop an egalitarian ideology. According to such an ideology, all the members of such a society are in principle equal. But we may say that no egalitarian socio-economic structure has characterized Palestine with in the last 5,000 years or so, therefore it remains only as ideal in the case of ancient Israelite society.

a) ***Trade*** Every town in the country side of Palestine produced pottery which in spite of local variations was only rarely of such exceptional equality as to be able to serve as trade goods. Food stuffs are not traded, but most commonly traded goods were such Specialities as rare metals and gem stones. Palestine was an important trade route between the countries like Egypt and Syro-Mesopotamian region.

Conclusion The very geographical position of Palestine makes obvious that it would be extremely unlikely for the region to have the opportunity to develop as an independent culture, so that we should expect the society in the land of Palestine greatly influenced by foreign impulses and cultural features. With Egypt on one side and Mesopotamia on the other, it forms what is often called the "Fertile Crescent" the land from Dan to Beersheba and its border is less than 150 miles and from the Sea to the Jordan valley the distance 13 not more than 50 miles. Eventhough, the land is small in its proportion the importance of it is immense historically. Most of the events of the people of the Old Testament must have taken place in this small land about which we shall discuss in the chapters that will follow. Moreover, this small region has become significant because most of the major nations in the ancient West Asia have to meet this region in one way or another through this small region for the purpose of commerce and trade.

3. PALESTINE LYING BETWEEN POWERFUL NATIONS

The Old Testament tells the story of one people, their origins and fortunes during their history, and in particular what they thought about the events through which they lived. These people are conveniently called as Israelites or Hebrews. We are also frequently introduced to other ancient peoples, living within the Fertile Crescent, or beyond, with whom Israel came into contact. The Excavation of sites in the Ancient Near East has given and continues to give a fuller picture of what these other peoples were and how they lived and thought. To know about them is very important because Israelite history very much happened in the midst of such powerful nations. By studying few aspects of ancient history we can understand this concern.

3.1. The History of ancient world before 2000 B.C.E

We do not really know where civilization began but we can trace very ancient centres of culture 1n Egypt in the river valleys of Mesopotamia, and in Palestine itself. Form early times at least as early as 5000 B.C.E various settlements can be traced along the Nile, whose peoples were already making fine pottery and using copper. With boats made of papyrus, they sailed on the river. Eventually the smaller settlements were unified into two states: Upper Egypt, whose symbol was the lotus, and Lower Egypt, whose symbol was the papyrus reed. These two symbols were later united together when a United Kingdom was formed, but the ruler was still reckoned as the Lord of the two lands. But we should be careful about this age in the Bronze Age (From 3000 B.C.E to about 1500 BCE), we do not possess any written sources capable of telling us anything about Palestinian society. However, there are evidences to show that between 2300 and 2000 B.C.E, the rise of political and social system was mainly based on the presence of number of urban societies.

In about 2700 to 2200 B.C.E the time when the pyramids were built, Egypt was united under the name as Old kingdom, which became popular very much. During those years Egypt was engaged in trade with Syria and Palestine and even controlled these lands politically.

During the same time some developments took place in Mesopotamia, the land between the rivers Tigris and Euphrates. Cultivation is here dependent upon the rivers and the use of the artificial canals. As mentioned above between 2600 to 2000 B.C.E. small settlements were followed by more organised city states, especially, between 2600 to 2400 B.C.E. Sumerian rulers built up a high level of civilisation in centres such as Ur and Lagash. Between 2400 to 2200 B.C.E. due to the gradual infiltration of Semites and their rise to power led to the establishment of first great empire under Sargon of Akkad.

Following this great period in Mesopotamia and in Egypt the population was decreased and life was at a low ebb. We cannot ascertain what caused this kind of situation. But may be some environmental and other natural disasters would have resulted in such a low-life situation and only after several hundred years the situation got normal.

3.2. Between 2000 to 1200 B.C.E

Soon after 2000 B.C.E, Amorite kingdoms began to grow up in Mesopotamia, as at Mari on the Euphrates in the eighteenth century, to be followed by the Old Babylonian empire of which Hammurabi, was the greatest ruler (around 1790-50 B.C.E). The northern area of his empire came to be occupied as time went on by non-Semitic peoples such as Hurrians, who adopted Babylonian culture. They appear in the Old Testament record as Horites; after the fall of the Babylonian Power they controlled a great state known as the Mitanni. Babylon was destroyed by the Hittites of Asia Minor in about 1600 and then came under the control of another non-Semitic people known as the Kassites.

Meanwhile, Egypt rose to power again in the 'Middle Kingdom' between about 2000 to 1780 B.C.E., exercising control over Palestine and Syria. This flourishing period was followed by the rule of another series of foreign rulers, probably related to the western Semites of Canaan, and known as the Hyksos, a name simply means"rulers of foreign lands". These rulers, much hated in Egypt were nevertheless able to build up a powerful empire, their military power was in part due to their use of chariotry, and cities in Palestine and Egypt which they fortified included large enclosures for horses. Syria and Palestine enjoyed great prosperity under their rule and the population increased in number.

When Egyptian native rulers in Upper Egypt became strong enough, they drove out the Hyksos in about 1550 B.C.E and gradually took over control of their empire, extending Egyptian rule to meet Mitanni in northern Mesopotamia and the Hittite empire of the Asia Minor. These Hittites were an Indo-European people who had begun to settle in Asia Minor about 2000

B.C.E., and by 1600 had established a strong empire strong enough to raid Babylon as we have seen, and to conquer the Kingdom of Mitanni by about 1370. During the rule of the kings who followed the Hyksos in Egypt (the 18th dynasty 1550 to 1320; and nineteenth 1320 to 1200), Egypt enjoyed two periods of power and expansion, being weaker in the fourteenth century. This is known fromthe discovery of Amarna Letters which tell about connections between Pharaoh, the Egyptian king and the local princes in Palestine and Phoenicia (Lebanon), they also tell us about the crisis which Syro-Palestine experienced at this time. Amarna letters therefore help us to reconstruct some of the factors which led to the collapse of late Bronze Age society.

The Hittites and Egyptians thus inevitably came into conflict eventually after an indecisive battle at Kadesh (Syria) in about 1286 B.C.E., an 'eternal Treaty'was made (c.1280 B.C.E.) between the two powers marking the agreed frontier.

3.3. 1200-900 B.C.E.

The year 1200 B.C.E. marks a turning point in the lands of western Asia. During the preceding centuries a great civilization known as the Minoan had existed in Crete, reaching its climax in the fifteenth century. The Mycenaean's in Greece along the coastline of Asia Minor and the Aegean island had controlled sea trade by about I400 B.C.E., they continued to dominate in trade with Palestine and Egypt by exporting pottery and other wares. But by about 1200 B.C.E. this trade was interrupted by a movement of so-called 'Sea Peoples', who probably came from the Greek islands and Asia Minor (cf: Amos. 9:7 which mentions Caphtor) or they might have come from the Balkan and Illyrian – Aegean region. Travelling in hordes by both sea and land, they ravaged throughout the eastern part of the Mediterranean territory, leaving behind them numerous towns, cities and states in ruins. Only Egypt was able to resist the advance of the sea-people. Some of the sea people groups subsequently settled down in Palestine, as, for e.g. the well-known Philistines.

The sea people - Philistine settlement contributed to the existing tensions in Palestine. In reality, this process led to the final dissolution of the Egyptian empire in 12th cent. B.C.E. Not only that, even the Hittite power was ended due to this movement.

After this for few centuries, Egypt was unable to intervene in the affairs of Palestine; and much of the time Egypt was ruled by Libyan and then by Ethiopian kings. For a short span of time there was an opportunity-for Palestine to develop. Once the Philistines had been defeated and confined to the sea-coast, the independent Kingdom of Israel and Judah came into being.

The Canaanites who had occupied prior to the Israelite invasions were subjected to Israel or mingled with the Israelite tribes in the inland areas.

But on the Sea-coast north of Mount Carmel they established an independent kingdom of their own, known to us as Phoenicia, with its capital as Tyre.

3.4. After 900 B.C.E.

Independence could not endure for little Kingdoms like those of Israel and Judah, for a new power was soon to appear in the last, that of Assyria. In about 1100 Assyrian domain even extended for a short time into northern Syria, However, the main Assyrian expansion came after 900 B.C.E.when small states of Syria and Palestine fall under Assyrian control. Egypt too was conquered in the early seventh century. But soon Babylon drove out Assyria, and Egypt recovered her freedom, but after a while Babylon overthrew Egypt, thus Babylonian Empire, was established by great ruler of Babylon Nebuchadnezzar II (605-562 B.C.E.). While Assyria declined, Other Kingdoms grew up - the Kingdom Lydia in Asia Minor and that of the Medes to the north and east of Babylonia. Alliance between Babylon and the Medes had caused the downfall of Assyria, but in the later years of the Neo Babylonian Empire, the alliance had been broken, and one of the subject rulers of the Medes, a Persian named Cyrus, overthrew his overlord and established himself as ruler of Medes and Persia. With extreme rapidly he conquered Croesus of Lydia (546 B.C.E.) and Babylon (539 B.C.E.).

The Persian Empire in its turn was brought to an end by the lightening campaigns of Alexander the great of Macedon, having united Greece under his rule as he invaded Asia Minor in 334 B.C.E. At his death in 323 B.C.E his rule had been extended throughout the Persian Empire, and beyond even to India, eventually, when Rome had return to supremacy in Italy and the west Roman power spread eastward. Greece was conquered and ultimately so too were Syria and Palestine.

Although we deal with one group of people, we need to remember that the movements of peoples with whom Israel came into contact were in part dictated by the complex political and economic forces of the whole Mediterranean and West Asian area. Despite its small region major nations in the West Asia came in contact with Israel on several occasions.

Chapter 2

People/Nations Surrounding Ancient Israel

People of Egypt, Syria, Arameans, Philistines, Phoenicians, Moabites, Canaanites and other small states across Jordan: Edomites, Ammonites, Hittites, etc.[3]

Many nations surrounding ancient Israel played a key and significant role both in the history and formation of the ancient Israel. The formation of Israel was in one way or another has happened under the influence of the great and small nations. We shall briefly summarize the importance of such nations by describing their nature and identity in so far as they are related to ancient Israel.

1. Ancient Egypt: was a civilization of ancient Northeastern Africa, concentrated along the lower reaches of the Nile River in what is now the modern country of Egypt. It is one of six civilizations globally to arise independently. Egyptian civilization coalesced around 3150 BC (according to conventional Egyptian chronology)[1] with the political unification of Upper and Lower Egypt under the first pharaoh.[2] The history of ancient Egypt occurred in a series of stable Kingdoms, separated by periods of relative instability known as Intermediate Periods: the Old Kingdom of the Early Bronze Age, the Middle Kingdom of the Middle Bronze Age and the New Kingdom of the Late Bronze Age.

Egypt reached the pinnacle of its power during the New Kingdom, in the Ramesside period where it rivalled the Hittite Empire, Assyrian Empire and Mitanni Empire, after which it entered a period of slow decline. Egypt

3 The information presented on these nations is very general and can be found in any introductory history of ancient Israel and for more information on these and other related nations separate books are available with more details. The readers may pursue such material for an elaborate information.

was invaded or conquered by a succession of foreign powers, such as the Canaanites/Hyksos, Libyans, the Nubians, the Assyrians, Babylonians, the Achaemenid Persians, and the Macedonians in the Third Intermediate Period and the Late Period of Egypt. In the aftermath of Alexander the Great's death, one of his generals, Ptolemy Soter, established himself as the new ruler of Egypt. This Greek Ptolemaic Kingdom ruled Egypt until 30 BC, when, under Cleopatra, it fell to the Roman Empire and became a Roman province.

The success of ancient Egyptian civilization came partly from its ability to adapt to the conditions of the Nile River valley for agriculture. The predictable flooding and controlled irrigation of the fertile valley produced surplus crops, which supported a more dense population, and social development and culture. With resources to spare, the administration sponsored mineral exploitation of the valley and surrounding desert regions, the early development of an independent writing system, the organization of collective construction and agricultural projects, trade with surrounding regions, and a military intended to defeat foreign enemies and assert Egyptian dominance. Motivating and organizing these activities was a bureaucracy of elite scribes, religious leaders, and administrators under the control of a pharaoh, who ensured the cooperation and unity of the Egyptian people in the context of an elaborate system of religious beliefs.

The many achievements of the ancient Egyptians include the quarrying, surveying and construction techniques that supported the building of monumental pyramids, temples, and obelisks; a system of mathematics, a practical and effective system of medicine, irrigation systems and agricultural production techniques, the first known ships, Egyptian faience and glass technology, new forms of literature, and the earliest known peace treaty, made with the Hittites.[7] Egypt left a lasting legacy. Its art and architecture were widely copied, and its antiquities carried off to far corners of the world. Its monumental ruins have inspired the imaginations of travellers and writers for centuries. A new-found respect for antiquities and excavations in the early modern period by Europeans and Egyptians led to the scientific investigation of Egyptian civilization and a greater appreciation of its cultural legacy.

2. Syrians: In its early written history, the region was known as Eber Nari ('across the river') by the Mesopotamians and included modern-day Syria, Lebanon, and Israel (collectively known as The **Levant**). Eber Nari is referenced in the biblical books of Ezra and Nehemiah as well as in reports by the scribes of Assyrian and Persian kings. The modern name of Syria is claimed by some scholars to have derived from **Herodotus**' habit of referring to the whole of **Mesopotamia** as '**Assyria**' and, after the Assyrian **Empire** fell in 612 BCE, the western part continued to be called 'Assyria' until after the **Seleucid Empire** when it became known as 'Syria'. This theory has been contested by the claim that the name comes from Hebrew, and the people of the land were referred to as 'Siryons' by the Hebrews because of their soldiers' metal armor ('Siryon' meaning armor, specifically chain mail, in Hebrew). There is also the theory that `Syria' derives from the Siddonian name for Mount Hermon - `Siryon' – which separated the regions of northern Eber Nari and southern **Phoenicia** (modern Lebanon, which **Sidon** was a part of), and it has also been suggested that the name comes from the Sumerian, `Saria' which was their name for Mount Hermon. As the designations `Siryon' and `Saria' would not have been known to Herodotus, and as his *Histories* had such an enormous impact on later writers in antiquity, it is most likely that the modern name `Syria' derives from `Assyria' (which comes from the Akkadian `**Ashur**' and designated the Assyrian's chief deity) and not from the Hebrew, Siddonian, or Sumerian words.

3. Arameans: were a Northwest Semitic people who originated in what is now present-day western, southern and central Syria (Biblical Aram) during the Late Bronze Age and the Iron Age.[1][2] Large groups migrated to Babylonia in southern Mesopotamia during the 11th and 10th centuries BCE, where they established small semi-independent Aramaic kingdoms, in the Levant and in Mesopotamia conquered Aramean populations were forcibly deported throughout the Assyrian Empire, e.g. under the rule of king Tiglath-Pileser III. Some Syriac Christians known as Suryanis, mostly adherents of the Syriac Orthodox Church with smaller percentages followers of the Syriac Catholic Church,[3] in the Middle East (particularly in Syria and Israel) still espouse an Aramean ethnic identity to this day and a minority still speak various Aramaic dialects or languages.

In northeast Syria, northern Iraq, northwest Iran and south eastern Turkey, Akkadian influenced Eastern Aramaic-Northeastern Neo-Aramaic dialects are still spoken fluently by between 575,000 and 1,000,000 people, but most of the speakers of these dialects are ethnic Mesopotamian Assyrians, the indigenous people of Upper Mesopotamia (present-day Iraq), rather than Levantine Arameans (present-day Syria and Israel). The Western Aramaic language of the Arameans in Maalula is in danger of extinction, although Aramean personal and family names are still found among the Syriac Christians throughout the Middle East.

The Arameans never had a unified nation; they were divided into small independent kingdoms across parts of the Near East, particularly in what is now more Syria and Jordan. After the Bronze Age collapse, their political influence was confined to a number of states such as Aram Damascus and the partly Aramean Syro-Hittite states, which were entirely absorbed into the Neo-Assyrian Empire by the 9th century BC.

By contrast, Imperial Aramaic came to be the *lingua franca* of the entire Near East and Asia Minor when introduced as the official language of the vast Neo-Assyrian Empire by Tiglath-Pileser III in the mid-8th century BC. This empire stretched from Cyprus and the East Mediterranean in the west to Persia and Elam to India in the east, and from Armenia and the Caucasus in the north to Egypt and Arabia in the south. This version of Aramaic later developed in Mesopotamia into the literary languages such as Syriac and Mandaic. Scholars have used the term "Aramaization" for the process by which the Assyrian and Babylonian Akkadian-speaking peoples became eastern Aramaic-speaking during the later Iron Age and intermingled with the Arameans.

4. Philistines: one of a people of Aegean origin who settled on the southern coast of Palestine in the 12th century BCE, about the time of the arrival of the Israelites. According to biblical tradition (Deuteronomy 2:23; Jeremiah 47:4), the Philistines came from Caphtor (possibly Crete). They are mentioned in Egyptian records as *prst,* one of the Sea Peoples that invaded Egypt in about 1190 BCE after ravaging Anatolia, Cyprus, and Syria. After being repulsed by the Egyptians, they occupied the coastal plain of Palestine from Joppa (modern Tel Aviv–Yafo) southward to the Gaza Strip. The area contained the five cities (the Pentapolis) of the Philistine confederacy (Gaza, Ashkelon [Ascalon], Ashdod, Gath, and Ekron) and was known as Philistia, or the Land of the Philistines. It was from this designation that the whole of the country was later called Palestine by the Greeks.

The Philistines expanded into neighbouring areas and soon came into conflict with the Israelites, a struggle represented by the Samson saga (Judges 13–16) in the Old Testament. With their superior arms and military organization the Philistines were able (*c.* 1050) to occupy part of the Judaean hill country. They were finally defeated by the Israelite king David (10th century), and thereafter their history was that of individual cities rather than of a people. After the division of Judah and Israel (10th century), the Philistines regained their independence and often engaged in border battles with those kingdoms.

By the early part of the 7th century, Gaza, Ashkelon, Ekron, Ashdod, and probably Gath were vassals of the Assyrian rulers; but during the second half of that century the cities became Egyptian vassals. With the conquests of the Babylonian king Nebuchadrezzar II (605–562) in Syria and Palestine, the Philistine cities became part of the Neo-Babylonian Empire. In later times they came under the control of Persia, Greece, and Rome.

There are no documents in the Philistine language, which was probably replaced by Canaanite, Aramaic, and, later, Greek. Nor is much known of the Philistine religion, since all their gods mentioned in biblical and other sources have Semitic names and were probably borrowed from the conquered Canaanites. Until their defeat by David, the Philistine cities were ruled by *seranim,* "lords," who acted in council for the common good of the nation. After their defeat, the *seranim* were replaced by kings.

The Philistines long held a monopoly on smithing iron, a skill probably acquired in Anatolia. At sites occupied by the Philistines at an early period, a distinctive type of pottery, a variety of the 13th-century Mycenaean styles, has been found.

5. Phoenicia: was an ancient Semitic thalassocratic civilization situated on the western, coastal part of the Fertile Crescent and centered on the coastline of modern Syria and Lebanon. All major Phoenician cities were on the coastline of the Mediterranean, some colonies reaching the Western Mediterranean. It was an enterprising maritime trading culture that spread across the Mediterranean from 3200 BCE to 300 BCE. The Phoenicians used the galley, a man-powered sailing vessel, and are credited with the invention of the bireme.[3] They were famed in Classical Greece and Rome as 'traders in purple', referring to their monopoly on the precious purple dye of the murex snail, used, among other things, for royal clothing, and for the spread of their alphabets, from which almost all modern phonetic alphabets are derived.

Although, Egyptian seafaring expeditions had already been made to Byblos to bring back Lebanon Cedars as early as the 3rd millennium BC, continuous contact only occurred in the Egyptian New Empire period. In the Amarna tablets of the 14th century BCE, people from the region called themselves *Kenaani* or *Kinaani*.[4] Much later, in the 6th century BCE, Hecataeus of Miletus writes that Phoenicia was formerly called *χνα* (Latinized: khna), a name Philo of Byblos later adopted into his mythology as his eponym for the Phoenicians: "Khna who was afterwards called Phoinix".

Phoenicia is really a Classical Greek term used to refer to the region of the major Canaanite port towns, and does not correspond exactly to a cultural identity that would have been recognized by the Phoenicians themselves. The term in Greek means 'land of purple', a reference to the valuable murex-shell dye they exported.[6] It is uncertain to what extent the Phoenicians viewed themselves as a single ethnicity and nationality. Their civilization was organized in city-states, similar to ancient Greece.[7] However, in terms of archaeology, language, life style and religion, there is little to set the Phoenicians apart as markedly different from other Semitic cultures of Canaan. As Canaanites, they were unique in their remarkable seafaring achievements.

Each city-state was a politically independent unit. They could come into conflict and one city might be dominated by another city-state, although they would collaborate in leagues or alliances. Though ancient boundaries of such city-centered cultures fluctuated, the city of Tyre seems to have been the southernmost. Sarepta (modern day Saraf and) between Sidon and Tyre is the most thoroughly excavated city of the Phoenician homeland.

The Phoenicians were the first state-level society to make extensive use of alphabets. The Phoenician alphabet is generally held to be the ancestor of almost all modern alphabets. They spoke Phoenician, a Semitic language of the Canaanite subgroup, closely related to Hebrew.[8][9] However, due to the very slight differences in language, and the insufficient records of the time, whether Phoenician formed a separate and united dialect, or was merely a superficially defined part of a broader language continuum, is unclear. Through their maritime trade, the Phoenicians spread the use of the alphabet to North Africa and Europe, where it was adopted by the Greeks, who later transmitted it to the Romans.[10] In addition to their many inscriptions, the Phoenicians are believed to have left numerous other types of written sources, but most have not survived.

6. Moabites: These are the descendants of Moab the son of Lot, Genesis 19:30-38. The land of Moab lay east and southeast of the Dead Sea, and chiefly south of the river Arnon. At one period, however, it extended north as far as the Jabbok, and for a long time the region beyond the Jordan opposite Jericho retained the name of "the plains of Moab," Numbers 22:1 De 1:5 29:1 Jos 13:32. The Moabites had dispossessed a race of giants called Emin, Deut 2:11, and had themselves been expelled by the Amorites from the territory north of the Arnon, Numbers 21:13, 26 Judg 11:13-18, which was again conquered by Moses, and assigned to the tribe of Reuben. On the approach of Israel from Egypt, the Moabites acted with great inhumanity, Numbers 22:1-24:25 De 2:8-9; and though God spared them from conquest, he excluded them and their seed even to the tenth generation form the peculiar privileges of his people, De 23:3-6. They were gross idolaters, worshipping Chemosh and Baalpeor with obscene rites, Numbers 25:1-18 2 Kings 3:27. See MOLOCH.

At times, as in the days of Ruth, there was peace between them and Israel; but a state of hostility was far more common, as in the time of Eglon, Jud 3:12-30; of Saul, 1 Samuel 14:47; of David, 2 Samuel 8:2,12; of Joram and Jeroboam, 2 Kings 3:13,20 14:25. They aided Nebuchadnezzar against the Jews, 2 Kings 24:2 Ezekiel 25:6-11; and after these began to be carried captive, appear to have regained their old possessions north of the Arnon, Isaiah 15:1-16:14. The Jewish prophets recorded many threats against these hereditary enemies of God and his people, Numbers 24:17 Psalm 60:12 83:6 Jeremiah 25:9-21 48:1-47 Am 2:1-3; and all travellers concur in attesting the fulfillment of these predictions. Desolation and gloom, brood over the mountains of Moab, and its fruitful valleys are for the most part untilled. It is under Turkish government, but is inhabited chiefly by migratory Arabs, Zephaniah 2:8-9. Few travellers have ventured to traverse it in modern times. They describe it as abounding in ruins, such as shattered tombs, cisterns walls, temples, etc., proving that it was once densely populated."

The original inhabitants of Moab were the Emim (Deuteronomy 2:10), "a people great.... and tall, as the Anakim." When these were deposed by the Moabites we do not know. The latter are not mentioned in the Tell el-Amarna Letters and do not appear on the Egyptian monuments before the 14th century B.C., when they seem to be referred to under the name of Ruten, or Luten or Lotan, i.e., Lot (Paton, Syria and Pal); Muab appears in a list of names on a monument of Rameses III of the XXth Dynasty. The country lay outside the line of march of the Egyptian armies, and this accounts for the silence of its monuments in regard to them.

The chief deity of Moab was Chemosh (kemosh), frequently mentioned in the Old Testament and on the Moabite Stone, where King Mesha speaks of building a high place in his honor because he was saved by him from his enemies. He represents the oppression of Moab by Omri as the result of the anger of Chemosh, and Mesha made war against Israel by command of Chemosh. He was the national god of Moab, as Molech was of Ammon, and it is pretty certain that he was propitiated by human sacrifices (2 Kings 3:27). But he was not the only god of Moab, as is clear from the account in Numbers 25, where it is also clear that their idolatrous worship was corrupt. They had their Baalim like the nations around, as may be inferred from the place-names compounded with Baal, such as Bamoth-baal, Beth-baal-meon and Baal-peor. At a later date Moab was overrun by the Nabathean Arabs who ruled in Petra and extended their authority on the east side of Jordan even as far as Damascus (Josephus, Ant, XIII, xv, 1, 2). The Moabites lost their identity as a nation and were afterward confounded with the Arabs, as we see in the statement of Josephus (XIII, xiii, 5), where he says that Alexander (Janneus) overcame the Arabians, such as the Moabites and the Gileadites. Alexander built the famous stronghold of Macherus in Moab, on a hill overlooking the Dead Sea, which afterward became the scene of the imprisonment and tragical death of John the Baptist (Josephus, BJ, VII, vi, 2; Ant, XVIII, v, 2; Mark 6:21-28). It was afterward destroyed by the Romans. Kir became a fortress of the Crusaders under the name of Krak (Kerak), which held out against the Moslems until the time of Saladin, who captured it in 1188 CE.

7. Edomites: are the descendants of Esau, the firstborn son of Isaac and the twin brother of Jacob. In the womb, Esau and Jacob struggled together, and God told their mother, Rebekah, that they would become two nations, with the older one serving the younger (Genesis 25:23). As an adult, Esau rashly sold his inheritance to Jacob for a bowl of red soup (Genesis 25:30-34), and he hated his brother afterward. Esau became the father of the Edomites and Jacob became the father of the Israelites, and the two nations continued to struggle through most of their history. In the Bible, "Seir" (Joshua 24:4), "Bozrah" (Isaiah 63:1) and "Sela" (2 Kings 14:7) are references to Edom's land and capital. Sela is better known today as Petra.

The name "Edom" comes from a Semitic word meaning "red," and the land south of the Dead Sea was given that name because of the red sandstone so prominent in the topography. Esau, because of the soup for which he traded his birthright, became known as Edom, and later moved his family into the hill country of the same name. Genesis 36 recounts the early history of the Edomites, stating that they had kings reigning over them long before Israel had a king (Genesis 36:31). The religion of the Edomites was similar to that of other pagan societies who worshiped fertility gods. Esau's descendants eventually dominated the southern lands and made their living by agriculture and trade. One of the ancient trade routes, the King's Highway (Numbers 20:17) passed through Edom, and when the Israelites requested permission to use the route on their exodus from Egypt, they were rejected by force.

Because they were close relatives, the Israelites were forbidden to hate the Edomites (Deuteronomy 23:7). However, the Edomites regularly attacked Israel, and many wars were fought as a result. King Saul fought against the Edomites, and King David subjugated them, establishing military garrisons in Edom. With control over Edomite territory, Israel had access to the port of Ezion-Geber on the Red Sea, from which King Solomon sent out many expeditions. After the reign of Solomon, the Edomites revolted and had some freedom until they were subdued by the Assyrians under Tiglath-Pileser.

During the Maccabean wars, the Edomites were subjugated by the Jews and forced to convert to Judaism. Through it all, the Edomites maintained much of their old hatred for the Jews. When Greek became the common language, the Edomites were called Idumaeans. With the rise of the Roman Empire, an Idumaean whose father had converted to Judaism was named king of Judea. That Idumaean is known in history as King Herod the Great, the tyrant who ordered a massacre in Bethlehem in an attempt to kill the Christ child (Matthew 2:16-18).

After Herod's death, the Idumaean people slowly disappeared from history. God had foretold the destruction of the Edomites in Ezekiel 35, saying, "As you rejoiced over the inheritance of the house of Israel, because it was desolate, so I will deal with you; you shall be desolate, Mount Seir, and all Edom, all of it. Then they will know that I am the Lord" (Ezekiel 35:15). Despite Edom's constant efforts to rule over the Jews, God's prophecy to Rebekah was fulfilled: the older child served the younger, and Israel proved stronger than Edom.

8. Ammonites: Throughout the early history of Israel, we find references to the Ammonite people. Who were they, where did they come from, and what happened to them? The Ammonites were a Semitic people, closely related to the Israelites. Despite that relationship, they were more often counted enemies than friends.

Lot, Abraham's nephew, was the progenitor of the Ammonites. After Abraham and Lot separated (Genesis 13), Lot settled in the city of Sodom. When God destroyed Sodom and Gomorrah because of their wickedness, Lot and his daughters fled to the hill country on the southern end of the Dead Sea. Probably thinking they were the only people left on the earth, Lot's daughters got him drunk and had incestuous relations with him to produce children (Genesis 19:37-38). The older daughter had a son named Moab ("from father"), and the younger gave birth to Ben-Ammi ("son of my people"). The Ammonites, descendants of Ben-Ammi, were a nomadic people who lived in the territory of modern-day Jordan, and the name of the capital city, Amman, reflects the name of those ancient inhabitants.

In the time of Moses, the fertile plains of the Jordan River valley were occupied by the Amorites, Ammonites and Moabites. When Israel left Egypt, the Ammonites refused to assist them in any way, and God punished them for their lack of support (Deuteronomy 23:3-4). Later, however, as the Israelites entered the Promised Land, God instructed them, "When you approach the territory of the people of Ammon, do not harass them or contend with them, for I will not give you any of the land of the people of Ammon as a possession, because I have given it to the sons of Lot for a possession" (Deuteronomy 2:19). The Israelite tribes of Gad, Reuben, and half of Manasseh claimed the Amorite territory bordering that of the Ammonites.

The Ammonites were a pagan people who worshiped the gods Milcom and Molech. God commanded the Israelites not to marry these pagans, because intermarriage would lead the Israelites to worship false gods. Solomon disobeyed and married Naamah the Ammonite (1 Kings 14:21), and, as God had warned, he was drawn into idolatry (1 Kings 11:1-8). Molech was a fire-god with the face of a calf; his images had arms outstretched to receive the babies who were sacrificed to him. Like their god, the Ammonites were cruel. When Nahash the Ammonite was asked for terms of a treaty (1 Samuel 11:2), he proposed gouging out the right eye of each Israelite man. Amos 1:13 says that the Ammonites would rip open pregnant women in the territories they conquered.

Under King Saul's leadership, Israel defeated the Ammonites and made them vassals. David continued that sovereignty over Ammon and later besieged the capital city to solidify his control. After the split of Israel and Judah, the Ammonites began to ally themselves with the enemies of Israel. Ammon regained some sovereignty in the seventh century B.C., until Nebuchadnezzar conquered them about a hundred years later. Tobiah the Ammonite (Nehemiah 2:19) was possibly a governor of the region under Persian rule, but the inhabitants were a mix of Ammonites, Arabs, and others. By New Testament times, Jews had settled in the area, and it was known as Perea. The last mention of Ammonites as a separate people was in the second century by Justin Martyr, who said they were very numerous. Sometime during the Roman period, the Ammonites seem to have been absorbed into Arab society.

9. Hittites: were an Ancient Anatolian people who established an empire centered on Hattusa in north-central Anatolia around 1600 BCE. This empire reached its height during the mid-14th century BCE under Suppiluliuma I, when it encompassed an area that included most of Asia Minor as well as parts of the northern Levant and Upper Mesopotamia. After c. 1180 BC, the empire came to an end during the Bronze Age collapse, splintering into several independent "Neo-Hittite" city-states, some of which survived until the 8th century BC.

The Hittite language was a distinct member of the Anatolian branch of the Indo-European language family. They referred to their native land as *Hatti*. The conventional name "Hittites" is due to their initial identification with the Biblical Hittitesin 19th century archaeology.

Despite the use of *Hatti* for their core territory, the Hittites should be distinguished from the Hattians, an earlier people who inhabited the same region (until the beginning of the 2nd millennium BC) and spoke a language possibly in the Northwest Caucasian languages group known as Hattic.

The Hittite military made successful use of chariots.[2] Although belonging to the Bronze Age, they were the forerunners of the Iron Age, developing the manufacture of iron artifacts from as early as the 18th century BCE, when the "man of Burushanda"'s gift of an iron throne and iron sceptre to the Kaneshite king Anitta was recorded in the *Anitta text* inscription.

After 1180 BCE amid general turmoil in the Levant conjectured to have been associated with the sudden arrival of the Sea Peoples,[3][4] the kingdom disintegrated into several independent "Neo-Hittite" city-states, some of which survived until as late as the 8th century BCE. The history of the Hittite civilization is known mostly from cuneiform texts found in the area of their kingdom, and from diplomatic and commercial correspondence found in various archives in Egypt and the Middle East.

10. Canaanites: Canaan in the Hebrew Bible: In Biblical usage, the name was confined to the country west of the Jordan. Canaanites were described as living "by the sea, and along by the side of the Jordan" (Numbers 33:51; Joshua 22:9), and was especially identified with Phoenicia (Isaiah 23:11).[17] The Philistines, while an integral part of the Canaanite milieu, do not seem to have been ethnic Canaanites, and were listed in the Table of Nations as descendants of Misraim; the Arameans, Moabites, Ammonites, Midianites and Edomites were also considered fellow descendants of Shem or Abraham, and distinct from generic Canaanites/Amorites. *"Heth"*, representing the Hittites, is a son of Canaan.

Canaan first appears as one of Noah's grandsons during the narrative known as the Curse of Ham, in which Canaan is cursed with perpetual slavery because his father Ham had "looked upon" the drunk and naked Noah. God later promises the land of Canaan to Abraham, and eventually delivers it to descendants of Abraham, the Israelites. The biblical history has become increasingly problematic as the archaeological and textual evidence supports the idea that the early Israelites were in ct themselves Canaanites.

The Hebrew Bible lists borders for the land of Canaan. Numbers 34:2 includes the phrase "the land of Canaan as defined by its borders." The borders are then delineated in Numbers 34:3–12. The term "Canaanites" in biblical Hebrew is applied especially to the inhabitants of the lower regions, along the sea coast and on the shores of Jordan, as opposed to the inhabitants of the mountainous regions. By the time of the Second Temple, "Canaanite" in Hebrew had come to be not an ethnic designation, so much as a general synonym for "merchant", as it is interpreted in, for example, Job 40:30, or Proverbs 31:24.

The passage in the Book of Genesis often called the Table of Nations describes the Canaanites as being descended from an ancestor called Canaan, the son of Ham and grandson of Noah (Hebrew: כְּנַעַן, *Knaan*), saying (Genesis 10:15–19): Canaan is the father of Sidon, his firstborn; and of the Hittites, Jebusites, Amorites, Girgashites, Hivites, Arkites, Sinites,Arvadites, Zemarites, and Hamathites. Later the Canaanite clans scattered, and the borders of Canaan reached [across the Mediterranean coast] from Sidon toward Gerar as far as Gaza, and then [inland around the Jordan Valley] toward Sodom, Gomorrah, Admah and Zeboiim, as far as Lasha.

The Sidon whom the Table identifies as the firstborn son of Canaan has the same name as that of the coastal city of Sidon, in Lebanon. This city dominated the Phoenician coast, and may have enjoyed hegemony over a number of ethnic groups, who are said to belong to the "Land of Canaan".

Similarly, Canaanite populations are said to have inhabited:

- the Mediterranean coastlands (Joshua 5:1), including Lebanon corresponding to Phoenicia (Isaiah 23:11) and the Gaza Strip corresponding to Philistia (Zephania 2:5).
- the Jordan Valley (Joshua 11:3, Numbers 13:29, Genesis 13:12).

According to the *Book of Jubilees*, the Israelite conquest of Canaan is attributed to Canaan's steadfast refusal to join his elder brothers in Ham's allotment beyond the Nile, and instead "squatting" on the eastern shores of the Mediterranean, within the inheritance delineated for Shem. Canaan thus incurs a further curse from Noah for disobeying the agreed apportionment of land.

While the Hebrew Bible contrasts the Canaanites ethnically from the Ancient Israelites, modern scholars Jonathan Tubb and Mark Smith have theorized the kingdoms of Israel and Judah to be a subset of Canaanite culture, based on their archaeological and linguistic interpretations.

The descendants of Canaan. Their first habitation was in the land of Canaan, where they multiplied extremely, and by trade and war acquired great riches, and sent out colonies all over the islands and coasts of the Mediterranean. When the measure of their idolatries and abominations was completed, God delivered their country into the hands of the Israelites, who conquered it under Joshua. See the previous article. The following are the principal tribes mentioned.

i) The HIVITES dwelt in the northern part of the country, at the foot of mount Hermon, or Anti-Lebanon, according to Joshua 11:3, where it is related that they, along with the united forces of northern Canaan, were defeated by Joshua. They were not, however, entirely driven out of their possessions, Jud 3:3 2 Sam 24:7 1 Kings 9:20. There were also Hivites in middle Palestine, Genesis 34:2 Joshua 19:1,7 11:19.
ii) The CANAANITES, in a restricted sense, inhabited partly the plains on the coast of the Mediterranean sea, Numbers 13:29 Joshua 11:3.
iii) The GIRGASHITES dwelt between the Canaanites and the Jebusites; as may be inferred from the order in which they are mentioned in Joshua 24:11.
iv) The JEBUSITES had possession of the hill country around Jerusalem, and of that city itself, of which the ancient name was Jebus, Joshua 15:8,63;18:28. The Benjamites, to whom this region was allotted, did not drive out the Jebusites, Jude 1:21. David first captured the citadel of Jebus, 2 Samuel 5:6.
v) The AMORITES inhabited, in Abraham's time, the region south of Jerusalem, on the western side of the Dead Sea, Genesis 14:7. At a later period, they spread themselves out over all the mountainous country which forms the southeastern part of Canaan, and which was called from them the "mountain of the Amorites," and afterwards the "mountain of Judea,"

   Deut 1:19,20 Numbers 13:29 Joshua 11:3. On the east side of the Jordan also they had, before the time of Moses, founded two kingdoms, that of Bashan in the north, and another, bounded at first by the Jabbok, in the south. But under Sihon they crossed the Jabbok, and took from the Ammonites and Moabites all the country between the Jabbok and the Arnon; so that this latter stream now became the southern boundary of the Amorites, Numbers 21:13,14,16,26 32:33,39 Deut 4:46,47 31:4. This last tract the Israelites took possession of after their victory over Sihon.
vi) The HITTITES, or children of Heth, according to the report of the spies, Numbers 1:29, dwelt among the Amorites in the mountainous district of the south, afterwards called the "mountain of Judah." In the time of Abraham they possessed Hebron; and the patriarch purchased from them the cave of Machpelah as a sepulchre, Genesis 23:1-20 25:9,10. After the Israelites entered Canaan, the Hittites

seem to have moved farther northward. The country around Bethel is called "the land of the Hittites," Jude 1:26.

vii) The PERIZZITES were found in various parts of Canaan. The name signifies inhabitants of the plains, from their original abode. According to Genesis 13:7, they dwelt with the Canaanites, between Bethel and Ai; and according to Genesis 34:30, in the vicinity of Shechem.

Besides these seven tribes, there were several others of the same parentage, dwelling north of Canaan. These were the Arkites, Arvadites, Hamathites, and Zemarites. There were also several other tribes of diverse origin within the bounds of Canaan, destroyed by the Israelites; such as the Anakim, the Amalekites, and the Rephaim of giants.

Section II

History of Ancient Israel

Chapter 3

Israel Before Settlement

1. THE WANDERING ARAMAEAN: STRUGGLE FOR SURVIVAL

There are two ways in which the question 'who were the people of the Old Testament?' may be answered. We must see what these people said about themselves, and we must see how far we can fit them into the pattern of life in the ancient West Asia as we now know it. In spite of this we cannot give a complete answer to the problem but maybe we can gain a fair idea of what are the issues involved in the origin and make-up of the people of the Old Testament. So the information we may present about the people of the Old Testament can only be deduced in plausible terms.[4]

1.1. Wandering Aramaean

Deut. 26:5 "wandering Aramean was my father" was the confession of faith which was spoken by the Israelite worshipper during the harvest festival. In this statement we can find out two catching words, Wandering and 'Aramaean' perhaps these words may reveal something of the origin of the people.

The word "wandering" may be rendered 'fugitive' which indicates a tradition that in the earlier period of their existence the Hebrews were a pastoral people, engaged in tending flocks and herds and moving from place to place in search of pasturage. But it is unlikely that the nomads have settled in one place for a long time. They move from one place to another and the main occupation was breeding of the cattle (Gen 46:34, 47:4). When the streams dry up, when the rain fails and there is famine, the herdsmen must move into

4 Some information on this topic is adapted from P. R. Ackroyd, *The People of Old Testament* (Bangalore: United Theological College, 1986).

another area. At a later period in the history Israelites may have moved in the same way to Egypt for their settlement.

In the period before the Israelite tribes entered Egypt, their forefathers may have wandered in the hill country, i.e., in and around Canaan, not settling in any definite area or locality. For instance, Abraham is to be found mainly in the area around Hebron, in the Negeb, or Southern part of the land. W.F. Albright in his article "Abraham the Hebrew: A New Archaeological Interpretation", *Bulletin of American School of Oriental Research* CLXII, 1961, 36-54, collected impressive evidence for the spread of donkey caravanning in the nineteenth century B.C.E. Albright portrayed Abraham as an itinerant merchant who frequented the trade routes southward through the Negeb towards Sinai. The specific sites mentioned in Genesis accounts of the patriarch wanderings—Shechem, Bethel, Hebron, Beersheba, and Gerar— according to Albright were settled in MBI, as attested by archaeology. Isaac is associated with the Negeb area particularly with the neighbourhood of Beersheba. Jacob's sons are to be found wandering in the central highlands, between Bethel and Shechem and even so far north as Dothan (Gen 37: 12-17).

In Dent 26:5 with confessional statement as pointed out earlier another element is found – 'Aramaean'. In various stories the tradition is preserved of the people having come into the Palestinian area from elsewhere. Of Abraham it is said that he came from Ur in Southern Mesopotamia to Haran in the northern, and thence into Canaan (Gen 11:31, 12:9). Same may be found in the speech of Joshua in the book of Joshua 24:2-3, but in Joshua there is no mention of Ur, and it is possible that its appearance in the Abraham story is not original. Certainly there is nothing in the stories of the patriarchs to suggest that they had any real connection with the Sumerian civilization of Ur and the other cities of Southern Mesopotamia; if they did not migrate from that area, it must have been that they had for a time lived as a pastoral people there, having originally came from elsewhere.

The common elements in the two statements point to the area around Haran situated on the tributary of the Euphrates in northern Mesopotamia. This area is known in the OT as 'Paddan-aram' the field of Aram (Gen 25: 20, 28: 2 and Hosea 12: 12) or as 'Aram-Naharaim'- 'Aram of two rivers' (Gen 24: 10). From the point of view of Palestine, it is 'Beyond the River - that is, beyond the Euphrates. It I here that the relatives of Abraham were to be found, for he sent his servant there to find a wife for Isaac; here too Jacob took refuge with his mother's family.

The connection of the people of the Old Testament with this area is in some measure confirmed by the evidence of archaeology. The names of the ancestors and relatives of Abraham in Ge. 11, include those of Haran, Nahor, Serug, and Peleg. These appear as names of cities in ancient records, particularly from Mari, a little farther down the Euphrates. Same of the vital clues may have been provided in the Mari to understand patriarchs in the bible. Following are the vital points:

a) Both patriarchal and Mari societies are "dimorphic". For instance, in Genesis some events reflect this such as: the frequent custom of camping in the vicinity of towns (Gen 12:6-9, 13:12-18, 33:18-20, 35:16-21, 37: 12-17); the occasional practice of agriculture (Gen 26:12f); the case of social and economic exchange with towns people (Gen 21:25-34; 23: 1-20, 26:17-33; 33:18-20); and the fact that Abraham, Lot and Isaac even dwell in the towns for various periods of time as 'resident aliens' (Heb. ger, Gen. 23:4 cf; Yasab to dwell Gen 12:10). Perhaps the episode is best clarified by the notion of a dimorphic society are the separation of Abraham and Lot and Lot's taking up residence within the orbit of the Canaanite towns (Gen 13:8-13, 19:1-4). Lot was sitting in the gate simply means that he dwelt near the gate outside the town, as Mari tribes people are sometimes described as doing; the contrasting yet complementary vocations of Jacob and Esau (Gen 25: 27-34); and particularly the relation of Jacob to the Shechemites (Gen 33: 18, 34:31).
b) In both dimorphic societies the groups representing the village pastoral morpheme are virtually identical. The tribal people of both Mari and the tribes of Genesis are pastoralists, i.e., sheep-breeders who move their encampments periodically in search of water and pasturage. In Israel this pastoral life is further characterized by the semi-nomadic life of shepherds who live in tents and move with their flocks, sometimes over considerable distances seeking traditional and sometimes disputed pastures and well. (Gen 3:5-11, 18: 1-8, 21:25-31, 24:62-67, 26:1-33, 29-31 chs; 33:12-17, 36:6-8).
c) Both societies in question are tribally organized.
d) The social institutions of the two-tribal societies might be compared, especially Patrimony, the custom of census taking, and the prominent place given to genealogies.

In recent years, many attempts have been made at explaining elements in the patriarchal stories from personal names and from information about customs and legal practices known to us from this northern Mesopotamian are particularly from Mari (around 1700 BC) and from Nuzi (further to the east, belonging to about 1500 to 1350 BC) some vital points are follows:

a) The names in the patriarchal narratives fit perfectly in a class known to have been current in both Mesopotamia and Palestine in the second millennium, specifically among the Amorite element of the population. For eg: The names of the patriarchs themselves,

"Jacob occurs in an eighteenth century text from Chagar Bazar upper Mesopotamia (*Ya'Qubel*), as the name of the Hyksos chief (Ya'Qub-'al), and as a Palestinian, place name in fifteenth-century list of Thutmosis III. The name "Abram" (Abraham) is know from Babylonian texts of the first Dynasty and possibly from the Execration Texts. The word "Nahor" occurs in the Mari texts as the name of the town (Nakhur) in the vicinity of Haran (as in Gen 24:10).

b) *Patriachal customs against the background of the second millennium*: The Nuzi texts which reflect the customary law of a predominantly. Hurrian population in the East-Tigris region in the fifteenth century are useful to get some clues for the patriarchal narratives and their surroundings. One such evidence can be traced for example:

i) From the story of Abraham's fear (Gen 15:1-4) that his slave Eleazar would be his heir becomes understandable in the light of slave adoption as practised at Nuzi. Childless couples would adopt a son who would serve them as long as they lived and inherit on their death. But, should natural son be born, the adopted son would have to yield the right of inheritance.

ii) Sarah gave her slave Hagar to Abraham as a concubine (Gen 16:1-4), so at Nuzi a marriage contract obliged the wife, of childless, to provide her husband with a substitute. Should son be born of such a union, the expulsion of the slave wife and her child was forbidden which explains Abraham's reluctance to send Hagar and Ishmael away (ch. 21:10f).

iii) In Laban-Jacob stories, Nuzi texts are especially illuminating. The adoption of Jacob into Laban's household, the condition laid on him to take no other wives other than Laban's daughters (Gen. 31), the resentment of Leah and Rachel against Laban (Gen. 31:15), and finally, Rachel's theft of Laban's gods (M. Greenberg argues: that possession of the gods conveyed title to headship in the family); all are Paralleled by Nuzian customs.

One may argue that such customs are not only limited to Nuzi texts, i.e., to the Hurrian population, but in general they are wide spread in the entire Palestinian area, but the fact remains only such parallels are found in Genesis accounts are not related to the other stories of the bible. But we need to recognize the fact that the information available to link the Hurrian customs and patriarchal stories is not adequate.

1.2. The Hebrews

The name Hebrew may also provide a clue to the background of the patriarchs, even though the evidence is complicated. In Gen 14:13 Abraham is described as "the Hebrew", and although no direct connection is here suggested, it is likely that one popular view was that such a title was appropriate because he was descended from an ancestor named "Eber" are closely connected in spelling. Eber is d scribed as the father of Peleg, whose name as we have seen is that of an ancient city. He is the ancestor of many clans besides those which were descended from Abraham, so that the term Hebrew would be broader than the terms Israel. This particular name is not, in fact, often used in the Old Testament itself, and sometimes it appears to have a slightly unfavourable tone which suggests that it might originallyhave been a sort of nickname, applied to a people by someone outside.

In many ancient record, a name appears variouslywritten as Habiru, Hapiru, Aperu, or Apiru; these probably represent the same name, and probably, though not certainly, the same word as 'Hebrew'. Most often the term is used to describe groups of raiders, bandits and other undesirable disturbers of the peace. We may describe them in some more detail as follows:

The Habiru as Refugees and outlaws: (cf: Exod 21:2) By the term 'Hebrew' one is tempted to imagine that an 'lsraelite' is intended, atleast on the basis of the present use of the term in the Old Testament. However, this term had a much more extensive significance, in that it is identical with the sociological class designation habiru which was in use throughout the second millennium BCE. The term habiru appears in one form or another throughout the entire region Spanning from Mesopotamia to the Mediterranean and from Asia Minor down to Egypt; it is designated those people who had abandoned their home regions and become refugees.

What reasons had they, though, to abandon their lands? Of course, a state could always elect to banish one or more of its inhabitants if they prove to be troublesome. In general, we may say on the basic of the occupations which the habiru undertook in their exile, or which were imposed upon them, that they mainly belonged to the peasantry but with the difference that they took refuge in other places, and in due course they become bandits by settling in mountainous regions in the north (king/the middle of the country. The Amarna archives are well supplied with data about the activities of such habiru. These events probably took place in the late Bronze Age.

Some would argue that the name 'Hebrew' originally a sort of occupational name for robbers, subsequently applied to certain tribes or Aramaeans?

In Ezek 16:3 we note that the prophet mentions about the origin of Israelites from the land of Canaan, their father an Amorite, and mother a Hittite. This cannot be regarded as a factual statement, but it does indicate something of the mixture of groups which together made up the people. For there are many indications in the OT of the intermarriage of different groups. The tribes of Ephraim and Manasseh ascribed their origin to the marriage of Joseph with Egyptian wife (Gen 46:20), Moses wife, a Midianite (Exod 2:21, and Cushite (Numb 12:1). Therefore we can say, the people of the OT was welded out of many elements, gathered of various stages of their history.

We shall now turn to another important concern of the patriarchs, i.e., their religion so as to get some clues about their possible origin.

a) The Religion of the Patriarchs: At the outset it must be said that to deduce the nature of the patriarchal religion from the Genesis narrative is not easy. According to Yahwist source (J) the God of the Patriarchs was none other than Yahweh. But elsewhere in Exo 6.2f, it is stated that though it was really Yahweh who had appeared to the patriarchs, he had not been known to them that name. The other strand of thought (E and P) avoid mention of Yahweh until they come to Moses, and speak of the patriarchal deity simply "God" (Elohim). All accounts agree, however, that the patriarchs worshipped God under various names; *El Shaddai* (Ex 6: 7, Gen 17:1, 43:14 etc.); *El 'Elyon* (Gen 14:18-24); *El 'olam* (Gen 21:33); *El Roi* (Gen 16:13 cf. *Yahweh Yir'eh*, (Gen. 22 1.4), *El Bethel* (Gen 31: 13, 35: 7).
b) *The God of the Patriarchs*: In Genesis narratives each Patriarch is represented as undertaking by a free and personal choice the worship of his God to whom he thereafter entrusted himself. Each Patriarch seems to have a clan God, these are: The God of Abraham *('elohe abraham*eg.; Gen. 28:13, 31:42, 53); the kinsman of Isaac (*Pahad yishaq*: Ch 31: 42, 53); and the champion of (might one) Jacob *('abir ya 'qob*: ch. 49:24). The God was the patron deity of the clan. This is illustrated in Gen. 31: 36-55 where Jacob swears by the Kinsman of Isaac, and Laban by the God of Nahor; i.e., each swears by the God of his father's clan.

Although it is impossible to describe the religion of the patriarchs in detail, owing to gaps in our knowledge, it was clearly of a type at home in the world of the day. We may note that the central cult in Ur was Sin cult (moon cult), thus we may suppose that the family of Abraham had once been devotees of Sin. But later Abraham might have moved from Ur due to economic factor, and also due to their personal experience. Thus, the Patriarchal religion was a clan religion, in which the clan was quite really the family of the patron God. The cult of the Patriarchs is depicted as exceedingly simple, as one would expect it to be. At its centre was animal sacrifice, as among all the Semites; but this was performed without organized clergy, and whatever place, by the hand of the clan father himself. As the Patriarchs moved into Palestine they came into contact with various shrines; Shechem, Bethel, Beer-Sheba, etc., there no doubt their cults were practiced and perpetuated in identification with the cults already at home at those places. The Patriarchal cult, however, was never a local one, but always the cult of the ancestral deity of the clan.

Conclusion: In the light of the above discussion on the concerns and issues raised concerning the origin of the people of the Old Testament/Israel we may make the following tentative conclusions: First, due to the lack of concrete evidence on the ancient people and their society we can only reconstruct the actual identity of Israel in plausible terms; Second, the archaeological and epigraphic evidence though reliable to some extent cannot be taken at the face value since the margin of error can be more than the actual time of happening of the events; Third, the information we have about the cultures of the societies that are paralleled to the people of the Old Testament can only be viewed with careful consideration; Fourth, the diverse elements in the religion of the ancestors of Israel are also complex and subject to uncertainties.

2. MIGRATION TO EGYPT

As we have noted earlier in the scriptural reference of Deuteronomy 26:5-9, the term wandering Aramean was somewhat related to the origin of the people of the Old Testament. The same passage goes on to mention other details" . . . and he went down into Egypt and so journeyed there . . . and became a nation, great, mighty, and populous. And the Egyptians treated us harshly and afflicted us, laid upon us hard bondage. Then we cried to the Lord God of our fathers, and the Lord heard our voice, and saw our affliction, our toil, and our oppression; and the Lord brought us out of Egypt with almighty hand and an outstretch arm, with great terror, with signs and wonders".

The real history of the people of the Old Testament begins here with this great experience of oppression and deliverance. They were never to be allowed to forget that they had been slaves in Egypt, and owed their life to divine action: "You shall remember that you were a slave in Egypt and the LORD your God redeemed you from there" (Deut 24:18).

The settlement of tribes' people in the border country of Egypt has taken place two times; In stories of Abraham one such tradition of earlier migration of the shepherds people into the rich delta country has taken place when famine was severe in Canaan (Gen 12: 10-13:1). In Joseph stories (Gen. 37-50) we know about the occasion which led to another such settlement, and probably the Egyptians welcomed the presence on their borders of groups like these which would in time of danger offer them some extra protection against invasion.

We need not be surprised either to find that in a time when building labour was needed urgently, Egyptian rulers were prepared to enslave such people and use them ontheir projects. The Old Testament pictures this as harsh oppression. The tomb of Rekhmire, vizier of Thothmes (1490-1436 B.C.E.), has a picture of brick layers at work. Among the workmen are Semitic foreigners, and the inscription refers to 'captives brought by his majesty for the works of the temple of Amun'.

In one of the Egyptian inscription it is inscribed: 'He supplies us with bread, beer, and every good thing'; the task master is saying: 'the rod is in my hand; be not idle'.

To the people which prided itself on being independent, free to wander to new pastures when it seemed desirable, the restraint of staying in Egypt against their wills would be irksome, even if conditions had not been severe. What they locked for was one who would lead them out of this state of slavery into new life and freedom, and this leader they found in Moses.

Historical Uncertainties: When we come to describe the events more exactly, however, faced with two major difficulties which need to be recognized. The first, we cannot now decide with certainty when the events took place. If we recon back from the time when the people of Israel settled in the land of Canaan (although this is not so easy to interpret), we are still unable to be sure just who was the Pharaoh of the oppression and who the Pharaoh of the Exodus (there isa change of king noted during Moses' career. Exodus 2:23). The period of forty years allotted to the wanderings cannot, in any case, be taken as an exact reckoning, but rather as a convenient period for the same number of years is used frequently in the Old Testament as an approximate statement, especially in the stories in the book of Judges. No Egyptian evidence of the Exodus is available, though it is probable that the cities of Pithom and Raamses, built by Israel for Egypt (Exod 1:11), were rebuilt extensively in the reign of Rameses II (1290-1224 B.C.E.). But we cannot easily interpret all these events as historically accurate.

The second, we have such a wealth of material, gathered from several different traditions about the events, that no completely satisfactory picture can be drawn. Some parts of the story appear more than once, and a great deal of later material has also been gathered into books from Exodus to Deuteronomy. The interpretations of these events was so important to the development of Hebrew thought that the old stories do not appear in simple form, but have been woven in to an elaborate pattern of which the main theme is the glory and power of God and his choice and deliverance of Israel.

We shall consider now few more details concerning the historical background, problems involved in Exodus. As we have already mentioned the Semites immigrated to Egypt in the first place owing to the lack of food caused by a deficiency of rain and they desired to be admitted, and were admitted, to the blessed land of the Nile which did not depend on rainfall. In the Papyrus Anastasi VI from the period of the Pharoah Seti II (C. 1205 B.C.E.) there is a report to his superior by an Egyptian frontier official of the eastern frontier of the delta, in which it is stated among other things, that on the frontier the transit of Bedouin from Edom through the fortress of Merneptah in ***tkw*** (the name for Egyptian city appears in the OT 1n the Hebraized form Succothg) the marshes of ***pr-tm*** (this is Pithom known from the Old Testament) of Merneptah in ***tkw*** had been stopped (?) in order to keep them and their flocks alike in the possession of the king . . . ". 'The Bedouin tribe of Edom' were probably groups of breeders of small cattle with their flocks no doubt quite small flocks from the steppe beyond the Sinaitic desert, like the Israelite tribe before their occupation of Palestine lack of food had persuaded them to try to preserve their life in Egypt. They were admitted to Egyptian state territory in the Wadi tumelat. This particular place or part of it seems to have had a name in ancient times which appears in the Old Testament in the form of 'Goshen' and according to Exod, 8:18, 9:26 it was in the land of Goshen that the Israelites had resided in Egypt. Therefore, the reference made in frontier officials report may have been similar kind that mentioned in the Old Testament.

These Israelites lived in Egypt in circumstances of which we have in details, as people with inferior rights who were usually called 'Hebrews'. The OT often used the word 'Hebrews' when referring to the Israelites in Egypt (Exod 1:19; 2:7, 11:13, 31:3 and elsewhere) is entirely in accordance with the actual situation. The Egyptians were quite familiar with this foreign term which they transliterated as ***'Pr'***. These ***'Pr'*** undertook or were compelled to undertake all kinds of service for the state of Egypt. This is mentioned in various Egyptian texts: For instance, under Rameses II ***'Pr'*** - people appear who haul stones for the great fortress of the city of Raamses, 'the beloved of Amon' and 'haul stones for the god Re, the Re of Rameses, the beloved of Amon, in the building of cities and temples. Under Rameses III we hear of '**Pr**' - people who had settled in the lower Egyptian city of Heliopolis. All this information is entirely in accordance with the tradition of the compulsory labour to which the Israelites were subjected in Egypt, and in particular in line with the information given in Exod 1:11 that the Israelites were used in the building of the cities of Pithom and Raamses in the eastern delta. The point is not that the Egyptian texts refer specifically to the Israelites as 'Hebrews' but they do show that "Hebrew" performing compulsory labour in Egypt were nothing unusual, and they therefore confirm in a most striking way the information about the fate of the Israelites in Egypt contained in the Old Testament.

Thus all the above information clearly indicated how Israelites or 'Hebrew' came down to Egypt for their settlement due to the genuine reasons as mentioned above. However, great caution must be exercised to take the above mentioned information with absolute certainty.

3. LIBERATION FROM EGYPT

Having seen several details about the possible entry of Semites or the so called 'Hebrews' in to the land of Nile for their survival, it becomes extremely difficult task to deal with yet another important aspect of view and when the people of the old testament came out of the Egyptian bondage.

The Israelites, who has gone to Egypt under the pressure of dire distress and had been forced to submit to compulsory labour in the midst of conditions of slavery, finally longed to recover their old freedom. At the same time, Egyptians in a period of busy building activity, as under Rameses II, whose interests were concentrated on the eastern deltadid not want to lose their labour force. The Israelites therefore tried to escape against the will of the Egyptians. In the old Testament the story of the Egyptian plagues and the futile negotiations with the Egyptians concerning the release of the Israelites, where only bore fruit at the very end, were developed in conjunction with the historical explanation of the: old traditional custom of the sacrifice of the Passover observed by the nomadic shepherds. In Exodus 15:15a however, remnant of an earlier account has 'apparently been preserved, according to which the Israelites had 'fled' from Egypt without the knowledge of the Egyptians; and this account is in one likely to be in accordance with the facts. It is true that it is no longer possible to discover any historical details regarding the circumstances of, and opportunities for, this flight.

Israel escaped the Egyptian army by crossing the Red sea, which means the Sea of Reeds (not to be identified with the Red sea) It is impossible to ascertain the locality and the incident more precisely and it would still be impossible even if we had exact information regarding the extent of the arms of the sea and the lakes in the modern Suez Canalarea at the time in question.

But we may suggest the following conclusions:

Some of the groups may have gone to Egypt as early as the late eighteenth century B.C.E., at the start of the foreign (Hyksos) rule; others may have arrived in the late fourteenth or early thirteenth century, only a few years before the oppression reflected in Exodus.

Groups of these ancestors may have left Egypt at different times, separated by many years, and under varied circumstances. The later Israelites preserved few stories from the period of their ancestors' earliest movements into Egypt until the oppression and exodus, but they knew it had been very long (430 years, Exod 12:40, 400 years, Gen 15:13). If there were repeated departures from Egypt, surviving traditions merged them into one complex movement. But all these events surrounded by various traditions is a complex matter to deal with and it is difficult to propose one single route for the exodus it he light of be complexity of the problem. Most scholars date the (final) Exodus from Egypt early in the reign of Pharaoh Ramesses II (ca 1290 B.C.E.)., so that the oppression would have begun not long after the nineteenth dynasty took power (ca 1350 B.C.E.)., and the invasion of Canaan would have started some years before the end of Ramesses' reign (ca 1230 B.C.E.). Another view is that the Hebrew tribes entered Egypt from Canaan at the time of the Hyksos, that the rise of the eighteenth dynasty (ca 1850 B.C.E.) began the oppression, and that the Exodus occurred during; the reign of Thutmose III (ca. 1450 B.C). This is in harmony with the statement (1 Kings 6:1) that the construction of Solomon's Temple (ca 970 B.C.E.) began 480 years after the Israelites left Egypt. This figure (12 generations of forty years) is too exact and probably a secondary calculation to the event.

Different routes have been proposed for the Exodus, as well. One route turns south after crossing the line of the modern Suez Canal (near Bitter Lakes), Parallels the eastern coast of the Gulf of Suez to the vicinity of the turquois mines at Serabit -el khadem, and continues inland to the traditional site of Mount Sinai at Gebel Musa. After the stay at Sinai, the people would have journeyed in a north eastern direction to the northern trip of the Gulf of Aqaba, then around Edom and Moab and on to Transjordan. While this route located Mount Sinai at the place accepted since Byzantine times, it lacks earlier support and conflicts with the biblical view that the people first headed for Canaan and were only condemned to wander after they had been at Sinai and had rejected the report of the spies sent in to the land of from Kadesh in the wilderness of Paran (Numb 13-14). There are other routes as well. The different Pentateuchal sources may have put the route of the Exodus on different combinations of these trails, but all apparently located it in the northern half of Sinai with a step at Kadesh Barnea and an approach to the northern end of the Gulf of Aqaba.

In the light of the above historical problems we can still look at the Israelite exodus from Egypt as miraculous and decisive act of God in their lives. This is clearly evident in terms of the frequent number of exodus verbs employed by the writer in order to make the point clear.

Some verbs of deliverance of Yahweh of Israel/Exodus testimony verbs: An impressive assortment of verbs are used in the Hebrew text in order to talk about the decisive action of Yahweh in the lives of the people of Israel, particularly from their exodus from Egypt. These verbs speak about God's concrete action in their deliverance process from the oppression of Egypt.

i) יצא This verb speak of a geographical exit. The sense of this verb is reflected in Exod 13:3 (and also compare: Exod 12:41; 14:8; Deut 16:3,6). Whatever doubts we may have about the historicity of the Israelite departure from Egypt, their testimony is uncompromisingly about a geographical departure, "from there to here." The verb in *qal* form is simply "you went out";

with reference to Yahweh the verb is put in the causative *hiphil* form, so that Yahweh is the agent who sanctions, propels, and enacts the departure of Israel.

ii) נצל "Yahweh delivers." "I have come down to deliver them from the Egyptians." (See Exodus 3:8 and also 5:23; 6:6; 18:9). This verb refers an abrupt physical act of grasping or seizing—often, as here, grasping or seizing in order to pull out of danger. Same verb is used for David who "snatched" from the danger of a paw of a lion (1 Sam 17:37) and used by Amos referring to Israel being "snatched" by God like a brand from the fire (Amos 4:11). Amos perhaps refers to the Exodus narrative, where Israel is "snatched" out of the danger of Egyptian slavery in a forceful and physical gesture by Yahweh.

iii) גאל "Yahweh redeems." "I will redeem you with an outstretched arm and with mighty acts of judgment." (Exod 6:6 also see 15:13 and also completed action in Psalm 106:10). This verb speaks of a transformative action that is as radical as that of יצא but the ambience of the term is quite different. In the first instance this term means to refer to economic action within a family in order to maintain family property (Lev 25:25 f), or retributive term to avenge in order to maintain family honour (Deut 19:6, 12). The image of the verb suggests something like family solidarity, in which Yahweh acts as kinsperson for the maintenance and wellbeing of the family. Without this intervention, these "kinsfolk" of Yahweh would have disappeared.

The above three verbs witness to a decisive, intrusive act of transformation, whereby Yahweh has interrupted the life of Israel with its "burden of Egypt" and its "slavery to them."

iii) ישא "Thus the Lord saved Israel that day from the Egyptians..." (Exod 14:30 and see Ps 106:8 and used as a noun in Exod 14:13; 15:2). The term is one of power, perhaps be speaking of political action, but more likely a forceful military action. The verb in this most characteristic sentence in Exod 14:30 tells of Yahweh's forceful activity, which ended a situation of fear, suffering, and helplessness and created the possibility of an alternative life that is received by Israel with joy.

iv) פדה "Yahweh redeems." "Every first born of my sons I redeem." (Exod 13:15 and also see Deut 7:8; 15:15; 24:18; Ps 78:42). This verb reflects an economic transaction whereby one is freed from a situation of hardship or risk—for example slavery—when someone pays a cash equivalent. Thus one who pays performs an act of great generosity, which is done freely and without obligation.

v) עלה "Yahweh brings up." (used in hiphil form). "I have come down to deliver them from the Egyptians, and to bring them up out of that land..." "I declare that I will bring you up out of the misery of Egypt..." (Exod 3:17). This verb has a close meaning as that of ישא from the (see Exod 17:3; 32:4,8; 33:1; Numb 14:13; Judg 6:13; 1 Sam 8:8; 10:8; Jer 11:7 and in Judg 6:8, the two terms are used in parallelism). This verb of which Yahweh is subject has a geographical connotation: to move from a lower place to a higher. The implication is that, one "goes up" from slavery to freedom, from the land of Egypt to the land of promise. In liberation from Egypt, Yahweh elevates or exalts Israel—changes its circumstances for the better. In Ps 71:20 the same verb is used metaphorically for the personal rescue and transformation by Yahweh.

4. WANDERINGS AND SINAI TRADITIONS

Just as Exodus tradition is crucial in the faith journey of Israel to determine their future, the wilderness wanderings and the Sinai traditions are equally crucial and significant and also formative in guiding the people of Israel towards their future. Between Exodus and occupation of the land of Canaan this "in between" moment in the life and faith of Israel packed with many twists and turns cannot be forgotten. We shall discuss few concerns in this regard.

4.1. Wanderings in the Wilderness

Between the Exodus and the revelation at Sinai and then between the revelation at Sinai and the settlement there is inserted the area of tradition known as the "guidance in the wilderness". But this does not form a continuous unit; rather it is made up of all sorts of individual sagas and scenes. These essentially describe the resume of the people from various troubles and dangers: hunger (the feeding with manna and Quail Exo. 16, Numb.11) and thirst (water from the rock Exod 17, Numb 20 cf: Exod 15.22 ff), but also threats from enemies (war with Amalek Exod 17:8 ff). Given the context into which they are placed, these individual traditions illustrate Israel's lack of trust in the divine promise, or the "murmuring" of the people as they look back with longing to the "flesh pots" of Egypt (3 I63 Numb 11).

These years of wilderness wandering were years of disappointment, and these are stories of discouragement and disobedience. When there was no water people rebelled against Moses and thus murmured against God (Exod 17:2-3). The story of the making of the golden calf (Exod 32-34) symbolises the people's tendency both at that time and subsequently during their life in Canaan, to away from their first loyalty. Rebellions against Moses (Numb. 12, 14, 16), and discouragement at the prospect of entering the land of Canaan with its powerful inhabitants (Numb 13-14), are also associated with this period.

But the story is also a story of protection and deliverance. God watched over his people to give water and food (Exod 15-17, Numb. 11). They were delivered from the attack of the enemy. For Eg: King of Moab employed the prophet Balaam to utter curses against Israel and so bring disaster upon them, but Balaam found himself prevented by God by cursing, and all his words turnedto blessing (Numb. 23:7:8 and 24:3, 5-6, 8, 9). Like Exodus testimony the people of Israel always looked back with gratitude and fear how in those dreadful years God has led them and protected them even providing their elemental needs in places where such possibilities are scarce. By means of an impressive use of verbs the wilderness wondering tradition has become alive for the readers to listen and meditate on the God's liberative activity in the formation Israelite community.

"Yahweh, the God who leads": Basic reference which affirms this fact is Deut. 8:2-3 "Remember the long way that the Lord your God led (הלך) you these forty years in the wilderness, in order to humble you, testing (נסה). He humbled you by letting you hunger, thereby feeding (אכל) you with manna, with which neither you nor your ancestors were acquainted... "This shows Yahweh's availability to Israel in every circumstance, Yahweh's readiness to enter into situations of risk, vulnerability, and exile, in order to be in dangerous and transformative solidarity with Yahweh's at risk people.

In their liberation experience, Israel had wonderfully witnessed the contest between Yahweh and the Pharaoh. An impressive assortment of verbs is used to describe this activity. Moses just attempted to convince Pharaoh that Yahweh might fall upon (פגע) the Hebrews with pestilence or sword, if they did not go into the wilderness to sacrifice (5:3). That, of course, did not happen. Two verbs meaning "strike" are used in connection with the first two plagues. The Lord struck (נכה) the Nile, turning it to blood (7:25), then struck (נגף) the whole country with the frogs (Exod 8:2). The former verb is also used of killing the first born in 12:12, 29, and the latter is used in the same context of striking the Egyptians in general (12:23,27). In Moses' instructions for the observance of Passover he tells the Hebrews to remember that the Lord killed (הרג) all the first born in the land of Egypt (13:15). He sent his "destroyer" (or destruction, *mashhith*) among them (12:13,23). At the sea, the Lord fought against the Egyptian army (לחם 14:14,25), confused them (14:24), and shook them off into the returning sea (נער, 14:27). then the song of the sea abounds with Violent language. God threw (רמה) horse and rider into the sea (15:1); he cast (ירה) Pharaoh's chariots and army into the sea (15:4). He shattered (רעץ) the enemy (15:6), he overthrew them (הרץ) and his fury consumed them (אכל,15:7). When he blew (vn) with his wind, the sea covered them (15:10). These chapters (5:1-15:21) are filled with destruction and death, all of it the work of Yahweh, ultimately for one purpose, to liberate Israel, his people from the oppressive structures of Pharaoh.

Additionally there are few more verbs that are used to testify how God led the people in their wilderness experience. The sojourn experience was at the same time an occasion for risk and desperation, and foe peculiar sustenance and care. This two fold horizon, which does not permit easy resolution, generating a two-sided testimony concerning Yahweh. On the one hand Yahweh tests (נסה) Israel (Deut 8:2, 16; Exod 15:25; 16:4) in order to find out if Israel is serious in its loyalty to Yahweh. Thus the sojourn experience is a trial in a juridical sense, in order to measure Israel's allegiance to Yahweh. This verb attests to Yahweh's concern for Yahweh's own sovereignty. Yahweh will break no rival, no anaemic or cowardly practiceof faith. Presumably Israel would fail the test if it sets up alternative loyalties that, in the imagination of Israel, would provide better provision in the wilderness, or if it abandoned Yahweh's leadership and resubmitted to the authority of Pharoah (Numb 14:4). The use of the governing term "lead" is intensified by the additional verb "he humbled you" (ענה)—to reduce Israel to drastic need and unambiguous dependence. This verb witnesses to the disputations in which Yahweh relates to Israel, the ominous tendency of Yahweh to deal with Israel for Yahweh's own sake.

Yahweh feeds Israel, and turns out to be a source of adequate food in a context where no other source is available (Exod 16 and Deut 8). Here, feeding is narrated as a "mighty deed." In other contexts it is an act of blessing, as a gift from the natural produce of the fruitful earth (see Josh 5:12; Pss 104:27-28; 145:15-16). This action is connected with wonder on par with Exodus deliverance.

The verb "eat" is intensified with (שׂבע) in both Exod 16:8 and Deut 8:10 which means "to be satisfied or satiated." This verb together "eat and be satisfied" affirm Yahweh's extravagant generosity, which gives abundantly beyond Israel's need and Israel's complete delight in Yahweh's abundance. Yahweh is the God who performs in situations of hazardous scarcity in order to generate abundance.

Another verb "lead" here expressed as (הלך) and (נהל) and also (נחה) found in Exod 15:13; 13:17, 21; Pss 77:20; 78:14, 52-53. This cluster of verbs bespeaks Yahweh's inordinate fidelity to Israel, in being with Israel in circumstance of risk and to assure Israel's safety and wellbeing. The wilderness is the place of without life supports, cannot be safely traversed by Israel on its own resources. Here Israel would employ pastoral-shepherd image for referring Yahweh's guidance in the wilderness. The motifs of testing and feeding, leading/providing are kept in tension. In the end, the positive testimony comes to prevail in the memory and witness of Israel. The verbs and their narrative usage witness to a time in the life of Israel when Israel is completely dependent and Yahweh is unexpectedly and attentively gracious ministering to Israel's most elemental survival needs. Psalm 23 a statement of profound confidence in Yahweh, takes up the aspects of leading and feeding and accompaniment. He leads (נהל) me besides still waters. He leads (נחה) in right paths they comfort (נחם) me; you prepare (ערך) a table before my enemies (Ps 23:2-5). These verbs give the affirmation of "you are with me." The imagery of pastoral-shepherd dominates in wilderness wandering; it speaks of tenderness, gentleness, and attentiveness—like motherly care (Numb 11:11-14). Yahweh has conceived (הרה) and birthed (ילד) his people and is now responsible for them and obliged to feed them.

Time and again Yahweh conformed his intention to deliver the people of Israel from the tyranny of Pharaoh's hand. In 6:6 very strong intention of God is recorded in this direction: "I am the Lord, and I will bring you out from under the burdens of the Egyptians, and I will deliver you from their bondage, and I will redeem you with an outstretched arm and with great acts of judgement". Here the sins of the Egyptians are cited, noting "burdens" and "bondage", and God is the Redeemer carrying out great judgements against them.

But after six plagues, the author feels that a comment on this lengthy process is needed, and three positive things are offered: "that you may know that there is none like me in all the earth", "to show you my power", and "so that my name may be declared throughout all the earth". This is a contest. God needs to make a point ("to show you my power"; "there is none like me in all the earth"), and he needs to prove is not just to Pharaoh, or even to Israel, but to all the earth. These points are reinforced in two other passages. Between the plagues of hail and locusts, God says to Moses, "Go into Pharaoh; for I have *hardened* his heart and the heart of his servants, that I may show these signs among them; that you may know that I am the Lord (10:1f). Here a reason for the hardening of Pharaoh's heart is offered; it is to provide the opportunity for God to reveal himself by signs, acts (miracles to us) and as signs so that they will be known to Pharaoh (9:14). All of this seems to have been initiated because of Israel's sufferings in Egypt, and more particularly God's glory is manifested over Pharaoh in Exod 14:4 and17.

In the light of above discussion it is clear that like the Israelite bondage the exodus from Egypt is also subject to historical problems and the details on this issue is only a matter of reconstruction. However, in the midst of the uncertainty there is possibility that the events related to exodus may be seen as a decisive event in the history of the people of Israel.

4.2. Sinai Traditions

a) *Sinai its location and Geography*: Throughout its history, Sinai was crossed or occupied by many other peoples - like Assyrians, Babylonians Persians, Greeks, Nabateans, and Romans but the most famous sojourn in the wilderness wasmade by the Hebrews after the Exodus. indeed, Sinai was the setting for some of the most important events in Israelite history. The Old Testament does not however, refer to the entire peninsula when it uses the word "Sinai" (The Sinai Peninsula, large, wedge shaped block of territory that forms a land bridge between Africa and Asia. Sinai is bounded on the west by the Suez Canal and the Gulf of Suez, while the Negeb and the Gulf of Aqaba form the peninsula eastern border. Sinai's northern and southern limits are clearly defined by the Mediterranean Sea and in Red Sea, respectively. Its total area is 24,000 square miles - It is part of Saharo-Arabian desert, climate is arid. Its extensive wadi system drains rainfall of 2.5 inches, except along the Mediterranean coast). Instead, the Old Testament mentions five smaller district tracts of wilderness in the large territory (Shur, Sin, Sinai, Paran and Zin).

The wilderness of Sinai, the biblical name for the small distinct wilderness region in which Mount Sinai was located. Its exact location cannot be ascertained. Since its limits are defined in relation to other place names that also defy accurate pinpointing. In general, the bible locates this tract of wasteland in between the wilderness of Sin and Paran and in the vicinity of Elim, Raphidim, and Kibroth-hattavah (Exod16:1, 19: 1-2, Numb 10: 12, 33:15-16). This traditional location of the wilderness of Sinai is in the south central part of the peninsula. It was in this wilderness that the Israelites were encamped when they received the law (eg. Exod. 19:1-2, Lev 7:38), they were numbered (Numb 1:19, 3:14, 26:64) and celebrated the Passover (Num 9:5). It was also in the wilderness of Mount Sinai that Moses encountered the burning bush (Exod 3:1-20).

On Mt.Sinai law was delivered to the people of Israel through Moses (Exod 31:18, 34:29, 32 Lev. 26:40, 27:34 Neh 9:13). The biblical writers refer to Mount Sinai by various names: "the mountain", "the mountain of God", "Mount Horeb", "the mountain of Horeb", and "the mountain of God in Horeb". Its sacred character was magnified when Sinai became the locus of divine revelation par excellence (Exod 19:18, 20,23, 24:16. Deut 33:2, Judg 5:5, 68:8).

b) Sinai traditions: The divine name Yahweh was originally connected with Mount Sinai (Judg 5:4, Deut 32:2); It is said that Moses "went up to God" in order to bring the people to God (Exod 19:24 cf. 33: 12ff).

Another question raised regarding Mt. Sinai is that did Sinai the exact location of which still unknown lie in the area where the nomadic Midianites lived? Is it possible that Israel's ancestors, received their faith in Yahweh through the Midianites (see Exod 18:2) or the Kenites (see Gen. 4:15). In any event the tradition preserved the reliable recollection that Moses had been the son-in-law of a Midianite priest (Exod 2: 16 ft; 18) or a kenite (Judg 1:16, 4:11). Is Moses who played a mediatorial role in the revelation of Sinai also a nuclear part of the tradition? These questions are difficult to answer with precision, but we can only say that on the basis of biblical tradition Moses story becomes an integral part in the Sinai tradition.

The Sinai pericope as we have it contains essentially three themes (or three traditions):

i. The Theophany that is the manifestation of God in natural events, whether volcanic activity or a thunder storm (Exod 19:16 ft).
ii. The conclusion of a covenant, that is the establishment of a community embracing God and the people (Exod 24, 34 chapters).
iii. And the proclamation of God's law (esp Exod 20-23rd Chapters, 34th Chapter).

In its original form, the tradition certainly included the theophany and, in all probability the encounter with God, who initiated an abiding relationship, which probably only later on was given the name "covenant". But, Is the proclamation of the law not an original and independent element in the tradition? In any case in as much as the Decalogue, the Book Of the covenant, and other collections of legal prescriptions and cultic ordinances have been inserted into the Sinai Pericope, ethical laws governing human social life and divine worship are seen as flowingfrom the relationship with God.

So we could say that the Sinai tradition is a concentration of reminiscences about the beginnings and foundations of Israelite religion, though it is impossible to paint a clear historical picture from it. One thing is Quite clear; that the God with whom these Sinai traditions deal is YHWH. However, in the present narrative complex the name of YHWH is already made known to Moses at his first divine encounter on the mountain of God (Exod 3: 13-15) cf 6:9). The name can therefore be presumed to be known in Exod l9ff. This again shows the significance of the way in which the complexes of tradition have been interwoven in a narrative.

Chapter 4

Settlement and Formative Period

1. THE SETTLEMENT IN PALESTINE

According to the Old Testament account, the Israelites travelled purposefully to the land promised to them by God, in order to take possession of it. Numbers 13:1ff reports that according to a divine command Moses sent out representatives of the twelve tribes to spy out the land. There was a dispute and finally an unsuccessful attempt to capture the land from the South (Numbers 13). Then began a further period of wandering, lasting forty years (14:33). Until the generation responsible for this interlude had died (cf 26:64). Meanwhile, the Israelites had approached the land by going a wide sweep to the east and after fighting with a number of kings in Transjordan took possession of their territory (21:21). This was subsequently assigned to the tribes of Reuben and Gad (32:33-38). After the death of Moses, the Israelites then crossed the Jordan under the leadership of Joshua (Joshua 3:8) again after sending out scouts in advance (Joshua 2) and began to capture the country (chs. 6 ff). Finally, the land was divided among the remaining ten tribes with great exactness (Chs. 13-19). Thus we can see the settlement of Israelite tribes in the land of Canaan as the capstone of the Israel's national epic, if Exodus is the foundation.

What is said above is only one side of the picture painted in one Biblical tradition mainly in the book of Joshua. In Judges (1:1-2:5 and 2:6-3:6) we have another picture painted which says that the conquest to the land of Canaan is not possible due to the people's infidelity to Yahweh. Thus we have no single and coherent picture presented about the conquest in the Old Testament. One of reasons for raising problems about the integrity of the biblical reports of the conquest is that it has been played down in the rest of the Old Testament.

Unlike the Exodus, there is hardly a recapitulation of its traditions elsewhere in the Old Testament (except in Micah 6: 1-4).

Two major opinions prevail about the conquest, whether Israelites entered the land from outside or from inside. We shall now briefly present some Views in each of these strands along with the proposals made by scholars.

1.1. Theories in which Israel enters Canaan from outside

a) *The Conventional Conquest Hypothesis (13 Century)* This Hypothesis very much adhere to the biblical traditions According to this view Israel was believed to enter in the land of Canaan violently and in concert. Most of these historians support the view that the conquest occurred in the 13th century B.C.E. The prime supporters of this theory was W. F. Albright andhis pupils John Bright and G Ernest Wright. This theory was supported by the above mentioned scholars due to following reasons:

i) 13th Century conquest was possible due to the support 0E archaeological excavations of Bethel & Debir and their destruction;
ii) The excavations at Tell ed-Duweir identified Lachish and the destruction layer was dated 1230/1220 BCE. Moreover, Yigal Yadin excavated Hazor which is to be dated to 1220 BCE.
iii) According to G.E. Wright's analysis of the data, if the conquest was set at around 1220 BCE., the Exodus would have occurred around 1260 BCE i.e., 40 years earlier according to Numbers 14:33. This was further confirmed by Nelson Glueck (1930) who after some excavations at Transjordan, concluded that the region was devoid of any settled population between 19th and 13th centuries BCE.

But there are several objections to this theory even through it look; convincing. The main objection being Joshua apparently had no connection with the fall of Jericho. If we take the date of the conquest as the thirteenth century, the ruins were then 50 years before Joshua crossed Jordan. Moreover, accordingto K. Kenyon there is no single entry of the Israelites to Canaan, but rather a diverse and sporadic infiltration of groups which ultimately coalesced. As per her evidence based on her excavations the evidence at Jericho suggests a destruction on the last quarter of the 13th century BCE at Tell Beit Mirsim and Tell Duweir. There is a destruction in the second half of the 13th century BCE. No evidence was found which would support the existence of a town in the second half of the 13th century B.C.E.

b) *The Conventional Conquest Hypothesis (15th Century):* This was proposed by scholars like L T Wood, J. B Payne, J. J. Bimson, et al. The main basis for this date is based on the internal chronology furnished to the Old Testament itself, especially in 1 Kings 6:1 and Judges 11:26. J. J. Bimson is of the opinion that the date of the conquest is 15th century B. C. E. on the basis of the fall of the Palestine fortress cities at the end of middle bronze age (15th century B.C.E.) by a big and unified group from Egypt.

But the problem with this proposal is that they deal extensively with biblical chronology and fails to adequately explain the gap in occupation with Transjordan. He also fails to furnish any evidence for the violent entry of the people into Canaan in the fifteenth century B.C.E.

c) <u>*The Infiltration Hypothesis*</u>: The proponents of this hypothesis share with the earlier discussed schools the view that Israelite tribes came into Canaan from outside. They also by and large hold to the 13th century dating of the entry. But, those who support this thesis have concluded that there was no real conquest but that the semi-nomadic tribes infiltrated peacefully into uninhabited or sparsely inhabited territories and into the gaps between the Canaanite cities at a time when no firm control was being exercised by Egypt. This peaceful occupation of taking possession of the land was followed by a period of consolidation, when, settling and developing the country, the tribes came into conflict with the Canaanite cities. The occupation was thus a long process and was characterised by various displacements of people and geographically distinct movements. The proponents of this theory argue that stories of the conquest in the book of Joshua are aetiological and Joshua himself played practically no historical part at all in them.

Albrecht Alt was the first one to formulate this theory back in 1925 who firmly believed that Israelite tribes undertook a course of peaceful and seminomadic infiltration into the land of Canaan. This theory was further modified and developed by Martin Noth, who dates the conquest approximately to the second half of the fourteenth century B.C.E. after Amarna period. Yet another scholar who supports this theory with some modifications was M. Weippert. According to him, the first, non-violent settlement was undertaken by the tribes of the group of Leah and those associated with it, the group of Billhah and Zilpah. The cult of Yahweh and the institution of holy war was introduced later on by the group of Rachel tribes. This initiated the Period of violent occupation.

The most important to this theory was offered by W.F. Albright, Y. Kaufmann and John Bright. They point out the fact that this theory is too much dependent on aetiology and it either minimises or neglect the external evidence of archaeology. Bimson questions the aeotiological points raised by Martin Noth concerning the city of Ai, he feels that Martin Noth's theory fails to account for certain of the narrative features, such as the appearance of a king of Ai and the apparent existence of a city gate, which implies the existence of fortified walls. Norman K. Gottwald contends that Noth's theory depends very heavily on the theory of a twelve tribe Israelite amphictyony and he levels a heavy barrage of criticism against it.

1.2. Theories in which Israel is Indigenous to Canaan

a) *The Peasant Revolt Hypothesis*: In 1962, G.E. Mendenhall propose what would be termed an internal revolt theory regarding Israel's origins and the occupation of Canaan. He argued that the conquest of Palestine by Israel was not a matter of one ethnic group, Israel destroying another, Canaan, but rather a case of the indigenous masses of Canaan raising against a ruling aristocracy comprising primarily of foreign military conquerors who had recently invaded the land such as the Hittites, Hivvites, Girgashites, Perizzetes and Jebusites. What caused in rebellion was the small mixed group who had made a covenant at Sinai with Yahweh. The terms of the covenant between Yahweh and this newly formed community of Israel were such that they created a solidarity of loyalty which was attractive to all persons suffering under the burden of subjugation to a monopoly of power which they had no part. The early Israelites were thus seen as the native peasantry of Canaan withdrawing from the oppressive structures of the city state system.

Norman K. Gottwald took up this thesis and developed it further along distinctive lines. He explains that the early Israel was an eclectic formation of marginal and depressed Canaanite people including feudalized peasants (hupshu). Apiru, mercenaries and adventurers, trans-human pastoralists, tribally organized farmers and pastoral nomads (shoshu), and probably also itinerant craftsmen and disaffected priests, (N.K. Gottwald, *Tribes of Yahweh*, p. xxii). Furthermore, Gottwald proposed that Israel's social structure was a deliberate retribalization process rather than an unreflective uni-linear carry over from pastoral nomadic tribalism.

Further he says, Yahwism as a religion was a crucial societal instrument for cementing and motivating the peculiar constellation of unifying and decentralizing sociocultural patterns necessary to the optimal functioning of the social system and in an extreme situation to its survival. Gottwald departs from Mendenhall by rejecting the Mosaic covenant and its religious ideology as a significant factorin Israel's emergence from Canaanite society. He expresses doubts about the historical value of the Exodus Sinai traditions. Further, Mendenhall treats the 'revolt' as something happening virtually overnight while Gottwald extends the process, supplementing the 'Peasant rebellion' model with one of 'Social revolution' which ebbs and flows over a com le of centuries.

Even though, this theory was spoken and presented with lot of enthusiasm, serious criticism was levelled against it by several scholars. Hauser attacks Mendenhall's thesis by saying that, if the revolt was on a large scale as was proposed by Mendenhall, then there is no such biblical evidence. Furthermore, Hauser says that Mendenhall underestimated the strength of the Canaanite rulers as it would have been extremely difficult for the peasants to overcome their military power. A serious blow to Gottwald's theory is that there is a total lack of externalevidence to substantiate a revolt by peasants, which took place in the 13th Century B.C.E. Infact, the archaeology of 13th century Canaan does not support the distinction between rural Peasantry and an urban aristocracy which is the basic presupposition of this theory.

b) Evolutionary Israel Hypothesis: This theory was proposed by Niels Peter Lemche, who, while critiquing the earlier revolutionary model of Israel's beginnings prefers to speak of an 'revolutionary Israel'. For Lemche, the biblical traditions must be considered as basically a historical and may be used only exceptionally if verified by external data as they are composed so late. He reconstructs the origins of Israel solely using archaeological materials of the social, economic, cultural and political developments in Palestine towards the close of the second millennium. According to Lemche, from the first half of the 14th century B.C.E. the 'Apiru' inhabited the central highlands. He defines them as 'a para social element . . . of runaway former peasants or copy holders from the small city-states in the place and valleys of Palestine. (N.P. Lemche, *Early Israel*, p.427). At one time they were settled agriculturists and are attested in the Amarna letters. However, they do not appear in archaeological evidence for that period as then they were not sedentary but roving outlaws. A century later at the beginning of the Iron Age, they formed new settlements, with new political structures and returned to agriculture, retribalizing themselves. Israel was the result of that process.

Based on the above discussion we can make few observations as follows: The earlier theories for the occupation deals with Israel's entry into Canaan from outside somehow forced the archaeological data into the biblical traditions. However, the infiltration model proposed seem to have had some influence than other theories and it is seen as a reasonable theory in the light of the problem. The Israelites not having an organized force should have made a peaceful entry into the land of Canaan. Internal Revolt Theory or Peasant Revolt Theory of Mendenhall and Gottwald also seem to be attractive and must be considered with a great caution.

2. THE ROLE OF JUDGES

The role of Judges intended to account for the period between the death of Joshua and the appearance of Samuel. Because the narratives concerning the Judges are of such unequal length, it has become customary to use two different terms for the Judges.

The heroes of the detailed narratives are called the "major" Judges: Othniel, Ehud, Deborah (and Barak), Gideon (and Abimelech), Jephthah and Samson; those that are merely mentioned in brief notices are called the "Minor" Judges; Shamgar, Tola, Jair, lbzan, Elon and Abdon. Within the frame work of the presentation, they all appear to exercise their Judgeship over the entire nation as regents of Israel and forerunners of the Kings.

More precisely, we can distinguish two types of figure included under the Hebrew term "Judge", which actually means, "executor of Justice", "helper", "ruler". This first group comprises warlike heroes, be they leaders of tribal militants, tribal heroes, or individuals about whom we have sufficient information. They are Othniel, Ehud, Shamgar, Deborah, Gideon, Abimelech, Jephthah, Samson. A second group with data concerning the length of time the person in question Judged Israel, his family and his burial place, obviously represents a different type.

In the book of Judges, the retrospective verdict on this period is negative the unifying power of the monarchy was absent, so that each person did what he wanted (17:6; 21:25) this judgement is based on the presupposition that 'Israel' was a unity which only lacked, leadership.

The word 'Judge' as it is used for the book in the Old Testament ought perhaps often to be rendered as 'deliverer', since the most important function of these leaders was saving of their people from some disaster or oppression. Some at least among them are described as exercising rule over the tribesmen, so that the function of the 'Judge' might well include the administering of justice as well. In those two aspects of the Judge's activity, we have an anticipation of the function of the king the deliverer of his people and the upholder of justice and right. Not all the judges conform to this picture. Some of them were popular figures, whose exploits formed the subjects of favourite tales; such a one was Samson. Nor did these leaders have authority over all the tribes. What they did was local in its effect, there was deliverance and protection for a time and then a new threat appeared, perhaps in the same area or somewhere else, and a new leader was needed. There was no continuity, no king to rule all the time over the people and be succeeded by his son. As time went on the stories of these local heroes, handed down in their own tribe became part of the common stock Hebrew tradition and was natural that they should be thought of as national heroes and so as rulers over all the people.

The Benjaminite Ehud (Judg. 3: 12-30) murders the Moabite King Eglon and then from the 'hill-country of Ephraim' declares war on the Moabites (v. 27); the battle essentially takes place at the fords over the Jordan. According to the account no one takes part in it, other than the Benjaminities and their northern neighbours, the Ephraimite Shamgar is said to have carried out a one-man action against the Philistines (3:31). Gideon's expedition against the Midianites (Judg 6-8) involve only his class of Abiezrites to begin with (16:11) and is then extended to the tribe of Manasseh and the neighbouring northern tribes of Asher, Zebulun and Naphtali (v. 35; Zebulun is missing from 7:23); finally, the Ephraimites are also summoned for the last act (7:24), complaining about their late inclusion (8: 1). Jephthah's battle against the

Ammonites (10:6-12:6) is a purely Transjordanian affair (11:29: Gilead and Manasseh. i.e., the North east of the Jordan) and again the Ephraimites complain about not having been involved (12:1 ff); this is perhaps and expression of Ephraim's claim to leadership.

Only on one occasion is a larger number of tribes mentioned. In Judg 4:5, there are two descriptions of a battle on plain of Jezreel under the leadership of Deborah (and Barak, the commander appointed by her, cf. 4:6 ff). This time the enemy does not come from outside. The real opponent is Sisera from the Harosheth-Goyim (4:26) on the north-west slope of the plain of Jezreel. (In 4:29 there is a mention of King Jabin of Hazor. who is even called "King of Canaan" (v 23 ff); this is probably meant to indicate the basic importance of the battle in the struggle against the Canaanites; Jabin himself evidently has nothing to do with the battle). InJudg 4 only Zebulun and Naphtali are mentioned as tribes involved in the battle (vv 6, 10). In Judg 5:14ff, however, the circle is extended. Ephraim, Benjamin, Machir, Zebulun, Issachar (and Napthali cf. v. 18) are involved, i.e., the whole of the Northern tribes. It is significant that other tribes are also mentioned, and are criticised which did not take part: the Transjordanian tribes of Reuben and Gilead along with the remaining Northern tribes, Dan and Asher (vv 15b 17). Here we can recognize the view that all the tribes should really have taken part in the battle. This unfulfilled postulate of unity, however, shows at the same time that this unity did not exist. Besides, the southern tribes of Judah and Simeon are not mentioned, so that the passage clearly does not envisage union of twelve tribes. Nor do we find anywhere in the book of Judges the reference to 12 tribes or true sense of being all Israel which would embrace this.

The deliverer figure of Judges appears spontaneously, always in situations of extreme need. It is evident that they do not hold any 'office' in the institutional sense and that there is no continuity between the individual deliverers. They are therefore often described as 'Charismatic Military leaders'. This primarily, denotes that their function was essentially military namely to summon and lead the 'army', i.e., all able bodied men capable of bearing arms (cf. 3:27; 4:10; 6:34 f;11:29) The use of the term 'Charismatic' is particularly the 'deliverer' (3:10,6:34;11:29).

According to Von Rad the wars described in the time of Judges can called as 'holy war', that they are not really waged by Israel itself but by YHWH for Israel. It is therefore better to describe them as Yahweh's wars. In this sense we can say that God becomes central who heard the cry of the people, on each occasion raises up ajudge whom he endows with the spirit.

The lesson we can learn from each of the Judge is, above all, that those who are dedicated to Yahweh can be used by Yahweh, the individuals despite of their short comings because of their dedication, Yahweh could use them to deliver Israel from its oppressors and to keep the tribal federation alive until Israel was ready for the next stage in his great redemptive purpose.

3. INTERACTION/CONFLICTS WITH THE CANAANITE CITY DWELLERS

The country in which the Israelite tribes settled was an inhabited land. In the Old Testament the people that had lived in the land in pre-Israelite times and usually called 'Canaanites' without regard to their economic differences. In this sense, the term is used here for our discussion. The Canaanite popu1ation was concentrated in the numerous fortified cities but population is not even distributed throughout the country. Some have settled in the plains and sort fertile and mountainous parts of the land. Hence, these cities are not fully occupied and the irregular distribution of the Canaanites helped the Israelites to gain a footing in parts of the country which were inhabited only sparsely or not at all. With this kind of settlements Israelites developed particular and entered into neighbourly relations with the Canaanites in many places. But we have very less information and it shows that their mutual relations varied enormously exceeding to time and place.

On the whole the Israelite tribes remained alien to the Canaanite way of life. On the one hand we see the culture of Israelite tribes was essentially agriculture and cattle-rearing and on the other hand Canaanites were interested in industry, commerce and profit-making which was rooted 1n their urban civilization. Thus the Israelites seem to have stayed separated to the Canaanite way of life. The Israelites, whose tribal organization was based on the equal rights of all the free members of the tribe, regarded the social stratification in the Canaanite cities as alien to their own social outlook; In Canaanites instead there was a ruling, property owning aristocracy on the one and with a feudal lord at the summit, who called himself a king, and on the other hand, in Israel we see a subject population devoted primarily to agricultural work. The military technique of chariot fighting as practiced by the ruling classes of the (Canaanite) cities was alien to the Israelites, and was also an object of terror to them. The Israelite tribes who fight with their own weapons, felt inferior to the contingents of iron chariots and they dare not to undertake war attacks on Canaanites cities (Joshua I7:16, 18, Judg. 1:19, 4:3, l3). Above all, it was the life and faith of the Canaanites that was very much alien to the Israelites. For instance, a girl who appears unprotected in the vicinity of a Canaanite city may easily be raped by one ofthe inhabitants, possibly even the son of the city King himself (cf. Gen. 34: 12 ff). For the Israelite tribes, who were used to the strict discipline of a patriarchal society, all this moral laxity was shocking. The cults which flourished among the Canaanites were the immemorial rites of the great fertility-bestowing mother deity generally called Astarte in Canaan, and of a youthful deity who represented the annual blossoming and dying of vegetation. These cults included the celebration of a 'holy marriage' at a holy place with female representations of the deity and 'sacred' prostitution and the cultic sacrifice of female chastity. There was also the cult of the multiform Ball, the fairly ancient Baal of heaven and the numerous local Baals which were also given of life and fertility and held survey in the sphere of sexual life. The Israelites were bound to reject all this, especially the Worship of female deities.

Despite the feeling of alienation to the culture and the way of life of the Canaanites, Israelites were not entirely hostile to the Canaanite culture. There are instances in which Israelites gained few things from the way of life of the Canaanites. For instance, in the period of occupation of the land the tribes of Issachar, Zebulun and Asher, which settled on the borders of the plain of Jezreel and the plain of Acco, apparently entered into feudal relationship with the city government in the plains and probably received share of the profits occurring from their rich estates in return for their services.

In the plains of Palestine Canaanites had upper hand where as in the mountains the Israelite tribes prevailed over the more scattered cities. But in intermediary area between the Southern Palestinian Mountains and the Southern part of the maritime plain a peaceful process of mutual assimilation existed between the Canaanites and Israelites. It was here that the vigorous tribe of Judah was seeking to expand and here the Judaeans and Canaanites had co-existence (cf. Gen 38 chapter).

However, it is true that the contacts between Israelites and Canaanites so far as they occurred at all, were not entirely of a peaceful nature. Warlike encounters between them evidently occurred at a very early stage. The information in this regard is very sporadic. In general, we learn that Israelites gained victory over the Canaanites but even the contrary situation also occurred. The fact that the Canaanite city rulers were able for the most part to maintain their properties is in general to be attributed to the fact that the cities were able to defend themselves against the encroachments of the Israelites by force of arms. On the other hand, the Israelites tribes are capable of warding off such attacks by their neighbours. For instance, in Joshua 10:1-5, in the story of the battle of Gibeon, the Israelites tribes especially the tribes of Benjamin and Ephraim defeated the army of the enemies in a mighty way. But such incidents are very much limited in extent and significance.

The Israelite tribes succeeded more than once in conquering individual Canaanite Cities by force of arms and obtaining possession for their settlement and territory. According to the available information, the cities in question were in more or less isolated spots away from the great city state territories. For instance, in Judges 1:10-15 (Joshua 15:14-19 of Joshua 14: 12) there is a reference to the fact that the Calebites (in Judges 1:10 the name 'Judah' may be assumed to have been originally 'Caleb' as in Joshua 15:14) had conquered the city of Hebron and the Othnielites, to whom they were related, had conquered the neighbouring city of Debir. According to the note in Numb. 13:22b, Hebron was formerly a Canaanite city; and the same may be true of Debir though there is no positive archaeological or literary evidence on this point. According to Judges 1:22-26, the 'houseof Joseph' conquered the city of Bethel which was situated right on the Southern border of its settlement. According to Joshua 11:1-15 in the remoted uppermost part of the Jordan valley the city of Hazor (the modern tell Wakkas) was conquered and destroyed by Israelites, and probably by the neighbouring tribe of Naphtali, and its territory annexed. In Judges 18:27f we hear the report about the tribe of Dan conquering the city of Laish (Modern tell el-Kadi) which was situated near the sources of Jordan. In the Old Testament tradition all these conquests are directly related to the occupation of the Land. These attacks by the Israelites tribes on the Canaanite cities did not take place until the tribes had established themselves in their vicinity.

We only hear of a war of any importance waged by Israelites tribe against Canaanite cities within the city state system proper, that is, in one of the plains; but such incidents were obviously quite exceptional, this is reported in Judges Chapter 5. We know little about the background of this victory; Sisera was King in Harosheth at the North Western end of the plain of Jezreel. His name is probably Illyrian and, if so,he may have been a member of the ruling class of the 'Sea peoples'. It may be that he exercised a kind of sovereignty over the cities in the plains of Jezreel which were occupied partly by 'Canaanites' and partly by 'sea peoples' and perhaps in the plain of Acco too.

According to Judges, 14:6, 10 the conflict was started by the neighbouring tribes of Naphtali and Zebulun. There is no reference to the results which followed from this event. But the most important result of the victory from the point of view of Israelites tribes was undoubtedly the experience which they gained ofbeing, with the help oftheir God, a match for and even superior to the might of the Canaanite chariots. This meant the disappearance of their feeling of insecurity and fear of military technique and power of their earlier inhabitants of the land; and so it became possible for the tribes to attain a position of superiority over the Canaanite city-state system. Moreover, regarding the time in which this victory of Israelites over the Sisera's army took place probably sometime during which the tribes were settling down and securing and developing their territories. Even though, there existed some good ground for the Israelites footing in the Canaanite cities the small scale tensions continue to exist.

Such conflicts can be heard in the story of Abimelech the 'son of Jerub-Baal (Judges 9). This story reveals the fact oftension that existed between the political and social structure of the Israelites and Canaanites. It is also important to note from the story of Abimelech, he was the first Israelite-though on his mother's side he was an Israelite-Canaanite half caste; to call himself a 'king', moreover one can hardly call this adventure of Abimelech reported in Judges 9 a prelude to the subsequent formation of a kingdom in Israel; but the story of Abimelech is remarkable as evidence of the tensions existing between the Israelites and Canaanite, systems.

Thus on the basis of above discussion we may conclude that the interaction between the Canaanites and Israelites had gone through different stages where at times it was a positive assimilation between them and at times resulting in a conflicting situation. But the fact remains that deep rooted relationship and interaction between two nations cannot be denied and that relationship had far reaching impact in the years to come in the history.

4. TRIBAL SOCIAL ORGANIZATION

A study on the Israelite tribal social organization is vital for the clear grasp of the early or pre-monarchic history of Israel. In Israel, an individual cannot stand alone, instead an individual is firmly integrated in the bonds of the society at large. The social organization of early Israelite tribals, i.e., their economic mode of life, political order, military defence, judicatory procedure, religious organization, etc., is complex matter of concern.

The word "tribe" is derived from the Hebrew words: *Shevat/Matteh* : both words are used together in Numb. 36:6, literally means a "rod" or "staff", conceived as a weapon or a ceremonial object. When the force of the words applied to the social unit, it emphasizes a group's autonomy as potency in military self-defence and in political self-rule. In other words, a tribe was normally understood as "an autonomous group of families who believe they are descended from common ancestor". In Judges 13:2, 18:2 another word *Mispahah* is used to denote that it is the protective association of families, smaller that *Shevat*, other words used to dente a tribal organization are *bayith* or *beth-av* which means; the household, or father's house (Judges 11:2; Joshua 7).

N.K. Gottwald traces few biblical references to show how that scheme of twelve tribe league existed in pre-monarchic Israel, however he observes that such texts may be explained as late surviving memories of a pre-monarchic scheme. Such references are as follows: twelve sons of Jacob (Gen 29:3130; 24; 35:16, 26; 42:13, 32); sending twelve scouts from twelve tribes taken from Jordan and set up either in the rives bed or at Gilgal (Joshua 3:12; 4:3-4, 8-9, 20); Judges 19:29 mentions about twelve dismembered parts of the Concubine's body sent throughout Israel to summon twelve tribes to punish Benjamin.

According to Baruch Halpern, the song of Deborah in Judges chapter 5 "represents the most formidable testimony to the existence of a league of tribes in the pre-monarchic ers, probably from 12th century B.C.E. (Judges 5:2-11)".

Since there is a mention of ten tribes in this place it must be considered as most important and genuine evidence for the organization of the tribes in Israel. Furthermore, Halpern points out there is another textual evidence as well to support the tribal social organization, but they must be used with caution, they are: Exod 15:17-18, Ps. 78, Joshua 24:6.7, Ps. 68:27, Deut. 33, etc.

We also have archaeological evidence to say with some extent that tribal organization or tribes existed in Israel, especially in the pre-monarchic Israel. One such evidence is found in a famous Merneptah inscription found in the year 1210 B.C.E. In this inscription Pharaoh mentions of having destroyed a number of Palestinian town through the way in which "Israel" is written in this inscription is in question; but it reflects Israelite tribes did exist in the central Palestine around 1200 B.C.E. (cf. Joshua 13-21 Chapters).

Another inscription from Egypt found in Beth-Shan during 1300 B.C.E. seem to have mentioned about the Israelites tribes. The names mentioned in Beth-Shan may be Habiru, who lived in accordance with the technological changes of 13th century B. C E. This fact is confirmed by the use of waterproof asphalt coated cisterns. But all this information IS only indirect evidence rather than direct support to the tribe/tribal organisation in Israel.

Several Scholars of the Old Testament studies have come up with different models for the origins emergence and formation of a possible social tribal organisation in Israel. In dealing with several theories one basic question is to be kept in mind; the question is what was the formation of Israelite society? or Whose social system from which it emerged and against which it was counter-posed? Now let us go on to consider the models proposed by the scholars in brief.

4.1. The Pastoral Nomadic Model

According to the theories of conquest and immigration, Israelites are understood as pastoral nomads who invaded or infiltrated Canaan from the desert. This theory was mainly proposed and supported by the Baltimore school led by W.E. Albright and his disciples. But this traditional view is questioned by N.K. Gottwald, M.L. Chaney, N.P. Lemche and other recent scholars.

Gottwald rightly observes that the general features ascribed to nomads such as keeping cattle, asses, sheep, living in the wooden and grass houses are the common features of any settled people, not particular to nomads or semi-nomads. Moreover, there are agricultural farmers who undertook nomadic life temporarily, for a while and returned back to their original farming when economic and political circumstances prompted. For Gottwald, Israelites are not pastoral nomads but that Israelite tribal society as a unique and politically decentralized power, and socially an egalitarian society as against stratified society.

4.2. Israelite Tribes as a Confederation

In the year 1930 Martin Noth has proposed a theory for the tribal league in early Israel This theory is based on the following factors:

a) To begin with Noth identifies two important groups of texts for the tribal lists (i). Gen 49: 16-27 (ii). Numb 26: 45-51 with the two principal tribes namely Leah tribes and Rachel tribes.
b) Noth observes that the tribes were not organised socially until the time of occupation. Therefore, it is difficult to determine the actual period in which they were united.
c) Noth proposes that number twelve and six are prominent numbers for Israelites, thus even when the tribal system changed from time to time number twelve was kept up and maintained regularly. But in the beginning six tribe federation was important and it served as a fore runner of the later twelve tribe association.
d) One of the unique contribution of Martin Noth was to ascribe the term Amphictyony (derived from the Greek word *Amphictiones*, means an organisation in which people were settled or dwelt around a focal point to the twelve tribe federation among Israelites. This word equates the social organisation used in Israel and in Greek shrines, particularly the shrines of Appollo and Delphi.
e) Noth gives the details of the amphictyonic model as follows: Like any other amphictonies there was a central shrine set at places in Israel via., Shechem (Joshua 24), Bethel (Gen. 35:1-5), Gilgal (Joshua 3,4) and Shiloh (I Sam. 3:3) respectively. So also in accordance with the regulations of an amphictyony, there was a central amphictyonic council, Noth calls this in Israel as the federal assemblies represented by elders called *Nasi'im* (1 Kings 8:1; 2 Sam. 3:17, 1:33, 17:4, 15).

While Noth's theory has been widely accepted with great appreciation, son problems involved in this theory are also pointed out. Gottwald observes that Noth has failed to see the variation in structural and functional positions of two religious (Mediterranean and Israelite) confederations in two different society systems. Moreover, Gottwald remarks that there is no single cultic obligatory site for the Israelite worship as described by Noth. Furthermore, the amplictyonic council found in Greece is quite different from the Israelite one if even such a council existed in Israel. In Greece the amphityonic council composed of delegates appointed by each member who is responsible for the up keep and protection of the central shrine. In Greek amphictyony members are from city states as against Israelite federation whose members are tribes.

4.3. The Socio-religious Retribalization Model (Israel a revolutionary peasants)

This theory was proposed by Norman K. Gottwald who says "that Israel burst into history as an ethnically and socio-economically mixed coalition composed of a majority of tribally organised peasants (eighty percent or more of the populace) along with lesser number of pastoral nomads, mercenaries and free hooters, associated craftsman, and renegade priests. These sections of indigenous populace joined in a combined socio-political and religious revolution against the imperial and hierarchic tribute-imposing structures of Egyptian dominated Canaan". Gottwald's theory is further explained on the following grounds:

a) Yahwistic Israel consciously organised large scale egalitarian movement. This movement was lacking in all the Amarna period. Israel's movement was pro-egalitarian, anti-feudal and social organization. This movement of Israel challenged Egyptian imperialism and rejected city state feudalism.
b) There was a unitary cult and ideology of this rebellious community of Israel in order to re-enforce their social, economic and military unity through this cult.
c) One of the basic element contained in this model of Gottwald is the decentralization of power in the hands of elders, priests and military leaders. This perhaps would have led a possible opposition against state power bureaucratic credential and ambitious power seekers.
d) In the socio-economic spheres, efforts were made to strengthen the egalitarian values. Eg: Land was not allowed for sale; it can only be transferred from one family to another with in the extended families. No interest was allowed on such loans given for emergency purposes, special provisions were made for socially vulnerable groups (viz. widows, orphans, etc.).
e) In the process of revolution Canaanites joined with Israelites by lending their support to the sovereign unity of Israel and to Praise their covenant Lord Yahweh.

Despite several positive conclusions made by Gottwald, problems are quite transparent in his theory.

J.J. Brimson is of the opinion that there is no evidence for the peasant revolt in 13th Cent B.C.E., this is further attested by the evidence from archaeological excavations., that in the 13th Century, there is no clear distinction between a rural peasantry and an urban aristocracy as envisaged by Gottwald., T. L. Thompson comments that Gottwald has failed to consider the geography of Palestinian. Transjordan and Sinai and concomitantly the agricultural and pastoral economics and associated social structures, comparable to that of Mari.

According to Gottwald, Israelite society was a nomadic/segmentary one, thus an egalitarian society. But N.P. Lemche responding to such conclusion of Gottwald says, "We must reject the notion that the Israelite tribes were governed by a self-regulating egalitarian ideology, if the source do not permit us to conclude that this sort of political organization existed". Responding to Gottwald's proposal that Israelite tribal society played unique role in its own time, Lemche remarks "that Israel was actually one among many stateless societies which arise towards the end of late Bronze Age and the beginning of early Iron age..." Instead of a revolutionary beginning of Israel proposed by Gottwald, Lemche suggests that Israelite tribal society as an evolutionary one, by this Lemche means there is a continuous transformation of Israelite tribal society into a centralized state especially at the beginning of Iron Age.

4.4. Structure of the Tribal Society in Israel

In Joshua chapters 7, we find a good description of a model structure for the existence of a tribal society. The following are the important Components of such a tribal society. But care should be taken to use this model

a) *The Individual*: In general, it should be noticed that no individual can stand alone in Israel, rather an individual's security was assured through an individual's relation to other people, i.e., to one's 'kin' Two circles are operated in this individual's relationship, i.e., inner circle: wife, children & parents; outside circle: members of another tribes or tribal coalition through Kinship.

b) *The family*: In ancient Israel, everyone was a members of a family. 80% of the population are small nuclear families, and the remaining 20% of the wealthy class are from extended families. In the nuclear family, there are uptosix to seven members, in the extended family, there are upto 20 members. The family circle in Israel widens (i. e., extended family) by exchanging women or unmarried daughters of one family to another.

c) *The Lineage*: The Lineage arose when the great and lesser families are interrelated by marriage. The Israelite family was a member of larger fam and each family was fully autonomous to take care of their own affairs, i.e., they can have their own land and cultivation. When there are problems of boundaries of the field, etc., they are resolved within the family members, but if there is any conflict between non-martially affiliated families, they will be solved either through peaceful negotiations or through feuds. Perhaps there existed a pater family system, i.e., elders are chosen from a leading family, who are vestedwith the authority to deal with the cases of their members.

d) *The Clan*: N. P Lemche points out that "the clan's position in the Kinship structure is that, it serves as a frame of reference establishing the individual to describe his relationship to a particular group of people who inhabit a particular locality or who are primarily associated with a particular place". However, Lemche observes that this system may be fictitious one and a stereotyped (i.e., Numb. 1:1-47, 48-54, 3:14-39), nolonger exists as the living reality in Israelite tribes but only a stereotyped conception of the social structure of pre-national Israel.

e) *The tribes*: In the social Organization ladder, above the clan we find the tribe. But when a tribe's name is mentioned, we are not sure whether it refers to the membership of the tribe or its territorial habitation. Moreover, there is no single satisfactory term that adequately explains the meaning of tribe. One of the difficult question raised by Lemche with regard to the composition of a tribe, is that; whether it (a tribe) accepted any new members to join in it and whether all the members present in it are the descendants of the same tribal ancestor?

f) *Tribal Leadership*: We have no evidence concerning the forms of leadership present among Israelite tribes. Moreover, there are only occasional evidence for the presence of collective tribal leadership, such as 'elders', 'chiefs', 'heads' and so on. J.W. Flanagan argues that the Israelite tribal society is mainly based on chiefdoms, and thus there was absence of centralized monopoly of power. It should be noticed, however, that the basic leadership among tribes was concentrated in the local group, except in few rare occasions. For Example: Judg. 9: Abimelech has become a great king in the vicinity of Shechem. But this event reminds us the fact when a tribal society experienced a crisis they seek for a chief or leadership.

4.5. Tribal Society and its Economy in Israel

N.K. Gottwald identifies three kinds of economic life before and after monarchy in Israel. In ancient Israel it was a communitarian mode of production, whereas from monarchy it was a tributary mode of production, until Hellenistic and there was another kind called a slave mode of production in the late Hellenistic to Roman period.

In the tribal society of Israel, the major chunk of the population were cultivators of soil and followed the vocation of animal husbandry. Moreover, the major economic resource of the tribal society in Israel was highland agriculture dependent on mix of crops. As pointed earlier pre-monarchic

Israel was a communitarian mode of production, which in turn is tributary-free political economy. Furthermore, the tributary free political economy has a strong basis in the family and village mode of life in which certain legal procedures were practiced, i.e., land holdings are passed in perpetuity from generation to generation, free from any tax, ultimately guaranteed every Israelite a means of livelihood.

Thus the tribal social organization in Israel has made tremendous influence in Israel in the course of her history, and such ideals of organization if at all they are truly practiced, never repeated in the later course, i.e., from the time of monarchy in the history is Israel. If an egalitarian policy followed and practiced during their tribal period has so much to offer in today's world where the crony capitalism and market oriented competition prevails.

5. TIIE EMERGENCE OF MONARCHY AND ITS CONSEQUENCES

The emergence of the monarchy in Israel at the end of the eleventh century B.C.E. was considered to be one of the most crucial events in the history of Palestine. The radical shift of the ancient Israel from a loose tribal confederation into a centralized monarchy is not possible to precisely or exactly dated, but the major events can be placed within the eleventh century BCE.

The major biblical materials that support to tell us the story of Israelite monarchy is the Deuteronomistic History of Israel that includes Joshua to 2 Kings. The book of Chronicles too gives us certain points of monarchic history from a different perspective than that of Deuteronomistic history. The prophets such as Amos, Isaiah and Jeremiah give us certain indirect clues to understand the political and social points of the monarchic history. Other minor prophets like Hosea and Micah describe the socio-economic and religious realities created by the monarchy.

Epigraphic material also gave some clue to the survival of monarchy in Israel. Some of important sources of epigraphic material was: the inscription from the Siloam tunnel and Ostraca (8th Cent.) from Samaria which are administrative texts. The recovery of deciphering texts is related to the monarchy of Israel. One text mentions the events in Israel's monarchy dated from the 10th Century are Pharaoh's Shishak's pylon at the temple of Aton at Karnak and his stele found at Megiddo. The first inscription to mention an Israelite King is the stela of Mesha of Moab (9th Cent. BCE) that refers to "the house of Omri".

Besides, epigraphic material there are certain archaeological resources identified for the evidence of monarchy in Israel. The archaeological record makes in general the 9th cent B.C. as the apex ancient Israel's security and prosperity. Remains from 8th to 6th century B.C. suggest economic decline and military weakness with significant destruction of cities.

5.1. Biblical Tradition for the Emergence of Monarchy in Israel

In spite, of an apparent confusion of the chapters dealing with Saul's accession to the throne, it is still possible to delineate a structure which reveals that in the last analysis a unifying plan and theme bind the separate parts together. This is further explained by D.J. McCarthy, who has observed that I Sam 8-12, is separated from what precedes by the formulae at the end of I Sam 7 which are used to mark the end of the story ofa Judge, and from what follows by I Sam 13:1 which is the formulae used for beginning the report of a Kings reign. In these Five Chapters (1 Sam 8-12) two alternative reports, one in favour another is in opposition to the emergence of monarchy is expressed, criticism of the monarchy is found in Samuel's speeches contained in the reports, while the stories remain positive and favourable about the monarchy. The tension between these two attitudes in finally resolved in Chapter 12 of 1 Samuel.

A.D.H. Mares has classified the whole block of material into five independent sections to understand the independence of the source used by the Deuteronomists and the way they have put them together:

a) I Samuel 8: The popular demand for a king resulting from the corruption of other forms of the administration of Justice, which is resisted by Samuel. (This is Anti-monarchic Source).
b) I Samuel 9:1-10: I6: (Pro-monarchic Source) Saul was introduced as an young farm boy, who was sent to look for the lost asses, being honoured and anointed *nagid* (Prince/Chief) over Israel by Samuel.
c) I Samuel 10:17-27: (Anti-monarchic Source) Samuel summoned the people to Mizpah and reminding them of their sin in demanding a King, but presides over the election of Saul.
d) I Samuel 11:1-15: (Pro-Monarchic Source) Saul is introduced as the tribal leader of lsrael in a battle with the Ammonites. After the success in this battle Saul was re-elected as the King of Israel at Gilgal.
e) I Samuel 12: 1-25: (Anti-monarchic Source)It is the speech of Samuel warning the people with the King to obey Yahweh, that even though they have a King, Yahweh alone has the power to deliver and that they will be destroyed and punished for disobedience.

5.2. Theory of Philistine Pressure

The fact that monarchy was finally established in Israel changed the entire course of her history. The possible reason for the emergence of monarchy in Israel has to do very much with the problems emerged in her own surrounding conditions. In this way, most scholars agree to the fact that an external element Philistine threat was the reason for the emergence of monarchy in Israel. Thus, Israel was forced to take up the new challenge raised by the Philistine threat. If they (Israelites) continued to remain as tribal society, it would be difficult for them to face the Philistine threat.

There may be five various reasons to explain why there was a clash between Israelites and Philistines:

a) Philistines expansion was an expression of their ambition to political domination in the entire country.
b) Philistine aggression aimed at preventing Israelite expansion to the coastal plain.
c) The Philistines reacted to Israelite raids on important trade routes.
d) The Philistine expansion eastward was set off by population growth.
e) The Philistine goal was economic exploitation of the hill country.

But all these points do not really answer to the questions of socio-political economic conditions that caused to the emergence of Israelite monarchy. Therefore, we need to consider some other points.

Scholars in general have identified that two kinds of societies that would normally be emerged, One is pristine state: that emerges in a political vacuum with no contemporaneous or previous developed political entities in their vicinity. Eg: Ancient Egypt, Mesopotamia and the Indus valley. The otherone is secondary state: This emerges from the collapse of other states or because of the influence of a neighbouring state and sometimes as a result of confrontation with a nearby state. Probably we may put Israel under this category.

J.W. Flanagan describes Saul's Kingship as a typical chiefdom category and the reign of David was a transition from a chiefdom to a state and that only Solomon's Kingdom can be classified as a fully development state.

5.3. Models and Theories for the Emergence of Monarchy in Israel

a) *The Urban Organization model of V.G. Childe*: According to this model, it is the production of agricultural surplus which lead to urbanization. The intensification of agriculture directly created concentration of wealth of prosperity around which rise the central settlements. This process lead to specialized production of goods for trade and to a gradual development of stratified society with rulers, priests, craftsmen, merchants and farmers. Trade requires administration which in turn, brings about the invention of writing, etc., and thus develop to a state.

b) *Carneiro's warfare or Environmental Circumscription Model*: This theory proposed that warfare is an essential factor, although not sufficient factor in the emergence of states. Further it describes that fertile agricultural region is the main reason and factor, which are surrounded by geographical barriers like deserts, seas and mountains due to constant population growth which compelled them for the utilization of all the land available for agriculture resulting in struggle between the different local communities, where the victorious take control over the land and create a chiefdom and the continuation of the process ultimately lead to the creation of a state. Butat the same time changes within the society take place-administration in the conquered territories, land given to those who» distinguish themselves in the war and other factors create social stratification, taxation and urban concentration.

c) *The Theory of the Role of trade Inter-regional or Intra-regional in the emergence of a State*: According to this model certain products are not available in a certain region. In order to obtain them through trade some regions are compelled to produce surplus of their own products. This brings about the development of administration, social stratification, etc. According to the intra-regional version of this model environmental and demographic variations in different parts of the same region engender specialization in sub-areas in order to produce surpluses to use for barter for the absent products.

Scholars have borrowed several useful elements from the above mentioned models in order to relate to the emergence of monarchy in Israel. M.L. Chaney attributed two factors that led to the rise of the Monarchy-Philistine threat to; Israelite economy from outside and the emergence of economic elite from inside. Technological advancements in the hill country in terms of terracing, plastered water cisterns and use of iron brought about the intensification of human activity and the production of agricultural surpluses. This improved the region's economic condition and inturn it attracted Philistine aggression which inturnled to the emergence of monarchy in Israel. Thus all the above discussed theories in someway help to understand the emergence of monarchy in Israel.

The consequence of such an emergence of monarchy in Israel are numerous and we can categorize them under three structural changes:

i) *Political Centralization*: Unlike the decentralized structure of the tribal society where every tribe or group had its autonomy in managing their own affairs, due to monarchy such an autonomy of independent group was lost, the structures are now centralized, a monopoly of force was created over and above the people of Israel.

ii) *Social Stratification*: The monopoly of power in the new state was the monopoly of particular social groups. A group of wealthy and influential people always dominated the society at its top the state. Policy of deliberately transforming wealth form the mass of production people to a parasitic non-production class spawned not only a structure of government officials but also strata of enterprising merchants and landlords.

iii) <u>*Shifts in land tenure*</u>: In the inter-tribal confederacy land has been held in perpetuity by extended families and would not be sold out of the family; but now due to the emergence of monarchy loans and interests were extended to Israelites and their property mortgaged; many of them ended up as tenant farmers, debt servants, or landless wage labourers. Tribal economic security and tribal religious identity were undermined. The social unity and political trust of the people in their leaders put in radical doubt. As the entrepreneurial wealth accumulated through taxes, plunder and trade, the upper class looked for "investment opportunities."

iv) <u>*Domestic repercussions of foreign trade, diplomacy and war:*</u> Syro-Palestine was caught up by the international web of trade, diplomacy and war during David and Solomon. Israel has amazingly emerged as successful in the political and military game. At the same time, there was a continuous friction between Israel and other small states that resulted in a volatile situation of largely looming war between Israel and the smaller states. During this period smaller powers surrounding Israel with limited economic and military resources added with the natural calamities like drought, earthquakes, etc. For such small powers including Israel changes in the international scenario means a lot to adjust themselves. Moreover, the small powers had to pay heavy tributes means to gather all their economic resources towards the payment and eventually weaken their military and political structure. Apart from this there seems to factional struggles between the local leaders either in support or to oppose the imperial policies, thus a net effect of all these developments had serious impact on the poor and impoverished populace. The native leaders and administrators when pressurized by the imperial economic tributes eventually lay heavy economic taxation on the poor common people. If and when any refusal on the art of the poor population who may refuse to pay unreasonable taxes and tributes the war of attrition was imposed against ordinary Israelites who bore the overall burnt of their leaders' vaulting ambitions along with other repercussions of war, foreign trade and diplomacy.[5]

Thus, we could see once the tribal solidarity and freedom was replaced with more of stratification in the social structure in the society of Israel as a result of the formations of a state, although such as emergence of monarchy was the only option left for the people of Israel in Eleventh century BCE.

5 For more details on the consequences of Israelite monarchy see, Norman K. Gottwald, *The Hebrew Bible: A Socio-literary Introduction* (Philadelphia: Fortress Press, 1985), pp. 323-325.

Moreover, the emergence of monarchy has totally changed the course of events in Israel and their tribal ethos. This change has radically altered the socio-economic and religio-political structures of Israel and the changes continued till the end of their kingdoms and even beyond.

Chapter 5

The United and Divided Monarchy

1. THE CONFLICT BETWEEN SOUTHERN AND NORTHERN TRIBES

With the death of Solomon around 925 BCE the opposition between the king in Jerusalem and his northern subjects burst into flame. The son and successor of Solomon, Rehoboam, was forced to journey to Shechem to parley with the leading circles of northern kingdom who were presumably the same group of elders, tribal and lineage leaders who had previously been influential during the coronation of his grandfather. The account of these discussions preserved in I Kings 12 explain the reasons for north Israelite discontent with the rule of Solomon. The Israelite representatives, demands relaxation of the burden of taxation and the *corvee* requirements and the king was unwilling to give the way on either issue. The king appears to have estimated his own importance with the result that he provoked the decisive break himself, and when he sent his overseer of the region the latter was lynched by representatives of the northern kingdom and the king himself had to flee to save his life. This resulted in the beginning of the serious conflict between the Southern and Northern tribes which continued for a long time. The outcome of the events already mentioned above cannot be described properly with the term, division of the kingdom. Actually it involved not the division of an inherently unified national structure but the non-renewal of a personal duality union between Judah and Israel and the restoration and solidification of the duality of south and north which this a personal union had temporarily overcome but had not dissolved. The old antagonism between north and south, which even in the lifetimes of David and Solomon had been kept alive and had found expression in saying "what portion have we in David?" (2 Sam. 20:1; 1 Kings 12:16; cf: 11:26ff) broke out again, and in the division of the kingdom (926 BCE I Kings 12). After two hundred years later the prophet Isaiah looked back to that movement as a day of judgement (Isa 7:17). Judah in the South, along with Jerusalem its capital, and Israel in the north were henceforth independent states.

If we look at the history of Israel and Judah as the histories of two independent kingdoms which existed alongside of one another for the next two hundred years, we cannot avoid noticing some significant difference between them both with respect to external and internal affairs. Israel's assets consisted in her control of the richest and largest parts of Palestine. Israel (North) also posed by far the largest population base and or so it appears, she had also assumed the power apparatus of the Davidic – Solomonic empire, namely its professional military Judah's (South) assets, by way of contrast, consisted in the greater homogeneity of the kingdom than was the case in the north. In reality the kingdom of Judah consisted of only a single tribal territory plus a capital city with its attendant lands. On the contrary, Israel consisted of a number of tribes which, admittedly even before the introduction of the monarchy had been able on occasion to coordinate their forces, but they had also been able to go on their own way when they desired and to make independent decisions accordingly.

2. DIVISION OF THE KINGDOM INTO JUDAH (SOUTH) AND ISRAEL (NORTH)

We need to look into few important causes that contributed to the division of the kingdom basically as elements responsible for the clash between the Northern and Southern tribes in Israel. The following are the vital points for consideration.

2.1. Social causes for Schism

Israelite society that was groaning under the burden of monarchy was an important factor that made the Schism inevitable. It was mainly the forced labour (*Corvee*) introduced by Solomon caused serious problems. In I kings 12:14 Rehoboam replied to the representation of Israel in a harsh way: "My father made your yoke heavy, but I will add to your Yoke; my father chastised you with whips but I chastise you with scorpion". The Phrase "Chastising with whip" has an indirect reference to *Corvee*. When monarchy produced a group of aristocrats to work in king's administrative machinery, it also has contributed to people of lower status. This was one of the major problems that contributed for schism. People lost their tribal freedom and they wanted to regain it. Solomon multiplied his building projects, which demands lot of money. When the money he got from other provinces decreased, he extracted the money from the local population to meet the needs of his buildings projects. His extravagant projects needed more and more revenue, thus he charged the common populace with heavy taxes. Both the *Corvee* and the imposition of taxes upon the people created a great social burden among them and thus they began to look for an alternative rule and measure of freedom where they can excise their tribal values.

Social differences between South and North is one other vital reason for the division of the kingdom. The North and South were not similar in their sociocultural setup. The people of north was a heterogonous group, whereas the South was more homogeneous coming from a single tribe. Northern kingdom had more outside contact whereas southern kingdom was geographically isolated. This resulted in different types of attitudes. Northern economic resources were stronger comparing to pastoral and agricultural society of South. The Social differences provided different cultural expression.

2.2. Political Causes

Not only social causes even the neighbours of Israel also contributed to the schism. The Egyptian Pharaoh Shishak was ready to accept any one who would come for his rescue, after this rebellion in Israel. This means then the internal revolt with in the United Kingdom was encouraged by the neighbouring Egyptian Kingdom. The Egyptian King Shishak, who, invaded Judah after the death of Solomon possibly had the motif of reducing the strength of Solomon's strong Kingdom. Hadad and Jerobam, who were against Solomon are accepted by the Egyptian King of Egypt. Another political factor that prompted the conflict between the southern and Northern tribes is that, the ruling king who happens to be from the tribe of Judah showed special favour to the Southern tribe. Many scholars think that Judah was not divided into districts, thus it was exempted from heavy taxation and *Corvee*; on the other side, Northern tribal region was subjected to *Corvee* and taxation.

The political ideology is different in both the states. Each one had different ideas of kingship. This attitude in the two group has been noticed from the time of the Emergence of monarchy. The people of Judah accepted the dynastic rule of David's family, because they think that David was divinely chosen King, but the people of Northern tribes rejected the Principle of dynastic succession and claims of Davidic home.

2.3. Religious Causes

Religion was an integral part of the Israelite society. Here prophets played a vital role. Some of the prophets were behind the scene of schism. Jeroboam, the King of Northern Israel was encouraged by the prophet Ahijah in the name of Yahweh (I Kings. 11:29-30) and Rehoboam, the king of Southern state was discouraged by the prophet Shemiah to muster the force and to recover the northern Kingdom (I Kings 12:21-24).

Another religious factor that could have mustered the clash between the South and North Israel was the Lord's covenant with David as mentioned 2 Sam. 7:14-17. This covenant with David was based on the patriarchal, in that both the covenants are promissory covenants and they are unconditional ones. Moreover, it is understood that through the Davidic Covenant, God promised the Davidic line of succession will continue in Israel. Such an exclusive tendency of the Southern tribe was not at all accepted by the northern tribes. Moreover, the people of Israel especially the northern tribes, who traditionally accepted the Sinai covenant as the basis of their promise of God, could not easily reconcile with the exclusivist tendency showed in the Davidic covenant, thus the conflict arise between the two states.

Thus far we have noted the events that led to the clear cut division of united Israel into Southern and Northern states. We shall now turn to few events as to see how the Kingdoms of Judah and Israel are established and continued their rule for the following two centuries. Even through there was a split in a United Kingdom to form the North and the South the conflict between the two states continued on several occasions. We shall note few events later in our discussion.

3. THE ISRAEL AND JUDAH SIDE BY SIDE

Immediately after the report of the apostasy of Israel there follows in Ii Kings 12:20a the account of the appointment of Jeroboam as king over all Israel. This incident has connection with the narrative of Jeroboam's rebellion against Solomon (1 Kings 11:26) which mentions first his flight (1 Kings 11:40) and then his return. The account of revolt thus proves to be a prelude to the reign of Jeroboam. Even before this incident, prophet Ahijah of Shiloh designates Jeroboam as king over Israel (1 Kings 11:29-34).

With the enthronement of Jeroboam as king, for the first time there was now two independent Kingdoms of Israel and Judah.

3.1. The Rule of Jeroboam at the Outset of Northern Kingdom

As soon as Jeroboam became the king of Israel he undertook two important steps:

a) *Choosing the capital city*: Jeroboam choose Shechem as his capital city (I Kings 12:25) but in the same place it is told that he moves from Shechem to Penuel in Transjordan perhaps this may be because of pharaoh's Shishak's invasion of Palestine at this time. Thus Jeroboam could have moved from Shechem to Jordan. However, it remains very obscure why he did not return to Shechem, but later resided in Tirzah (1 Kings 14:17 cf. 15:33, 16:8 etc.).

b) *Policy of Worship*: Jeroboam established central sanctuaries in Bethel and Dan, i.e., in the south and in the extreme north of his kingdom. The account in I Kings 12:26-33 portrays it from the perspective of Judah as apostasy from the legitimate cult in Jerusalem. Jeroboam must have felt to achieve cultic independence (1 Kings 12:26) along with the political independence, thus he founded his own sanctuaries with a priesthood to go with them (1 Kings 12:31), feasts (v. 32f) etc. In the newly built sanctuaries Jeroboam erected the bull images, thus following after the Canaanite conceptions of God. Jeroboam's activity of erecting bull images in the sanctuaries is viewed as negative remark. The same prophet who designated him as the King over Israel now rejected him in the name of Yahweh (1 Kings 14:1-18). With Jeroboam began what is later referred to by the stereotyped phrase the 'Sin of Jeroboam', the cultic revolt from Jerusalem which is also described as sin (1 Kings 12:30).

3.2. Important events of the Northern Kingdom after Jeroboam until the fall of Samaria in 722 B.C.E.

a) *Chronological sequence of the Northern Kingdom (Israel)*: Jeroboam I (931-909 B.C.E) - Nadab (909-908 B.C.E) - Baasha (908-885 B.C.E) - Elah (885-884 B.C.E) - Zimri (884 B.C.E) - Omri (884-873 B.C.E) - Ahab (873-853 B.C.E) - Ahaziah (853-852 B.C.E) - Joram (852-841 B.C.E) - Jehu (841-813 B.C.E) - Jehoahaz (813-798 B.C) - Jehoash (798-782 B.C) - Jeroboam II (782-753 B.C,E) - Zachariah (753-752 B.C.E) - Shallum (752 B.C.E) - Menaham (752-741 B.C.E) - Pekahiah (741-739 B.C.E) - Pekah (739-731 B.C.E) - Hoshea (731-722 B.C.E) - Fall of Samaria (722 B. C.E).

b) *War between Israel and Judah*: Even after the division of the United Kingdom of David into two after Solomon, there was a constant state of war between the two states. (1 Kings 14:30, 15:7,16), which were probably expressed above all in frontier classes (cf: 15: 17, 22). The comments about this state of war end with the death of Baasha of Israel (15:16), nothing is said about Omri, but his son Ahab lived at peace with Jehoshaphat of Judah (22:45) this is an indication of changed relationships between the two states.

c) *The Dynasty of Omri*: At this point of Northern Kingdom when Omri succeeded Zimri in 884 B.C. the most basic change in the kingdom took place. Omri who had come to power through a military revolt (1 Kings 15:16-22 like Baasha before him, I Kings 15:27) succeeded in founding a dynasty which ruled for three generations (Omri, Ahab, Ahaziah (Joram). Thus after initial confusion the monarchy in Israel attained long-term stability until in the last decades before it was again involved in a new confusion.

Omri founded a new capital. He bought a hill from a man called Shemer and called the city which he built on it Shomoron after him (1 Kings 16:24). We are not told the reason why Omri moved his capital from Tirzah to Samaria. However, the geographical situation of Samaria was an important strategic site of trade. Perhaps, Omri wanted to follow David's example to create an independent capital. The excavations at Samaria show the construction of a very impressive fortified residence at the time of Omri and his son Ahab. In view of this Altmakes the comparison between Jerusalem and Samaria and argued that Samaria had been an independent city state modelled on Jerusalem. It had Canaanite features to meet the desires of the Canaanite part of the population. Alt explained this above all in terms of the Baal cult which was officially practised in Samaria (cf: 1 Kings 16:32, 2 Kings 10:18, Reports of prophets of Yahweh in Samaria cf:1 Kings 22, 2 Kings 5:38 etc.).

d) *Religious policy of the Omrides*: The Old Testament tradition devotes only a few verses to Omri (1 Kings 16:16f, 21-28). The religious judgement notes that his actions were worse than those of all his Predecessors (V. 25), without making it clear what this means. This emerges more clearly in the case of his son and successor Ahab (1 Kings 16:29 ffesp. in v. 31) He took to wife Jezebel the daughter of Ethbaal, King of Sidonians, and went and served Baal and Worshipped him. Here two things are connected. Political marriage with a Phoenician princess and the Baal cult. The two things were evidently indeed closely associated. Jezebel was a central figure in the court of Ahab, and she was responsible for the persecution and extermination of the prophets of Yahweh (I Kings 18:4, 19:2), while the prophets of Baal 'ate her tabel' (18:19). Thus the domestic policy at the time of Ahab and his sons was shaped by the controversy between Yahweh religion and Baal religion.

e) *Battles with Aramaeans*: The conflict between Israel and Aramaeans is reported from the second half of the 9th century B.C.E. But the references to the battles with the Aramaeans are too sporadic to allow us to make any exact reconstruction. At the time of Prophet Elisha, in II Kings 6:8-7:20 Kings of Israel, Joram (8:4-28f, 9:14f) was said to have fought against the Aramaeansin Transjordan. More than thirty years later, during the reign of Jehoahaz, Israel fought with Aramaeans. (2 Kings 13:3 ff). There are several reports about the besieging of the capital Samaria by the Aramaeans (1 Kings 20:1f, II Kings 6:24 ff), the Israelite Victories and a personal surrender by the Aramaean King Benhadad (1 Kings 20:31 ft), and finally even of offensive wars by the Israelites against the

Aramaeans in northern Transjordan (1 Kings 22). Then again we hear of campaigns by the Aramaeans in Transjordan (II Kings 10:32), and of an almost complete annihilation of Israelite forces by the Aramaeans (13:7). Thus, various texts make it difficult to get any coherent picture of the overall situation. However, it is clear that in the period there was a constant threat to Israel from the north, even Judah was affected by it (cf. II Kings 12:18 ff).

f) Jehu's Revolution: The situation with the northern kingdom changed again as a result of Jehu's revolution (II Kings 9 ff). The report of this is completely dominated by the religious aspect of the abolition of the Baal cult. The direct prophetic involvement in Jehu's revolution takes place (II Kings 9:1-10). The occupation of the capital Samaria come to a dramatic and gruesome climax with the murder of the assembled Baal worshippers in their temple and the destruction of the temple and the symbols of the cult (10:18-28). The real aim ofthe revolt seems to be 'wiping out Baal from Israel' (v. 28).

g) Jeroboam II: The long reign ofJeroboam II in Israel (782-753 BC) and from 793-782 he was coregent, i.e., forty-one years were probably a time of political stability, at the same time a period of economic boom and heightened social tensions. Prophet Amos appears in this time offers a sharp accusations of social injustice experienced 1n the Northern Kingdom.

h) The Assyrian Advance: After the death of Jeroboam II, the long-drawn-out period of stability and continuity in the northern kingdom under the dynasties of Omri and Jehu came to an end. A series of military coups followed in swift succession (II Kings 15:8-12, 13-16, 17-22), almost similar like the time before the beginning of the dynasty of Omri (cf: I Kings 16: 8-22). Finally, Meneham was able to assert himself as king (II Kings 15:17-22). The first expedition of the Assyrian King Tiglath-Pileser III to Syria 1n 738 B.C.E falls in this time. Menahem paid a substantial tribute in order to forestall an attack by the Assyrians (v. 20). During his second campaign in 733 BC, Tigleth-Pilesar (II Kings 15:29) attacked Israel. After 733/32 B.C.E Israel became vasal to the Assyrians. According to II Kings 17:1-6, Hoshea, the last King of Israel joined the anti-Assyrian coalition (by seeking the help from Egypt) and refused to pay tribute to Assyria. In 722 BCE. the Assyrian King Shalmaneser V undertook a campaign in this region. He captured Samaria, deported part of the population, and made the whole of Israel into an Assyrian province, thus bringing the history of the northern Kingdom, Israel to an end.

3.3. Important events of the Southern Kingdom from Rehoboam until the fall of Jerusalem in 587 B.C.E.

a) *Chronical Sequence of the southern Kingdom (Judah)*: Rehoboam (931-913 B.C.E) - Abijam (913-911 B.C.E) - Asa (911-869 B.C.E) - Jehoshaphat (869-848 B.C.E) - Jehoram (848-841 B.C.E) -Athaliah (841-835 B.C.E) - Joash (835-796 B.C.E) - Amaziah (796-767 B.C.E) - Azariah (Uzziah) (767-740 B.C.E) - Jotham (740-731 B.C.E) - Ahaz (731-715 B.C.E) - Hezekiah (715-686 B.C.E) - Manasseh (686-641 B.C.E) - Amon (641-639 B.C.E) - Josiah (639-609 B.C.E) - Jehoahaz (609 B.C.E) - Jehoiakim (609-597 B.C.E) - Jehoiakin (597 B.C.E) - Zedekiah (597-587 B.C.E) – Fall of Jerusalem (587 BCE).

b) *Reign of Hezekiah*: We have no information of the effect of the decline of the northern kingdom on Judah-perhaps the Assyrians regarded Judah as a loyal vassal since King Ahaz had paid tribute. Three things in particular are repeated of Hezekiah the son and successor of King Ahaz, in 2 Kings 18:1-8; a reform of the cult (v.1), defection from the Assyrians (v.7) and a victory over the Philistines (v.8). The second point is the easiest to deal with-Hezekiah's defection occurred in a wider political context about which Assyrian Sources also inform us. After the death of the Assyrian King Sargon II in 705 BC, there was much unrest in the Assyrian Empire; Egypt and Babylon, for example, which has formerly been subject to the Assyrians, again achieved independence. Hezekiah evidently took part in negotiations against Assyria, as is shown in the visits of Egyptian (cf. Isa. 18, also 30:2; 31:1) and Babylonian (II Kings 20:12) delegations to Jerusalem. Once again in the year 701 BC. Sennacherib, the successor of Sargon II, undertook a campaign in this region to restore his rule. He conquered an Egyptian army which opposed him, and occupied the rebellious cities of the Philistines. Then he turned against Judah, took, forty-six of its fortified cities and countless small cities in its territory (2 Kings 18:13), and shut up Hezekiah himself in Jerusalem 'like a bird in a cage'. Sennacherib heavy tribute on Hezekiah.

Two difficult elements can be distinguished in the note about Hezekiah's reform of the cult (18:4) -firstly, we hear of the removal of the high places (bamot) and the cultic symbols of stone (*mazzebot*) and wood ('asera) secondly, removes the 'brazen serpent', named Nehushtan. By this it is said that Hezekiah removed theriomorphic cultic symbol from the time of Moses (cf: Numb 21:4-9).

c) *Rule of Manasseh*: Reports about Manasseh, the son and successor of Hezekiah, are exclusively concerned with cultic matters and are completely negative (2 Kings 21:1-18). He is depicted as the great 'heretic king', Here all that is said about him serves in every detail as a negative foil for the subsequent reform by Josiah. Manasseh had an unusually long reign (fifty-five years!) and evidently had no competition either abroad or at home. However, in retrospect his reign could be seen as a time of cultic apostasy from the legitimate religion of Yahweh.

d) *Josiah's reign and reformation*: (2 Kings 22:1-23, 30) Josiah is known forhis reform of the cult which stood in a wider political context, it took place at a time when the Assyrian empire was in the verge of disintegration; As early as 625 BC. Babylon had capital Nineveh was destroyed; the last Assyrian king, Asshur-uballit, withdrew to Harran in Western Mesopotamia and attempted to defend his empire from there with the help of the Egyptians.

Josiah evidently exploited this power vacuum to consolidate and extend his rule. The action against the altar in Bethel, the former state sanctuary of the northern kingdom (11 Kings 23: 15-18), could be seen in the context of an extension of the sphere of the rule of the king of Judah over parts of what used to be the northern kingdom. Moreover, the circumstances of Josiah's death indicate his political ambitions. He opposed the Egyptian Pharaoh Necho, who moved north to support the Assyrian king (not to oppose him, as the translation of 2 Kings 23:29 usually reads). Perhaps he wanted to prevent Assyrian power being strengthened with the help ofthe Egyptians, or he feared and Egyptian domination in the wake of that of Assyria.

e) *Battle of Carchemish*: After the death of Josiah, Judah was drawn into the struggles of the great powers for control of this area. Josiah's younger son Jehoahaz was appointed as king soon after the death of Josiah (II Kings 23:30), but three months later Pharaoh Necho deposed Jehoahaz and deported him to Egypt. Necho appointed Jehoahaz's brother Eliakim in his place and changed his name to Jehoiakim. Moreover, Necho imposed a heavy tribute on the country (II Kings 23:31-35). However, power relationships soon changed in favour of the Babylonians, once they had defeated the Egyptians in 605 at Carchemish on the Euphrates; and Jehoiakim became a vassal of the Babylonians.

f) *Nebuchadnezzar and his deportations of the people of Judah to Babylon*: Three years after the events of 605 BCE. Jehoiakim defected from the Babylonians, probably as a reaction to a defeat which the Babylonians suffered in the winter of 601/600 in a campaign against Egypt. Still, Nebuchadnezzar, who had been king of Babylon since 605, soon undertook another campaign in this region and at the beginning of 597 appeared before Jerusalem, wherc immediately before hand Jehoiachin had succeeded his father as king. Jehoiachin seems to have handed over the city voluntarily (24:11 ff), he was taken as prisoner and deported. Nebuchadnezzar appointed his uncle (i.e. another son of Josiah) Mattaniah King; again he changed his name (as Necho had done in an earlier case), to Zedekiah (v.17) parts of the population were deported along with Jehoiachin (24:14) these mentioned are the officials (Sarim), the well-to-do tax paying citizens (*gibbore-hayil*) and also particular groups of craftsmen (harass-armourer! master=fortress builders), only the poorer stratum of the population (*dallat am-ha-ares*) remained behind.

Again in 588 B.C.E a Babylonian army approached Jerusalem and laidsiege to the city (II Kings 25:1). Apparently the siege was interrupted for a time because of the approach of an Egyptian army (Jer. 37:5, 11. the dates in Ezek. 29:1, 39:20). But as part of their second deportation in summer 586 B.C the Babylonians first made a breach in the city wall; then finally, about a month later, they completely occupied the city, burnt the temple (which they had earlier plundered, vv.13-17), the royal palace and the rest of the city, and destroyed the city walls (cf: II Kings 25:3f. 8, Jer. 52:6f, 12). Zedekiah attempted to escape from the city (II Kings 25:4 cf. Jer 39:4), but was over taken by the Babylonians in Jericho, i.e., before he could cross the Jordan to safety, prisoned and brought to Nebuchadnezzar's headquarters at Riblah. There he was cruelly punished for his defection. His sons were killed before his eyes, and he himself was blinded and brought in chains to Babylon (v. 7). We hear nothing further of his fate.

From the in habitants of Jerusalem some military, court and temple officials and sixty members of the upper class were also brought to Nebuchadnezzar at Riblah and executed there (II King 25:18, 21). Moreover, 2 Kings 25:11f. states sweepingly that the surviving remnant of the population was deported, along with those, who had defected to the king of Babylon and the remainder of the craftsmen, while parts of the poorer stratum of the population were left behind to work in the vineyards and the fields.

The fall of Jerusalem makes a great division in the history of Israel. Will it the rule of the Davidic dynasty, which had more than four hundred years came of an end. For the next four centuries down to the completion of the last bookof the Old Testament, Israel (or Judah) lived under the rule of different foreign superpowers.

4. POLITICAL ALLIANCES/STRUGGLES OF ISRAEL AND JUDAH WITH THE NEIGHBOURING STATES/EMPIRES

The disintegration of the empire of David and Solomon turned Judah and Israel into minor kingdoms within the political world of Syria and Palestine. They were forced to fight for their survival in repeated conflicts with the other powers in this area. Sometime Israel and Judah had entered into alliance with their neighbouring states. We shall consider few details in this regard:

A. The change in the Solomonic kingdom after his death caused the Philistines in the south-most to stir themselves again. Earlier the power of the Philistines was broken by David. In the divided kingdom Rehoboam had already protected the little kingdom of Judah by means of a complete system of fortified strongholds (2 Chronicles 11:5-10), and the system in particular was powerful in the western border of Judah. According to 2 Kings 12:18f however, Gath was still in the hands of Judah at the time ofthe Judean King Jehoash (839-838 to 800-739 BCE). At that time the Aramaean King Hazael-an allay of the philistines, conquered the city of Gath and even threatened Jerusalem, so that king of Judah had to pay clearly to persuade Hazael to retreat by sending tribute from the temple and palace treasury in Jerusalem. Possibly Judah lost Gath at that time, anyway, about a century later we find Gath in Philistine, hands again. The kingdom of Israel waged repeated border warfare with the Philistines near the city of Gibbethon, on two occasions this was evidently stated (1 Kings 15:27, 16:15I7), this time the struggle between Israel and Philistines was for the two cities Gezer and Ekron.

B. The power from the south-west intervened for a time in the history of Israel and Judah. In the year of king Rehoboam, i.e., in the year 922-921 BCE, the pharaoh Shishak I, a Libyan mercenary leader, who had founded the 22nd Dynasty in Egypt, undertook an expedition to Palestine. In I Kings 14:25-28, it is recorded that Rehoboam assembled all the treasure of the temple and palace in Jerusalem to pay tribute to pharaoh. Shishak I therefore spared Judah and Jerusalem, and it is quite unlikely that Shishak wanted to intervene in the internal relations between the kingdom of Judah and Israel and take sides with one or the other. The aim of his expedition was simply to plunder the land in western Asia nearest to Egypt.

C. In North-east the power developed namely the Aramaean monarch of Damascus was far more menacing for Judah and, in particular, for Israel than the military troubles from the south-west-Benhadad, who designated himself (I Kings 15:18) as son of Tabrimmon, was a member of a dynasty of kings of Aram, which had already reigned for several generations, must have had connection with the Phoenician coastal cities and moreover, had been the ruler of the Aramaeans as far as northern Syria. It is the same Benhadad I whom we met as the first dangerous military enemy of the kingdom of Israel. He was the

Aramaean king and king Asa of Judah persuaded to attack Israel in the reign of Baasha by making him a lavish present. He made his troops to occupy the Israelite cities of Ijon, Dan, Abel Bethmaacah (I Kings 15:20). We are not sure of this future course, perhaps Benhadad temporarily occupied these places and later withdrew on his own accord.

The Israelite kings of the dynasty of Omri made the warding off of this threat of Aramaeans the main aim of their policy. They brought to an end of frontier disputes with the neighbouring kingdom of against the Aramaeans. The northern kingdom thought to establish contacts with the Phoenician coastal cities, which resulted in Omri's son Ahab's marriage to Jezebel, the daughter of the King of the Sidonians, Ethbaal of Tyre. But, this relationship hardly helped the Israelites to avert the influence and upperhand of the Aramaeams over there, the increasing strength of the Aramaeans had made the situation altogether too difficult for the kingdom of Israel. The battles also do not give any particular context whether it is with Israel or Judah. But the battles were full of changing fortunes for both sides-sometimes the Aramaeans would take a few cities front in the Israelites and vice versa; the sites in questionwere no doubt city-states in the northern land east of the Jordan on the border of the 'ajlur or 'jolan (I Kings 20:34). But on the whole Israel appears to have suffered most of the defeats. For eg: in IKings 22:2-38, there is a reference to a fruitless attempt to regain Ramoth in Gilead that was occupied by the Aramaeans.

D. According to 2 Kings 3:4-5, Mesha, king of Moab, ceased paying tribute to Israel after the death of Ahab. Furthermore, Moab was able to seize the fertile tabeldand north of the Arnon, which had been in dispute between Israel and Moab for many years. We get the details of Moabite rule from the inscription on the stele of king Mesha of Moab, which was discovered in 1868 in Dibon (the modern diban) north of the Arnon. According to this inscription the southern most part by the city Dibon had been occupied once by the Moabites. Further, the Mesha inscription mentions the name of king Omri, who had oppressed Moab for a long time, and further inscription mentions about the sons of Omri who ruled Israel after him. It implies that Mesha's victorious campaign came at very end of the dynasty.
E. The first serious encroachment of the new Assyrian empire on Syria-Palestine occurred in the period of the dynasty of Omri. In the 9th century B.C the power of the Assyrians began to rise again. They advanced beyond the Euphrates to the Mediterranean coast. The Assyrian King Ashurnasirpal II (884-859 B.C.E) had already made

a thrust into northern Syria and had reached the coast and received tribute from a number of Phoenician cities on the coast. In a number of expeditions his son and successor, Shalmaneser III (859-824 BCE) advanced further towards central and southern Syria. In the 6th year of Shalmaneser, in 853 BCE, a battle took place between Shalmaneser and a coalition of Syrian and Palestinian rulers. Among his enemies Shalmaneser mentions, in addition to Hadadezer of Damascus and king lrhuleni of Hamath, the Israelite Ahab, who participated with 2000 chariots and 10,000 soldiers. The battle took place near the city of Karkar (Karkara) in the province of Hamath in the northern Syria. But, in battle had led to no tangible results, and in his following years, 10th, 11th and 14th year, Shalmaneser attacked Syria again to fight the 12 kings of the land of Hatti. By their combined efforts the allies in Syria and Palestine still succeeded in resisting the Assyrian, and at any rate delaying his advance.

When is his 18th year (841 B.C.E) Shalmaneser appeared in Syria for the fourth time, Jehu evidently made no attempt at resistance but paid tribute to the Assyrian monarch like the Phenonician cities. On the basalt obelisk of Shalmaneser (the so called Black obelisk) which was discovered in the Assyrian royal city of Calah (Kalah, the modern tell nimrurd) the payment of Jehu's tribute is portrayed, and in the description his name is mentioned explicitly *(ia-u-a-mar-hu-um-ri-i)*.

Thus through the history of Israel and Judah they had very strategic alliances with the superpowers that surround them and at the same time those superpowers created great unrest for Israel and Judah eventually the same superpowers brought both the kingdoms to an end in a decisive manner.

Chapter 6

The Downfall of Israel and Judah

1. THE ROLE OF THE PROPHETS AND THE PROPHETIC MOVEMENT

The emergence of prophets is a particularly characteristic feature of the life of ancient Israel. The phenomenon of prophecy is certainly not limited to Israel, but also occurs in other spheres of ancient west Asia, however, as far as the sources indicate, nowhere did prophets become as significant as they were in Israel.

The people of Israel had often followed other gods and especially many Canaanite religious practices were absorbed into the Israelite religion. But this did not happen altogether. Every now and then a protest was made, some outstanding men dared to say boldly that certain beliefs and practices were wrong, for instance, Nathan who dared to accuse king David of stealing the wife of his soldier Uriah the Hittite and of having the husband deliberately killed in battle. Then in the time of Ahab there appeared the first of a line of men who in both Israel and Judah protested in the name of God against wicked practices-oppression, bloodshed and injustice and against the worship of other Gods. These are the Prophets about who we shall briefly mention in so far as they are related to the downfall of Israel and Judah. More details about the prophets and their significance in their books will be discussed in an appropriate section.

A. *Elijah, Champion of Israel's God*: A man suddenly appeared during the time of Ahab, pronouncing judgement upon Israel, and appearing again to challenge the people to abandon their evil ways and worship Yahweh their God alone the situation is connected with

> Ahab's marriage with Jezebel. The Princess from Phoenicia wished to continue to worship the God of her native country, referred to in the Old Testament simply by the title Baal, lord, 'master'. The trouble was that she was not content to worship her own God in private, but was determined to bring all Israel to worship him.

According to 1 Kings 17:1, Elijah not only came from a remote area of Gilead, east of Jordan, but also belonged to the class of small farmers (*toshab*) who owned no land of their own He shows how people of lowly origin could, through their prophetic activity, come to play a decisive role for the whole society.

The content of Elijah's ministry begins, as pointed earlier, by putting down to the first persecution of Yahweh's nabis in Israel by the notorious Jezebel., she wanted to spread the cult of Baal of Tyre (the God of her native country) and whose efforts met with great success in the country. At that time Tyre was enjoying an economic heyday. Its merchants dominated the shipping trade in the Mediterranean. Phoenician colonization spread as far as Spain. The deity who was at work in all this could be no minor God. As the royal court of Samaria, people no doubt put the Tyrian Baal on the same level as Yahweh and therefore simply used the title of dignity 'Lord and master'(ba'al) and not the proper name Melkart, under which the God was worshipped in Tyre.

But Elijah expressed the conscience of the Old Yahwistic religion on Israel's soil there can only be the one worship: the worship of Yahweh-every alien God who exerts his influence from outside) makes people and country tabu (*'akar*, I Kings 18:17) and destroys the healthful condition of its life.

Elijah's stories show the prophet engaged in dispute, not merely about cultic sites and rites (I Kings 18, II King 1), but also about the right of the individual, Israelite to the land which is his ancestral heritage.

The act of Elijah is not only displayed on the Mount Carmel (I Kings 18) but also about the right of the individual Israelite (Naboth) to the land which is his ancestral heritage (I Kings. 21st chapter). The story of Naboth also represents a protest against the idea of a king as one who is above the law and free to do as he pleases. The story further shows that a protest was made against the break down the laws of Justice and family property which belonged to the ancient Hebrew heritage law, and formed one of the strongest forces in Hebrew life. It also shows us the beginning of a breakdown in Hebrew society, with the old family rights and customs being destroyed by a new social order where wealth and privilege counted for more than citizen rights.

The act of Elijah on Mount Carmel even though looks cruel, it was necessary undertaking at that time. If Elijah had not been victorious, he would have been killed. Moreover, Elijah had maintained that the country was being defiled by cults and that its vital power was being sapped. Because the deity declares that Elijah is right, it is essential that the pollution should be eradicated by means of some impressive act. Whenever Elijah appears there is an eruption like a volcano. No other Prophet of the early period of the monarchy approaches him in effectiveness, or in his readiness for complete involvement in Yahweh's cause. Elijah's main appeal is to the claims of Yahweh, God of Israel, and to those ancient principles of Justice and fair dealing which belong to Hebrew law. That such protests made by Elijah show us that all was not well in the life of Israel at this time of increasing prosperity. In later tradition, Elijah became a symbol of the prophetic movement.

B. *The Ministry of Elisha*: Elisha son of Shaphat from Abel-meholah, was a follower and the designated successor of Elijah (1 Kings 19:16-21, II Kings 2). He appears to have been active during the reigns of the Kings of Northern & Southern Israel: Ahab, Ahaziah and Jehoram, ca. 850-800 BCE. The extensive narratives which preserve numerous stories about the prophet Elisha are found in the Deuteronomistic History (DH) I Kings 19:19-21, II Kings 2-13 Chapters). The record of events about Elisha confirm to the fact that he was the prophet of Yahweh. His authority is confirmed by his ability to part the waters of the Jordan (II Kings 2:13-13), to clear the spring outside Jericho of impurities (II King; 2:19-22), and to fatally curse the children that taunted him (II Kings 2:23-25). He also helped the widow of one of the prophetic guilds to pay her debts (II King. 4:1-7), other acts are recorded in the sections as follows: 11 Kings 4:8-37, 4:38-41,42, 44, II Kings 5:1-19, 20-17, 6:1-7, 8-23, II Kings 13:20-21.

Elisha is depicted as constantly in conflict with the Omride dynasty, and it culminates in his central role in legitimizing the rebellion of Jehu (II Kings 9:1-10), who massacred Ahab and the remaining Omrides in a palace coup. Robert Wilson points out that Elisha's role as peripheral to central prophet changed afterJehu's assumption of power. Now Elisha became more closely associated with the royal court, particularly in the military sphere (II Kings 6:8-7, 13:14-19).

The importance of Elisha lies really in his continuing the work of Elijah Stories like that of his faith in God, when the city of Dothan was surrounded by the armies of Syria, show that he insisted like Elijah upon the sole claim and power of Yahweh, God of Israel (II Kings 6:13 ff). But this is shown above allin his appointing of Jehu as new king over Israel in the place of the dynasty of Omri and Ahab.

Elisha sent one of his band of prophet to Ramoth-gilead (II Kings 9:1 ff) where Jehu was commanding to army, to anoint him as king over Israel, and to order him to wipe out the house of Ahab. The messenger took Jehu into a house in private and anointed him. Jehu mounted his chariot and drove furiously to Jezreel, where he killed Jehoram, the nephew of Ahab who was then king over Israel, close by the vineyard which had belonged to Naboth. Then Jehu killed Ahaziah, the king of Judah, the grandson of Ahab. Jehu also had Jezebel murdered, and the remaining members of the royal house of Israel were also killed. The dreadful series of events mentioned in II Kings 9. It is known sometimes as the 'Prophetic Revolution', because it was instigated by Elisha and other prophets. These incidents mark the end of the rule of Ahab's family, and the end, so far as we know, ofthe public worship of Baal in Israel.

C. *Amos' Judgement on Israel*: Amos came from Southern Israel; he was a native of Judah, a countryman, engaged in herding cattle and tending wild figs. But he had felt the hand of God upon him to send him as a prophet to the people of the north, and nothing would turn him from that task (cf: Amos 7:15). The claim made by Amos that he was sent by God was expressed by him when he confronted the Priest at the royal sanctuary of Bethel, where he has prophesied the judgement which was to come upon Israel and upon the royal house. The priest sent to Jeroboam to inform him the threat in Amos' words, and ordered Amos himself togo back to his native Judah to prophesy there and not to return to Bethel. (cf. Amos 7:13). Amos replied by claiming God's authority for his words of Judgement and spoke a word too against the Priest who dared to challenge that authority.

Amos sees the people of the north living in false security, imagining that because they are the people whom God brought out of Egypt he will always deliver them and deliver them. They are proud because they have won back the cities beyond Jordan which Syria had taken, but Amos mocks them, Punning on the names of the cities; they rejoice in Lo-deber, but that means 'something of no value', and they speak of taking Karnaim, thinking that because the name means 'horns' they have really gained in strength (Amos 6:13). But the fact that they are in a special way the people of God will means a more severe Judgement. "You only have I cared for of all the families of the earth. Therefore, will I punish you for all your iniquities" (Amos 3:2). Israel's hope of a day of victory and deliverance from God is therefore vain; the day of the LORD when it comes will be a day of Judgement from which none can escape, a day of darkness of not a day of light (Amos 5:18-20).

Not only Israel, but other nations too will discover that the wicked things they have done are not to be overlooked. God is concerned not with Israel and Judah alone, but with other peoples, for just as he brought Israel out of Egypt, so too he brought "the Philistines from caphtor and the Syrians from

Kir" (Amos 9:7). They too will be Judged, and even now a great power is being raised up by 50d. They whole land, from north to south, will fall, and the people will be taken into exile to the east, beyond Damascus (Amos 5:27). Assyria is to be the tool used by God in bringing disaster upon Israel.

False security led to wrong ideas about God and what he requires from men. The land was prosperous, and religion too was flourishing, but this Amos saw to be an empty show. The worship Israel offered was loathsome to God (Amos 4:4-5 and 5:21-22). Such a worship is unacceptable, because it is a shame. For there are men who long for the days of religious celebration to pass, so that they may act back to their trade, and in trading to cheat to make "the *ephah* shall and the shekel great and deal deceitfully with false balance" (Amos 8:5). It is a religion which does not produce good lives; there is no justice in the land, the poor and the defenceless have no protection. The wealthy by bribes control affairs, so that all is turned to their advantage, and they will not listen to those who speak the truth: (Amos 5:10-42).

D. <u>*Hosea's message of Judgement and promise*</u>: Amos prophesied in the later years of Jeroboam II's reign, before the great upsurge of Assyrian power which finally brought disaster to Israel. Hosea in all probability delivered his message a little later. Jeroboam II'sson Zechariah was murdered and a time of uncertainty and political strife followed as the end drew nearer and the shadow of Assyria loomed large. Hosea, too, is concerned about the evil practices which go on in Israel but more about the political and religious consequences of Israel's behaviour.

Israel is trying to play at politics, and to be clever enough by such means to escape disaster; on the one is Assyria, her power rapidly increasing, on the other side Egypt, again beginning to take an interest in the affairs of Palestine because it is to her advantage to have small buffer states under her own protection against any great power in the north and west. Thus Israel has ceased to trust in her God, and seeks helpby playing off one of the great powers against the other; her political folly is really a lack offaith. (Hosea 7:11 – "Ephraim (Israel) is like a dove silly and without sense, calling to Egypt, going to Assyria").

There is a deeper cause for uneasiness, since Israel has fallen away from the true worship of God and has gone after idols. Hosea sees this as the inner reason for the present situation, with Israel regarding 'the calf of Samaria' as a God, and going to worship the gods of the land, the Baals, imagining that it is they who give her the produce of the earth, corn and wine and oil, and Yahweh her own God. The people, even though know (from Elijah's story) that Baal has no power, but people still hanker after other Gods, and forget the one who delivered them and had watched over them since childhood: "when Israel was a child I loved him and out of Egypt I called my son . . ." (Hosea 11:1-3).

Hosea's understanding of the unfaithfulness of Israel was bound up with his own personal experience, which became to him a parable of the relationship between God and Israel Hosea speak of his marriage and of his children, whose names express his belief that God repudiates his relationship with Israel (Hosea 1:2-9). He sees coming Judgement as being a deprivation of the full bond between husbandand wife (Hosea 3). Hosea pictures Israel as a woman, a bride of God, who loves her deeply, and instead of finding love in return, finds that she goes away, leaving him to go to other Gods, as if it were they who gave her all the gifts that she enjoys (Hosea-2). As Hosea loves his life, so much more God love God's people. Hosea recognises that Judgement must come, yet he believes that throught his disaster there may come a new life for Israel. Hosea thinks that there must be a period of discipline, when Israel will be deprived of all the benefits which come from civilised, settled life; there must be a period of discipline, when Israel goes back to the desert, to live in tents and so recover that close fellowship with God which once she enjoyed.

E. *Isaiah's Judgement on Judah*: After the death of Uzziah, the king of Judah, the threat of Assyria was looming over Israel, and Judah became anxious over herfuture. A new prophet appeared in Jerusalem, namely Isaiah, and it was in the year of Uzziah's death he saw a great vision of God in the temple (Isaiah 6: 1-7). He felt that he was being told to take a message to his people. He was to tell them that Judgement, would come upon them because of the evils of his time, and he was to discover that this message would fall upon hard hearts and deaf ears (Isa 6:8-13).

It is clear from the saying of Isaiah that Judah's prosperity had brought with it many of the same evils as had been condemned in Israel by Amos and Hosea. There are 'woes' spoken against those who had wrongly accumulated land and built great houses for themselves, and against those whose one aim in life was making and feasting (Isa 5:8-23). Justice is forgotten; worship has become a mockery (Isa. 1:14-15). Isaiah pictures Judah as the vineyard which God has planted (Isa 5:2), it was protected and cared for but instead of good yield it yieldedwild grapes.Therefore, God will destroy his vineyard; Judah, his land and people, shall be rejected (Isa 5:7).

The same conditions are described by another prophet in Judah, Micah who express particular hostility to the great capital cities, Jerusalem and Samaria Where the rulers and leading men rob the poor, seizing the inheritances of those who are unprotected. Worst of all those who should warn, the prophets and priests join the evil-doing by supporting the wicked with their words when they are paid to do so, and confidently claim that no harm can come because 'the LORD is in the midst of us' (Micah 3:11).

During the early days of king Ahaz's reign there was crisis for Judah. In the year 733 BCE, the kingdoms of Syria and Israel joined together in rebellion against Assyria. Pekah of Israel and Rezin of Damascus wished to persuade Ahaz to join them in this rebellion, and when he refused, they marched their armies against Judah and besieged Jerusalem. Their plan was to depose Ahaz and put on the throne a King of their own choice. Ahaz was terrified (Isa 7:2). But Isaiah hadamessage of warning and encouragement for Ahaz and his people.

According to II Kings, 16, Ahaz appealed to Assyria, sending a gift of silver and gold from the Temple and the royal palace, and soon after this, Damascus was taken and much of the kingdom of Israel was made into Assyrian provinces. Ahaz became subject to Assyria, and travelled to Damascus to make his submission.

Isaiah's prophecy that Israel and Syria would be subdued by the Assyrians proved to be true. Judah became subservient too. From the fate of the drunkard rulers of Samaria the men of Jerusalem and Judah ought to have learnt wisdom but they did not (Isa. 28). Micah too follows his description of the reducing of Samaria to a heap of rubble with a warning of a like disaster for Jerusalem (Micah 12-9 and 3: 12).

After the disaster in the northern. Israel Judah was saved but it was reduced to a tiny city state: still subservient to Assyria and forced to pay heavy tribute. This situation was to last for three, quarters of acentury, and it is probable that some part of her territory was later restored to her, perhaps as a reward for continued obedience to Assyria in the years that followed. Isaiah saw this deliverance as an opportunity. He describes the land desolated by war and nothing but the city of Jerusalem remaining isolated (Isa 1:8). A remnant only of the people was left to Judah, and this alone made her fate different from that of other lands: (Isa 1:9 cf: Isa 7:3).

Thus, the role of the prophets in the crucial events of the history of Israeli especially the ninth and eighth century is very important. They played a key and vital role in the religious and political shaping of the independent kingdoms of Israel and Judah.

2. THEOLOGICAL RESPONSE TO THE EXILIC SITUATION AND NEW HOPE

The Babylonian exile was one of the most decisive events in the history of Israel. It is also most traumatic, not only because of the fate of the people in exile, but more decisively because of the events that led to the destruction and deportation. The exilic age served as a turning point in the Jewish history, as it provided an opportunity for the new orientation of their faith in the coming period. W.H. Schmidt observes that "the external losses of many kinds (in the exilic age) were spiritually profitable, because the period of exile became one of uncommon literary productivity." The basic question posed by the people who are exile was, Yahweh as God of Israel was he still in control of events in the history in the midst of events that had occurred one after another, finally shattered the nation in this exilic age? Ralph W. Klein observes that all the institutions based on which the Israelite faith was rested (Temple, Covenant, etc.) had no longer functioned. What kind of future was possible for people which traced its unique election to God who had just lost? The dogma upon which state and cult were founded had been dealt a mortal blow. This, as we have said repeatedly, was the assurance of Yahweh's eternal choice of Zion as his earthly seat, and his unconditional promises of David of a dynasty that would never end. Sheltered by that dogma, the nation rested secure and, rejecting prophetic warnings to the contrary as unthinkable heresy, confidently awaited Yahweh's mighty intervention, and a future that would bring the ideal saviour of David's line-perhaps the next one-under whom Yahweh's righteous and magnificent rule would be triumphantly established and all the dynastic promises made actual.

2.1. Religio-cultural and Theological Developments

There was no administration of the cult in the proper sense in the exile. No evidence for the existence of any temple cult in the exile. On the basis of the Oracles of salvation in Deutero-lsaiah. Rolf Rendtorffis of the view that there might have taken place services of lamentation. Moreover, it is supposed that the liturgy of the Word without sacrifice might have had origin in this time, thus leading to the foundation of the Synagogue, worship. On the other hand, in Palestine, the forms of cult continued; the ruined site of old Temple, with its large saved ark served as, a place of worship to which the pilgrims came from as far as Samaria (Jer. 41:4-8). Compositions such as lamentations, and pss-79, 105-106 were publicly proclaimed on fast days commemorating the catastrophic events of Jerusalem siege and destruction (Zech 7:2-7, 8:18-19).

Culturally, the exilic age was a period of creativity, with the production of several important parts of the literature. For example, Deuteronomists were active during this period, perhaps the main part of Deuteromistic History came in to being in this period. The basic parameter underlying deuteronomistic history was, the history is viewed as people's rebellion to God, and the punishment from the latter, followed by God's forgiveness. Moreover, it is God who is sovereign who acts in the historical events, of the people (cf. Joshua 27:15, I Sam. 12:2 f, I Kings 9:8f, II Kings 17:10f, 21:4f, 24:3, 20 et al.).

The priestly tradition as it stands now must have composed in the late exilic and post-exilic context this tradition reinterpreted certain older traditions to suit need of the hour Reaction against foreign influences was strongly portrayed in this tradition. For example, in Gen 17 (p), the circumcision of males even though this was very old custom in Israel and in ANE Priestly tradition gives it more cultic embellishment, and brings out its importance for the Jews because they are living in the midst of Babylonians who didn't practice circumcision. History was presented by these writers of exilic age (including prophets) as a response to the catastrophe, which gives causal explanations of current disasters. The message of apostasy (past) of the people and resulting in God's rejection (at present) but the forgiveness (in future) are brought out very clearly.

Prophets like Jeremiah, Ezekiel and Deutero-Isaiah have sharply responded to the exilic situation. Each one had touched the common concerns while maintaining their distinctive approach in their response:

a) *Jeremiah*: Jeremiah's activity extended to over four decades. He received his call in the 13th year of Josiah's reign (1:2, 25:3). Perhaps, the last words of Jeremiah's words (chap. 44) may have come from the time shortly after the conquest of Jerusalem in 587, when the remnant Jews fled to Egypt, who has compelled Jeremiah to go with them. Jeremiah more or less reflected the internal political events occurred during these four decades.

One of the main objective of Jeremiah's message was to offer an explanation of the catastrophe, which will fall on Judah in 587 B C. Because people have failed to comply with the law and the words of Yahweh mediated to her by the prophets (cf: 3:12 ff, 11:3ff). However, Yahweh will certainly restore the fortunes of the people and give back their land to them (29:4).

Jeremiah's message on Babylon is very positive. He warns people of Israel to subject to the Babylonian authority (27:11). Moreover, Jeremiah sees the Babylonian authority as a legitimate monarchy upon the earth established by Yahweh himself. In one of the remarkable, passage i.e., Jer. 27:46, Jeremiah even gives the title 'ebed' to the Babylonian king Nebuchadnezzar (Previously this word is applied only to Davidic dynasty). In the words of Klaus Koch "Jeremiah gives the phrase (my servant) a universal connotation in a way that was unheard of in the ears of Israel. Even Amos, and Isaiah has viewed the Assyrian kings as tools of destruction instigated by Yahweh; but they did not see the foreign power as a positive ordering force". At the same time, Jeremiah brings out the limitations of the Babylonian power. After seventy years (i.e. from 605 to 538 BC), even this power will be shattered and the relief will come to Israel (27:21f, 51:59f).

Jeremiah proclaims in his message that exile is not purposed for mere punishment even though it is intended to punish the sins of Judah it is more as an opportunity to turn to God (29: 1014*. This message is more impressively presented by Jeremiah in his preaching on new Covenant (Chapter. 32), Jeremiah shows symbolically the message of new covenant by purchasing a piece of land (32 3:744). Jeremiah's basis of new covenant will be made effective by Yahweh (cf. 31:31-34; 32:37-41).

Jeremiah sharply responds to Gedaliah's episode and its consequences. When people are panic after Gedaliah's murder, Jeremiah comforts the people not to be panic (42:10). Jeremiah also warns the people who fled to Egypt by resting their hope on the Egyptian cities and Pharaoh. Jeremiah says that everyone who had fled to Egypt from Judah will never again return to their homeland (44:14), even the Pharaoh of Egypt will be given to the hands of enemies (44:30).

Thus staring from the saying that people's sins are the cause of the wake of 587 (21:5), Jeremiah moves forward by assuring hope and new creative action of God to restore his people from their misfortunes (36:3, 18:11-12, 24:6, 27:22) and in particular assures them the return to their home (31:17).

b) *Ezekiel*: Ezekiel was said to be active during the years of 593-571, i.e., during the period of the 'rule of Nebuchadnezzar's dynasty (605-362 BC) Probably, Ezekiel lived during his prophetic activity at Tel Abib (1:1, 3:15), by the great canal (River Chebar), not far from Nippur. Here, he had been settled with exiles of 598 BCE (1:1). Three significant periods of Ezekiel's activity can thus be recognized as follows: The first period of his activity is from 593-587 BCE during which time he proclaims the total disaster and destruction (Chaps. 4-12, 16-17, 19, 21-24). The second period from 586-585 BCE, Ezekiel proclaims conditional salvation, i.e., salvation for the faithful and the death of the wicked. (3:16b-21, 33:1-20 et.al.). The third period of Ezekiel's activity was between 584 until 571 B.C.E during which time Ezekiel proclaimed a message of unconditional salvation (Chapter 38-39 and 40-48).

For Ezekiel, the central attention of Exile is to see the reality of the disaster occurred. The reality of being in foreign land (Chapter 4) is a shattering experience to him (obviously Ezekiel himself was in the exile). In all his proclamation Ezekiel takes pains to demonstrate how the catastrophe fits into the plan and purpose of God, and to demonstrate the sinful condition of the people is such that, any alternative is unthinkable (cf: 5:10 ff.6:12f, 16:2f, 17:12f et. al). Furthermore, Ezekiel preaches an irrevocable end of Israel (Chp. 7) and she is accused by the Egypt (Chp. 20). Not only that Ezekiel speaks about the Judgement of God on the chosen city, Jerusalem, the punishment is so served that even the prophet is crying out for halt (9:8).

Ezekiel saw that in a real way God's presence moved (1:1-3) from Jerusalem to be present among the exiles in Babylon, thus giving protection to the people who are in exile. Ezekiel assigns significant role to Babylon and Nebuchadnezzar. It is in Babylon the word of God that laid the foundation to the history has to be heard, and it is here the prophet is appointed to speak. In the message of Ezekiel, the restoration of the community of people from exile is also very important. On the one hand the prophet has proclaimed the downfall of the nation and the disastrous consequences of exile, on the other hand Ezekiel affirmed that God would be faithful to his covenant promises, that he would bring a new creative order among the people and the land (36:23-28, chapter 37).

For the sake of his faithfulness (not because of the merits of the people) and for the sake of his holy name he would restore his chosen people to their own land (Ezek. 20:41, 36:20, 36). This hope of restoration is envisaged even to the extent or reunion of two kingdoms, north and south (37: 15 ff), obviously Ezekiel had Josiah's reformation in his mind.

In the oracles of Ezekiel against foreign nations. (Chapter 25:32): Tyre. Ammon, Moab, Edom, Philistia and Egypt, Ezekiel asserts that the destruction or other nations is the beginning of salvation for Israel (28:25). Moreover, through the events connected with the defeat of the foreign nations, Israel in exile will know Yahweh's sovereign power (28:24, 26).

Ezekiel, a prophet from exile explains the real nature and necessity of the exile on the one hand, and on the other hand, predicts a future hope and assurance that the temple will be rebuilt and the glory, of God would return to Jerusalem (chapters 40-48).

C) Deutero-Isaiah: The time of Deutero-Isaiah's activity can be placed between the destruction of Jerusalem in 587 BC and the downfall of the Babylonian empire in 539 BCE. To be more precise Eissfeldt would like to place the activity of Deutero-Isaiah between the beginning of series of victories of Cyrus in about 550B.C.E and the conquest of Babylon in 538 by Cyrus.

While on the one hand, Ezekiel's message of restoration of the exiles and the temple (Ezek. 40-48) was not actualised, some of the exiles must have lost their hope for the bright future. On the other hand, the rise of Cyrus as a powerful king over the ancient orient would have rejuvenated some hopes in the minds of the exiles. At this decisive moment of Israelite history, Deutero-Isaiah proclaims his message of salvation and the hope of restoration for the people of Israel. At the outset Deutero-Isaiah proclaims that the exile and the disasters connected with it are due to the sin of the people (40:20). At the same time, Deutero-Isaiah also proclaims that exile as an occasion of fulfilling their (people's) task of witnessing Yahweh's creative action in the world history. In other words, the basic principle underlying Deutero-Isaiah's message was that the events of exile is the confirmation of Yahweh 5 election of h1s people (cf: Isa 44: 18, 55: 4f, 54: 15-17 et. a1).

In the context of exile, Deutero-Isaiah makes use of creation tradition as the central theme of his message. The creative work of Yahweh will bring about a new hope and a new situation for the exiles (41:18-20). By transforming a desert into a fruitful field Yahweh affirms his support and strength to his people. Von Rad points out that the creation theme in Deutero-lsaiah particularly reflects God's power in history. (Isa. 40:21 ff, 44:24 ff, 45: 12 ff), more specifically in the context of Babylonian exile. Isaiah's polemic against idols (44:88 f) is very much coming from the exilic situation. When the people of Israel thought that Yahweh Was a defeated God, and Marduk, a victorious God; Deutero-Isaiah sharply comes up against such a View that even Marduk, the Babylonian creator God was created by Yahweh.

Concerning Cyrus, Deutero-Isaiah's response was very positive, Cyrus is seen as the chosen by Yahweh to set his people free from the exile (45:1-7) Deutero-Isaiah saw in Cyrus the political reality behind which lies the divine plan and purpose. Deutero-Isaiah thus sharply reacting to his own historical situation confirms the fact of the uniqueness of Yahweh for the deliverance of exiles and of the same time expands the horizon of God's saving act through a Persian monarch.

The historical developments in the exilic age in a way open up a wide possibility to the world history, in that it shatters the exclusive claims of Judah as the only elected nation of God. In a way this election of Judah by God has to be viewed in terms of Israel's attitude towards foreign nations (Babylon, Persia). Yahweh, by choosing Nebuchadnezzar and Cyrus manifests his sovereignty over the entire world and made Judah to realise that Yahweh can initiate his plan even through the socalled 'enemies' of Judah. Thus along with Klaus Koch we would argue that the prophets of the exilic age initiated the new history of Israel in meta-historical realm of the world, which calls for the openness to outsiders.

Chapter 7

The Return and Restoration

1. THE RETURN AND RESTORATION OF THE EXILES

The end of the period which we usually call the 'Babylonian exile' is connected with the person of the Persian King Cyrus, who in the middle of the sixth century rose within a decade to become ruler over large areas of the near East after the subjection of Media in the East (550 BCE) and Lydia, ruled over by We" the fabulous King Croesus in the extreme north-west of Asia Minor (547 BCE), he We" turned against Babylonia, which was now in a decadent state, and in 539 occupied its capital Babylon. Thus, Cyrus came to rule over the biggest empire there had ever been in this part of the world. (His son and successor Cambyses also conquered Egypt in 525 BCE and added further to this kingdom).

A. Sources: The sources at our disposal for the post-exilic period are the book of Ezra and Nehemiah. In their account they limit themselves to two focal points: (i) the time from the 'edict of Cyrus' (538 B.C.E) to the conclusion of the building of the temple (515 B.C.E) (ii) and the activity of Ezra and Nehemiah (From 458 or 445 BCE). The books of Haggai and Zechariah are supplementary for the first phase. Apart from these sources, the picture is very fragmentary.

B. Edict of Cyrus: At the beginning of the book of Ezra (and similarly and the end of II chronicles) we are told that in the first year of his rule (i.e. probably in his first full regnal year, 538 BCE) Cyrus publicly proclaimed that he had been commissioned by Yahweh, the God of heaven, to build him a house in Jerusalem (Ezra 1:1-3; II Chronicles 36:20; at the same time, he had invited the Jews to go up to Jerusalem and build this house for their God. There is another version of this decree in Aramaic in Ezra 6:3-5. In that passage there is more detailed mention of the building of the temple; the size (v.3) and the method of the building (v. 4a) are given; and it is decreed that the costs are to be paid from the royal purse (v. 4b); the return of the temple vessels is ordered (v. 5). However, there is no mention of a return of the exiles.

1.1. Rebuilding of the Temple and the Return of the Exiles

Thus according to the sources immediately after his accession, Cyrus ordered the rebuilding of the temple in Jerusalem. (the Cyrus Cylinder which is made of baked clay gives useful information about the conciliatory policy of Cyrus. This historical cuneiform text is called, 'magna carta of freedom and tolerance'. This gives us the information about the policy of Persians under Cyrus and about the background of restoration). It is often assumed that the report about the return of exiles in Ezra 1:3 and the account of its implementation in v.5 is governed by the view of the chronicler that the land was empty during the exile, so that the return was the indispensable Presupposition for the rebuilding Jerusalem. However, it can be argued that in the inscription on the 'Cyrus Cylinder' there is also mention of the return of former inhabitants to other regions, so that immediate permission to return seems quite possible.

Few important persons connected with the returnees of the exile. We shall briefly discuss on each one's significance as follows:

a) *Sheshbazzar*: The question is; under whose leadership the return of the exiles took place? According to Ezra 1:8 the temple vessels were handed over by the Persian treasurer to Sheshbazzar, who is designated nasi (prince) of Judah. In the Aramaic text of 5:13-16 a remark by the 'elder' of Jerusalem (v.9) is quoted; according to this he not only brought the temple vessels to Jerusalem (cf. v. 11) but was appointed governor (Pehah) by Cyrus (v. 14) and laid the foundations of the temple.

b) *Zerubbabel*: There is another name connected with the return of the exiles, i.e., Zerubbabel. The list of those who returned (Ezra 2:2 cf. Neh. 7:7) begins with him, and there is a detailed report of the beginnings of his activity after his arrival in Jerusalem: the beginning of sacrificial worship on a provisional altar (Ezra 1:3), the celebration of the feast of tabernacles (v.4) and the continuation of regular sacrificial worship (v.5). Above all we are then told that the building of the temple was begun and continued. (chap. 4f) under his leadership (which he shared with the priest Joshua, vv.83). There are close connections here with the accounts by the prophets/Haggai

(1:14, 2:2 ft) and Zechariah (4:80, who are also mentioned in Ezra 5:1, 6:14 the title *Pechah* (Governor) is also repeatedly used for Zerubbabel, in the form ('governor of Judah') (Hag 1:1, 14, 2:2, 21).

So, the relationship between the activity of Sheshbazaar and that of Zerubbabel in the tradition is unclear. We get the impression that Zerubbabelhas been put in the foreground at the expense of Sheshbaziar.

c) <u>Ezra</u>: First of all, Ezra and Nehemiah have one important thing in common. Both come from the circles of the Jewish exiles. It is said of Ezra that he set out from 'Babylon' i.e. from Babylonia, where the centre of the Jewish exiles had been since 597/586. Nehemiah, on the other hand, had and exalted position as cupbearer at the Persian court in the capital, Susa (Neh 1:1). (the book of Esther later, also presupposes the presence of Jews in Susa and their activity in the service of the court, of also Dan. 8:2). Both figures are connected with the Jewish homeland, though in quite different ways.

In his professional capacity Ezra was evidently concerned with Jewish questions. His title, 'scribe of the law of the God of Heaven' (Ezra 7:12, 21) is probably to be understood as an official Persian title (secretary or the like), and 'law of the God of heaven' as an official Aramaic designation for the Jewish religion, whose God is revered as creator of the world and thus as 'God of heaven'. So, Ezra was secretary (or recorder) for matters relating to the Jewish religion. Accordingly, he too travelled to Jerusalem on an official mission.

Ezra's commission is described in the credentials given him by king <u>Artaxerxes</u> (Ezra 7:12-26) which have been handed down in Aramaic. First of all, any Israelites wanting to return home may join him (v. 13). From the list of those returning in Ezra 8:1f a total of five thousand people (including number of families) has been calculated, in addition to this are the Levites and the temple servants (8: 1820). Ezra appointed Judges and experts in the law in order to instruct those who know the law to Judge by it and teach it to others (v 25). In addition, there are penalties against those who do not follow 'the law of your God and the law of the King' (v.26).

The first and only area in which there is any mention of the implementation of Ezra's commission is the question of mixed marriages (Ezra 9). The report of this appears as the implementation of the 'visitation': The leaders of the people tell Ezra about a problematical state of affairs which represents a violation of religious obligations (*ma'al*, 9:2, 4, 10:2,6). At the next investigation of the situation (ch. 10) we are told of a great readiness to cooperate on the part of all concerned (vv. 1-4, 12-14) which finally leads to the appointment of a commission (vv. 16f, Judges are also mentioned in v. 14, cf. 7:25), and the listing of all those involved. Here, we can see Ezra's concern for the purity of the Jewish community which is already evident in the accounts from the first phase after the exile (Ezra 9:1).

Ezra is mentioned again in Nehemiah chapter 8. It is reported here that he read from the 'book of the Torah of Moses' (v.1) in a solemn liturgical setting. Most scholars identify (usually implicitly) this Torah with the 'Law' which according to Ezra 7:14, 25, was 'in the hand of 'Ezra'. It is usually concluded from this that Ezra's task was to bring this law to Jerusalem to 'proclaim', 'promulgate' it there and thus make it the legal basis for the Jewish community in Jerusalem.

So there are two sides to the picture of Ezra. Firstly, he is the 'visitor'. appointed by the Persian King who is to implement the Jewish law sanctioned by the king in his own interest among the subjects of Persia who are adherents of the Jewish religion. Secondly, he is the pious scholar and teacher of the Torah (Ezra 7:10), who performs the first reading of the law in the Synagogue recorded in the tradition. These two aspects must be clearly distinguished. However, this does not mean that they are exclusive. Ezra could easily have performed his official function and at the same time have played an important religious role in the consolidation and further development of post-exilic Jewish religion. The description of Ezra's activity in reading out the law showsan important feature of Post-exilic religious development. The Torah, its reading and exposition, forms the centre around which the Jewish community assembled in Jerusalem and throughout Judah. Here we can see a piety connected with the Torah of a kind which is already suggested in Deuteronomy (eg. in the Shema Israel: 'Hear Israel' of Deut 6:4 ff).

d) *Nehemiah*: Nehemiah's connections with his mother country of Judah at first seem to be more of a 'private' nature. On the basis of the report from relatives about the situation in Jerusalem (Neh 1:2 t) he asked permission from the king to rebuild of the place of my father's "Sepulchres" (Neh 2:3, 5). Then he received permission from the king and the relevant papers, along with the military escort (2:7-9). However, later on in the narrative he appears as 'governor' (5:14).

The most prominent subject in Nehemiah's autobiographical "memories" is the rebuilding of the walls of the city and the difficulties which have to be over-come in connection with this (Nehemiah 1-6). The opposition comes above all from Samaria. In the foreground we have a man by the name Sanballat 2:10, 19, 3:33 f, 4:1f, 6:1-14); his title is not given, but he may probably be seen as the governor of Samaria, so here we can see rivalry between Jerusalem and Samaria. Possibly Jerusalem did not have a governor of its own. Before the arrival of Nehemiah and perhaps Nehemiah was only nominated governor at a later stage.

The title first appears in Neh 5:14, 18 (cf, 12:26), so that the people in Samaria feared a limitation of their own sphere of influence through Nehemiah's activity. Moreover, Nehemiah's position was made more difficult and endangered by a group in the upper classes of Jerusalem who conspired with his opponents in Samaria (cf. 6:17-19). However, despite all opposition he succeeded in winning over the great majority of the inhabitants of Jerusalem and Judah to his plans, so that the rebuilding of the city wall was completed with great involvement on all sides (3: 1-32, 4:9-17) in a period of only fifty-two days (6:15f).

This social situation is illuminated at a stroke by the account in Neh. 5 which reports far-reaching social tensions within the population of Judah. The population of the land complained about its increasing poverty, which led to situations of economic dependence and finally slavery for debt (vv.1-5). It was thought particularly scandalous that those who practised this exploitation were Jewish 'brothers' (vv. 1, 5). It is quite clear from Neh. 5:6 ff. that the creditors were members of the upper class 'noble' i.e. those held particular offices or performed special functions (v. 7). So, the crises did not involve everyone in the same way; on the contrary, it heightened the social distinctions and led to tensions and unrest. Nehemiah is implemented a general remission of debts, the binding nature of which the creditors had to accept in a public assembly and through an additional religious oath (v. 12).

This obligation imposed by Nehemiah and the measures which went it combine a number of intentions: the demand for a demarcation of the Jewish community, and for its purity, a concern for the regular observance of temple Worship, and explicit social concern. Thus, Nehemiah's achieve whole for the consolidation of Jewish life after exile. By rebuilding the walls of Jerusalem and increasing the number of inhabitants, he restored a political (and at the same time a spiritual) centre to the province of Judah. By regulating the offering to the temple he guaranteed that sacrificial worship would be performed in an orderly way, so that Jerusalem could fulfil its role as a religious centre. By remitting debts and arranging a year of remission he helped to diminish social tensions and thus made the Jewish community more viable.

2. THE SECOND TEMPLE AND RELIGIOUS REORGANISATION

As noted above, for two centuries Israel, together with the whole of the Near east, lived under Persian rule. Apart from Cyrus decree, Ezra, Nehemiah, we know nothing about the history of Israel in this long period. Even what we know is, generally speaking, limited to the narrow confines of the small province of Judah with Jerusalem as its centre. But, Israel extended far beyond the province of Judah apart from those parts which were scattered in the

Diaspora In the neighbouring provinces of Samaria and Acco (assuming that was the name of the Galilean Province at the time), and to some extent in the provinces of Ammon and Ashdod there divide the descendants of the old Israelite tribes, who as is evident from the history of the following period still regard themselves as belonging to the community of Israel and the Jerusalem religious community and took part in public worship Jerusalem (cf. Ezra 7: 12-26).

It was during the Persian period that Jerusalem cults acquired the form which presented in its essentials until the end of its existence. In Jerusalem there ruled a priestly hierarchy with the 'High Priest' at its head and a closed priesthood who derived from the Zadokite families of the Davidic period and now traced their origin even further back to Moses' brother Aaron, who was not assigned great prominence in the tradition (cf. Priestly code in Lev 8, 9 and in I Chronicles 5:27-41). In the course of the Persian period the *Clerus minor* of the now so called 'levites' developed alongside this priesthood in what was presumably fairly long process.

Public worship itself also assumed new forms during the Persian period. The temple in Jerusalem was no longer, as in Davidic Period, a royal shrine. After Ezra's reform the whole religious community became responsible for public worship in Jerusalem. Certain new (innovative) things are attached now to their religious practices, particularly important, 'Day of Atonement', which was observed five days before the beginning of the great autumn festival on the tenth day of the seventh month (Lev 23:27-32), and this now took the place of the autumn festival as the real beginning of the religious year (Lev. 25:98); this required increasing importance of expiation in general in Public Worship.

Persian period was important because it saw the beginning of a canonisation of a Particular literature. Pentateuch has acquired the definite form. Ezra's law book, even if this 'Law' of Ezra was a compilation of ordinance of while we have now no detailed knowledge and not the complete Pentateuch itself, it was soon followed by the final redaction of the great Pentateuch. Which pursued the same line and included Ezra's law (However, Synagogue worship and scribal exegesis do not emerge into the clear light of history until the later Hellenistic period).

The traditional records of Prophets' sayings also continued to be read and collected in the Persian period. It can hardly be doubted that a fairly large part of the secondary material to the books of the prophet, as they have come down to us, derives from the Persian period, though it is naturally, impossible to trace this process in detail. Later this process continued and finally in the Hellenistic period, the prophets were combined with Deuteronomistic history, which was now regarded as prophetic, to form to prophetic canon as the second part of the authoritarian holy writings. Thus the Persian period clearly has, in many repeats, adecisive influence on the later course of Israelitehistory and Israelite life.

Archaeologically, no building is available from this period, even the new sanctuary at Jerusalem since the site is still occupied by a famous Muslim shrine and not available for archaeological research. The only available one from Parisian period with the inscription Yhd ='Judah' on the coins, this shows that the promise of Judah was granted autonomy by the Persians. These coins with Yhd came to the use in the course of fourth century. Numerous Jar handles stamped with the letters Yhd or Yrslm (Jerusalem) have also been found. The clay vessels which stamped in this way were presumably used with the cultic taxation system.

One other archaeological traces, a remarkable legacy of this period has been found at Tell ed-duwer, the site of ancient Lachish, namely, the remains of an imposing Persian palace from the end of the 5th or the beginning of the 4th century Lachish is an important palace/centre of Persian government; it may be this was the seat of the Persian Governor of the province of Edom.

3. THE SAMARITANS AND THE SCHISM

In the inner history of the Jerusalem religious community, the separation of the Samaritan community led to its establishment of independent cults on the ancient holy mountain Gerizim near Shechem.

It is impossible to assign an exact date to the carrying through of this Separation, but it is the completion of a long development. This process has its ultimate roots in the age-old division between the southern group of tribes and the rest of the tribes. After the exile, Jerusalem temple was still recognised as the centre shrine. But it has now no longer a royal Judean shrine and could therefore be recognized more readily as the one central shrine common to all. But old antithesis between north and south still continued below the surface and broke out again when plans were made for the rebuilding of the sanctuary in Jerusalem following Cyrus' decree. This time the resistance came from the Judean side. The inhabitants of the neighbouring provinces, in which the foreign upper classes had gradually been absorbed or were in process of being absorbed by the local Israelite population, were regarded by the Judeans, who had no foreign upper has imposed on them, as 'culturally unclean' (cf: Haggai 2: 10-14).

Perhaps the political conflict between Judeans and Israelites still playeda part at this period, but the religious and cultic aspect appears to have been more to the fore, the more so since Judah was probably still in the subject to the governor of Samaria and the restoration of the temple took place under the jurisdiction of the provincial government in Samaria. The situation changed when Nehemiah constituted Judah as an independent province and the antithesis arose again between Samaria and Jerusalem.

The Samaritans established their cult by bringing out Samaritan Pentateuch. It is the Hellenistic period during which we have first explicit evidence of the existence of the Samaritan sanctuary on Gerizim dates from the period of Antiochus IV Epiphanes (II Maccabees 6:2). Only in the second century B.C.E. the complete separation may have taken place between the Samaritans and the Jerusalem religions community. By the Jerusalem religious community Samaritans were considered to be apostates and religiously unclean. The whole of the Chronicle's history composed about 300 B.C.E prove this that Jerusalem traditions are historically unique and legitimate as opposed to the Samaritan cultus.

The Samaritan religious community managed to survive through the vicissitudes of history; they gradually became vanished, today, there is a tiny remnant of Samaritans in the city of Nablus (Shechem), they celebrate their Passover on Gerizim, but otherwise became a mere historical curiosity.

Chapter 8

The Maccabean Period

1. PEOPLE'S MOVEMENT AND THEIR INDEPENDENCE: THE MACCABEAN REVOLT

The conflict between the Jerusalem religious community and the Seleucids took place because of the latter's serious encroachments on the property, rights and regulations of the sanctuary. Antiochus III maintained a positive attitude to Jerusalem religions community, his son took over the throne in 187 B.C.E. Seleucus IV Philopator, who then was murdered by his minister in 175 BCE. and the throne was occupied by his brother Antiochus IV Epiphanes, seized the power, by passing over the real heir to the throne Demetrius who was living in Rome, thus initiated inner conflicts in the Seleucid dynasty.

The Hellenistic influence. in Jerusalem religious community by diaspora Jews who were also visiting the Jerusalem temple, several Hellenistic cities began to develop, which also attracted the Israelites (cf. 2 Maccabees 4:12 ff), but large group of Jerusalem religious community rejected this new way of life, gradually the conflict developed. The fundamental question faced by Jerusalem religious community as to what its attitude ought to be towards the foreign Hellenistic customs and the ways of life. Disturbance in the Jerusalem religious community also arise at this time because of all kinds of struggles around the office of high priest.

At the time of Seleucus IV, we have a priest named Onias, who was faithful to the law (II Macc. 3:1f, 4:1 ff), but he had enemies from his fellow priests who tried to get him removed by conveying slanderous reports on him to the King (2 Macc. 3:4 f, 4:1 f) but according to 2 Macc 3:3 Seleucus did not yield to the demands of the slanderous reporters, but with Antiochus IV Epiphanes (from 175 BCE), Jason son of Onias sacked Onias and made himself high priest by giving lot of gifts to the kin and vigorous promotion of Hellenization in Jerusalem (II Macc 4:7 f). Jerusalem religious community was highly disturbed by this intervention. Three years later Menelaus offered still larger sums to the king, thus Menelaus was appointed as high priest, (2 Macc 4:23 f). But in 169 B.C.E. because of the rumour that Antiochus IV lost his life in his campaign in Egypt, Jason took over and banished Menelaus, and Menelaus in turn fled to Antiochus but Antiochus IV Epiphanes restored Menelaus by force, Jason now flew to east of Jordan where he had retired after his first deposition (2 Macc. 5 5 ff).

Antiochus IV Epiphanes after this took a radical step (earlier Seleucus IV had already made an attempt to draw riches of temple by Jerusalemite enemy of then high priest Onias but attempts failed). Now Antiochus IV took the advantage of making Menalaus to the office of the high Priest in 169 B.C.E to take with him valuables of the temple, and he himself entered into the temple (I Macc. 1:17-28, 2 Macc 5:15 ff). This made Israelites furious, and considered Kingas their enemy.

In 168 BCE When Antiochus IV Epiphanes once again had attacked Egypt but he was forced to leave the country by advice of Roman senate delivered by Popilius Laenas, even he ordered his leading tax-official (II Macc. 5:24) to 'Mysarch, named Apollonius to make surprise attack on Jerusalem, severe loss, city burnt, women and children are captured (I Macc. 1:29 ff).

After all these events Antiochus IV Epiphanes took a decisive step against the Jerusalem religious community. In a decree (I Macc. 1:41) he prohibited all important religious observances, forbid sacrifices, observance of Sabbath, custom of circumcision, and he had the holy books destroyed, if any one breaks these rules he charged them with death punishment. He introduced foreign worship with sanctuary and dealt same way with Samaritan sanctuary at Mount Gerizim, he expected everyone to take part in his own way of sanctuary worship on the 15th day of the month Kislev in the 145th year of Seleucid era (I Macc. 1:54) in Dec 67 BCE the "Abomination of desolation" was set up in the temple in Jerusalem, new cult was begun the towns in country side altars were set up at which everyone now had to sacrifice. The religious privileges of Jerusalem religious community are totally abolished, so much of persecution followed, some have escaped from it by leaving their homes.

Some determined and resolute leaders revolted against this cruel act by Antiochus IV, especially from a priestly family lived in Modein (the modern el-midye), who traced their descent (I Macc. 2:1) from the priestly house of Joiarib (Neh 12:6:19 I Chr. 24. 7). Its more recent ancestor was a certain Hasmon, they called themselves Hasmonaeans after him; a senior member of his family, at this time was Mattathias, who has number of sons, he killed an Israelite who offered a Pagan sacrifice including Seleucid official (I Macc 2:15-18), and he escaped later to the mountains in the inaccessible wilderness of Judah, in the year 166 B.C.E, they destroyed pagan altars, killed apostates, used force to circumcise children they strictly followed Sabbath, but to defend themselves they did fight on the day of Sabbath(I Macc 2:29-48). In 166 B.C.E Mattathias dies, taken over by Judas called Makkabaios (I Macc 2:4, 'the hammor') with him started the Maecabean period; Judas Maeeabeaus was a great warrior (1 Macc 3 4).

l Macc 3:10-12, Judas was successful by defeating a Seleucid under leadership of Apollonius (place not specified) may be seen (I Mace 2:29), later, Antiochus IV took strong measures, he sent three generals Ptolemy, Nicanor and Gorgias with a considerable army against Judas and his followers in the 147th Year of the Seleucid era (the summer of 165 B.C.E). Battle took place at Emmaus (modern 'amwas) once again, Maccabeans registered victory over their enemies (I Macc 3:27-4:25); another victory to Judas (I Macc 4:26-35), these successors made confirmation that God was on their side. It was during the time the visions recorded in the second book of Daniel (7-12). Dan 7:18 "royal power of the saints of the Most High". In the midst of these troubles, there developed a thought called Apocalyptic, which continuing the prophecy of the earliest period, explain the world and its history as leading to an end brought about by God.

After this Judas envisaged the liberation of Jerusalem and the restoration of the sanctuary After the desecration of the temple in 167 B C.E the faithful had erected a kind of substitute sanctuary at Mizpah (tell en-nasbe) north of Jerusalem, but no sacrifices only a meeting place (1 Macc 3:46-49), but real holy place was still Jerusalem; once again Judas restored the worship at sanctuary on 25th Kislev ofthe 148th Seleucid year i.e. Dec 164 BCE i.e. three years after its destruction, the temple was restored, legitimate sacrifices were made an eight-day festival with sacrifices, prayer and singing (I Mac C 4:36-61).

Judas sent his eldest brother Simon in 163 B.C.E to 'Gilead' then Simon was successful in this campaign. But later Antiochus V with Lysias had crushed the rebels in 163-62 B.C.E later Judas has failed in another battle near Beth-Zechariah, 6 miles South west of Bethlehem, now they further attacked Jerusalem sanctuary (I Mace. 6:17-54), but later Lysias had to wind up the campaign in Judea, but offered peace to the besieged (Judas) to give them freedom to worship, then Judas accepted the offer, and surrendered the fortified areas of the temple, then the Jerusalem religious community was restored to its old portion.

In 162 BCE Demetrius I Soter ascended to the throne, the son of Seleucus IV. in Jerusalem, after the high priest Menelaus had been removed by Antiochus V, probably in connection with the agreed re-organisation of cultus (2 Macc. l3:1-8), a man Alcimus (prob. Eliakim) was appointed as high priest (I Macc 7: 14), in order to make peace with Jerusalem religious community, but Judas had no confidence in the peace, because he was aiming at complete political independence, but this resulted in a cleavage within (Judas) unified group. One group called Hasmonaeans others were who wanted to work for total freedom and to live strictly according to the law. The latter group is simply called the Pious (hasidim). In addition, Hellenizing groups, and among the priestly families, the Sadducees have emerged (Probably Alcimus) was in the group. But Judas was uncompromised (I Mace. 8:1-32), Alcimus sought help from Demetrius, later gave Nicanor, but Judas defeated him in March 161 near Adasa, but later Demetrius sent Bachides to fight, later Judas was defeated in the battle (I Macc 9: 1-22) and his followers were taken for task; they escaped to the desert of Judah, but they chose Jonathanas successor of Judas – the internal difficulties once again came to the aid of Jonathan's purposes. The Bachides agreed to negotiate with Jonathan; thus Jonathan established his residence in Michmash (Mod. Mukhmas), 8 miles North East of Jerusalem, from there he judged people (I Macc. 9:70-73), this happened in the year 157 B.CE.

In 153 BCE Alexander Balas, passed himself as a son of Antiochus 1V Epiphanes claimed same and rebelled against Demetrius, under this conditions he attracted Jonathan as a friend of support, Alexander Balas made Jonathan as high priest, he entered his office at the great autumn festival in the year 152 BCE, so the supreme religious office was conferred on a member of non-'Zadokite', non-'Aaronite' priestly family. Of the Hasmonaeans until the reign of Herod (I Macc. 10: 1 5-21: Alexander gave a subject king position to Jonathan), for some time Jonathan ruled under Demetrius and Alexander, but finally helped Alexander to kill Demetrius in 150 B.C.E Alexander invited Jonathan to his marriage with Cleopatra, daughter of Ptolemy VI Philometer, and Jonathan was made as 'general', 'jointruler' in the Seleucid state (I Macc. 10: 59-66) - glory of Jonathan raised to its peak (I Macc 10:61-64), but Alexander Balas was finally defeated by son of Demetrius Iin the year 145 B.C.E, afterwards Ptolemy VI died then Demetrius ascended the throne as Demetrius II Nicator (I Macc. 10: 67-11:9), even this king was in favour of Jonathan. Later Jonathan wanted the withdrawal of the Seleucid garrison from the 'Akra' in Jerusalem and from Beth-zur, but Demetrius II did not agree for this concession, there on Jonathan has departed from Demetrius II, but finally Jonathan was defeated by Diodotus Tryphon in 143 B.C. (I Macc. 12:39-13: 32) at the land east of Jordan at a place called Bascame whose location is not known to us.

Simon became successor of Jonathan, (already appointed by Tryphon) but want to seek the support of Demetrius II after the Jonathan's death, and the king gave several concessions to him, but Simon functioned more independently, with the consent of the people Simon gave him a name 'great high priest', general and leader of the Judeans (1 Macc. 13:42), he reckoned 170th Seleucid year (142-141 BCE) as his first year (I Macc. 13:91f), he once again gained control over, 'Akra' of Jerusalem (I Mace 13:49-52), thus he extended his territories too far and wide. Simon was considered to be a just and benevolent ruler; after initial battles, his reign was regarded as a time of peace and prosperity (I Macc. 14:4, 8 ff) also I Macc 14:25-49. But once again Simon was in trouble, after Demetrius II's death, his brother Antiochus VII Sidetes set himself on the throne in Antioch, but soon he asked Simon to surrender some of the won territories by him. But when Simon refused he sent his general, Cendebeus against the province of Judah (I Macc. 15:25-41). Now Simon, his two sons Judas and John also fought with him but Ptolemy killed Simon with his two sons Mattathias and Judas, but John had established himself as a ruler in his father's office in Jerusalem (I Macc. 16:11-22) as John Hyrcanus I, but later Antiochus VII Sidetes made him to pay an amount to settle the dispute amicably.

Israel's inner life in the Hellenistic Period, the community life was becoming more and more individualized for a longtime, this process of individualism in further promoted by involvement in the intellectual atmosphere of the Hellenistic world (though difficult to prove this point in detail) Eg. Book of Daniel chapters 1-6; the individual and his important place in their faith, above all the wide spread Diaspora, the individual was dependent on his own resources in a foreign environment.

There were certain Hellenising circles, adhered more to the Jerusalem Religions Community. Eg. In the mid-2nd cent, the philosopher Aristobulus in Alexandria attempted to show that the Old Testament law, when its basic content is analysed, agrees with the various schools of Greek philosophy the method used was allegorical exegesis. Sadducees sympathised with this Hellenising tendency in the Maccabean-Hasmonaen period.

The Anti-Hellenistic forces won the victory in struggles of the 2nd cent B.C.E, especially in the context of Seleucid attacks. They formed a major group called Pharisees.

The rise and birth of Apocalyptic arose at this time and context, individual expectation of life after the death of the body thus took its place alongside the expectation of the ending of history by the coming of the kingdom of God, Later, a rich apocalyptic literature has developed; the basic themes like eschatological individual expectations, angiology. Probably the development of groups and parties with in Judaism took place from now on? These groups (including the Essenes) originated in the external and internal upheavals of the 2nd Century, they are at the same time an indication that the inner life of the Jerusalem religious community had become sterile, but victors assumed their own path. For example, Pharisees turned increasingly to a legalistic moralism which led to an increasingly subtle casuistic treatment of the traditional laws of God, later developed by the Qumran Community.

Section III

The Old Testament Literature and the Canon

Chapter 9

The Formation of the Old Testament

1. FORMATION OF THE INDIVIDUAL BOOKS OF THE OLD TESTAMENT

1.1. The Process from Oral, till written Form of the Books

The Old Testament whose formation will be discussed into following pages, comprise neither the whole Israelite literature; which has so far been the subject of our study, not a specified stratum of this literature. The OT is rather the extant remains of Israelites literature, whose development continues in Jewish literature, much more of which is preserved. Quite generally we must recall that Israelite literature, and therefore the books of the OT were not written as autofocus works of art but to serve practical religious purposes. The emphasis can reign nationalist culture or ethical elements.

The crucial fact is that this literature is intimately linked with human existence, and attempt to make possible and guarantee a comprehensive regulation of life on the basis of the divine will we see this reflects in various ways in the laws, narratives, poems, wisdom aphorisms and prophetic oracles.

For this reason, also it is almost impossible to distinguish between religious and secular rhetorical forms and literary types and to distribute them according to such a criterion. This is not even possible in the case of the common types of lyric poetry, all of which exhibit religious elements. For life was not divided into secular and religious spheres but in general constituted a unity under the sign of religion.

1.2. The Formation of the Historical and Legal Books

The writings referred to as historical and legal books constitute a considerable part of the Old Testament. In bulk and according to the present classification in number they form the largest including the Pentateuch. The following books of Joshua, the Judges, Samuel and Kings, together with Chronicler History (the Books of Chronicles, Ezra and Nehemiah) and the books of Ruth and Esther, which stand in isolation.

In order to present the Old Testament Literary types clearly six groups are identified (i) the first group, the 'regulating types' comprises those forms that refers to life and conduct as well as the whole realm of law; (ii) the second group requesting types comprises of those forms and formulas however various, that express a request or wish (iii) the third group proclaiming and instructing types comprises in which on the basis of special authority, something is proclaimed, instruction is issued or knowledge is transmitted. (iv) the fourth group the narrative types comprise those forms that depict events or situations whose historical nature is comparable or questionable. (v) the fifth group include those accounts or descriptions that atleast in form claim faithfully to reproduce reality. (vi) the sixth group the communicating types comprises the forms involving direct communication with other men or with God for the sake of simplification and concentration. We shall categorize them in to the laws, instructions, narratives, and report, and they are dealt in relation to the ancient west Asian situation.

a) Law

These are textual or other evidence for legal maxims and laws, law codes and strictly the regulated legal procedure. Private contracts and state treaties at any early period for each culture. In Mesopotamia several types of cuneiform law can be distinguished after Sumerian, Old Babylonian, New Babylonian, Assyrians forms begin to diverge. For about a millennium until the end of the period of Hammurabi, the "old law" was in force. Its old documents include economic texts from Shuruppak and Lagash (middle of the third millennium), the account of "reform" of Uurkagina (twenty fourth century) fragmentary code of Urnammu (about 2000 BCE), then, after scattered additional Sumerian laws, the Neo Sumerian legal documents of the Ur III period. Basically all law as in the Old Testament is considered a gift of the gods. The power to issue laws is of the divine origin. This idea at first associated with the god of the particular city, gradually becomes restricted first to a few specific gods and then to the Sun God <u>Shamash</u>.

Two common and important points are stressed in all the international treaties <u>first</u>, the oaths must be taken by the gods, of both partners to the treaty; sacrificial rites and symbolic action must be performed when the treaty is concluded. <u>Second</u>, legal practice seems to be based not on law codes but on traditional common law, for which collections of various judgements probably were at the disposal of judges in the particular cities.

b) Instructions

Throughout the AWA oracles are obtained, blessings or curses are pronounced, instruction and advice in religious and cultic questions is given, and the cult is performed according to specific rituals and regulations. Practices forbidden in Israel is being contrary to Yahwism are found than the OT would indicate. Prognostication, which reached its highest development in Mesopotamia, making use of astrology as well as omens from the animal and human worlds, hepatoscopy, and artificially produced (Omens, Smoke, Oil); calculations to determine auspicious and inauspicious days.

c) Narrative

It has long been well known that myth and epic, which frequently assume the role played in Israel by Saga and legend, are of immense significance in the ancient West Asia. It has been said that myth always accompanies ritual, joining with it as a kind of verbal ceremony to produce a powerful event. Myth and ritual frequently go together, especially in the context of the religious position; but is not true always as a general rule. The myth of the Deluge for example, was never recited as part of the edit, other myths furnish religious propaganda for a particular sanctuary or a theological tenet, or else political propaganda, like the Babylonian myth of the plague god Ekra Eg: In Mesopotamia myth and epics, the Sumerian heritage of the third millennium is the most extensive, even though it has been subjected to Sumerian by Semites. The myth of Enki and Eridu. The Babylonian creation epic, called Enuma Elis, etc. In Egyptian texts we find for the most past only isolated motifs taken from myths, the myths of Heliopolitan or Memphite theology; the Canaanite myths and epics for instance, the great cycle introducing the gods Baal, Anat, and Mot which is the most important. We have such myths as the marriage of the moon god with the goddess Nikkal and the Birth of the god: Shahar and Shalim.

d) Report

The first attempt to comprehend the course of history as the formal chronology, which we first encounter in Mesopotamia in the form of the king list from the Akkad period, the great Assyrian king list. In Egypt in the so calledyear tables of the first Dynasty, the regnal years of the kings were at first named for from the second dynasty on, this practice is superceded by simple examination. Annual writing, the first major form of Egyptian historiography, follows the pattern of the year tables.

e) Letters

Few letters are to be mentioned from AWA among the many letters; the Akkadian letters from Nimrud, Mari, Alalakh and Amama; the letters from

Ugarit letters from Akkadian and in Canaanite and the Hittite letters. Later on, there are the letters of the Neo-Babylonian and Persian periods, mostly written in Aramaic and the Greek letters of the Hellenistic period. The Israelite epistolary style is almost identical with contemporary style elsewhere.

The forms customarily used in Israel for law and instruction, narrative and report, obviously are basically identical with or similar to those employed elsewhere with ancient West Asia. Many of the literary types found in the historical and legal books are not typical of the Old Testament, but of the ancient Near East in general. It is therefore all the more important to notice where changes or innovations have taken place and to inquire whether they have come about through the influence of Yahwism or for some other reason. Thus the study of rhetorical and literary types leads directly to the question of uniqueness of this against its ancient West Asian environment.

1.3. The Formulas and Sayings of Everyday Life

To a large extent the formulas of everyday Israelite life are preserved only because they were appropriate to certain contexts in the books and narratives of the Old Testament. In many cases there are certain stereotyped formulas that have come down to us.

The birth of child especially a son, gave the parents of the relatives occasion for various sayings. Sayings related to the individual situation naturally have not survived, but we do possess stereotype formulas such as that was to encourage their mother. "Fear not: for now you will have another son" (Genesis 35:17), and the similar expression used in I Sam 4:20. We also have the mother's exclamation, I have got a Man (Genesis 4:1). The formulas use at betrothal and marriage are echoed by the declaration of relationship with which the man receives the women formed from the rib (Genesis 2:23). The formulas mentioned 'fear not', which at times is meant only to calm and encourage (1 Sam 28: 1213), also can take on the character of the summons or a directive. This is especially true when Yahweh or is angel appears. (Judge 6: 23), is the context of battle, of when a powerful man promises protection to another (1 Sam 22:23).

1.4. Rules of Conduct in Apodictic Form

Alt has termed all the sayings in this category apodictically formulated legal maxims: according to him they are transmitted primarily in short or long Series of maxims with parallel structure, they are uniquely Israelite and Yahwistic and their categorical directives correspond to their intimate associations with the divine will. This type of law as some times been called somewhat incautiously, divine, law. The material and form of the apodictic series (Do this . . . Do not do ...) are not legal in origin, but moral and ethical; it came into being in the context of Pre-Yahwistic nomadism (cf. Lev 18:7-12, 14-16; Exod 20:11-12).

1.5. Legal Maxims and Decisions

The realm of legal practice exhibits a variety of customs and legal maxims. The latter appear death penalty Eg. Gen 9:6 "whoever sheds the blood of the man, by man shall is blood be shed". There were also legal maxims employed in civil law; for instance, the widow who removes the sandal from the foot of the man referring to perform the duty of levirate marriage and is to spit at him and say, 'so shall it be done to the man to who does not built up his brother's house' (Deut 25:9).

Legal decisions formed after the pattern of the series of apodictic rules. They are so-called (surely you shall die) series scattered throughout the Book of the covenant and the Holiness Code (Exod 21:12, 15-17, 22:19-20, Lev. 20:2, 9-13, 15-16, 27, 24:16. The sentences of this series are constructed in participant style, eg. "Whoever curses (literally: one cursing) forever or his mother shall be put to death."

The group of another set of laws are called Casuistic Laws. These laws precisely the usual style of ancient West Asia law, elucidating in detail various legal questions in order to regulate daily life and the performance of the cult. (eg.Exod 21:12-17).

The etiological legal narrative, which is connected with the legal material proper. These narratives derive legal practices from things done by Israel's ancestors, their function at some time was certainly to regulate conduct, and they must have had the character of directives. Such narratives can determine cultic practices; Exod 12:27, for example, institutes a Passover custom, and Exodus 13:14-15 justifies the sacrifice of the first born. In addition, such narratives sometimes relate legal cases and decisions, in these instances the real purpose of the narratives is made quite clear, as in Numbers 9, which directs that those who are unclean or away on a journey are to celebrate the Passover later: Numbers 15:32-36, which describes the stoning of a man who had violated the Sabbath and Numb 22 and 36, which guarantee the right of a daughter to inherit.

1.6. Rhetorical Forms in Legal Proceedings

Numerous forms that are particularly employed in the discourses of the prophets are associated with legal proceedings. These are different types as follows: (a) The forms used in the dispute before court action; the summons to hand over the accused, the formation of opposition and appeasement used in the pre-trial dispute, the forms intended to avert the trial, the appeals of the accused and the plaintiff. (b) the rhetorical forms used in the trial itself: the accusations the defences (both Personal and on behalf of them). The formulas of admission, and the settlement proposals. These are followed by the concluding forms: the various forms of verdict and sentence. All these forms show how greatly legal procedures influence the life of an Israelite.

1.7. Treaties and Contracts

In Israel, as through the entire ancient near East, treaties and contracts played an important role. The OT, however usually diverts the concluding of a treaty of contract without relating its content. Formally we may distinguish four types of contracts. (a) The mutual contract between the equal partners– wife - in the early period expresses a reciprocal relationship of solidarity with all the rights and duties that this implies for the contracting parties, so that they are linked together by a common bond (b) The treaty and contract by which a powerful person binds himself, placing himself in a relationship towards a weaker party according to which he undertakes to perform certain conditions while the weaker party has no active significance (c) The Suzerinity or vassal treaty, in which certain obligations are placed upon the weaker party, by the powerful party restricts himself to general pledges of loyalty; the traditions made by the Hittites with their vassal fall in to this category. (d) The treaty and contract that a third party establishes between two others, like that formed in one of the Mari letters without mention of obligation imposed on the parties to the treaty. When such treaties or contracts concluded, not only of the conditions stipulated, but many kinds of ritual are also performed such as mingling of the parties blood or sparkling with blood (Exod 24:8), hand clasp (Ezek 17:18), exchanges of personal property (1 Sam 1823-4) setting up a stele (Josh. 24:26) and oath (Gen 21:22-24) a meal (Exo 24:1 1) etc. With regard to the persons or groups between which sud1 treaties of contracts are concluded in the O.T, we once more find four types:

a) Treaties are concluded between political entities or their representatives. such as that between Solomon and the King of Tyre (I Kings 5:212) Treaties of Abraham and lsaac with Abimelach of Gerar (Gen 21 :2223, 26:26-80) of Jacob with Laban (Gen 3 1:44-50) and Joshua with the people of Gibeon (Josh 9:15) are to understood in the same way.
b) When a king is chosen or appointed, treaties are concluded between the future ruler and the people or their representatives as in the case of David (II Sam 5:3) Joash (II Kings 11:17) and Josiah (II Kings 23: 1-3).
c) There is a frequent reference to the contracts between individuals as that between Abraham and Ephron for the purchase of cave of Machpelah (Gen 23), that made by Jeremiah for the purchase of the field (Jet 32) and that made by Boaz and Ruth (Ruth 4).
d) The treaty of contract form was extended to the relationship between God and man (Abraham) or God and Israel although the prophet

prefer personal categories and use kingship terminology to define this relationship. The Sinai covenant is based on the primitive treaty relationship, which forges a common bond between the two parties and places them in a common milieu. Later apparently the royal treaty provided the pattern. Scholars have identified that there exists parallelism between the Hittite vassal treaties and O.T. "Covenant formulations", especially in the Decalogues in Exodus 20 and 34, as well as Deuteronomy 4:29-30, and Joshua 24. The pattern reads as follows opening formula events leading up to the making of the treaty, declaration of the purpose, individual stipulations, list of witnesses, blessings and curses. Seen from this point of the view, the form of the covenant appears constant from the earliest period down to the latest.

2. Compilation and Transmission

A. Legal Codes: The process of the compilation and transmission that brought the legal dicta in to the present form of the legal codes, some dependent and some independent was long and complicated. Originally the legal dicta where the most part transmitted orally and in isolation for help in reaching a legal decision.

Interpolation and combination of the separate legal dicta brought the first small compilations into being. Further unification turned those small compilations into larger ones, such as the section Exod. 21: 1-22: 17, which is set off by the heading "ordinances" (Lev 1 1-15, 20-21 and Deuteronomy 21-25). The same may be the case with legal codes, so-called Covenant Code (Exod. 20:23 23:9), and the Holiness Code (Lev. 17-26) can be termed dependent law codes, because they have been observed into extensive literary works, while the law code of Deuteronomy together with its framework constitutes an independent work. The Priestly source of the Pentateuch, including the legal sections it has been observed as represents an independent unit. These law codes simply did not develop at one time, but these law codes contain new ordinances, judgements or decisions intended to alter or replace traditional customary law, which is never recorded. This purpose affected the very process of transmission and often left traces in alterations, revisions, or supplementations of the basic text, which had to be adapted to a new situation or redefined to apply to the present. For eg: Lev. 23, the basic text of it, was revised in this fashion even after it had been absorbed into the priestly source, vss 18 a-b to 19a were added from Numb. 28:27-30. Another example Leviticus 18, which at first consisted of a series often rules of conduct, exhibits several stages of revision. (i) expansion into a Decalogue by the addition of vss. 13 and 17a, and at the same time elevation to the status of Yahweh's ordinance by means of vs. 6, with the purpose of prohibiting certain degrees of consanguinity, (having the same lineage) in order to strengthen the matrimonial bond (ii) incorporation into a general law against unchastely by the addition of vss 17b-23, in order to preserve the cultic holiness of the congregation of Yahweh. (iii) inclusion in a frame work of exhortations, vss. 2b-5, 2430. This and many other instances illustrate clearly the continual processes of reinterpretation and adaptation to changing conditions, which in turn shows the original purpose of codification, the establishment of new laws through alteration of traditional customary law.

B. Narrative and historical sections: With few exceptions, the process of compilation, revision and redaction of the narrative and historical sections of the books in question begins with the isolated individual narrative or account, no matter what literary type those sections may belong to. In innumerable instances these units can still be recognised. At first they were certainly transmitted by oral tradition. The simplest means oflinking several stories was juxtaposition by means of connecting phrases such as "it came to pass" or "after this", the reluctant discrepancies or contradictions were only partially resolved. We may call this procedure "combination". In addition, we find interpolation, the insertion of brief notes or narratives into a context already present. It can often be recognized through the fact that the last sentences before the insertion is cited is literally or wortl1 minor variation after the interpolation. Eg. Gen 37:36 and 39:1, 11 Sam. 3:1 and 3:6a. A further stage' is represented by the construction of small or large narrative cycles, like those that grew around Jacob and Esther, Jacob and Laban, Elijah, or Elisha. Even the court history of David is understood in this way, because it employed a series of individual narratives.

Besides this process of gradual growth coupled with simultaneous revision in the course of which the individual narratives were personalized, nationalized, theologized, and applied to Yahweh. We may also observe the growth of transmission through use of literary sources. While such a use can only be inferred for the Primal History (Gen. 11 l), the mention of the book of the wars of Yahweh 1an the book of the upright (Numb. 21:14, Joshua 10: 13 and II Sam 1: 18) is direct evidence for the written sources. This is true even for the historical works cited by the authors of the books of Kings and the sources mentioned in the Chronicle's history (I & II Chronicles and Ezra-Nehemiah). We are therefore dealing with a process of compilation and selective transmission of material lying ready to hand.

Both processes—compilation of narratives or narrative cycles and utilization of sources—resulted, after additional intermediate stages, in the formation of more extensive works. These include first of all the basic narrative of Pentateuch or Hexateuch, which was then subject to further revision; it appears in various final forms in the different sources. Mention must also be made of the Pre-Deuteronomistic drafts of the books of Judges, Samuel, and Kings, and the Chm History. At the end of the long road that began with the individual narratives and the first written sources we come, then, to extensive presentations.

C. Later Historical and Legal Books: Later historical and legal books that were not included in the Old Testament include III Ezra (a translation of the conclusion of Chronicles, Ezra and a small section of Nehemiah, Plus three additional sections), and three books of Maccabees (I-II Maccabees constitute historical narrative, II Maccabees having a more "edifying" approach, III Maccabees is legendary), Tobit (a fairy-tale or novella), Judith (historical romance), the narratives of Susanna and of Bel and Dragon (additions to Daniel with fairy-tale and saga motifs, in part of foreign origin), the letters of Jeremiah a polemic against the worship of images, based on Jeremiah 29), the letter of Aristeas (a legend concerning the origin of LXX), the book of Jubilees (a legendary reworking of Genesis Exodus 12), the Martyrdom and Ascension of Isaiah (a prophetical legend with two Christian supplements), the Testament of Twelve Patriarchs, as well as some of the Qumran documents, such as the so-called manual of discipline (IQS, together with the supplements IQS^{a} and IQS^{b}), the partially related Damascus Document, the so-called War Scroll (IQM, containing military regulations), the so-called Genesis Apocryphon (IQ Gen AP, containing a legendary reworking of parts of Genesis), and fragments of other documents perhaps including the much debated Copper scroll.

The entire process mentioned above concerning the compilation and transmission of the Old Testament, starting from its pre-literary to the literary state is based on hypothetical construction. To a large extent the process described above seems realistic, while some assumptions are made at few places of our discussion. One thing can be noticed concerning the above discussed process is that it is a complicated and long process that finally presented the written documents of the Old Testament.

Chapter 10

The Old Testament Literature and Canon Introduction to the Different Sections of the Old Testament

I. Brief and critical introduction on each book[6]

1. THE PENTATEUCH: THE FIRST FIVE BOOKS OF THE OLD TESTAMENT

A. Introduction

The Old Testament Pentateuch, or Torah, combines narrative and legal materials with occasional Poetic Sections. The narrative material tells the story of human history from Adam to Abraham, then recounts the fate of Abraham and his descendants (Primarily the ancestors of Israel) until the period just before the conquest of the territory West of Jordan River. The legal material primarily appears as two large blocks: the revelations given while the people encamped at Mt. Sinai (Exodus 19-40; Leviticus, Numb 111-10210) and Moses' proclamation of the laws in Moab just before the conquest (Numb 22-36 and Deuteronomy). At other places, laws, commands, and legal ordinances appear (Sec. Gen 1:28-29; 9:1-7; 17: 9-15 and throughout the Journeys recorded in Numb. 10: 10-21:35).

6 For some books a detailed survey with their historical background is presented along with more description of the content. The intention of doing this is to highlight the significance of some books, especially the prophetic and wisdom books. The reader of this book is expected to supplement with extra readings where more information is not presented. For the want of space the author of this book presented a simplified survey of some books.

Moses was considered to be the author of Pentateuch was a firm belief shared by Judaism and Christianity-synagogue and church throughout much of their history. But interestingly enough Pentateuch itself no-where claims Moses as its author. In the Sixteen and Seventeenth centuries, persons became increasingly aware of internal references in the Pentateuch which contain contradictions, and anachronisms, stylistic variety and indications of editorial activity.

Moses may have used some possible source although he does not mention about them. Moses must have used genealogical lists mentioned in (Gen 5:1ff, 11:10ff, 27, 25:72 and 36:1). The book of Numbers contains census lists (chapters 1-4, 26) which may have been preserved by the Levites or the elders who assisted him. "The Book of the wars of the Lord" (Numb. 21:14) may have been a source available which commemorates God's intervention on Israel's behalf as the people struggled against numerous enemies. Another similar kind of source was the book of Jashar (Joshua 10:13, II Samuel 1:18), probably the material preserved in this source talks about nation's experience under the blessing and protection of God.

Moses and single authorship of Pentateuch came to be challenged on a number of grounds: (a) As anachronisms, scholars pointed to the account of Moses' death (Deut 34) city of Dan Gen 14:14 (see Judg. 18:29), to Gen 36:31, which assumes the knowledge of Hebrew monarchy, to references to the Canaanites still in the land (Gen 12:6, 13:7), to the Philistines (Gen 21 :34, 26:14-18, Exod 13:17) so on all of which suggest a post Mosaic date. (b) Multiple accounts of the same events were noted. Beersheba is so named on two occasions (Gen 21:31, 26:31), references to the naming of Bethel appears in two passage (Gen 28:19, 35:15), Jacob's name is twice changed to Israel (Gen 32:28, 35:10), on three occasions a Patriarch passes off his wife as his sister (Gen 12: 10-20:20, 26) and in a span of nine verses. Moses is called to go up and goes up Mt. Sinai three times (Exod 24:19-18) without ever coming down. (c) Disagreements between narratives were frequently pointed out, the character and order or creation differ between Gen 121-2; 4a and 2:4b-25, the flood story contains contrary statements about the number of animals taken into the ark (compare Gen 6:19-20 with 7:2, 8-9) and so on. (d) Differences in the laws have been noted Exod 20:24 allows for altars to be built at every place God appoints, but Deut 12:14 forbids altars except at a single and centralized sanctuary, Exod 28:1 limits the offering of sacrifices to the descendants of Aaron Deut 18:7 permits this service to any Levite. (e) Some texts specify that God was known and worshipped by the name Yahweh from earliest times (Gen 4:26), while else where it is claimed that this name was only revealed at the time of Moses (Exod 6:2-3).

B. General contents of the Pentateuch

The dividing lines between the individual books of the Pentateuch are in general meaningful. At the end of Genesis Chapter 50, there comes to an end the story which tells of the Patriarchs, i.e., the forefathers of the people, and with Exodus chapter 1, there begins the history of the people itself (1:7). The division between Exodus and Leviticus is also justified in so far as the tent of meeting is completed with Exodus 40:33, and from Leviticus Chapter 1 onwards there are set out the regulations which apply to the cultus to be celebrated there – though admittedly together with other regulations. But this division does at the same time break the connection between thematerial which belongs together. For Leviticus chapter 8, in which is related the carrying out of the Priesthood and Aaron and his sons, belong as closely with Exodus. 25-31 as do Exodus 35-36. The fact is that the setting for the action of Leviticus and Exodus. 19-40 is the same, namely Sinai, also binds these two books together.

At the beginning of the books of Numbers there begins a new theme. For the reviewing and arrangements for marching and service related in Chapters 14 may be considered as preparation for departure from Sinai, and indeed be so regarded. The period of time between 1:1 and 10: 11, is also twenty days, whereas Israel's sojourn at Sinai lasted more than three quarters of a year (Exodus. 19:1, Numb. 1:1-22:2), So that the twenty days in Numbers 1:1-10:10, may simply be regarded as leading up to the departure. Although there is no change of place, Deuteronomy stands out sharply from the end of Numbers in that Deut.1:1, begins the great speech of Moses which covers chapters 1-30. On the other hand, Deut. 31-34 are clearly the direct continuation of Numb. 27 (26), because here the appointment of Joshua as Moses' successor, begun in Numb. 27, is brought to a conclusion, and besides, these chapters are concerned with the last words and death of Moses. Thus it may be seen that the division is meaningful, but at the same time it clearly appears that it has been made secondarily, and derives from the desire to divide into five approximately equal parts a complex which was felt to be too large.

For our understanding of the Pentateuch, this five-fold division may not be only the determinative, Pentateuch as follows Genesis 1-11: Pre-history, 12-50: the Patriarchs Abraham, Isaac, Jacob and his sons); Exodus 1-18: the oppression of the Israelites in Egypt, their flight from Egypt and journey to Sinai; Exodus 191-Numbers 10:10, Israel's sojourn at Sinai; Numbers 10:11-36 + Deuteronomy 1-34 chapters; Israel's Journey from Sinai into the plains of Moab opposite Jericho and Moses death on Mount Nebo.

In Exodus 19:1 - Numb. 10:10 and in Numbers 10:11 to Deut. 34 there is a little action related, in contrast to Genesis 1 to Exodus 18. Here a very large part is taken from legal material: Exod.20:1-17, the ethical Decalogue, 20:22-23:19 (33), the Book of the Covenant; Exod.25-31, 35-40, and Leviticus 8-9 contains direction concerning the tent of meeting together with cultic apparatus belonging to it, and the carrying out of these directions. Exod. 34: the cultic Decalogue; Lev.1-7: Sacrificial laws; 11-15 Purification laws; 16; the Great Day of Atonement; 17-26: The Holiness Code; 27: directions concerning vows, the first born, the ban, and tithes; a series of smaller groups of laws in Numbers including in 18th chapter, the duties and privileges of the priests and Levites, and in Numb 28-29 the sacrificial calendar, Deuteronomy 1-30, the Deuteronomic law.

1.1. THE BOOK OF GENESIS

The book of Genesis is divided into two main sections: The Primal history (chs. 1-11) and the Patriarchal ancestral history (chs. 12-50). Each, of the two parts developed in its own way, so to begin with each must be treated separately.

The primal history contains (chs. 1-4) a number of narratives which interims of forms may be described as sagas. The subjects of the narratives are predominantly ideal typical figures: husband and wife (chs. 2-8), the hostile brothers (chs. 4) exemplary just man (chs. 6-8)" humanity (11:1-9). The following are the important concern in the book of Genesis.

a) Creation

In this origin of the world in which human beings live is depicted from the perspective of the farmer; man (Adam) is destined by God to fill the earth ('adama 2:15, 3:17-19, 23). The transgression of the divine prohibition in the garden leads to the more burdensome aspects of life (the toil of work 3: 14-19) the curse on Cain even separates him (and the city dwellers, nomads, musicians, smiths, who are descendants) from the soil and thus God himself (4: 1 1f, 14, 16) the liaison of heavenly beings with human women (6:1-4) results in the reduction in the human life span (v.3) and the end of these narratives God responds to the hubris of humanity by scattering it and confusing its language (11:1-9).

b) Genealogies

In Genesis chpters.5, 10, 11:10-32 genealogies are given. On the one hand they draw the line from Adam (5:3) through Noah (5:24) and his son Shem (5:32, 11:10) to Abraham (11:26ff); on the other hand, in a 'table of nation' they outline the whole world of known humanity at that time (ch. 10).

c) Flood

After a series of 10 generations each of which lives to an extreme old age the flood brings a profound break. At the end of the very detailed narrative about the flood (6:25-8:21) God guarantees the future existence of order in creation in order to safeguard the life of humanity in the future (8:21 f, again from the perspectives of the farmer) after the flood there is again sin among humanity and this leads to a curse (9:20-27).

d) The Patriarchal/Ancestral Narratives

From the general history of humanity (chps. 1:1-11) there now emerges the history of one people whose ancestor is Abraham. The Patriarchal narratives, that is, the tradition of the Patriarchs Abraham, Isaac and Jacob and of Joseph takes up most space in Genesis (chps. 12-50). The Abraham story (12:1-25:10) contains a series of independent individual sagas, eg. Gen. 12:10-20 (connected with the context by notes of itineraries in 12: 13:1 3f); 22, 23, 24 alongside these we also see larger narratives, complexes of combination of individual sagas in to larger compositions: Abraham, Lot narrative in chapters 13, 18, 19 chapter 20 incidentally contains a variant or doublet to 2: 10-20; chapters 21 is probably a variant on the aetiology of Ishmael in chp. 16. Chp. 22 in which Abraham career arrives at its dramatic end and climax.

The Isaac Story (26) is strikingly brief and hardly developed at all. The story of Isaac contains only two narratives, both of which have a parallel in the Abraham story (26:7-11), 26-31). These are linked to a continuous narrative about Isaac among and with the Philistines by brief passages almost notes, which are concerned above all with wells in the Negeb, there are also references back (cf. eg: v-29 with 11, 12, 16), The main theme here is the territorial division between philistines and Israelites in the Negeb.

Jacob story (25:19-34, 27-35 Chaps.) is an important block of narrative in the patriarchal stories. Everything is subordinated to one overarching theme: Jacob conflicts with his brother Esau (25: 19-34; chaps. 27,32f) and with his uncle Laban (29-31 chapters). The two divine epiphanies at Bethel (28:1 ff) and Penuel (32:23 ff), at decisive turning points for Jacob, also serve to support the narrative. Without question this narrative comes from North Israel.

The traditions of the three "patriarchs" are followed in the Genesis by the Joseph story. Unlike Patriarchal stories, this is a large scale narrative conceived as the unity from the start and given a novelistic form. The story of Genesis 12-50 can also be equally called as an important account of the matriarchal stories where in no less important terms the activities of matriarchs is described. The matriarchs played very significant role both in the lives of the patriarchs and in the course of major and significant events along the history.

e) Promises

The promises increasingly played a role 1n the format1on of larger patriarchal narratives as elements of composition and interpretation. Thus, the promises of land and prosperity in 13: 14-17 and 28: 13, 14 a formulated in such a way to see the connection between Jacob and Abraham. The four divine speeches are also connected in this way: 12:1-3, 26:1-3, 31: 11, 13, 46:1-5. The main text for the divine promise is chapter 15, when God enters into a covenant with Abraham was developed into a kind of "promise narrative". In chapter 17 covenant concept is developed in another direction. From the side of Yahweh here the promise of countless descendants stands in the foreground (v. 2, 4), coupled with the promise that Yahweh will be the god of Abraham and his descendants. Circumcision is made as a sign of covenant - a priestly, stratum editing is clearly evident.

1.2. THE BOOK OF EXODUS

The beginning of the book of Exodus marks a deep change in the presuppositions of the narrative. In the patriarchal narratives the protagonists were always individuals, but now the people makes as appearance, the transition is explicitly marked at the beginning. The seventy "souls" of the families of Jacob and his sons (1: 115) become the "Israelites" (v.7, 'Children of Israel') are the people of Israel (v. 9) who fill the whole land.

The nature of the narratives changes at the same time. Only occasionally is there an encounter between individuals (eg: 22:1-10, 11-15a, 15b-22). Usually the people itself is one of the partners. Sometimes it alone is contrasted with the Egyptians or with the pharaoh (eg. 18-14), or this represented by an anonymous figure (5: 15-18) more often Moses represented the people, often along with Aaron (especially chs. 7 ff). The basic theological frame work under in which the narratives work: the oppression of the Israelites (chs.1f) the presupposition of the promise of deliverance (chs. 3 f) The sequence is therefore concerned only with how God carries out his plan to deliver Israel and how the Israelites react to the dangers on the way. Some of the important concerns in the book of Exodus are as follows:

a) Exodus

The first part of the book of Exodus (1-15) moves purposefully towards the 'exodus from Egypt, which is closely connected with Passover. After a brief description of oppression, the turning point is marked by Yahweh hearing the lament of the Israelites and 'remembering his covenant with the Patriarchs' (2:23-25); When Moses announces deliverance to Israelites they 'believe' (4:31). This statement about their belief is then emphatically taken up again after the deliverance from Egyptian pursuit at the red sea (14:31). With this the narrative has reached a clear conclusion.

b) Sinai

Exod 15:22 describes a further departure of the Israelites, they arrive at Sinai. Van Rod argues that in a number of creed-like passages the Exodus from Egypt is followed without a break by the entry into the promise land. (Deut 26:5-9, 6:20-25 cf. I Sam 12:8, Ex. 15:12, Ps.135:8-12), in other text there is none or less extended mention between these two events of the wandering in the wilderness (eg. Josh. 14:76, Ps. 78:52b, 136:16, 105:40, Jer 2:6, Amos 2:10), but here too there is no mention of Sinai. Thus, Rendtorff argues that in essentials the events on Sinai are evidently an independent tradition which was not initially combined in a narrative with Exodus from Egypt. The "Sinai Pericope" (Exo. 19:1-Numb. 10: 10) is having an extremely complex structure, which contains an important independent section: Exodus 19-24' this contains two legal passages: The Decalogue (20:1-17) and the Book of the Covenant (20:22-23:19; the name is taken from 24:7).

c) The Decalogue

The Decalogue, which with slight alterations also appear in Deuteronomy 5:6-18 (21) contains the series of prohibitions, the individual members of which predominantly begin with the negative "not", but the commandments of keeping Sabbath holy (v-8) and honouring parents are given a positive formulation. In content, Decalogue contains cultic (v3-1 l) prohibitions and commandments relating to behaviour between individuals (vv. 12-17), thus it embraces a wider sphere than other series of prohibition and is to be understood as a collection of basic rules.

d) The Book of the Covenant

It is a collection of legal Precepts of a very different kind. 21:1 ff contains legal statements predominantly with the casuistic formulation, about slave law (2112-11), bodily injury (21:18-36) and crimes connected with the property (21:37-22:16); between them a series of apodictic statements about crimes which bear death penalty (21: 12-17). Further, the book of the covenant contains religious rules of various kinds, about the idol; and the building of altars (20: 23-26); magic, bestiality, sacrificing to idols (22:17-19), blasphemy and cursing (22:7), the flesh of the savaged animals which have not been cultically slaughtered (22:30), and instructions about cultic offerings (22:28); the Sabbath year, feast days, festivals and sacrifices (23:10-19), there are further rules about behaviour towards aliens, the socially disadvantaged, and 'enemies' (22:20-26, 23:4 f, 9) as well as legal proceedings (23: 1-3, 6-8).

e) Wandering in the Wilderness

In Exod. 15:22-18:27, that stand between the exodus from Egypt and the arrival on Sinai. What holds together these individual narratives is the theme of "murmuring" of the Israelites against Moses (and Aaron) 15: 24, 16:2, 7-9, 12; 17:3. The reason for the murmuring is thirst (15:24, 17:30) or hunger (16:3) combined with a reproach to Moses for having led the Israelites out of Egypt and brought them to their present position (cf. also 14:11 ff). So in the last resort it is directed against Yahweh himself and forms a sharp contrast with the 'faith' of Israelites after the deliverance at the Red Sea (14:31).

1.3. THE BOOK OF LEVITICUS

This book contains almost exclusively of legal material which is predominantly concerned with cultic questions. The few narrative passages also deal with cultic themes. The performance of the Priestly ordination ordered in Ex. 29 (Lev.8) and the first general sacrifices on the newly built altar (9), two short narratives about problems over the right performance of sacrifice (10: 1-5, 16-20) and one about dealing with the blasphemer (24: 10-14, 23).

a) Sacrifice and Purity

Leviticus 1-7 contains a collection of rules for sacrifice which are further sub-divided into sacrificial rituals (1-5) and other regulations concerned with their performance (6 f). They reflect different stages in the history of Israelite sacrificial worship, the sequence of the kinds of sacrifice differ in two sections; 'Sin offering' and 'guilt offering' (6: 17-7:7). The regulations for purity in Levi 11-15 stand out as a further group of texts. The collection consists of individual chapters on clean and unclean animals (1 1, cf. Deut 14:3 21), the purification of awoman after the birth of a child (12), leprosy and other eruptions on people, clothes and houses (13 f), and impurity through bodily discharges (15 f).

b) The Holiness Code

Leviticus 12-26 is regarded as an independent collection of laws. At the same time, it is continually stressed that no internal order can be recognized in this collection Lev. 17-20 deals with cultic impurity, above all that which cannot be removed. Therefore, someone transgressing against a particular cultic rule is to be 'cut off from the worshiping community and his people (17: 4, 9, 10, 18: 29, 19:8, 20:3, 6, 17 f.) such transgressions are through eating blood (17), illicit sexual relationship (18), crimes carrying the death penalty (20). Lev. 21f, discusses further special rules for the purity of Priests (21) and sacrificial. offerings (22). More details on the Holiness Code can be illustrated as follows:

Within the priestly corpus, there is a distinguishable text in Leviticus 17 -26 known as the "Holiness Code" in view of the reiterated motive for obedience to its laws: "Be Holy". We shall now turn our attention to consider some of the major characteristic features of the Holiness code.

Leviticus 17-26 is usually distinguished from the rest of the book and designated the holiness code; Leviticus 27 is viewed as a later appendix. These chapters give a different perspective from Leviticus 1-16, the subject matter sometimes similar, but the point of View is more that of the layman than the priest. A number of sections are devoted to clear themes: the shedding and treatment of blood (17), prohibited sexual relations (18), regulations for the priests (21-22), festivals (23), sabbatical and jubilee years (25), and blessings and curses (26). Other chapters especially 19 and 20, have a miscellaneous character in terms of modern ideas about organization. We shall now briefly make a survey of each individual sections concerning their content and other matters.

i) Leviticus 17:1-16: The shedding of blood and its treatment: It was envisaged that all slaughter was to be done at the altar so that the blood could be dashed against the altar and the fat burned on it (17:3-7). Thus, all slaughter of animals for food would take place in a sacrificial context and no butchering or consumption of meat could be done away from the shrine. How could this stipulation be carried out in practical terms? This difficulty is highlighted by Deut.12:20-25, which seemed to change just such a regulation when it stated that profane slaughter was allowed, as along as the blood was drained out of the animal. This means that Leviticus 17 must either be an idealized system divorced from reality or have envisaged a society small enough in numbers and territory to allow a trip to the altar and back within a day or so. Although, no specific site is mentioned in Leviticus, it is clear that only one altar was envisaged, the context being the tabernacle in the wilderness. Sacrifices were not to be carried out elsewhere (17:7-9). The exception to this rule about laughter at the altar was the case of clean wild animals or birds which could be hunted, killed and eaten apart from the shrine as long as the blood was drained out into the earth (17:13-14).

Blood itself is a central element in this chapter. The life of both human beings and animals is in their Blood. For that reason, blood should not be eaten but dashed on the altar or poured on the ground and covered with dust. Blood functions as a potent symbol within the sacrificial cult. For the same reason that blood was not to be eaten, that which dies of itself or is killed by animals was not to be eaten: it polluted the eater (17:15-16).

ii) Leviticus 18:1-30: Forbidden sexual relations: Much of this chapter covers what is usually referred to as incest, that is, sexual relations forbidden because of the closeness of kinship of the persons involved. The following are forbidden to the Israelite male. *First*, sexual acts 'with his own flesh' (near of kin): mother or step-mother (Lev. 18:6-8); sister, half-sister, step-sister, or sister-in-law (Lev. 18:9, 11, 16), daughter-in-law (Lev. 18:10,15); aunt (Lev. 18:12-14); a women and her daughter or granddaughter (Lev. 18:17). Other regulations seem more concerned with what was deemed appropriate: not to take a wife's sister as rival wife (Lev. 18:18); not to indulge in sexual intercourse during the menstrual period (Lev. 18:19) or with the neighbour's wife (Lev. 18:20), with another male (Lev. 18:22) or with animals (Lev. 18:23). It was forbidden to offer one's children to Molech (Lev. 18:21).

Sexual relations are at the heart of social practice within any community. Each society has strict views about which kinds are allowed and which are not. Israel's rules here are lenient (despite the claim that 'the Canaanites' allowed sexual relations with close of kin), allowing even first cousins to marry. Israel was thus an endogamous society. This fits with their emphasis on rigid barriers to non-Israelites.

iii) Leviticus 19:1:20:21: Miscellaneous Laws: This section has a number of parallels with the covenant code. (Exod. 21:1-23:33) and Deut. 12:26 as well as with the laws known elsewhere in the ancient near east. It has been suggested by number of commentators (e.g. Patrick) that the regulations of 19:1-20:9 have parallels with the Decalogue. It is true that the contents of some of the Ten Commandments are echoed here (Lev. 19:11-12; Exod. 20:7, 13 for example), but this seems to be fictitious. There is no obvious relationship between the structure and wording of Leviticus 19-20 and the Decalogue.

iv) Leviticus 21:21-24; laws on the priesthood: the presumption was all Israel was to be holy, but the priests had to be even more rigorous. They were not allowed to defile themselves by contact with a corpse through participating in funerals other than of close relations: mother, father, son, daughter, brother, or an unmarried sister (Lev. 21:1-4). They were not to carry out mourning rites by disfiguring their hair, beards, or flesh (Lev. 21:5-6). They were not allowed to marry a harlot or divorcee and the priest's daughter who became a harlot was to be burned (Lev. 21:7-9). Leviticus does envisage certain regulations for a high priest (21:10-15). This person had been anointed by the sacred oil. He was not to participate in a funeral, even for a close relative, or engage in mourning rites of any kind. He was to marry only a virgin of his own people.

The regulations about those who could preside at the altar were also rigorous (Lev. 21:16-23). Just as animals to be sacrificed were to be without physical defect, so the officiating priests were to be without physical blemish.

v) Leviticus 22:1-33: Regulations about the sacred gifts: Certain portions of the sacrificial animals and other offerings were to go to the priests. These were sacred and to be eaten only by those qualified and only under certain conditions. The priests and their families who were in a state of purity, and they alone, were to take part of them (Lev. 22:3-16). Lay persons were not to eat of these holy things. Hired servants also were forbidden to do so, but slaves owned by the priests were considered a part of the family and could eat them. The priestly portions were prohibited to the daughter of a priest who married a layman, unless she became divorced or a widow and returned to her father's house. If a layman unwittingly ate of the sacred gifts he was to restore them, together with an additional twenty percent of their value (Lev. 22:14).

All offerings were to be of whole, normal animals without major physical defects (Lev. 22:17-25). Anything which was blind, injured, maimed, or had certain sorts of disease was rejected. Neither was a castrated animal to be accepted (the implication being that Israelites did not castrate their animals, contrary to the normal practice of theirs around them). An animal with a limb extraordinary short or long could be accepted for a free-will offering but not for a vow. This was only explicit concession made about blemishes, though how these regulations might have been interpreted in practice is unknown. A new born animal was not to be sacrificed until it had been with its mother seven days (Lev. 22:26), nor was it and its mother to be sacrificed on the same day (22:27). Any thanksgiving offering had to be eaten on the day it was offered; anything left over was to be burnt (22:29-30, in agreement with 7:15).

vi) Leviticus 24:1-9: Lampstand and Bread of Presence: The first part of this chapter relates to the area inside the holy place but in front of the certain separating the Holy of Holies. A very pure olive oil was to be provided to keep the lampstand burning continually (Lev. 24:2-4), there was also to be a table on which twelve loaves (together with frankincense) were to be placed each Sabbath. The frankincense was evidently burned at the end of the week, and the priests were allowed to eat the loaves. This was known as the bread of presence or show bread.

vii) Leviticus 24:10-23: Blasphemy: At times within Leviticus there occurs a narrative rather than a specific law. In such cases, the episode in question seems to have been intended to explain what should be done by example rather than by direct instruction. In this passage, an Israelite whose father was Egyptian used God's name in a blasphemous way. He was put in custody until God could be consulted. God's reply was that the man should be stoned by the entire community. In future, anyone blaspheming with God's name was likewise to be executed by stoning. Within this section there is an insert paragraph about life and reciprocation of punishment, otherwise known as the *lex talionis*. Lev. 24:17-22 stresses the importance of life, especially human life. One who kills another person is to be executed. The person who kills an animal must make restitution. The principle is also stated that injuries were to be compensated a reciprocal injury to the perpetrator - the famous 'eye for an eye and tooth for a tooth'. This law has often been misunderstood as a primitive barbaric practice, which embarrassed legislators later did their best to soften.

In fact, the earlier principle was that a person injuring another was to pay compensation. In the case of an extended family or community, that was the simplest way of handling the matter. The injured party, or the family, received some benefit. The *lex talionis* was an important advance in jurisprudence for two reasons: *Firstly*, it made everyone equal before the law the rich could not get away with the crime of injuring another simply by making monetary payment. The 'eye for an eye' principle was a great leveller. *Secondly*, the law marked the stage at which the tribe or state took over the function of justice from the local community.

viii) Leviticus 26:1-46: concluding blessings and curses: An appropriate literary closure of a book such as Leviticus is a section demonstrating the consequences of heeding or ignoring the commands contained in it. A similar conclusion may be found in Deuteronomy 28. Here in Leviticus 26 the blessings for obedience come first (26: 3-13), with promises of peace, plenty and fertility, the section given over to the curses for disobedience is longer and more clearly structured (26:14-38). Five sections are marked off with the phrase: 'If you (still) disobey, I will punish you sevenfold' or similar words (26:14-17, 18-20, 21-22, 23-26, 27-38). The aim seems to have been to create a crescendo effect, so that the longer the Israelites refused to obey, the stronger became the punishments, multiplying sevenfold each time. Finally, hope is expressed for repentance and a return from captivity (Lev. 26:39-45).

Such blessings and curses are well known from other ancient Near Eastern Literature International treaties usually ended with a list of blessings and, especially, curses for disobedience. The so-called 'law codes' often included a similar section. For example, the epilogue to the code of Hammurabi spelled out how the gods would punish the king in various for not heeding the marvellous laws which had just been listed. As with the list in Leviticus 26, the curses tended to dominate, with the blessings listed only briefly. Leviticus 26:31-45 ends with reference to an exile and return, which led many scholars to claim that this showed knowledge of the exile of the Jews in 587/586 BCE and their return in 538 BCE.

The other passages are dealt in appropriate places in the later discussion. They are: Lev.23:1-44: concerns the festivals; Lev.25:1-55: concerns the Sabbatical and Jubilee years; and Lev. 27:1-34 an appendix on vows and tithes, but not in line with 17-26, a later addition to the Holiness code.

c) Other Important Concerns

Lev. 16 mentions about the regulations for the 'Day of Atonement' (cf. Lev 23:27 i). All removal of impurity comes to a conclusion and climax in the great annual occasion of atonement at which at the same time the sanctuary is cleansed from the impurity caused by all the happenings for which atonement could not be made.

Primary details of calendars are collected in (Lev. 23-25, the sacrificial calendar (23), supplemented by regulations for lights and show bread (24: 1-9). regulations about the Sabbath year (25:1-7) and the year of Jubilee (8-31). In 24:15-22 further regulations about crimes carrying the death penalty have been inserted into the narrative about dealing with the blasphemer (24: 10-14; 23).

1.4. THE BOOK OF NUMBERS

Of all the books of the Pentateuch, the book of Numbers is hardest to survey. It contains a great deal of material of a very varied kind and gives the impression of being very heterogeneous. It is even difficult to decide how to divide it. A clear break comes after Num. 10: 10; the Israelites set out from Sinai. So the first part of the book belongs to the 'Sinai Pericope' in the wider sense, which begins with Exo. 19:1.

a) Cultic Laws

The section Numb. 1:1-10:10 predominantly contains regulations about the cult, which have a clear affinity with texts in the book of Exodus and Leviticus. The key word 'purity' determines the whole section. Chapters 1-4 deal with a census of the Israelites and their organisation into one great camp. According to 5:1-4 the character of this camp as a holy places in which Yahweh himself dwells (v:3) is to be safeguarded by the exclusion from the camp of all those who are unclean in the cultic sense. The subsequent regulations have then evidently been collected from this perspective; the problem of uncleanness is at issue in the suspicion of a wife's adultery (5:11-31) in the case of the Nazirite (ch.6). The consecration of Levites (8:5-22) and in the Passover (9:1-14), the sanctity ofthe camp and the presence of Yahweh are again stressed in the Priestly blessing (6:22-27). Yahweh's speaking from the 'mercy seat' of the ark (7: 89, cf. Exod. 25, 22) and by the cloud which covers the sanctuary (9:15 ff).

b) Wilderness Experience of the Israelites

Wandering of Israel through the wilderness comes to a provisional end with the 'Steppes of the Moab' (22:1), where Moses later dies, begins in Numbers 10:11-20, 13 resemble in many respects Exodus 15:22-18:27 (cf. parallel narratives Exodus 7: 1-7, Numbers 20:1-13). In both sections the rebellion of the Israelites against Moses and those against Yahweh himself stand in foreground, this is also mention of the 'murmuring' of the Israelites in the Numbers texts (14:2, 27, 29, 36, 16:11, 17, 6, 20, 25); however here this expression is not associated with complaints about hunger and thirst (cf. 1 1:4-6; 20; 2-5; 21:5) but with protest on one hand about danger of the way to the promise land (14:28) on the other about the special position of Moses (16:1-11, 17:6 cf. ch. 12). Thus there is a much more basic expression here of the rebellion of the Israelites against the will of Yahweh. Here, the concept of 'holiness' plays an important role (11:18, 16:3, 5, 7; 17:2f, 20:12f).

The narrative about the miracle with the water at Meribah in Numbers 20:1-13 marks a clear break: because of their unbelief (which according to the narrative probably consist in the fact that they did not tell the rock to produce water as Yahweh commanded in v-8, but used the staff for the miracle v-11). Moses and Aaron are not allowed to enter the promise land (v. 12, cf. v.24, 27:14). Thus they too belong to the generation which has to die in the wilderness (cf. 14, 22, f. 29 ff).

c) Assigning of Land

The assignment of land to the tribes east of the Jordan (Num. 32), Project? back into the early period a later extension of the tribal territories, instruction about the division of the land west of Jordan (33:50-34:29); the demarcation of Levitical cities and cities of sanctuary (35), and in between a list of stations in the wilderness wandering (33), which in its entirely must be seen as a late attempt to reconstruct the Journey. Perhaps using an earlier itinerary of a 'pilgrimage' to Sinai.

1.5. THE BOOK OF DEUTERONOMY

This book is a self-contained, independent, formulated as a speech of Moses to the Israelites. At the same time, it is connected with the previous books of the Pentateuch: The Speech of Moses is given at the place "beyond the Jordan in the land of Moab" (Deut 1:1, 5). Which has already been the scene of events since Numb. 22:1, and the book ends with the death of Moses and the appointment of Joshua as his successor in accordance with the announcement in Numb. 27:12 ff. The appointment of Joshua also provides a link with the following book.

a) Structure

The structure of Deuteronomy is easy to recognize. It begins with a double introductory speech (1:1-4; 40, 4:44-11:32), followed by the collection of laws proper (Chs. 12-26); the closing section (Chs. 27-34) is made up of variety of elements of which Chs. 28-30 are formulated as a speech of Moses and thus form the end of the speech which begins in 1:1.

The first introductory speech (1 :1-4, 40) gives a retrospective survey of the history of Israel from the departure from Horeb (1-3; the name Horeb is used for Sinai in Deuteronomy) and ends with a long paraenetic message (4:1-40). It is governed by an easily recognizable leading thought: the generation which was at Horeb did not believe the promised land and therefore was not allowed to enter the land (1:19-2:15) but in future, new generation is to observe the commandments of Yahweh and thus they will live in the promised land (4: 1-22) otherwise they will again be led out of the land into dispersion (4:23-31). Finally, in 4:3240, a central theme of Deuteronomic theology is developed: Yahweh, the Creator of the world, has chosen Israel out of love for the fathers (v. 37, cf. 7:6-8) and revealed his commandments to it (cf. 10: 12-17, etc.)

The second introductory speech (4:44-1 1:32) has a new beginning (4:44-49; cf. 1:1-5) and then repeats the dialogue (5:6-21). In 6:4 the central statement of Israelite religion is given is an extremely concentrated from with a further "Hear, Israel" (of. 5:1); worshipping strange gods is opposed (6:10-11), brief salvation historical creed (6:20-25). 7: 1-10:11 warns the chosen

Israel of the danger of arrogance towards the other people. The great closing paraenesis (10: 12-11:32) ends with the alternatives of blessing and curse as a consequence of harkening. or not harkening to the commandment of the Yahweh (11:26-28).

The introductory speeches are stamped by Deuteronomistic language not only in style, which is broad, often over loaded and seemingly prolix (easy Hebrew) but also paraenesis, i.e., constantly repeated admonitions to observe the commandments, often bound up with the promise of blessings on life in the promised land. Stereotyped frequently recurring phrases are used for eg: Deut 4:1 "and now Israel, give heed to the statutes and the ordinance which I teach you…"(cf. 4:40 5:1, 31-37, 6: 1 -3 etc.). The collection of laws (Chs 12-26) is also stamped throughout by the paraenetic Deuteronomistic language.

b) Centralisation of Cult

The collection of Laws begins emphatically with the demand of the 'centralization of the cult' i.e. the regulations that sacrifice shall be performed and cultic offering made at only one place of worship (12: 2-28). This governsthe first part ofthe collection (Chs. 12-18, Ch. 14: 22-26, 15: 19-23, 16:1-17, 8-13, 18: 1-8and 26: 1-11). It also has two aspects: cultic purity (i.e. delimitation from the outside world, chp 12:2-7) and cultic unity (i.e. concentration within the community, chp 12:8-12). Here the place of worship is not mentioned by name, but is paraphrased as "the place which Yahweh will choose", frequently with the addition to make his name dwell there, etc. (12:5, 11, 14, 18, 21, 14:23-25). Therefore, some would think it as other than Jerusalem (e.g. Shechem?) but it is unlikely that any place other than Jerusalem might achieve such central significance.

c) The book of Covenant

A comparison of the collection of laws with the book of covenant is particularly interesting. There are countless points of contact between the two but the difference of more striking. Only occasionally are sentences completely identical in both (e.g. Exodus 23: 19b; Deut. 14:21b), occasionally the formulation in Deuteronomy is shorter and seems like an extract from the sentences in the book the covenant (eg. Deut 16: 19 & Exodus 23:2f, 6-8) or a section from the book of the covenant appears in Deuteronomy divided into individual statements and part in other contexts (cf. Exodus 22:20-26, Deut. 24: 17f, 23:20; 24; 20:1-13). In most cases however, the version in Deuteronomy is more detailed. Thus, a statement about the offering of the first born of domestic animals (Exodus 22: 29) is developed from various aspects so that one could now call the passage a set of rules of the procedure, same thing about three regular festivals (Exodus 23:14-17; Deut. 16:1-17), the rules about sanctuary (Exodus 21:12-14; Deut 19-13), etc.

d) Josiah's Reform of the Cult

Once the book of Deuteronomy was seen as an independent book but it was also recognised to have a connection with the report about Josiah's reform of the cult in II Kings 22 ff. The measures taken in Josiah's reforms as supported in II Kings 23 show striking affinity to the demands of Deuteronomy. So the Connection in indisputable.

We can notice three significant features in the central law code of Deuteronomy. We shall briefly consider them:

i) Deuteronomic revision of earlier laws: As noted earlier that the law code of Deuteronomy is built upon a revision of many of the earlier laws to be found in the Book of the covenant (Exod. 20:22-23:19) G. von Rad, *Deuteronomy, a Commentary* (London: SCM, 1966), P.13 lists the correspondences in the following way:

Exod.21:1-11	= Deut.15:12-18;	Exod.21:12-14	= Deut.19:1-13
Exod.21:16	= Deut. 24:7;	Exod.22:16f	= Deut.22:28-29
Exod.22:21-24	= Deut. 24:17-22;	Exod.22:25	= Deut.23:19-20
Exod.22:26f	= Deut. 24:10-13;	Exod.22:29f	= Deut.15219-23
Exod.22:31	= Deut.14:3-21;	Exod.23:1	= Deut.19:16-21
Exod.23:2f; 6-8	= Deut.16:18-20;	Exod.23:4f	= Deut.22:1-4
Exod.23:9	= Deut. 24:17f;	Exod.23:10f	= Deut.15:1-11
Exod.23:12	= Deut. 5:13-15;	Exod.23:13	= Deut.6:13
Exod.23:14-17	= Deut.16:1-17;	Exod.23:19a	= Deut.26;2-10
Exod.23:19b	= Deut.14:21b		

This series of correspondences can be either increased or decreased depending on the degree of closeness we expect to find in the different law collections. Where the same matter is dealt with in two different law codes we should naturally expect to find a certain measure of overlap.

When we examine in detail the nature of this Deuteronomic revision of the earlier laws taken from the Book of the Covenant we are brought face to face with a number of interesting: features of the development of Israel's legal system. It becomes clear in the first place that the Deuteronomic law is the later version and has been designed to take account of wider range of features than those reflected in the earlier law this becomes clear for example, when we examine the law concerning homicide and the importance it demonstrates of the necessity for distinguishing between accidental and intentional killing. The law of the book of the covenant reads:

> "Whoever strikes a man so that he dies shall be put to death. But if he did not lie in wait for him, but God let him fall into his hand, then I will appoint for you a place to which he may flee. But if a man willfully attacks another to kill him treacherously, you shall take him from my altar, that he may die" (Exod. 21:12-14).

When we compare this with the revised form of the law as set out in Deut. 19:1-13, we find that it has been incorporated into a larger set of provisions concerning the allocation of six cities to serve as the specified places of refuge (they are called 'cities of refuge' in Numb 35:6,11. These are to serve as substitutes for the sanctuaries of the older law (cf: the reference to the 'altar' in Exod. 21:14). We notice that the whole question of investigation of the crime and of establishing guilt by showing a motive for murder has been dealt with more extensively. A matter of prime concern in dealing with cases of murder was the need to assert culpability. This could only be achieved by establishing some idea of motive; and this required a knowledge both of the circumstances of death and the culprit's intentions toward the victim. From the more advanced legal system presupposed by Deuteronomy we can see that much less responsibility has been placed upon the 'avenger of blood' and upon the priests of the cultus. M. Fishbane speaks (*Biblical Intepretation in Ancient Israel*, p.244) of an 'increasing rationalization of the Juridical process'. This led to the establishment of a system of officers and judges (Deut. 16:18) who were to handle all normal legal cases. They were clearly expected to make whatever assessments they could in the light of what they could discover about the relationships between the culprit and the victim, much as a modern murder investigation would be expected to do. Only when these officers were unable to reach a satisfactory verdict was resource to be made to the Levitical priests who were to be found at the central sanctuary (Deut. 17:8-13)

The ruling of the law of evidence in Exod. 23:1-3 runs quite tersely: "You shall not utter a false report. You shall not join hands with a wicked man, to be a malicious witness. You shall not follow a multitude to do evil, nor shall you bear witness in a suit, turning aside after a multitude, so as to pervert justice; nor shall you be partial to a poor man in his suit". When we compare this with what we find in Deut. 19:15-21, we can see that it has been elaborated to a quite considerable degree the "*revised law*" demands that a charge be supported by at least two, and if possible three, witnesses for it to be sustained. The Deuteronomic provision also envisages the further examination of witnesses to check on their veracity (Deut. 19:18). The new law then further lays down penalties where perjury has been committed (19:19) and this is amplified by the mention that such penalties are to serve as a deterrent. Quite clearly the need to check on witnesses, combined with the difficulty of weeding out malicious cases of collusion between unprincipled witnesses, had to be taken fully into account. In this respect we can see how the Deuteronomic legislation has become conscious of the need to resort a principle of deterrence in its efforts to establish a rational and fair judicial system.

We can see further aspects of the way in which Deuteronomy has built upon the greater simplicity of the order Book of the Covenant when we note the way in which the later law presupposes a more advanced economic order.

Ownership of property and systems of sale and exchange in the Book of the Covenant are relatively unsophisticated. They have become much more sophisticated in the Deuteronomic code; this is reflected in the development of the law concerning the release of slaves after they have fulfilled their allotted time of servitude.

The law in Exod 21:2f envisages the case of a slave bought from a previous owner, who is then obligated to fulfil six years of slave service. The development of this in Deut. 15: 12ff. recognizes the rather different situation of debt-slavery. In this the person concerned is considered to have sold himself into slavery in order to clear debts that have been incurred. The Deuteronomic legislation also considers the possibility of woman being entitled to inherit and own property in a manner which is not envisaged in the earlier code. Several examples of this sort can be cited both from the covenant code and from the Deuteronomic law code.

i) Regulations Governing Worship: In the book of the covenant a short calendar of the major religious festivals which Israelites were bound to observe is given (Exod. 23:14-17), An impressive and striking feature of the Deuteronomic law code is that a more elaborate version of this festival calendar (Deut. 16:1-17) has been incorporated into the very heart of the collection. Moreover, other features regarding worship, for example the law of the altar of Exod. 20:24-26, have been expanded extensively and woven fully into the Deuteronomic legislation (Deut. 12:2-14). Laws relating to religious observance have been set alongside more strictly 1egal matters and incorporated into a code in which both are given similar importance. The law of the central sanctuary in Deut. 12: 2-14 must certainly be regarded as one of the most distinctive features of the Deuteronomic legislation. It represents a milestone of great significance in the development of worship in ancient Israel. The toleration of a wide variety of altars and sanctuaries can be described as 'Pre-Deuteronomic', whereas insistence on a single sanctuary can be recognized as belonging to a period after this Deuteronomic demand had become an established fact.

It is also significant that the manner in which most of Israel's and Judah's kings are criticised in the history of I & II Kings up to the time of Josiah's great reform (II Kings 22-23), demonstrates the influential outworking of this Deuteronomy has sought to introduce such a restrictive rule concerning sacrificial worship which in other respects must have proved highly inconvenient (cf. 14:24-26). It is part of its endeavour to implement a widespread purification of the worship of God in Israel by removing the opportunity and occasion for retaining any vestiges of the older Canaanite worship of Baal and other gods and goddesses (12:2~3, cf. also 13:1-5, 6-11, 12-18). By restricting sacrificial worship to one single sanctuary far greater control could be exercised over its activities.

It is wholly in keeping with the Deuteronomic concern to bring together a wide range of religious and social concerns that it should include a comprehensive calendar of religious festivals (Deut. 16:1-17). This clearly represents an expansion and development from the laid down in the older shorter festival calendars preserved in Exod.23:14-17 and 34:8-24. At the same time, it is less developed than the much fuller calendar in Lev.23:1-44, showing how the Deuteronomic legislation represents a middle position in the records of Israel's developing system of worship.

What is especially noteworthy about these Deuteronomic rules for worship is the manner 1n which they combine into one single spring festival the celebration of the Feast of Passover. (Heb. *Pesah*; Deut.16:1-2, 5-7) with that of the Feast of Unleavened Bread (Heb. *Massot*; Deut.16:3-4,8). There can be no doubt that this marks a carefully considered concern to bind together two festival celebrations which were originally separate in their origin. One of these was a shepherds' sacrificial rite, most probably occurring at the time when the flocks were moved into new pasture lands. The rites relating to the eating of unleavened bread on the other hand, were celebrated by those living off the sown land and marked the consumption of the last of the previous year's grain stocks. It would appear that an economic situation had developed in which both patterns of agriculture had come to exist side by side, the accompanying religious rites were linked together.

Two other features relating to this spring festival deserve special attention. The *first* of these is that the purpose of such a celebration is very firmly laid down as an act of 'remembering' the event of the Exodus from Egypt (Deut. 16:1-8). In this way the more surface aspects of the agricultural significance are left in the background. The *second* is the firm insistence that the Passover should be celebrated at the sanctuary which God would choose (Deut.16:6-7), and not the domestic settlements of the worshippers. It is probable that, by combining these spring celebrations, Deuteronomy was simply acknowledging a practice that had already become an established convention for some groups in Israel.

ii) Distinctive laws in Deuteronomy: Besides developments and modifications of earlier laws and the elaboration of regulations governing worship there are in Deuteronomy many legal prescriptions which do not appear in earlier texts. Of special interest among these is a series of laws relating to the conduct war 6 and the obligations for military service. These cover such issues as circumstances entitling a man to exemption from military service (20:21-9), the conduct of an army when besieging a city (20:10-20) and the necessity for maintaining firm hygienic discipline in a military camp (23:9-14).

The inclusion of these regulations governing warfare would certainly suggest that Deuteronomy arose at a time when Israel was facing something of a military crisis. It is also significant that such regulations presuppose that Israel's defence was primarily a matter for the civilian conscripted militia, rather than for a central corps of professional soldiers, such as must have grown up as a part of Israel's royal establishment from the time of David and Solomon.

Besides a number of miscellaneous laws which appear in Deuteronomy for the first time aimed at protecting the environment (cf. Deut. 22:6-7) and requiring a responsible attitude towards the building and maintenance of property (cf. Deut. 22:8), the most striking new introduction is a law defining the position of the king (Deut. 17:14-20). This is the only biblical statement concerning the constitutional position of the Monarch, and it contains a number of striking features. In the first place the requirement that he should be 'one from among your brethren' (Deut. 17:15) excludes a foreigner from such office. At the same time, there is no hint that he is anything other than an ordinary mortal human being, so that all traces of an older divine mythology concerning the king's status are set aside. The highest that is affirmed regarding him is that he must be one whom God himself has chosen. This indicates the divine election.

Presumably at the end of the monarchy in Israel or (Judah) a theological movement came into being which made successful (and momentous) attempt to bring together the complex experiences of Israel in decisive formulae which were appropriate for understanding and interpreting the past and give a constructive shape to the future.

2. THE FORMER PROPHETS

In Jewish tradition the Prophets follow the Torah as the second part of the canon. In addition to the Prophetic books in the narrower sense, this part comprises the books of Joshua to Kings, the authors where were regarded as prophets. Joshua, Samuel, who was regarded as the author of Judges and the books which bear his name (and also the Book of Ruth), and Jeremiah, to whom the books of kings were attribute (Babylonian Talmud, Baba Bathra 14b/15a). Since the Middle Ages a distinction has been drawn between the former prophets and the later prophets. G Meir content the former prophets often-turned historical book.

2.1. The Book of Joshua

This book naturally divided into two approximately equal sections, chapters 1-12 deal with the conquest and 13-24, with the division of the land of Canaan. The first part relates how Joshua made preparations after Moses' death for the crossing of the Jordan. Chapter I reports how spies after inspecting the land of Jericho brought report to Joshua. Chapter 2, the crossing of Jordan, Chapter 3-4, halting at Gilgal and celebrated Passover and here the appearance of a heavenly being made Joshua aware of a sacredness of the place. Chapter 5, the first fortress which fell in to the hands of Israel assisted by miraculous divine action, was Jericho. Chapter 6, but the enterprise, seemingly not arduous, against the fortress of Ai, north-west of Jericho, failed because unnamed Achan took for himself some of the property plundered in Jericho, against the command of Yahweh. So, the enterprise succeeded only after this guilt had been removed from Israel and the criminal has been executed (7: 1-8; 29); 8:30-35: on Mount Ebal, Joshua erected an altar according to the command of Moses, 8.30-35, the Gibeonites, however, terrified by the conquest of Jericho and Ai, by the employment of a stratagem succeeded in getting Joshua to make a treaty with them so that he could touch them. In Chapter 9: the Canaanite kings of the southern region, including Japhia of Lachish, marched under the leadership or Adoni-Zedek of Jerusalem against Gibeon which had been disloyal to the cause and were annihilated by Joshua at Gibeon, so that southern Canaan now lay Open to Israel. Chapter 10: a coalition under the leadership of Jabin of Hazor of the kings of northern Canaan was broken by Joshua at the waters of Merom, so that north was delivered into Israel's power. Chapter 11: a list of Canaanite kings defeated by Israelites, Chapter 12 concludes the first half of the book.

Chapters 13-19 relate the allocation of the West Jordan to the 9 ½ tribes and of East Jordan to the 2 ½ (Reuben, Gad and half Manasseh). In Chapter 20 there is added to the division of the land the establishing of cities of refuge, and in 21, cities for the priest and Levites. Now that the allocation and what is related to it has been disposed of the East Jordan tribes are allowed to go, with thanks for the help they have given west of Jordan. They build an altar at first felt to be illegitimate by the other tribes but then recognized as a simple token of adherence to Yahweh (22). Two farewell speeches by Joshua (23, 24) conclude the book.

The book of Joshua is the greatest testimony to the mighty acts of God on behalf of the people of Israel recorded in the Bible as a culminating event began in the Exodus. It reports how God granted land to Israel (Josh 1-12) and allotted it as an inheritance (Josh 13-22) in accordance with the promises God made with Abraham (Gen 12:7; 15:12-16). The book concludes the calling of the people to express their faithfulness to the God who granted their land and inheritance (Josh 23-24). The book begins with the affirmation that everyone including Joshua will abide by the Law of Moses (Josh 1:7-8).

Traditional understanding of the book of Joshua supports a general view that the book should be read along with Deuteronomy as one continuous narrative of God's acts of salvation. The other suggestion is that the book should be read from the beginning of Genesis if not from Genesis 1, at least from Chapter 12 as the account that begins with the promise of God to Abraham.

The promise given to Abraham may have been concluded and fulfilled in the book of Joshua. If the second suggestion is taken into account it means that the stories of the fathers in Genesis 12-50 presuppose the book of Joshua and these stories of the Patriarchs will not be complete without this book.

Through the centuries the book of Joshua is understood and used by the Christians as fundamental and foundation to explain the doctrines of election, predestination in a broader sense and divine grace. The book is also used as one of the concrete examples of the salvation history, the way in which God's liberation activity takes its definite shape for Israel. Even though this salvation history is pervasive in the earlier and later parts of the Bible it is in Joshua one can notice more a practical demonstration of salvation history (apart from liberation of Israel from Egypt) of God for Israel. Joshua's attempt to give rest to the people of Israel (in Josh 1:13, 15 and compare with 21:44) is seen as paradigmatic of Jesus' provision of rest from the power of sin (Heb 4:1-11). Israelite entry into the land of Canaan is seen as a scheme for the Christians to enter into the heaven as a given reward who follow Jesus. Moreover the crossing of the river Jordan is seen as a symbolic act of conquering of the land and thus a code word for the passage into the next life.

With the above mentioned positive portraits of the book of Joshua some would reject it in the modern day context citing the reason that the book is predominantly the record of "war crimes" of a particular nation. Those who holds on to this view argue that the book cannot be accepted in the light of global peace and justice that we need to uphold in the present context. We shall return to the question of the use of violence and war in the book later in our discussion, particularly as it relates to the South Asian context. The book cannot be ignored or taken lightly as we see it referred either directly or indirectly in 14 other biblical texts: 1 Kings 16:34; Pss 44; 68:12-14; 78:54,55; 94:4,5; Hab 3:11; Acts 7:45; Heb 4:8; 11:30,31; 13:5; Jas 2:25. Moreover the book projects certain important demands that God made on the people of Israel: absolute loyalty of the people of Israel to Yahweh in all circumstances, total obedience of the people to the Mosaic law and covenant, people's acceptance of the leadership of Joshua, etc., and those demands must always be heard by any contemporary reader of the book of Joshua.

2.1.1 ***Themes in the book:*** In the light of what is discussed above the following major themes can be listed in the book of Joshua.

Firstly, the book projects the importance of following the Mosaic Torah or instruction in the God's chosen community. It is believed that Moses under the direction of God wrote the Torah and completed it. Deut 31:9-13, 24-29; 32:44-47 informs us that Moses wrote down all the words of Torah according to God's instruction. Joshua follows this document of Moses seriously in all its words. Moreover, this Torah of Moses serves as a document of authority for Joshua and the community of Israel in the subsequent periods after Moses. It all begins right at the time when Joshua is commissioned for his task to obey "law of Moses" (Josh 1:7). It is understandable why Joshua accepts the Torah of Moses as a sign of authority for the entire community of the people of Israel. In this way the book of Joshua is not only seen as a continuation of Mosaic Law but also continuation of history of the book of Deuteronomy. In this sense the book of Joshua is narrated as one continues history of God's salvation to liberate the people of Israel from the shackles of oppressive nations and settle them in a permanent land in accordance with the promise of given to the fathers of Israel. Right at the beginning of the book we can notice in the commission of Joshua (Josh 1:7-8) the Lord reminded him about the importance of the Mosaic Torah and also to the entire community. The emphasis on Torah appears again in Josh 8: 30-35, when Joshua leads Israel in a ceremony to renew the covenant mediated first by Moses. In the penultimate speech of Joshua in 23:6-13, Joshua once again sums up his speech by reminding the people the Mosaic contribution to torah and exhorting people to torah faithfulness.

Secondly, book of Joshua also affirms that ban on all captured things be it places, goods, or people. The possible reasons why total ban is imposed on all the captured goods and land in the warfare may be that the people of Israel need to burn all that has been captured like what they do in a burnt offering. By this act the people of Israel declare that what has been captured by war is not the achievement of the warriors but belongs to God who fought the battles on behalf of the people. We can see the total ban for instance, in the case of Jericho where there is a requirement of total destruction that includes all its residents, men, women and children, and all the living creatures and material goods (Josh 6:17, 18 and 21). The above mentioned ban is applicable in the case of Canaanite town and cities (also applicable to Israelite towns as mentioned in Deut 13:12-18) as suggested in Deut 7: 2-4:

> When the LORD your God has delivered them over to you and you have defeated them, then you must destroy them totally. Make no treaty with them, and show them no mercy. Do not intermarry with them. Do not give your daughters to their sons or take their daughters for your sons, for they will turn your children away from following me to serve other gods, and LORD's anger will burn against you and will quickly destroy you.

In another place in the book of Deuteronomy 20:16-18 clear and harsh instruction is given concerning the annihilation of "anything that breaths." These verses read as follows:

> However, in the cities of the nations the LORD your God is giving you as an inheritance, do not leave alive anything that breaths. Completely destroy them—the Hittites, Amorites, Canaanites,

> Perizzites, Hivites and Jebusites—as the LORD your God has commanded you. Otherwise, they will teach you to follow all the detestable things they do in worshipping their gods, and you will sin against the LORD your God.

However, certain exceptions are made to this rigorous practice of ban of the war goods and property. Rahab in Josh 6 and Gibeonites in Josh 9:3-27 are exempted for several reasons. The above discussion on ban in the book of Joshua illustrates that the God of Israel is jealous God and will not compromise on any account in matters of people's total loyalty and obedience to him. In the ancient West Asian context herem (ban) was imposed on particular towns by the conquering nation as sign of political dominance over the entire land. In the Moabite Mesha inscription of ninth century the word herem occurs in the sense of "consecrate to destruction." It was claimed by the Moabite king Mesha that he imposes herem on captured Israelites. Herem in the ancient West Asian world also means the conquering nation destroyed a particular nation and it is filled with people from the victorious nation. Apart from this the booty of the war is shared among the conquering nation as an incentive to the soldiers. Similar practice can be noticed in ancient Indian wars.

Thirdly, the book of Joshua insists on the concept of all Israel who will be gathered and be given the Promised Land. This was also done in accordance with the promise God made and is repeatedly cited on number of occasions (Deut 1:1; 5:1; 11:6; 27:14; 29:9; Josh 3:7, 17; 4:14; 7:22-26; 8:21, 24; 23:2). Even when there are possible conflicts between various tribes within Israel the book stresses for the unity of all people. Joshua calls all the tribes to be united for the sake of the nation and its unity. For instance in Josh 1:12-15 and 4:12 it is stated that Joshua allows Transjordan tribal groups to go separately only after they first help their brethren in the conquest east of the river. Probably there was a possibility of a potential conflict between different tribes indirectly hinted in the book of Joshua, although a more realistic picture can be seen in the case of the book of Judges where intertribal non-cooperation and then outright civil wars were recorded (Judg 20). The book of Joshua on the other hand strongly affirm that despite practical problems there must be unity of all tribes and that is the cause for the entire nation to be united under the name of one God, Yahweh. The unity theme of all Israel also appears at crucial places in the book. It appears at the beginning (Josh 1:12-18); at the beginning of tribal allotments (Josh 13:8-32); and also almost at the end of the book (Josh 22).

Fourthly, when Israel is obedient to the demands of Mosaic covenant initiated by God and are reaffirmed through Joshua at that point of time in history in the exile then Yahweh will be faithful to fulfill the promises for the people. Israel's suffering is the cause of their own sin that is clearly communicated to them through Joshua. But God is faithful to protect the people if they continue to live in obedience to God's covenantal love. However that cannot be taken for granted all the time. We do have exceptions to this God's grace as we note in the case of Achan (Josh 7) that Israel's faithlessness leads to divine judgment and loss. Joshua warns (Josh 23) the people that if they remain faithless then they will lose their land, although this kind of strict judgment is implemented in the book of Judges. On the whole the book of Joshua warns the people of losing their land, nevertheless it concentrates on the blessing that will follow if people adhere to the torah demands and that blessing is centered on the gift of the land that God would give the people.

Fifthly, the book of Joshua generates hope within the context of the Babylonian exile or in any situation of distress the people experience. Looking at the reality of the exile and the loss of land, driven away from their homeland and scattering of the people to different places, the book of Joshua generates hope and confidence in the minds of the people in distress that God would once again grant them their land and they can rightfully claim their lost territorial land. As a minority and powerless community they can once again gain their land not by their military power but by the divine initiative, by the very God who gave them the torah who will now act on their behalf.

2.1.2 *Problematic issues in the book:* Apart from the major theses discussed above in the book of Joshua we do have certain issues in the book that needs brief introductory note. These issues will be clarifies in details at appropriate places below in the commentary.

Firstly, the readers of the book of Joshua are often perturbed is the issue of violence. As a contemporary reader one may perceive this issue differently than what the book of Joshua would have meant in its original setting. The main reason why we need to talk about this issue is to clear the misapprehensions that may be created when the book of Joshua is judged from the modern readers' point of view. Violence is mostly spoken in terms of human arrogance and superior self-interest as has been mentioned in Ps 73:6. If this meaning is taken into consideration then the wars in the book of Joshua is not a violent act rather it is to establish a society that is based on the torah of Moses, where the Lord will be accepted as the God and all human beings and in turn the human beings will act justly towards one another. Deut 9:4-5 clearly states that the LORD had driven out the Anakites on account of their wickedness and arrogance. Moreover, Israelites are also warned in Deut 8:19-20 that they too will be destroyed like any other nation, a caution that is more than enough to know that Yahweh is impartial in dealing with the sin of all the human beings. God supports and fights on behalf of the people of Israel and at the same time God deals with them stiffly if they do not comply with the demands of the covenant set before them. Thus we see the understanding of violence in the book of Joshua is not unilateral one but very much marked by the context of human attitude towards their neighbor and God. In fact the Old

Testament differentiates between an attack on a city in a war context and attack on one's neighbor or his daughter by raping her (see Amos 3:10; Deut 22:25-27; Jer 20:8). While in the earlier case it is the war that also determines Israel's existence amidst her neighbours and the latter case is condemned because it is an unjust offence that the people of Israel created to their neighbor and thus not at all permitted. Thus the idea of violence in the book of Joshua has to be seen in the light of what is stated above in Deut 9:4-5. It can't be arbitrary application of Israelites on the part of their enemies.

Secondly, the book portrays the concerns that warfare is not to be seen a violent activity but as a Holy War fought by God on behalf of the small and emerging nation of Israel. In the Old Testament Holy war is also called "wars of Yahweh," in which God was conceived as primary actor (Exod 14:1-4; Deut 1:30; Judg 20:35; 1 Sam 14:23) and the human roles were deemphasized that the size of the Israelite army was immaterial (Judg 7:2-8; 1 Sam 14:6). However, Holy War also involves people's participation. For their part Israel was carrying the ark into the battle (Numb 10:35-36; 1 Sam 4) and accompanied by the blowing of trumpet. Human reaction to the battles of Yahweh is to admire God's victory in silent and submissive faith (Exod 14:13-14; 2 Chr 20:17; Isa 7:4). In the ancient world Israel is not alone to view God as their battle leader. It is common in Ugaritic and Mesopotamian texts. The Moabite Stone of 9th century BCE has similar vocabulary and concept of Holy War like the book of Joshua (divine order to fight, divinely granted victory, attack at dawn, devotion of enemy population to destruction, occupation of the conquering territory). Holy War in Israel emphasizes the confessional statement "Yahweh fought for Israel," (Josh 10:14, 42; 23:3, 10) with the view that it is God who has the power to victory to a small nation and is responsible for their survival. However it is not to be understood as a sanction for Israel to oppress other nations. Holy War is also not to be equated with modern Jihad which is thought of divine will to fight against evil. In Jihad end justifies the means and thus those who support this will launch onslaught on all life. Violence and terror is justified as right way in Jihad and all groups (dominant and marginalized/ oppressor and oppressed) are attacked in the process.

Thirdly, many misinterpretations and misreading are commonly seen in the case of the book of Joshua. Historically the way in which the war reports presented in the book of Joshua is somewhat exaggerated than what could have really happened. By the time the book has been composed the real story of the people of Israel was that they were scattered and made homeless and the two nations Israel and Judah almost disappeared from the main stage of the world politics. The book may have been composed in its original form during the time of Josiah as part of the Deuteronomistic History (Joshua – Kings) with Deuteronomy as introduction. But the final editing and composition of the book may have taken place only during the exile in 587 or 586 BCE. The battle reports mentioned in the book may have been slightly exaggerated than what was in the reality. It was customary in the ancient times to exaggerate certain facts by way of common statements. For instance in the Indian context the kings are ascribed to have fought battles and ruled the people "with peace and prosperity" and everyone in the kingdom had no idea of what is hunger in all the days of a particular king. Even if we consider the accuracy of the reports more or less true it was to be understood that God fought on behalf of the weak in order to pull down the mighty nations that were oppressive in their own day. Therefore looking at the face value one cannot reject the book of Joshua as violent report of the wars of Israel waged against other nations. The above discussed point that the book of Joshua is a faithful record of the wars of Yahweh on behalf of his vulnerable people needs further clarification. In order to control the tyrannical powers that are oppressive at the time of Israel some amount of violence in ancient terms could be justified without keeping it as pretext for any form of violence. Reading the book in this way will remove unnecessary misapprehensions of it and it will also clarify the wider purpose for which the book is composed. If Canaanites and such power-seeking oppressive forces are allowed to be continued the victimized and the small nations like Israel and Judah would have been totally swallowed by them. Viewing the book of Joshua in this light will certainly help us to affirm the positive value for which the book has been composed even when we may think that certain battle reports are seemingly exaggerated. But we cannot overstate this point in the case of Israel as well as mentioned above that Israelites too faced violent end because of their arrogant, rebellious and sinful attitude. Time and again Israelites are warned not to oppress the aliens, widows and orphans since they were once aliens in a foreign land (Exod 22:21-22).

2.2. The Book of Judges

We have already noted that Judges 1:1-2:9 ought to be assigned to the book of Joshua, and clearly was only taken as the beginning of new book because it begins with 'And it came to pass after the death of Joshua'. But in reality 2:10-3:6 also apart from the Deuteronomistic survey of the period of the Judges in 2:11-19, belongs to the book of Joshua and not in the book of Judges. For here we are concerned with the motive which lead Yahweh not to give complete success to the battle of Joshua or of the first generation of the conquerors, but still to leave in and around Canaan some people hostile to Israel. The real Judge narrative begin only at 3:7, and extend to 16:31. These then follow properly devoted as "appendices" to book of Judges to narratives one concerning the theft of cult objects by the Danites in 17 & 18, and the other concerning outrage at Gibeah and its punishment in 19-21.

Judges is the second book of the "Former Prophets" section of the Hebrew Old Testament. The fact that the Hebrews placed this book in this section of their canon is significant. It demonstrates that they recognized it as God's "selective history" of the period, designed to teach spiritual lessons more than simply to record historical facts. God revealed Himself through the events of life and history, as well as through the messages of the prophets.

2.2.1. Date and Author: Internal references help us locate the approximate date of composition of this book. The clause, "In those days there was no king in Israel" (17:6; 18:1; 19:1; 21:25), suggests that someone wrote Judges during the monarchical period that followed the period of rule by judges (the so-called "amphictyony"). Someone probably wrote it after 1051 B.C.E when Saul became king. However, at the time of writing, Jerusalem was still under Jebusite control ("the sons of Benjamin did not drive out the Jebusites who lived in Jerusalem," 1:21). David captured Jerusalem about 1004 B.C.E. Therefore, the writing of Judges must date between 1051 and 1004 B.C.E. Jewish tradition suggests that Samuel wrote Judges. This was the opinion of the writers of the "Talmud," the collection of Jewish writings (commentaries) that proliferated around revealed Scripture, beginning very early in Israel's history. Samuel is a likely writer because of his major role in Israel during the period that someone wrote Judges. Samuel's ministry began about 1090 B.C.E., and apparently ended just a few years before Saul's death (ca. 1021 B.C.E). If Samuel did write Judges, he probably did so between 1051 and about 1021 B.C.E.

Message of the Book: Joshua reveals that victory, success, and progress result when God's people trust and obey Him consistently. Judges shows that defeat, failure, and retrogression follow when they fail to trust and obey consistently. In this respect, Joshua and Judges are like two sides of one coin. The former is a positive lesson and the latter a negative one. Judges portrays the deterioration of the nation of Israel: what caused it, the course it followed, and the consequences that resulted. The Israelites failed because their hearts turned from Yahweh, and then their heads forsook God's covenant.

We could visualize the structure of the book as a descending spiral. Israel departed from God, fell under His discipline, repented, experienced deliverance from her oppressors, dedicated herself anew to Yahweh, experienced His blessing, and then apostatized again. In each cycle, Israel seems to have sunk lower than she had been previously, even though each cycle included a spiritual revival. Judges reveals the course and process by which Israel deteriorated as a nation.

The root cause of Israel's deterioration was religious apostasy. The Israelites turned from God. They did not drive out the Canaanites as God had commanded (1:21, 27-33). Instead they made covenants with them (2:1-3). Rather than destroying the foreign altars, the Israelites served idols and forsook the Lord (2:11-12, 17, 19). Their apostasy began with toleration of things that God had condemned and prohibited. In time, the Israelites began to admire these things. Finally, they conformed to them. The story of Micah and the Danites (chs. 17—18) is a short illustration of the religious apostasy in Israel at this time. Chapters 17—21 are an appendix to the book. Shortly after Israel departed from God, it began to come apart as a nation. The people stopped working together toward their God-given goal of possessing the entire land, and they began fighting with one another instead. At the beginning of the amphictyony (rule by judges), the tribes were fairly united, but by the end of this period of Israel's history, anarchy prevailed (21:25). The government in Israel deteriorated from aristocracy (rule by Moses and then Joshua)—to anarchy (no rule or government). Israel became fragmented, weak, and unable to withstand her enemies. This is ironic, because after Joshua died, Israel was in position to begin to enjoy the benefits of the theocracy in the land for the first time! Until Judges opens, God was preparing Israel to enjoy the theocracy in the land. There are several examples of tribal jealousies in Judges (e.g., 8:1-3; 12:1-6), but the worst example of political disorganization is the vignette that concludes the book. This was the Israelites' "civil war," in which 11 of the tribes almost annihilated the twelfth: Benjamin (chs. 20—21). Instead of utterly destroying the Canaanites, God's people had allowed them to live among them, while the Israelite tribes proceeded to destroy one another.

Immorality marked Israel's social life. Even Samson, one of the judges, was a victim of this cancer. The story of the "Levite and his concubine," who visited the town of Gibeah (ch. 19), is a slice of life out of the period of the judges that shows the immorality that characterized Israel's social life. The behavior demonstrated in this story was the fruit of departure from God. The very sin that had previously characterized the Canaanites of Sodom (sodomy; homosexuality, Gen. 19), now marked God's people! Chapter 19 comprises a third part of the appendix to the book. God revealed this process of deterioration to warn all people in every time. Spiritual apostasy leads to political disorganization and social chaos. Social and governmental evils rise out of spiritual conditions. When the Israelites repented and rededicated themselves to God, He brought political deliverance and restored social order. Therefore, it is very important to deal with the spiritual issues that lie at the root of other problems in modern life.

2.3. The Books of Samuel

According to Jewish tradition, deriving I Chronicles 29: 29-30, the book of Samuel were compiled by Samuel or Samuel, Nathan and Gad, and bear the name of the compiler or chief compiler. The two books originally formed a single unit in the Jewish Canon. Hebrew manuscripts and printed editions have only adopted the division into two since 1448, were as first and subsequently the Vulgate had long preceded them in this. In LXX the word for the book of Samuel and is kind is termed as (he four books of kingdoms, and in Latin as four books of kingdoms (Regnorum) later it has become Regnum formed on the basis of the Hebrew kings prevailed.

The division of the book into two is not inappropriate. The principle here operative is, of making the division after the death of a leading individual, in this case after the death of Saul, which is described in I Sam 31. To obtain a rapid survey of the contents, the books may be further divided thus:

a) I Sam l-7 ff: Samuel childhood and his victory over the Philistines who up till then had heavily oppressed Israel, Chapters 8-25, the installation of Saul as king by Samuel at the people's wish and his rejection by Yahweh; Chapter 26-31, the relationships between Saul and David, at first friendly and then hostile, and Saul's death in the disastrous battle on Mount Gilboa.
b) II Samuel 1-8 ff: David's rise to power as king of Judah with his residence at Hebron, and then as king of all Israel with his residence in the city of Jerusalem which he conquered, Chapter 9-24, with which I Kings 1-2 clearly belong, stories of David's family and in particular of the context among his sons for the throne, which lead finally, shortly before David's death, to the accession of Solomon.

2.3.1. Date and the Author: The writer did not identify himself as the writer in the book. Statements in the Book of Samuel imply that someone who had witnessed at least some of the events recorded wrote it. However someone, or more than one person, must have written most of it after Samuel's death (i.e., 1 Sam. 25—2 Sam. 24) and some of it even after the division of the kingdom following Solomon's death (e.g., 1 Sam. 27:6). These features have made it difficult to date the book.

According to M. H. Segal: "Our guess is that the author was a high state official in frequent attendance at the court, enjoying the full confidence of David and his household, who served David throughout his reign in Jerusalem and also Solomon during the early years of his reign, and whose duties may have been connected with literary work."[7]

2.3.2. Message of the Books of Samuel: First and Second Samuel are really one story. The translators divided them into two books for convenience, not because of subject matter. This is also true of Kings and Chronicles. First Samuel records Israel's transition from amphictyony (rule by judges) to monarchy (rule by kings). The key passage that explains this transition is 8:4-7. Two statements from this passage are especially significant. The human desire that produced the transition expressed itself in verse 5: "Now appoint a king for us to judge us like all the nations." God had brought Israel into

7 M. H. Segal, "The Composition of the Books of Samuel," *Jewish Quarterly Review* 55 (1964-65), p. 334.

existence as a nation to be unlike all the nations (Exod. 19:5-6). The essence of its uniqueness was Yahweh's rule over it as King. God wanted Israel to be a demonstration for all the world to see how glorious it can be to live under the authority of God. The real meaning of the people's request comes out in verse 7: ". . . they have rejected me from being king over them."

During the period of the judges, religious apostasy spread and characterized Israel. The people refused to obey their King. It is this attitude that finds expression in verse 5. This is the essence of sin, and it results in idolatry. Every idol is a witness to man's need of God. When people reject the true God, they must put something in His place to meet that need. Human beings must have a god. Israel turned from God as her King in 1 Samuel. She demanded a king like the other nations. This book shows the immediate effects of that demand. One of the great revelations of 1 Samuel is how, from the human viewpoint, God adapts in order to continue God's reign. That God has changed the rules by which He expects people to live, as history has unfolded, is a clear revelation of Scripture. Usually this change followed a major failure by human beings to live under the rules God had established for them. These periods of history, in which God's requirements for humankind were consistent, are the dispensations. The statement that "God adapts to continue His reign" may appear to contradict 8:7, but it does not.

The people rejected Yahweh, but they did not dethrone Him. The first act is possible, but the second is not. This is a major lesson of 1 Samuel. The great revelation of this book is not primarily its three central figures: Samuel, Saul, and David. It is Yahweh reigning by adapting to human situations, and moving—surely and steadily—toward the fulfillment of His purposes. In spite of disobedience or obedience, failure or success, rebellious or loyal people, the reign of God moves on. We see this great lesson in the history of 1 Samuel's three central figures: Samuel, Saul, and David. The writer introduced Samuel's story with his mother Hannah's experience with God. Hannah was a great woman of faith who lived in the Judges Period. Her faith became God's foothold for advance. Her song reveals a profound appreciation for Yahweh as the God who reigns over all (2:6-8, 10).

Yahweh chose their kings for them. Yahweh allowed their desire for a human king to work itself out in ultimate disaster through the years that followed. Yet, He never spoke to the people through the king. He always spoke to them through the prophets. Samuel was the first of these. David, of course, was both a king and a prophet in a wider sense of the term. The role of the kings was to govern the people. The role of the prophets was to reveal God's will to them. With Samuel, the office of prophet in Israel emerges as that of Yahweh's authoritative representative to His people. Samuel became the kingmaker, finding and anointing both Saul and David. From now on, when God had a message for the people, it normally did not come directly to the king, but to the king and the people through a prophet. The prophet's office was always superior to that of Israel's kings.

The prophets became God's mediators, His messengers, and the interpreters of God's will. Thus Yahweh reigned, though adapted His methods of ruling by raising up the prophets. Yahweh called Samuel as the first of these mediators. During the monarchy, God provided guidance through two offices rather than through one, which He had done previously. The kings provided political leadership, and the prophets gave the people spiritual leadership. God had previously provided both types of leadership through single individuals, namely: Moses, Joshua, and the judges. Saul's story is one of the most tragic in Scripture. At the beginning of his reign, Israel was virtually without a leader. The books of 1 and 2 Samuel portrays how despite the powerful kings and dedicated prophets in the United Kingdom of Israel suffered setbacks and defeats but yet was protected and safeguarded by Yahweh, who loved the people unconditionally.

2.4. The Books of Kings

The story in the books of Kings runs from the death of David and the establishment in office of Solomon, his successor (1 Kings 1), through the history of the two kingdoms, down to the destruction of Jerusalem and the Babylonian exile (2 Kings 25). The period of about four centuries that the story covers, falls almost automatically in to three parts:

a) I Kings 1-11 the reign of Solomon.
b) I Kings 12-II Kings 17 History of the divided Kingdoms of Israel and Judah.
c) II Kings 18-25: History of the Southern Kingdom, Judah continued.

The books of kings tell a story of guilt accompanied by forceful theological Judgements: we hear of the usually tense relations between prophets and kings, peaceful or violent changes of regime, cultic measures and wars, but hardly anything of social politics and problems of domestic politics, although these because increasingly important during the monarchic period.

In addition to all sorts of individual materials there are two main sources on which the presentation of the books of kings is based.

i) A rigorous and official character attaches to:
    a) The "Synchronistic Chronicle" which in recording the accession of a king indicates the year of the reign of the ruler in the neighbouring kingdom (I kings 15:1, 25 to II kings 18:1).
    b) The length of the reign and often the place of residence (1 kings 2:11 11 42, 14: 20) and frequently. These two regularly given pieces of Information are supplemented for the kings of Judah, by notices on:

c) The age of the rulers and his accession and
d) The name of the queen mother (I kings 14:21 etc.) who as "mistress" exercised certain functions of government (see 15:3, 2 kings 10:13, Jer. 13: 18). Finally, information is generally given regarding the death of the kings and regarding his succession (1 Kings 14: 20, 31), etc.

This official information and perhaps other data as well (12:25 etc.), may come from the annals that are likewise cited almost everywhere in the books of Kings. "The book of the acts of Solomon" (11:41), "The book of the Chronicles of the kings of Israel" (14:19 to 2 kings 15:26, 31) as well as "The book ofthe Chronicles of the Kings of Judah" (1 Kings 14: 29-11 Kings 24:5).

ii) From these more or less stereotyped pieces of information are to be distinguished the more loosely structured stories about the prophets, which of its surprising take up a goodly space in the books of Kings. These are stories about unnamed prophets (I kings 13:20) as well as about Ahijah of Shiloh (I kings 11:29, 14), Micaiah son of Imlah (I kings 22), Elijah (I kings 17-19, 21, 2 kings 1), Elisha (2 kings 2-9, 13, l kings 19:19), Isaiah (2 kings 18-20), Elisa (36-39).

2.4.1. Historical setting of the books: The events described in Kings occurred between the very end of David's reign and Jehoiachin's release from a Babylonian prison, that is, from c. 970 B.C.E to 561 B.C.E., a period of over four hundred years. This is the time of Israel's monarchy during which there was much internal strife and division as well as great external threats from the likes of Egypt, Syria, Assyria, and Babylon. Hence, Israel's covenant relationship with Yahweh is being played out on the stage of international affairs, a milieu well attested in extra-biblical history.

2.4.2. Special concerns: Several important concerns from the books of Kings can be discussed. But for the want of space we shall consider most important concerns that would occupy the books.

First, relationship to Deuteronomy: From the way in which the author of Kings chronicles the history of the monarchy it is obvious that the fates of monarch and people are directly related to their obedience or disobedience to the stipulations set forth in the Mosaic Covenant, particularly in the expression of it found in the book of Deuteronomy. Because the whole of Kings is in one sense an outworking of the blessings and cursings section (Deut 28), it is obvious that the author approaches history with Deuteronomy in mind and writes with that as the basis for evaluating king and subject and for defending Yahweh's judgments. However, it would be difficult to prove the exact influence of Deuteronomy in the books of Kings.

Second, the books of Kings follow certain stereotypical frame work of discussing the details of the events and with a clear theological ficus. The reigning kigs are described in a fixed pattern by comparing with David as an exemplary king among all others. Anyone who falls short of the expectations are narrated as below David or as good as David. Theologically, the book talks about a pattern of sin, judgment and punishement and restoration until there came a point of total collapse of the two kingdoms. This stereotypical pattern is the narrator's creative invention in that given situation.

Third, the miracle working of Elijah and Elisha. The only other place in the Old Testament where such a grouping of miracles occurs is in conjunction with the ministries of Moses and Joshua. These two periods were critical times of transition and decision in the life of the nation of Israel. The nature of these miracles and their purpose in the narrative will not be discussed as it is beyond the scope of this section.

To sum up, when the people of Israel and their kings spurned Yahweh's law, repudiated Yahweh's messengers, and turned to foreign gods, Yahweh judged them; however, they were not without hope because through repentance and faith restoration was possible since God had promised to raise up the messiah for them in the coming days.

The book of Kings was intended to serve as a theological justification for the way that Yahweh had treated His covenant people, Israel. It displays in no uncertain terms the reasons for the dissolution of the united monarchy, so glorious under David and Solomon, and then goes on to indicate why both of the resulting nations had gone into captivity. The reason was that both king and people, with the complicity of the priesthood and a large contingent of false prophets, had grievously violated the Mosaic Covenant as set forth in its first renewal document, the book of Deuteronomy. However, this situation was not without hope. Since the Abrahamic covenant was still in force, and new guarantees had been amplified in the Davidic Covenant, the Assyrian and Babylonian captivities were not Yahweh's last word on the matter. Canonically Kings serves as the theological backdrop for this message of hope as developed in the prophets and post-exilic history, especially Isaiah, Jeremiah, Ezekiel, Daniel, Zechariah, and Ezra-Nehemiah.

3. THE LATTER PROPHETS: MAJOR PROPHETS AND MINOR PROPHETS

3.1. Major Prophets

A. Isaiah

(Chapters 1-39): Isaiah, the son of Amoz (1:1) was called to be prophet according to the tradition in the year of the death of king Uzziah of Judah (6:1). Perhaps his ministry, which was confined to Jerusalem ended is any case in the year 701 B.C.E He must have gone to a school (30:80, was married to a prophetess (8: 3) The names of his sons are Shear-Jashub ('a remnant will return) and Maher-shalal-hash-baz (the spoil speeds the pray hastes'). A number of scholars regard the Immanuel mentioned in 7:14 as another son of prophet. The main message of the Prophet: Yahweh's intention to destroy the nation was already revealed to him at his call and the task of further hardening the nations heart was assigned to his own ministry (Chp. 6:1). Five periods are usually distinguished within his prophetic activity. The first (early period) includes the years from his call down to the outbreak of the Syro-Ephraimite war, usually 6:1-11, 1:2-3, 1:10-17, 1:18-20, 1:21-26, 2:6-22, 3:1-9, 12-15, 3:25-4:1, 5:1-7, 5:8-24 to 10:1-4 are assigned to this period. In this period inspite of occasional exhortations, the preaching of judgement is already predominant.

i) *The Second period*: covers the years of Syro-Ephraimite war (734-733) and reached return form in the so called memorial of the prophet. This opened with chapter 6 and continued 7: 1-9, 7: 10-17, 18-25, 8:1-4, 5-8, 16-18 and (9:1), 9:2-7. 17:1-3.

ii) *The Third period*: The sayings of the prophet from the time before the fall of the Northern Kingdom, in which he foretold the fall of Israel, are treated as forming the third period. 9: 8-21 +5: 25-30 and 28: 1-4.

iii) *The Fourth period*: It is the decade of the Philistine movement of revolt against Assyria from 721-711, Isaiah foretold the fruitlessness of the revolts and accordingly warned his nation against taking part in them. (Chp. 14: 28-32, 20:1-6 and perhaps also 18: 1-4). Finally, in the fifth and last period before during immediately after the Syro-Palestenian revolt of the years 703(5)-701. Isaiah quite certainly raised his voice to announce uncompromisingly its end to the blinded and rebellious nation (chp. 28: 7-13, 29:9-10a; 29:13-14, 15-17; 30:1-5, 6-7, 8; 31:1-3 and 22:1-4, 12-14).

i) More details on Isaiah of Jerusalem (1-39 chapters, the eighth century prophetic voice):

Isaiah 1-39 chapters belong to the prophetic voice of eighth century BCE. It would be appropriated to look into this prophet's contribution to the mission and development of the people of Israel in the paragraphs that follow.

a) The Historical background: The superscription in Isa. 1:1 asserts that Isaiah Prophesied during the days of Uzziah, Jotham, Ahaz and Hezekiah, Kings of Judah. But this superscription is quite later addition to the composition of the book. Since Isaiah did not receive his call to be a Prophet until, the year that King Uzziah dies" (6:1), it is in only case evident that little could have derived from that same Year and none at all from it, as is most Probable, Uzziah was already dead when the call came. While the dates of the other Kings are a dispute among scholars more or less the following dates can be agreed upon: Uzziah (Azariah). 787-736 B.C.E; Jotham (co-regent)-756-741

B.C; Ahaz (co-regent); 741-736 B.C; Ahaz (sole ruler); 736-725; Hezekiah: 725-697 B.C.E.

Unfortunately, yet another major Point of uncertainty over dating emerges with regard to the Year in which Hezekiah came to the throne. The evidence of II Kings 18:1f, 9, asserts that Hezekiah has already assumed the throne of Judah for some years when Samaria fall to the Assyrians in 722 B.C. This Conflicts with the evidence of II Kings 18:13 that it was only the 14th Year of the Hezekiah when Sennacherib marched into Judah and attacked Jerusalem, an event which can be Placed in 701 B.C.E. Therefore. several scholars tend to propose that Hezekiah's accession did not take place until 715 BCE. But R.E. Clements brings out a proposal on this by saying: Ahaz's death probably occurred in 726/5 and that Hezekiah's accession took Place in 725. From these conclusions we can then proceed to Isaiah's Prophesying between these two reigns. The Prophets call may be located in 736 BCE, and the latest Prophecies which have been Preserved from him in the year 701, or very shortly thereafter (1:4-8; 22:1-4, 12-14).

The major political events which affect the entire Period of Isaiah's activity were those occasioned by the military and Political threat Posed to Israel and Judah by the Assyrians. Four rulers of Assyrian empire are involved in this regard: Tiglath Pileser III: 744-727 B.C.E; Shalmaneser V: 726-722 BCE; Sargon II: 721-705 BCE; Sennacherib: 704-681 BCE. We shall now turn to examine briefly the events and political developments that occurred in Judah ultimately shared by Isaiah in his oracles and Prophetic ministry in this regard we shall briefly look into Isaiah's relationship to the court.

It is understood Isaiah must have acted as adviser to two Kings of Judah: Ahaz and Hezekiah (Isa. 7:3-17; 37:2-7, 21-35), and that his Prophetic message contains much directly Political advise, Isaiah seems to have had ready access to the King (7:3,10) and according to the narrative of chs. 36-39 the King sent to consult him when the Assyrians invaded. J. Fichtner and J.W. Whedbee argued that Isaiah was a 'wise man' in the technical sense, someone educated in the schools of ancient Israel, which are widely thought to have trained civil servants to work in the chancelleries of the royal courts in Jerusalem and Samaria, When Isaiah condemned the ruling classes of Jerusalem, and commented on the country's foreign Policy, he was criticizing members of the social class he himself belonged to.

Isaiah lived in the period when the growing might of Assyria increasingly threatened the stability and independence of the small states of Syria-Palestine. In the ninth century these states had been quite successful in containing Assyrian expansionism, and in 853 BCE had beaten off Shalmaneser III at the battle of Qarqar; Ahab of Israel was among the successful allies.

But the 745 B.C.E is usually regarded as the crucial turning point, the year in which Tiglath-Pileser III took the throne of Assyria and began a series of conquests which would effectively wipe out Israelite and Judean independence. Isaiah began to Prophesy at a time when both the aggressive incentives and the various Kings of Judah as they tried to handle the complexities of a situation from which, in the end, no one was likely to come to Palestine as happened to other Kingdoms.

Four important issues we need to consider briefly in order to examine the role of Isaiah in his historical and political situation:

b) The Syro-Ephraimite Crisis: The Syro-Ephraimite crisis had its beginning in the earl Conquests of Tiglath-Pilesar, who captured Hamath in northern Syria as early as 738 and then quickly took tribute from the cities of Phoenicia arid from Damascus, the immediate neighbour of northern Kingdom of Israel (Ephraim) and the leading Aramean (Syrian) state, Israel soon paid tribute in turn. Paying tribute was the least of the kind of vassaldom enforced by the Assyrians and involved no invasion or 'conquest' in the Physical sense-it is not unlike Paying Protection money. By these means the Assyrians spread their influence and control by the threat of military invasion, without needing to expend forces on its army, Paying the tribute also had the effect of weakening the national economy, and consequently also the Political institution leaving the country an easier Prey if the Assyrian King later decided on a more aggressive.

At this stage Judah was not affected. However, in 734 BCE Tiglath-Pileser moved west and terrorized the Philistine Pentapolis. Judah was thus threatened to both north and west of Assyria, on the other hand, may have looked slightly overstretched. At all events in 733 B.C.E Israel and the Arameans of Damascus decided to try to revive the old alliances of the ninth century and oppose the Assyrians through a 'Syro-Ephraimite' coalition. They failed to see how immensely Assyrian Power had increased, and how weak they themselves now were. Razon (biblical Rezin) of Damascus and Pekah son of Remaliah of Israel 'invited' Ahaz, who had just succeeded Jotham, to join the coalition. They intended if he refused to depose him, and place on the Judaic throne someone called 'ben Tabeel'- his personal name is unknown, as is everything about him. As the northern armies prepared to march on Judah to implement this unwise plan (Hos 5:8-9 may describe their route), Ahaz decided to send the Assyrians the tribute they had not (yet) asked for to persuade them to intervene on his behalf. Whether on his behalf or not, the Assyrians certainly did crush the rebellion, which in any case they could not have afforded to ignore. Samaria was sacked in 733, Damascus in 732 BCE Isa. 17:1-6 predict both events.

This Period is the setting for Isaiah 7 and 8. Isaiah goes to meet Ahaz 'at the end of the conduit of the upper pool' on the highway to the Fuller's field, Perhaps implying that the King was inspecting the city's water supply in case of siege.

Isaiah's message to Ahaz has two aspects. The first is the symbolic Prediction in his son's name, Shear-jashub ('a remnant will return'). The other is the advice given to the King, which bears directly on the Political decision he has to make. The adverse appears clear: Do not fear, because God can deliver his people; take no action to prevent by the coalition (8:4).

What is the action Ahaz is contemplating, and which Isaiah warns against? At the face value of the text, it may appear that Isaiah is warning the King Ahaz not to prepare for siege or war rather to put his trust in God. But there is another possibility; and that is that Isaiah was opposing not Ahaz's preparations for war, nor his plans for fortifying the city, but his intention of sending tribute to Tiglath-Pileser. Isaiah could have been saying that Ahaz has no need to do anything but 'keep quiet'. A small indication that this may be what was meant is Isaiah's advice not to fear Rezin and Pekah. Ahaz sending to Assyria for help would indeed show fear, and it may be this that Isaiah opposes.

The oracle which Isaiah gives to Ahaz seems to have both unconditional and conditional promise. On the one hand, Isaiah was saying that the King has no need to fear, since God will confirm him on his throne? Isa. 8:1-14 might tend to support this: "Before the child (the Prophets son, Maher-Shalal-Hash-Baz) knows to cry "My father" or "My mother", the wealth of Damascus and the spoil of Samaria will be carried away before the King of Assyria; or it could be conditional promise, and also a conditional threat. Isa. 7:4 and 7:9a suggests the conditional promise, but 7:9b, the climax of the oracle may means in the sense: unless you are prepared to stand firm, you will not be confirmed or upheld in your position.

Thus the whole oracle is Probably meant as a conditional promise of deliverance: only by not "fearing" only by being "quiet" (cf. Ps. 76:9), will Ahaz be showing faith in Yahweh, and thus deserves Yahweh's Protection. Paradoxically, to be afraid, and therefore to seek help from Assyria, is the one certain way of not obtaining help from the genuine source of help – the God of Israel.

c) The Fall of Samaria: The aftermath of the Syro-Ephraimite coalition was disastrous for the northern Kingdom of Israel, which effectively became an Assyrian province, with only Samaria and its immediate environs left as a nominally independent but tribute-paying vassal state. Israel had long had a stronger tendency to insurrection and internal strife than its smaller southern neighbour, and in the years following the defeat of the coalition the monarchy there became highly unstable This is the situation reflected in the book of Hosea (eg: 6:11-7:7; 8:4). 722 B.C.E. Samaria revolted against Assyrian rule, and the city was besieged, falling in 722 to Shalmaneser V. Judah was not implicated in this revolt, and so retained its status as a vassal but with its own monarchy and administration.

d) Alliances with the Philistines and the Egyptians: The third Phase of Isaiah's life saw Judah Preoccupied with intrigues and alliances involving the Philistine cities and the Egyptians. From about 720 B.C.E, a couple of years after Samaria fell, Syria-Palestine experienced stirrings of rebellion against Assyrian domination. There were revolts in Hamath, the first state to fall to the Assyrians, and in Gaza, the farthest point of the empire from their Mesopotamian Power-base. The Egyptians saw advantage for themselves in getting involved, but nevertheless the King of Gaza was captured, and the revolt fizzled out.

But in 713-711 there was a further serious bid for freedom when the city of Ashdod tried to break the Assyrian's hold on the Philistine Pentapolis (five cities). This time the Egyptians, under Shabaka were deeply entangled; there were also negotiations with the more easterly Palestinian states, Edom and Moab, and Judah was certainly part of the alliance. This is widely agreed to be the background to the oracles of Isaiah 18 and 19. It is also the contest for the story of Isaiah walking naked and barefoot through Jerusalem in ch. 20, dated to 'the year that the Tartan came to Ashdod', that is, 711 B.C.E—the year when the Assyrians under Sargon II finally stepped in to put the rebellion down. Ashdod was completely crushed, and the Egyptians for the time being handed over the kingdom to the King of Ashdod, who had fled to them for asylum, to the Assyrians; but there is no record of any reprisals against Judah, Edom or Moab.

Isa 19:16-24 consists of five oracles about Yahweh's future Purposes for Egypt, culminating in the extraordinary promise that the day Israel will be the third with Egypt and Assyria' (v-24)-one of the most universalistic oracles in the OT. Isaiah's Political advice is again that Judah should rely on God, not on human beings, and he interprets this to mean that no alliances should be made with Egypt. Isaiah's message in this crisis is thus completely consistent with his attitude in the earlier days when it was the alliance with Assyria that he condemned.

e) The Assyrian crisis: The final Phase of Isaiah's 'Political' Prophecy is also the most complex and the most discussed. The accession of Sennacherib to the Assyrian throne in 705/04 evidently seemed to the Palestinian states to herald a weakening of Assyrian power, or at least a time when determined vassals could exploit possible tensions and uncertainties at the heart of the empire. Along with the Philistine cities of Ekron and Ashkelon, Hezekiah withheld tribute, perhaps in consultation with Babylon, then ruled by Marduk-apal-iddin II (biblical Merodach-baladan), With who he said to have had diplomatic dealings (see Isa. 39; II Kings 20:12-19). Once again Egypt was heavily involved, its Promises of help as crucial as empty as ever. Thus, Sennacherib was faced with rebellion at the extreme western and eastern ends of his empire. Since it took him four years to put down the Babylonian rebellion and turn his attention to that in the west, the allies had Probably judged their moment well: if there ever would be a moment for rebellion, this was it.

Nevertheless, in 701 BCE Sennacherib was at last in a Position to involve Judah, and to involve the Judeans in what is usually called 'The 'Assyrian Crisis'. It drew from Isaiah a number of prophecies, broadly in line with his utterances in the earlier periods. The main sources for Isaiah's oracles are 28-31 chaps; 36-38 chaps and chp. 1:2-9. The last passage gives a graphic description of the state of Judah once Sennacherib's army had invaded, leaving Jerusalem the only unconquered city in a devastated country, which is comparable to Sennacherib's own account of this campaign as recorded in ANET, p.288:

"As to Hezekiah the Jew, he did not submit to my yoke. I laid siege to 46 of his strong cities, walled forts, and countless small villages in their vicinity, and conquered (them) by means of well-stamped (earth) ramps, and battering rams...Himself I made a prisoner in Jerusalem, his royal residence, like a bird in a cage (cf. Isa. 10: 14)".

In 28:1-6 we find the main contents are on the Northern Kingdom and its fall, its concerns the social morality of the north (specifically its leaders' habitual drunkenness) rather than its political attitudes. But the chapter continues (vv.7-13) with what seems to be an attack on Judah ('There also...'), reapplying the early, anti-Israel oracle to the southern Kingdom during the Assyrian crisis. A similar use of the fall of Northern Israel as a warning to Judah can be found in Micah 1 and in 2 Kings 17:7-41. Isaiah sees the leadership as so befuddled that they believe they can defeat the superior Power of Assyria.

In Isa 28:14-22 the core of Political message of Isaiah is found: 'he who believes will not be in haste' (v.16). It apparently condemns the alliance with Egypt as an attempt to make a 'covenant with death'-Death is a notoriously hard bargaining Partner. The only true security comes horn Yahweh, who provides a secure rock in Zion for those who trust him, but rejects those who prefer to seek safety in Egypt. It piled-up metaphors experience when the Assyrians come and sweep away all possibility of security: hail, rising flood-waters, a scourge, boots to trample them down, as they try in vain to rest on a bed too short to lie down on, under sheets too narrow to cover them.

How far did the events of 701 BCE vindicate Isaiah's words? Two things are virtually certain. Firstly, Jerusalem was not actually captured by Sennacherib. The Assyrian troops went away without sacking the city, and an oracle in Isa. 22:12-14 probably refers to the population's reaction: 'Joy and gladness slaying oxen and killing sheep, eating flesh and drinking wine', But secondly, the context in which the city was thus 'delivered' was such as to make these celebrations 'the unforgettable day of Jerusalem's complacency as R.E. Clements calls it.

There is a much more difficult historical problem about the Assyrian crisis. It arises from the puzzling inconsistencies and duplications in the biblical narratives. The short account of the events of 701 in 2 Kings 18:13-18 does not appear in parallel account in Isa. 36-37, except for the introductory verse ('In the fourteenth Year of King Hezekiah, Sennacherib King of Assyria came up against all the fortified cities of Judah and took them'). This account is broadly confirmed by Sennacherib's own annals (ANET. pp. 287-88). The account which does appear, which is also in Kings, is along and rambling one. It culminates in a miraculous deliverance of Jerusalem and the death of the Assyrian army through the agency of the angel of Yahweh' (Isa. 37:36). The Assyrian official, the Rabshakeh, makes two speeches in very similar words (Isa. 36:4-20 and 37:10-13), Hezekiah twice consults Yahweh through Isaiah (37:1-4 and 37:14-20), and Isaiah twice Prophesies the deliverance of the city (37:5-7 and 37:21-35).

The events of Isaiah's life were complex, as the political allegiances of the State of Judah shitted and adapted to accommodate the realities of Assyrian Power. His message, however, was remarkably simple and unchanging. It concentrated on a pure trust in Yahweh; which the ones believed must exclude all human attempts at self-defence and self-determination- whether these took the form of military preparations or appeals for help to one of the great powers.

ii) Theology and Preaching of Isaiah

A study of the background to the preaching of the Prophet has already raised a number of matters concerning his particular theology. That he was a citizen of Jerusalem, born and brought up in the city, has clearly pointed us to the main setting of his understanding of God and his relationship to Israel. His favourite title for God is 'the 'Holy one of Israel' (1:4 etc.), and this immediately draws our attention a major feature of his whole outlook. Yahweh was the God of 'Israel' and by this the prophet quite evidently understood both Kingdoms, Ephraim and Judah to be referred to (cf. 5:7; 8:14), so that the prophet is concerned about both Israel and Judah. Isaiah began his ministry at a time when the relationship between Judah and Israel was hostile than any other time (of. 7:17). He found himself confronted with a King, Ahaz who was bent on betraying this historic unity between the two Kingdoms still further by appealing to Assyria to rescue him from the sister Kingdoms in the north.

It is not surprising therefore that Isaiah should have felt able to affirm that the peoplc whom God had once owned as 'my people' had become a band of rebels, whom he only describe as 'this people' (cf. 6:9). Even the reigning King of Judah, in whose days he began to prophesy, had the Davidic heritage of ruling with a regard for all Israel. He played politics against the interests of God's people. Especially was this true Ahaz, whom Isaiah regards as having betrayed the very foundation of the throne of David. He had greater hopes for Hezekiah (cf. 9:2-7), although these were destined never to be realized so far as the remains of the Northern Kingdom were concerned (cf. 9:8). Nonetheless, the sense that in God's eyes both 'houses' of Ephraim and Judah formed only one People Israel established a basis for all Isaiah's preaching. In his eyes the royal claims of the Davidic family belonged within this 'all Israel' perspective.

It is within this broader perspective that we must understand the special significance with both the temple Jerusalem and the Davidic royal dynasty had for Isaiah. They were institutions which belonged to the entire nation. At no Point does Isaiah appear to have considered either of them to be entirely indispensable to the purposes of God with Israel. So we must dismiss completely any suggestion that he regarded Jerusalem as inviolable on account of the presence of God in the temple there, or the Davidic dynasty as irreplaceable. They each fulfilled a purpose in the plans of Yahweh, but this was open to the realities of each historical situation, as God made his intentions known regarding it.

Isaiah's theology therefore operating within this place, primarily looks critically at the making of foreign alliances. We have already presented a detailed picture on this in our discussion on the historical background. From this point on the reader is expected to consult the material on previous section in Isaiah.

Of the 66 Chapters of Isaiah chps. 40-55 (Deutero-Isaiah) and 56-66 (Trito-Isaiah) must in any case be separated off. It is only in chapters 1-39 that utterances of the prophet Isaiah are contained. In Isaiah 1-39 a three-element eschatological scheme can be seen, though not without a few difficulties in the material: Isa. 1-12 chapters contain predominantly sayings against Isaiah's own nation, 13-23 chapters are sayings against other nations and 24-35 chapters are prophecies of salvation:36-39 chapters are biographical appendix. If we view thecontents in terms of eschatological point, we can witness a powerful drama, which leads through a renewed threat to Jerusalem, in the result of the nations to its eternal liberations and glorification. The picture of the threat and the deliverance of the Jerusalem in 701 formed by tradition in the Isaiah legends in chps. 36 and 37 is thus made the antitype of the events of 587 and at the same time the model for the eschatological event.

The collection in Chps. 1-12 is evidently meant to outline a particular picture of the prophet Isaiah. On the other hand, he is the prophet of judgement of Israel, on Jerusalem, on the leading classes and on the royal house itself; here the focal point hisis meeting with king Ahaz and his vain attempt to move the king to hold fast to the divine promises about Jerusalem and the royal house (7:1-9). On the other hand, he is the prophet of future salvation for Israel, for Jerusalem and for the dynasty of David. Here it becomes quite evident that these promises will come into force after the fulfilment of the announcements of judgements; this is also demonstrated by the position of the words of promise (2:1-5, 4:2-6, 9:1-6 11:1-16) within the individual subsidiary collections (see also 6:11).

The structure of Isaiah 24-35 are clearly recognizable chapters 24-27 is often called the Isaiah apocalypse. Chapters 28-32 are designated as an Assyrian cycle is meant to express the origin of the majority of the texts in the time of Assyrianrule. We can see historical references in the threat to Samaria (2821-4) the warring against a coalition with the Egypt (30: 1-5, 31:1-3), the mention of Assyria (30:31, 31:8) and threat to Jerusalem (29:1-8, 31:48).

iii) Isaiah 40-55 (Deutero-Isaiah)

It is now almost universally recognised that Isaiah 40 ff cannot come from the prophet with whom chp. 1-39 are concerned. The situation which is initially the setting of chp. 40-55 is fundamentally different. Israel is in captivity, far from its homeland and is promised comfort and speedy deliverance. There can be hardly any doubt this is a reference to the Babylonian exile: that is suggested above all by the mention of the name of Cyrus the Persian king. (44:28, 45:1).

In spite of the anonymity of authorship, Isa. 40-45, display a marled independence and coherence in form and theological expression. The texts of the various genres all serve the one main purpose which is already formulated in the prologue (40:1-11) to proclaim to the Judeans bring in exile that this 'forced labour' is at an end (vv. 1 f) that Yahweh will bring them on a way through the wilderness (vv. 3-5) to Jerusalem and lead those are freed from exile like a shepherd (vv. 9:11). This is confirmed in the epilogue (55:8-13) Yahweh's word will come about, (vv. 10 ff) and those who are freed will return home in joy to the Jubilation of creation (vv. 12 f).

This so called servant songs pose a special problem in the book of Deutero-Isaiah. B. Duhm had singled out the sections 42:1-4, 49:1-6, 50: 4-9; 52: 13-53: 12) as 'Ebed Yahweh' songs and attributed them to a later author. Since then this hypothesis has held almost undisputed sway (though some exegetes extend the first song to 42:1-9, the second to 49: 1-12 and the third to (50: 4-11) and this has become one of the most discussed themes of the OT scholarship, though without leading to any tangible or even generally recognised results.

a) Historical Background: In 587 B.C.E the tiny Kingdom of Judah, the survivor of the two Kingdoms into which the united Kingdom of Israel had been split at the death of Solomon, succumbed to the military Power of the neo-Babylonian empires despite its traditional confidence in its special relationship with its God Yahweh, but in accordance with the Predictions of Prophets such as Jeremiah and Ezekiel, its capital Jerusalem Pillaged and burnt, the King and many high officials executed, and the whole apparatus of government brought to an end. Of those who survived, many including the former leaders of the nation, were deported to Babylonia. A substantial portion of the population, however, remained. The deportation of 587 B.C. was only one of several. There had been a previous one, following an earlier Babylonian Campaign, in 597 BC (II Kings 24:10-17), and another was to follow in 582 B.C. (Jer 52:28:30).

Deutero-Isaiah's Prophetic ministry was exercised during the period following 587 B.C.E, which is generally known as the Babylonian Exile. That is during the half century between the fall of Jerusalem and the conquest of Babylonian scene establishes beyond reasonable doubt that he was one of the exiles in Babylon. His career, however, falls in the latter Part of the Period. As has already been noted, he was familiar with the name of Cyrus, whom he regarded as the man destined by Yahweh to conquer Babylon and to release the Jewish exiles. Throughout his extant oracles he regarded these events as imminent. But in order to understand the situation in which he exercised his ministry it is necessary to survey the history of the Preceding half century.

In 587 B.C.E the Power of Nee-Babylonian Empire was at its Peak. But it was not destined to be of long duration. Nebuchadnezzar, the conqueror of Jerusalem was its greatest King; and a decline began soon after his death in 562 BCE. In 556 B.C.E, after a Period of confusion, the Babylonians Placed on the throne one Nabu:na'id (Nabonidus) a native of Harran Nabonidus caused divisions in the state by his antagonism towards the cult of Marduk, the patron on deity of the city of Babylon, and its Powerful Priesthood. He revived the cultus of other God's whose worship had a special devotion to the god Sin, the god of his native city Harran.

For about eight years (552-545), Nabonidus, for some reason left the capital, Babylon, and set up his court in the oasis of Teima in the north Arabian desert. The absence of King in the capital not only caused confusion in the administration of the court in Babylon which is a serious problem in view of the Medes and the Persians Posing a severe threat to the empire, but also, the absence of the king in the capital means, no celebration of the New Year festival, which resulted in a terrible calamity to the Babylon (a view held strongly by the natives of Babylon).

The external menace to the empire had begun with the increasing power of the people known as Medes, in view of this, Nabonidus allied himself with Cyrus, King of Persia, against Medes, but in 550 B.C.E Cyrus, who was a vassal king within the Median empire, defeated the Median army without Babylonian assistance and found himself master of the Median empire.

Nabonidus now realised that it was the Persians who were the real enemy. Now he desperately made an alliance with the only two powers of consequence at that time, Egypt, then ruled by Amasis, and the Lydia, in the western Asia Minor whose king was Croesus. But in 547 B.C.E Cyrus conquered Lydia. In 545 Nabonidus returned to Babylon, and celebration of the New Year Festival was resumed. In the years which followed Cyrus was absent from the scene, occupied with conquests elsewhere. But in 539

B.C.E, his army arrived at the gates of Babylon. Cyrus now claimed to be the deliverer of the Population from Nabonidus, and to be the true patron of their god Marduk whom Nabonidus had neglected. Cyrus had not miscalculated. The citizens of Babylon surrendered without a struggle and welcomed the conqueror, who took the titles of a Babylonian King and restored Marduk to his traditional position of honour. The neo-Babylonian Empire had come to an end swallowed up in the greater Persian Empire the city of Babylon continued to flourish, but now as a mere provincial city.

During this time the Jewish exiles in Babylon seem to have been well aware of the trend of political and military events. Most of the Jews in exile did not really took note of the developments with eagerness, because it matters nothing to them and they also thought that their condition will be same as before. But they may have been aware that the Cyrus, unlike the Assyrians and the Babylonians, did not make use of mass deportations as an instrument of policy. Deutero-Isaiah, however, took note of all these developments seriously. The meteoric career of Cyrus made a profound impression on him, and he delivered a number of oracles in which he predicted that Cyrus would overthrow Babylon and release the Jewish exilie's. (41:2-4; 41:25; 44:28; 45:1-6; 45:13; 46:11; 48:14-15). In a way contrary to Deutero-Isaiah's expectation, Cyrus did not destroy the city of Babylon (see especially chap.47), rather Cyrus made the city more splendid than ever. But Cyrus did allow the Jewish exiles to return home if they wished, though not in the triumphant manner which Deutero-Isaiah expected.

With all this information, now we may date the ministry of Deutero-Isaiah mainly in the years of 550-539 B.C.E, and probably towards the end of that Period. This again clearly indicates that Deutero-Isaiah is addressing to the Jewish exiles of second generation. The exiles in Babylonian become despondent and discouraged due to the non-fulfilment of the words of Jeremiah and Ezekiel. There seems to be a tendency that they will no more be delivered from the clutches of the Babylonian oppression (through in a real sense it in not, like the Egyptians bondage). To such people, who were in a state of confusion and discouragement, Deutero-Isaiah brings out his message with a Positive note of their future deliverance.

b) Forms of Speech in Deutero-Isaiah: Based on the form-critical analysis following are the important types of speech used by the Deutero-Isaiah. We shall discuss on few of them:

1) The oracle of Salvation: According to von Waldow (1953), some of the oracles of Deutero-Isaiah Point to an actual cultic setting: their initial words like quotations of phrases, or even whole sections, taken from lamentations which had actually been recited by the exile's at their meetings for worship. In other words, Deutero-Isaiah had picked up these self-pitying epithets and appeals for help, and, speaking in the name of Yahweh, had assured the

Petitioners that their situation was now to be radically transformed. Thus 49:14 makes a specific reference to the recital of such a lamentation: "But Zion has said, "Yahweh has forsaken me, my Lord has forgotten me"! 51:9-10 similarly is quotation from such a lamentation. reminding Yahweh of his great deeds in the Past and appealing for a further display of his power now, In other examples, prophet, in addressing his audience, picked up phrases which they had evidently applied to themselves in describing their state of distress: 'You worm Jacob" (41:14): 'You whose heart fails, who are far from deliverance' (46: 12); 'to one deeply despised' (49:7); 'You who have drunk from Yahweh's hand the cup of his wrath' (51:17); 'O barren one, who did not bear' (54:1). Much of this language is similar to the Psalms of lament and the language of lamentations in the Book of Lamentations, which are themselves lamentations of the people from the exilic period (in Palestine, not Babylonia).

According to Claus Westermann the promises of salvation in Deutero-Isaiah are not numerous, and almost all occur within chapters 41-44. They comprise 41:8-13; 41:14-16; general, a strict pattern whose cultic origins are shown by their similarity to examples of Babylonian oracles addressed by priests to kings in answer to their prayers.

According to Westermann's analysis of 41:14-16, the following are the elements of structure found in it.

(i) The address: 'You worm Jacob, you lose Israel' (14a) compare 41:8, 9; 43:1a; 44:1. The address is missing in 43; 5-7 and 54:4-6.

(ii) The assurance of salvation: "Fear not!" (14a) this Phrase, which occurs in all the promises of salvation (also in 41:10; 43:1; 43:5; 44:2b; 54:4) is in itself an assurance that the petitioner's prayers will be answered, since it is spoken as Yahweh's own authoritative word; it may occur either at the beginning of the address or immediately after it.

(iii) The basis of the assurance: (1) "I will help you" says Yahweh; (2) 'the Holy one of Israel is your Redeemer (14b), Here, Yahweh substantiates his word of assurance, answering the appeals for help by affirming his Presence, his intimate relationship with the Petitioners, and the fact that he is already taking steps to help them. In four cases (here and in 43:1; 43:5; 54:4) this section is introduced by the explanatory particle **ki**, 'For'. It may consist one or both of two elements: a statement about Yahweh's relationship to the petitioner (here 'the Holy one of Israel is your Redeemer' elsewhere 'For your Maker... is your Redeemer', 54: 5) and a statement in the perfect tense (indicating certainty) that Yahweh is about to help and is already helping (here 'I will help you'; elsewhere 'I will strengthen You..,' 41:10b; 'I will redeem you...', 43:1b). This section is lacking in 44:1-5.

(iv) The consequences of Yahweh's action: expressed more concretely and in greater detail, mainly in future (imperfect) tenses: vv.15, 16a. Compare 41:11, 12; 43:2; 43;5-6; 44:3-5; 54:4.

(v) Yahweh's ultimate Purpose: vs.16b. This can be seen clearly only in two of the other oracles: 43:7, 44:5.

Even though these things suggested by Westermann are useful, some of them are still disputed by the scholars, i.e., the announcement of salvation Westermann further clarifies that some more elements in it are:

(i) Allusion to a previous lamentation;
(ii) Announcement of salvation: God's turning to his People; Gog intervention;
(iii) God's ultimate purpose.

2) The Hymn: One important feature of Israel's worship in the days when the Temple at Jerusalem was still in use was the Hymn or Psalm, of Praise in which the assembled people, at the major festivals of the Year, offered their Praise to Yahweh. Some of these hymns are quite elaborate; but (basically their structure was very simple, consisting of only two parts: first, a summons to Praise, usually expressed in the imperative mood but sometimes in the cohortative ('Let us....'), and addressed to Israel' alone but sometimes to the Peoples of the world, or even to the whole created universe; and secondly a statement about Yahweh's benevolence towards his people or about the consequences of that benevolence-his great deeds performed in the Past in creation or in history. This section, the main section of the hymn, is often introduced by the word **ki**, 'For' since it states the reason why praise should be offered. This simple structure is well illustrated by Ps. 117;

"Praise Yahweh all nations! Extol him, all Peoples! For great is his steadfast love towards us; and the faithfulness of Yahweh endures for ever".

The style of Deutero-Isaiah, was greatly influenced throughout by that of these liturgical hymns. There are complete hymns within this book; three examples are; 42:10-13; 44:23; 49:13. The last of these runs as follows: "Sing for joy, o heavens, and exalt, o earth; break forth, o mountains, in singing! For Yahweh has comforted his people, and has compassion for his afflicted". (49:13). Westermann calls these hymns as 'eschatological Psalms of Praise (he does not use the word hymn) on the grounds of their form as well as of their function: according to him it is only these psalms (of which a few are to be found in other Prophetical books) that the summons to worship is followed by a statement Yahweh's actions rather than about his Personal qualities (as in Ps.117).

In addition to this group of complete hymns, there are many Phrases and stylistic devices of the hymn. The most striking examples of this are the Passages (eg. 42:5; 43:1; 43:16-17; 44:2; 45:18) in which he describes the nature and activity, especially the creative activity, of Yahweh in a series of

Participial clauses (usually rendered in English translations by 'who…'). A good example of this is 42:5:

"Thus says God, Yahweh, who created the heavens and stretched them out, who spread forth and what grows from it, who gives breath to the People on it, and spirit to, those who walk on it..."

cf. other texts in Psalms: 103:3-5; 104:1-4; 136:4-7; 147:8-9, 14-17 Unlike psalms, however, in Deutero-Isaiah the messenger formula is used to proclaim the prophetic message by the phrase 'Thus says Yahweh'. Here also their function is to (like Psalms) evoke those sentiments of awe and dependence on Yahweh as the creator of the world and creator and sustainer of Israel of which the cultic hymns had been the expression and which the exiles were in danger of losing, but which were indispensable if they were to be convinced by the promise of help which was to following in the ensuring oracle of salvation.

Sometimes such descriptions of Yahweh's nature and activity are placed in the mouth of Yahweh himself, so that he is represented as praising himself, as in 46:9-10.

" .... For I am God, and there is no other, I am God, and there is none like me, declaring the end from the beginning and from ancient times things not yet done, saying, 'My counsel shall stand, and I will accomplish all my Purpose..."

Other passages in which Yahweh Praises himself include 41:4b; 42:8; 43:10-13; 44:24-28; 45:6-7; 48:12-13; 51:15.

3) The Trial scene: Deutero-Isaiah had to deal with an audience which was reluctant to accept his message as authentic. Consequently, he was obliged to take on the role of Yahweh's advocate, attempting to substantiate his central message by means of argument. Such arguments are to be found in what A. Schoors calls 'the Polemical genres' in the book: forms of speech to which different scholars have given various names, of which perhaps the most appropriate are the 'trial scene' (*Gerichtsszene*) and the 'disputation' (*Disputationswort*): Their *Sitz im Leben* (setting in life) is unlikely to have been that of public worship.

The device of the trial scene had been used by earlier prophets (eg. Isa 3:13-15; Micah 6:1-5) to give additional effectiveness to their oracles of Judgment against Israel by planning them in the fictitious setting of a court of law. This procedure is probably based on the ordinary legal procedures in use in Pre-exilic Israel. (cf. Jer. Chap. 26).

Deutero-Isaiah used the form of the trial scene mainly for the purpose: to demonstrate the worthlessness of the God's worshiped by the other nations. The 'trial' here seems not so much are the foreign nations and their God's; and the question at the issue is, 'who is the true God?', this is the of Deutero-Isaiah is most characteristic types of argument.

Deutero-Isaiah records at least five clear examples of the kind of trial scene: 41:1-5; 41:21-29; 43:8-13; 44:6-8 -21-22; 45:20-25. 41:21-29 maybe taken as a model in which a number of the constitutive elements appear. The language vs.21, which sets the scene, it clearly that of the law court. Yahweh is presiding judge, though he is also one of the parties in dispute, the other side consists pagan God's. These are addressed and asked to present proofs of their activity and thus effectively of their existence vss. 22-23 state the nature of the matter in dispute and the kind of evidence to be admitted. But the god's are shown by their silence to be non-existent. Yahweh then presents, his own case, which is the main reason for the use of the device of the trial scene (vv. 25-28) and reaches his conclusion. The concluding Judgement in v.29 is that the other so-called god's have no existence.

A similar pattern but with slightly different features is followed in the other examples, 41:1 gives a fuller account of the setting. 43:9-12 mentions the witnesses: the nations on one side, Israel on the other. 44:6-8-21-22 ends somewhat differently from the others, with a divine promise to Israel (v.22). But all these trial scenes are intended to leave the exiles with the impression that Yahweh is firmly in charge of events.

4) The disputation: The disputation is a form of argument in which the speaker is usually not Yahweh but the prophet:

Westermann pointed out that Deutero-Isaiah had a predilection of one kind of argument in particular: the argument which proceeds by analogy. The speaker begins by stating a fact about which his audience would be in agreement a self-evident fact which either is a matter of common sense or forms part of the common religious tradition of Israel which no one would dispute; From this he proceeds, by means of analogy, to state a proposition which his audience had not previously been prepared to accept.

So in 40:12-17 and 40:18-26 the prophet argues from the Israelite belief that Yahweh is the creator of the world to the proposition that he must therefore be the one who controls historical persons and events. In 40:27-31 he argues from Yahweh's almightiness to the proposition that he can make to the weary and the dispirited exiles all the strength which they need. In 45:9-13 he argues from the common sense proposition that it is absurd for a created absurd for a created abject like a pot to criticise the potter who made it, or for a foetus to question its parents, to the proposition that it is equally nonsensical for Israel to question Yahweh, their maker, about his plans. And in 55:8-11 he argues from the regularly and inevitability of the fertilising power of the rain sent from heaven by Yahweh to the Proposition that Yahweh's word spoken by the prophets equally cannot fail to achieve purpose for which it was Sent. There are other passages in Deutero-Isaiah which take arguments, in different lines, passages, such as: 46:9-11, 48:1-11, 48:12-16.

c) The Main Theological message of Deutero-Isaiah: Before we consider the detailed study of several important theological themes in Deutero-Isaiah such as: The servant of Yahweh, Uniqueness of God, Sovereignty over the nations, understanding of history, election and covenant, comfort and hope, the word of God and other themes, let us briefly present the central message of the Prophet.

The central message of Deutero-Isaiah is neatly summarised in the scene in the heavenly council (40:1-8). Its essential features are:

i) The exiled people are to take heart because their sins now have been expiated and their term of punishment is over (vv.1-2).
ii) Yahweh is now about to come to the aid of his People in such a decisive fashion that the whole world will be astonished at this revelation of his glory (vv.3-5).
iii) The guarantee of this message of hope and restoration is the word of Yahweh spoken through the prophet, which is all-powerful and compared with which all human activity is ludicrously impotent (vv.6-8).

Having state this, now let us move on to consider some of the important theological concerns of Deutero-Isaiah in which his message is still grasped in depth.

1) The Servant of Yahweh: Is one of the special features of the oracles of Deutero-Isaiah that Israel as a nation is frequently referred to as Yahweh's 'servant' or 'slave' ('ebed). This epithet of Israel, though peculiar to Deutero-Isaiah, does not call for special remark. It is used in the Old Testament to God's children such as: Abraham, Moses, David, etc. Deutero-Isaiah's designation of the nation Israel as Yahweh's servant is an example of his general tendency to personify the nation as a single individual. He used this term especially in the salvation oracles (eg: 41:8-10) to remind the exiles of their special relationship with Yahweh and so give them confidence in his good will towards them.

There are, however, a number of other passages which speak of a Servant of Yahweh but do not unmistakably identity him with Israel. The interpretation of these servant songs is a matter of debate and scholars continue to bring out new proposals on this matter. We shall briefly summarise some of the opinions:

In 1892, Bernhard Duhm put the interpretation of the Servant Songs in a new and precise way. He singled out four passages: 42;1-4; 49:1-6; 50:4-9; 52:13-53:12 in which a single individual "Servant of Yahweh" is to be seen, sharply distinguishing these from the reminder of the book, in which the Servant is Israel. These four passages he called 'Servant Songs' (Ebed-Lieder). The identity of the Servant with an 'individual' is questioned by other scholars, although the number of passages for the Servant Songs is not disputed much.

B. Duhm also found that the servant songs are different in their language and in their content. The difference with other songs in Deutero-Isaiah is also noted. Some poems picture Israel as the servant. But in the servant's songs except in 49:3, nowhere it has been mentioned that Israel is the servant. The servant of the other songs is different from that is mentioned in the servant songs. For example, the servant Israel become weary (40:27: 41;12). The servant of Yahweh was from the beginning dis-obedient (48:4). in the other songs the servant is pictured as the only person who receives salvation (49:5,6; 53:12). In the servant songs the foreigners were looked upon with compassion. But in other songs they were looked very unwantedly.

However, these arguments can be repudiated on the following grounds: Though the content and style differ in servant songs with other poems, the author is mentioning about two different servants; In 41:9; 48:2, Israelites were called as "God's witnesses" therefore we can say that the Israelites had a mission. To do so the task of Israel is not only to receive salvation, but as a chosen minority to serve as servants for a majority of People (47:5,6).

The main contention however, is the interpretation of the Servant. i.e., whom the writer of Deutero-Isaiah had in mind when he spoke of the Servant of the Lord. We shall briefly present the different interpretations on the Servant and his identity.

(a) Collective interpretations: The view that the Servant is a personification of the people of Israel is a very ancient interpretation. Apart from the explicit identification in 49:3, its main strength lies in the resemblance between the events of the Servants career-call, special status before Yahweh, suffering, imminent restoration and (according to one interpretation) mission to the world. But a number of objections are raised against the identification of the Servants with Israel.

i) In 49:5-6 the Servant refers to a divine commission which he has received to restore Israel's fortunes. This is a difficult concept if the Servant and Israel are identical: Again in 53:1-6 the speakers ('we') refer to the things which the Servant ('he') has done for them. The view that they are the foreign nations and Kings mentioned in 52:15 is difficult to reconcile with their confession in 53:46, which appears to imply that they are representatives, or at least members, of the People of Israel. But if this is so, the servant cannot himself he the embodiment of the nation.

ii) in the songs the Servant is represented as completely devoted to the service of Yahweh as a wholly innocent sufferer. This Is in marked contrast with what Deutero-Isaiah says elsewhere about Israel, which according to him has thoroughly deserved its punishment. If the Servant of the songs were a Personification of a nation, Deutero-Isaiah's whole message would appear inconsistent.

iii) Apart from the occurrence of the word "Israel" in 49:3, the Servant is never named in the Songs. It appears to be taken for granted that his identity is known to those addressed. Such an absence of identification by name is extremely rare in Old Testament passages in which a corporate entity is personified. But particularly significant is the absence of such identification in the two songs (49:1-6 and 50:4-9) in which the Servant himself is the speaker. In the prophetical books it may be assumed that, speech in the first Person singular other than that of Yahweh is that of the prophet himself, unless the contrary is specifically indicated by the naming of another speaker in an introductory phrase (eg. 'But Zion said; 49:14) or in the body of the speech, or by the context that a personified Israel should be the speaker in these two songs without any such specific indication is therefore improbable.

The difficulties attending the simple identification of the Servant in the songs with Israel led some scholars (eg. S.R. Driver, Skinner, Blank) to suggest that he stands for a section of the nation: a righteous remnant 'ideal Israel', or something similar. Although this is a plausible theory, we can hardly accept it because no such distinction of 'remnant' made with in the nation by Deutero-Isaiah.

An attempt was made by H.W. Robinson and O. Eissfeldt (1932-33), Working separately, to reconcile the Portrayal of the servant as an individual with the corporate features observable both in the songs and outside, by means of the concept which Robinson called **corporate personality**. According to this theory the prophets, 'Primitive Psychology' enabled him to speak now of himself and now of Israel as the servant of Yahweh: The servant can be both the prophet himself as representative of the nation and the nation whose proper mission is actually being fulfilled only by the prophet and that group of followers who may share his views. But this hypothesis is seriously questioned.

The most recent of the corporate theories is proposed by Eaton, who, while pointing to certain supposed royal characteristics of the servant in the songs, believes that he stands, not for any individual king, but for the Davidic dynasty. His theory depends on the view that the pre-exilic autumnal festival as celebrated in Judah had included a rite in which the Davidic King was ritually humiliated and then restored to his throne. This theme together with others drawn from the festival, was used in Deutero-Isaiah's oracles as a symbol of the fate of the whole Davidic dynasty: after a period of divine favour it had been humiliated by the exile, but was about to be restored by Yahweh. The main message of the book is the coming restoration of the nation, after humiliation, by a divine act of salvation; and the restoration of Davidic monarchy is an integral part and symbol of this restoration. Apart from its dependence on a particular and disputed interpretation of the autumn festival this theory makes two assumptions which need further substantiation: that the Servant of the songs is in fact primarily described in royal terms; and that the fate of the

Davidic dynasty (explicitly referred to only in 55:3-5) played a significant role in the thought of Deutero-Isaiah as a whole.

b) Individual interpretations: The wealth and variety of the imagery employed in the songs to describe the Servant's character and role have provided the basis for a wide range of interpretations of the figure as an individual. Different scholars have seen him as a new Moses, as a Prophet, 4 as a teacher of the law and as much else besides.

The studies of Gressmann, Engnell and Nyberg based on the ancient Near Eastern myths, especially the myth of the dying and rising God and its supposed re-enactment in fertility cults supposed that one version of this type of theory is applicable to the description in chapter 53 of the humiliation and subsequent restoration of the Servant is a prediction of a Messianic figure, whose career and functions are expressed in terms derived from the sequence of events in the cultic myth of Tammuz. This myth could have been familiar to Deutero-Isaiah either directly through Babylonian sources or through Canaanizing elements in the pre-exilic cult of Jerusalem. Theories of this kind have however lost support in recent years because the evidence both for the existence of a cult of a dying and rising God for influence of this kind on the Israelite cult of Yahweh now appears very fragile.

There remains the possibility that the Servant was a contemporary of Deutero-Isaiah, well Known to him and to his audience. Duhm, Mowinckel (at one time) and more recently G.R. Driver believed that he was an anonymous contemporary of the author of the Songs of whom no mention is made elsewhere in the Old Testament. It would, however, be strange if a person so remarkable and so important to the author of the songs had remained anonymous and had left no other memorial. However, if the servant was a member of Deutero-lsaiah's own generation, there is an alternative possibility: that he was none other than *the prophet himself*. But this is very old theory.

What evidence do the songs offer in support of this theory? The evidence that the Servant was a prophet is strong. In 42:1-4 the terms in which Yahweh affirms his choice of the Servant, promises to support him in his assigned task, and assures him of success despite opposition suggest the commissioning of a prophet and are strongly reminiscent of the calls of Jeremiah (1:8, 17:19) and of Ezekiel (2:3-7; 3:4-11). Again, like Jeremiah (1:5, 10) the servant is to be Yahweh's instrument in the establishment of his sovereignty over the nations. This song, however is not the call-narrative (which is found in 40:1-8) but a subsequent oracle continuing the prophet's claim to speak with Yahweh's authority.

In 52:13-53:12, it may be inferred from the astonishment of the speakers (53:1) that an even later stage in the career of the servant has been reached. After passing through such intense suffering and humiliation that he was regarded by others as singled out by Yahweh for a special punishment (vv.2-

4), he has now in some unexpected way been rescued by the intervention of the 'arm of Yahweh', if the servant in these lines is the prophet Deutero-Isaiah, then the prophecy may be regarding the release from a Babylonian prison, consequent on the fall of Babylon to Cyrus.

Not all the scholars who identify the servant with Deutero-Isaiah himself accept the above interpretation of the final song. The traditional view that the song was composed after his death by his followers still commands support 53:7-9 are held to refer to his death, while 53:10b-12 promise his future resurrection.

Against the identification of the servant with Deutero-Isaiah or indeed with any merely human figure - it has been argued that the servant's character and role especially as described in chapter 53, for transcend those conceivable of ordinary humanity. Some would answer this issue by saying that the servant transcends the suffering of an ordinary human being: in his supposed role 'vicarious sufferer', certain Christian exegetes interpret this as the suffering of the servant vicariously for others: that is, through his own unmerited suffering he enabled others to escape the divine punishment which they had deserved.

The statements made from Isa 53:9b are to be seen in the context of the life and times of Deutero-Isaiah. It is clear that he was an exceptionally righteous man and that his exceptional suffering was understand. They were caused solely by the fact, that he had accepted the prophetic office and so undertaken the Proclamation of a politically dangerous message: the prophecy of the fall of Babylon. He thus bore the sins of many not in the sense of suffering instead of the many-as we have noted, was not the case, but of enduring additional and exceptional suffering. This suffering, as in the case of other prophets, was the consequence of the nation's sin, for it was the nation's plight which had made his prophetic activity necessary. At the same time, it could be said that his sufferings led to their restoration to 'wholeness' or their 'healing-that is, to' their release from exile: for had he not preserved in his dangerous work at the risk of suffering and death, the divine word which, like a sharp sword in Yahweh's hand, brought about the fall of Babylon would not have been pronounced.

The portrait of the Servant of Yahweh which emerges from the songs on the basis of the above interpretation is not one of a person who transcends ordinary humanity, but of an exceptionally faithful prophet of Yahweh who, like his Predecessor Jeremiah, endured great suffering in the course of his ministry but also experienced the intervention of Yahweh on his behalf to deliver him from danger. His ministry was entirely bound up with the life of his people, and it may well be that his rescue from death was regarded by those who composed chapter 53 as the turning-point in the fortunes of their community.

2) Uniqueness of God: In spite of their traditional belief, expressed in Psalms and creation-narratives, that Yahweh was the creator of the world, the Jewish exiles in Babylon, surrounded by the grandiose worship of the Babylonian God's, to whom of course the Babylonians attributed their conquests, were easily tempted to wonder whether their own beliefs were mistaken: Whether their humiliation was due to Yahweh's having been defeated by God's more powerful than himself. These doubts would have been nourished by the celebration of the annual New Year Festival at Babylon, a festival which commemorated the creation of the world by Marduk, his installation as King of the God's, and the supremacy, of his city, Babylon. Although, the actual rites of this festival were celebrated in private, there were public processions along the great sacral way, and the festival was the occasion of Public rejoicing. Moreover, it is probable that the Babylonian creation myths such as the 'Creation Epic' (Enuma Elish) which describes Marduk's exploits, were familiar to the ordinary citizens through public recitation. Festivals and myths alike must have seemed to the Jewish exiles to correspond to the political reality of Babylon's supremacy.

The question is: how could, Deutero-Isaiah combat the effects of this pro-Marduk propaganda? All that the prophet could do was to set the mythological tradition of Babylon against the more sober theological tradition of Israel, and to attempt to show in point after point that the latter was more credible (Yahweh) than the former (Marduk). In addition to rational argument, he also used his poetical skill to evoke the mood of joyful confidence in Yahweh's incomparable power and majesty which had been the keynote of the Judean festival cult in the days when Yahweh's Kingship had been celebrated in Jerusalem. It was in this context, Deutero-Isaiah produced some of his finest poems.

In 40: 12-31, he used the disputation form as a vehicle for his argument, In the first of these disputations (vv.12-17) he restated the Israelite creation tradition in a series of rhetorical questions creation in order to make the point that if it is indeed Yahweh who created the world of nature with such skill (vv.12-14) he must also possess absolute control over his human creatures, and so over the historical process. (vv.15-17).

This disputation also puts forward an argument to show that the Israelite creation tradition itself is superior to that of Babylon. In vv.13-14 the question is asked, rhetorically, Whether Yahweh had needed help to carry out his work of creation. This is an indirect allusion to the Babylonian polytheistic tradition such as is found in Enuma Elish, where **Marduk**, himself appointed as King by a 'committee' of 'God's', nevertheless received help in his creative work from the wise, **Ea**, his father, who is in fact alone credited in one Passage with the creation of humankind. None of the Babylonian God's therefore could be 'God' in an absolute sense as was Yahweh, to whom therefore Deutero-Isaiah can simply refer absolutely as 'God' (eg. in v.18). The implication is clear: the Israelite tradition of sole creator is the one which has the ring of truth.

In 40:21 comes a series of further questions, which are in fact reproaches: Deutero-Isaiah asks his audience how they can possibly be in any doubt Yahweh's incomparability. Surely they know their own tradition! In v.22 he reminds them of that tradition, using the participle style and vocabulary of the creation hymn. (cf. Ps.136 and 104, esp. 104:2b).

The concluding verse 40:26 about Yahweh and the heavenly bodies may at first seem to be an anti-climax; but in fact it is equally polemical. In Enuma Elish (Tablet V) the heavenly bodies are not Marduk's creatures: they are the great God's themselves. Marduk established them in the heavens with their prescribed, movements, but they were still God's. Against this polytheistic belief Deutero-Isaiah set the monotheistic Israelite tradition. The heavenly bodies are simply Yahweh's creatures. He uses the special word 'bara' 'create', here, a word which is used only of the divine creation, and so makes an absolute distinction between creator and creatures. Having created the heavenly bodies Yahweh put them, as it were, 'on Parade', bringing them out to shine 'by number! 'Not one is missing! Yahweh, then, really is incomparable: for him there are no divine rivals.

The polemic against Babylonian polytheism is taken up again in 43:10-13, Part of a trial scene (vv. 8-13) in which Yahweh is the speaker. Yahweh's claim, which Israel's traditional belief, is that "Before me no God was formed, nor shall there be any after me" (v.10). This is a clear allusion to Babylonian mythology, according to which Marduk belonged not to the first but to the fourth generation of God's (Enuma Elish, Tablet I), his father, Ea and his mother Damkina being mentioned by name. Marduk himself had children: so there were God's before Marduk was born, and God's after him. Deutero-Isaiah is, by implication, asking his audience which they would rather believe: the fairy-tale mythology of Babylon, or their own tradition of Yahweh who had existed since eternity and would always exist: the only God, without birth and without sexuality. The phrase 'I am He' (v. 13 and repeated frequently in other passages): means in effect 'I am the only one'. Deutero-Isaiah pursues the argument: the sole creator must also be the sole saviour: there is no other God to hinder him from saving his people. A similar point is made in 44:6-8; 44:24; 45:5; 46:9; 51:6.

The Israelite belief in Yahweh as creator is also made the basis of some of Deutero-Isaiah's other leading arguments. As has already be pointed out, he used it in 45:9-13 (a disputation in which Yahweh is the speaker) to defend Yahweh's right as creator to do whatever he wishes with his creatures, as does a potter with his pots or a father with his children. The point here, as the final verse makes clear, is Yahweh's choice of the foreign King Cyrus as his instrument in the salvation and restoration of Israel, a choice which will certainly have needed some defence. Other passage which affirms Yahweh's supremacy as creator is 54:16-17.

Deutero-Isaiah also used the doctrine of creation to support his teaching about the efficacy of the prophetic word. In 45:18-19 he began from the purposefulness of Yahweh's act of creation of the world: he created it not to be chaos but to be inhabited-a different view of mankind from that of Babylonians, for whom man's sole duty was to act as slave to the God's.

Thus, Deutero-Isaiah by using the Israelite creation traditions in a number of different ways is attempting to convince the exiles of the truth of his basic message of imminent salvation: he used them to expose the absurdity of Babylonian polytheism, to show that it was Yahweh who possesses sole control over world history, and to stimulate trust in Yahweh and in the word of promise which he was speaking through his prophet.

3) Deutero-Isaiah's Presentation of history: Israel's pre-exilic narrative traditions, now incorporated in the biblical books from Genesis to Kings: comprised accounts of Yahweh's great deeds in the past: his creation of the world, guidance of the human race in its infancy, and finally his creation of Israel as his special people and his subsequent dealings with them. The Babylonian exile, because this story had now been brought to an abrupt end, was a time for reflecting on the meaning of this history, bringing together the various strands of tradition into comprehensive and theologically oriented literary works, and attempting to draw lessons, and perhaps hope, for the future from it all. Deutero-Isaiah, who was evidently familiar with the earlier traditions has used them in quite different way, he used the material as an appeal to history which forms an additional argument to support his main message.

Other prophets before Deutero-Isaiah used examples from past history to illustrate their teaching, especially as dreadful warnings (Eg. Jezreel: Hos. 1:4: Sodom and Gomorrah: Isa. 1:10; the fall of Shiloh: Jer 7:12-15; Parables of Israel's history in Ezekiel). Deutero-Isaiah used his examples in various ways, but above all to remind the exiles of incidents in which Yahweh had shown power not in anger but in love towards humankind or to his people, so that his hearers could take heart and be brought to a state of mind in which they could accept that Yahweh was both able to perform such deeds once more.

To consider Deutero-Isaiah's usage of historical tradition, we shall look into few important ones as follows: In the use of the flood story (54:7-10), Yahweh is speaking. The question at issue is Yahweh's reliability. His aim is to persuade the exiles, who believe that, despite his covenant with them, he has forsaken them, that it is now his intention to return to them and to behave towards them with a love which will never cease: "My steadfast love shall not depart from you, my covenant of peace shall not be removed!" In order to convince them that he will keep the oath which he had sworn to them, he uses the analogy of the oath which he swore to Noah after the flood, that he would never again send a flood which would destroy humankind. That oath he has kept; he can therefore be relied on to keep the new one.

The next historical references are to Abraham (48:18-19) and in 51:1-3, the prophet, addressing a dispirited audience convinced that there is no hope for them in their wretched and depleted state, used the traditions of the miraculous parenthood of Abraham and Sarah and the marvellous gift to them of numerous and prosperous descendants to support the new promise and numerous population. What Yahweh once did for their ancestors he can and will now do for them. The description of Abraham (41:8-13) as Yahweh's 'friend' (literally, 'the one whom I loved'), which occurs again in II Chron. 20:7, reminds the exiles both of the intimacy and the constancy of Yahweh's love for them; which stretched back to their most remote ancestor.

The period of Israel's history from which Deutero-Isaiah most frequently drew lessons was that of Israel's beginnings: the release of the nation's ancestors from slavery in Egypt, their crossing of the Red Sea, and their journey, under Yahweh's guidance, through the wilderness. These events-often called as the 'Exodus events' - offered an obvious analogy to the picture which the prophet was presenting to the exiles of what was, about to happen to them. Deutero-Isaiah not only reminded the People of their past events in which Yahweh's greatness is manifested, but, he taught that the 'New Exodus' would be even more spectacular and lasting in its effects than the first Exodus; so much so that he could claim that Yahweh was saying (43:18-19): "Remember not the former things, nor consider the thing of old" Behold, I am doing a new thing".

In 52:11-12 the prophet gives a form of command to his fellow-exiles to begin their home. This is a projection into the future: he speaks as if Babylon has already fallen, or is falling, to Cyrus. They are to leave the city, preceded by the Ark on their wilderness Journeys (Numb. 10:33-35), the reference to the Exodus is even clearer in v.12. The departure from Egypt had taken place secretly, by night, and in haste. (The word 'haste' or 'hurried flight' (*hippazon*) used here occurs elsewhere in the Old Testament only in connection with the Exodus events-Exod.12:11, Deut 16:3). The departure from Babylon, on the other hand, will be more like a ceremonial procession.

Another clear allusion to the Exodus is to be found in the announcement of salvation in 43: 14-21. In vv.16-17, in a series of epithets attached to the messenger -formula, which refers in plain terms, closely following the account in Exod. 14:21-29, to God's action at the Red Sea, when the Israelites were enabled to cross on dry ground while the Egyptians were drowned. This is a Prelude to the admonition 'Remember not the former things.' The 'new Exodus' will be far more glorious. The oracle ends with the promise proper (vv. 1ad-21), which speaks of a repetition of the feeding of the people of old in the wilderness during the period after the crossing of the Red Sea, rendered even more marvellous by the motif of the homage of the animal world (vs.20). Here the theme of Yahweh's glory and its effect on the beholders' is a major theme of Deutero-Isaiah's. For Deutero-Isaiah the salvation of Israel was not an end itself. The ultimate Purpose was the manifestation of Yahweh's glory to the world. Deutero-Isaiah was clearly determined to turn the thoughts of the exiles away frown their preoccupation with themselves to a deeper acknowledgement of the transcendent Saviour-God. It is significant that three of these passages emphasize this theme: "And the glory of Yahweh shall be revealed" (40:5); "that men may see and know... that the hand of Yahweh has done it (41:20), "...they might declare my Praise" (43:21).

Deutero-Isaiah makes very few direct references to the Period of the monarchy. For him, like other prophets this was essentially a time of apostasy leading to the disruption of the kingdoms and to the exile, (52:3-6; 43:28). In 55:1-5, the reference to David is made. In this passage, Deutero-Isaiah speaks of an everlasting covenant which Yahweh will make with his people, and links this with God's 'steadfast, sure love for David', the great leader of the Past, whose greatness had been acknowledged by the surrounding nations. The mention of this 'golden age' of the time of David was intended to evoke the same feelings as were evoked by the references to Abraham: confidence that Yahweh who in the past had made Israel. Great and prosperous could and would now do so again. There is no promise here of the restoration of the Davidic dynasty rather it is the whole people who will now be united with Yahweh, as David had been in v the past, in an everlasting covenant.

As one looks back on this survey of Deutero-Isaiah's references to past history, it is clear that he had a remarkably detailed knowledge of the nation's historical traditions, and he used them in a special and creative way. Deutero-Isaiah was very much aware that, despite the terrible interval of the Exile, there was a continuity in Yahweh's dealings with his people: it was not Yahweh who had ceased to love and care for his people but Israel which had ceased to love Yahweh. Yahweh is consistently picture as always ready to demonstrate his love for Israel, and now even more abundantly than before.

4) Election and Covenant: Deutero-Isaiah's theological message is dominated by his Presentation of election, the theology of election in Deutero-Isaiah takes a totally new and radical approach Deutero-Isaiah's message is primarily directed to the Babylonian exiles, who confronted with the might of Babylonian Power. Therefore, the prophet wanted to assure them of a great comfort. Israel too was seeking God's abundant grace in this time of trouble. By combining two themes, i.e., creation and election, Deutero-Isaiah at this time addresses the discouraged People. By using certain selected vocabulary, the Prophet comforts the people: "Fear not", "I redeem", "I strengthen You", "I am with You", "You are mine" (Isa: 41:10,13; 43:1,5; 44:2ff). Deutero-Isaiah affirms the fact that Yahweh is on their side. For Deutero-Isaiah, it is the election that precedes creation in the sense that at the time of exile whom people pondered over their situation as "the elect" evokes them to reflect upon creation.

Some of the crucial passages in which Deutero-Isaiah brings out the election tradition of Israel are: 41:9; 43:1,7,15,20-21; 44:1-5,21,24,28.

In 41:9, the verb **bachar** (to choose) is used with the shade of Deuteronomy. Here the idea of election refers to God's choice of Israel out of many other people, and that Israel is chosen with a future hope. Further the prophet refers to the fact of election that was initiated with Patriarchs, but it is actively intensified in the creative action of Yahweh by his special intervention in the history.

In 43:20-21, the activity of God in creation and redemption are explained as inseparable formulas. The main setting here is deliverance (God's election) and placed it in the wider setting of God's activity in creation. The language used for elected people (v.21: "whom I formed for myself", "they might declare my Praise") is reflected in the purpose of God's creation that the elect people in the creation may glorify God.

44:1-5 is perhaps the most crucial passage in Deutero-Isaiah's theology on election theme. In this passage the election is understood as something more than a mere exodus event. It is in the election frame work Israel's act of deliverance took place in the course of history. This fact is further strengthened by the prophet by referring to creation (as creative redemption of Yahweh). This being primarily an oracle of salvation, it has special theme of election. In vv.l-2, the conspicuous note of election is noted "Israel whom I have chosen". According to Stuhlmueller, the major stress of election of particulars in the past and it is the continuation of that choice in the present.

In vv.3-5, Yahweh's choice of Israel is explained by means of powerful symbols. The words used here: water, spirit, blessing in the sense of recreation, purification and renewal and God's creative Power. Yahweh provides a new dimension to the election or to the chosen ones even in the hopeless situation. These verses theologically affirm the fact that Yahweh's creative redemption in election, i.e., Yahweh controls, guides and pervades in all the areas of Israel's life and existence.

Klaus Koch argues that Deutero-Isaiah's uniqueness to the elect and the world Yahweh does a new creative action of calling Cyrus to create the ground for the liberation of Israel from exile. Yahweh has also chosen the servant as the representative of the Israelites to the restorative action for the elect and to create a new world order for the nations. In the course of this he had been put to death. The cultic community recognises this act as a vicarious suffering of atoning the sins of the elect. Yahweh makes an assurance that the Servant will be resurrected to life and glorified, this will enable the nations to be partakers of this redemptive Process.

Just as election is a central theme in Deutero-Isaiah's theology, covenant too finds a very important place in the oracles of the prophet. Deutero-Isaiah uses the idea of Covenant (54: 10,55:3) in order to link it with the past, i.e., with the election of Abraham (41:8f; 51:2). The old covenant is totally overshadowed by the new covenant which Yahweh himself will initiate. However, this covenant is mediated through the Servant, who functions as mediator not only to Israel but to the entire world (all the nations; cf. 42:6 & 49:8). For Deutero-Isaiah the covenant is operative in the context of *misphat* (Justice) and *sedaka* (righteousness 45:22; 51:5). Furthermore, the Servant, i.e., Covenant of a people and light to the nations. It is obvious here that the task of the Servant is seen in the context of liberation (Light=mishphat; cf. Micah 7:8ff; Hosea 6:5; Zeph 3:5).

Thus, Deutero-Isaiah the ideas of covenant and election are blended together. Just: as God elected and entered into covenant with Patriarchs (Abraham: 44:1-5, 24-28), same election-covenant act of God continues in the Present.

5) Comfort and hope to the exiles: It was the sufferings and disappointments of the Present which made the people in exile reluctant to believe in the readiness of Yahweh to help them. Deutero-Isaiah had to interpret these sufferings; he had to account for them, and also to convince his audience that they were now coming to an end.

First of all, the prophet emphasized that it is Yahweh who had inflicted them: it was not the Babylonian kings, who were only Yahweh's instruments, and certainly not their seemingly all-powerful God's. Deutero-Isaiah makes his point clear in 42:18-25 by saying that a nation so stupid that they had been unable to see that what was happening to them was the result of their sin.

But to tell the exiles that they deserved what they had got was to risk leaving them in despair, and also to leave them still with the feeling that Yahweh was unfair to them, since the generation felt (as we learn from other exilic writings such as Jer. 31:29; Ezek. 18:2-4; Lam. 5:7) that they were being punished for their Parents' sins. Precisely the new generation which was to be treated differently from that of their parents. The sufferings of the Exile had never been intended by Yahweh to last for ever. He had always intended that they should have a limit and that limit had been served and the exiles were therefore about to become freemen again (40:1-2). This is also the point of the passage about the supposed 'divorce; between Yahweh and his people (50:1). Hosea (2:2), Jeremiah (3:8), and Ezekiel (16) had all used the metaphor of divorce to stress that Yahweh had rejected his people and broken the relationship between him and them. They had, it is true, envisaged the possibility of a reconciliation. Deutero-Isaiah however, seems in 50:1 to have denied that there had even been a real divorce: since there is no 'divorce-certificate' (see Deut. 24:1-4; Jer 3;8), these had only been a temporary separation.

In an answer to the question of people's repentance, Deutero-Isaiah stressed the **grace** of Yahweh which does not wait for repentance Isa 43:25, a declaration of free pardon is given in an oracle which begins as an oracle of Judgment. Deutero-Isaiah's theology is a theology of grace which outweighs all other considerations.

6) Cyrus: The Persian King is named twice in the book, probably in a single oracle, 44:24-45:7. But many other Passages refer to him: 41:1-5; 41:21-29; 45:9-13; 46:9-11; 48:12-17 and probably 42:5-7. Cyrus is directly addressed and given his commission to carryout Yahweh's purpose. In all these passages Yahweh is the speaker. Deutero-Isaiah's main point was to say that the future lay in the hands of a great and irresistible conqueror who, however, was simply an instrument of Yahweh, created by him in order to carry out his good Purpose towards Israel.

Deutero-Isaiah went to great lengths to emphasize the complete dependence of Cyrus's achievements on the support given him by Yahweh. Yahweh not only calls him 'my shepherd' (44:28), a title used both in Israel and elsewhere in the ancient Near East of Kings who ruled by divine appointment, but even his 'anointed one' (*masiah*, 45:1), a title which had Previously been reserved exclusively for the reigning kings of the dynasty of David, God also states that he 'loves' him (48:14). The idea of Yahweh's making use of foreign Kings to carry out his Purpose for Israel was not in itself new; but in the Past this had been in order to Punish Israel for its disloyalty to Yahweh: Assyria had been 'the rod of Yahweh's anger' (Isa. 10:56), and Nebuchadnezzar, as Yahweh's instrument, but Yahweh's intentions towards his people were now wholly good, and it was Babylon which was to receive the divine chastisement (48:14). The use of the title 'anointed one' is astonishing, and was no doubt intended to administer? salutary shock to those who heard it: the exiles had no anointed king of their own who could save them; but Yahweh who could do all things (45:9-13) had created one out of the unlikely material of a foreign ruler, who was already Poised to deliver the blow which would open the prison gates, set the captives free (42:7; 45:2,3; 48:14), rebuild Jerusalem and other cities of Judah, and even lay the foundations of a restored Temple (44:26-28). The fact that Cyrus was a pagan who 'did not know' Yahweh (45:4) and might be expected to attribute his successes to his own God's was of no consequence in any case, together with the world at large he would eventually come to acknowledge Yahweh as the God (45:3).

iv) Isaiah 56-66 (Trito-Isaiah)

The last major section of the book of Isaiah is similarly anonymous. It seems much less of a unity and less coherent than the previous section. All events, a specific individual can be recognized in 61:1, where there is mention of a commissioning and sending in the first person, however, this text is less reminiscent of the accounts of prophetic calls. The term 'Trito-lsaiah' essentially denotes the collection of texts Isa. 56-66.

One special problem in the collection Isa. 56-66 lies in the fact that quite different themes appear in it side by side: On the one hand there is lamentation and accusation because of severe infringement of justice (chp. 56-59) and correct worship (chp. 65) on the other hand there is the promise of imminent salvation (chs. 60-62, 64). The themes are associated and related in the composition of collection. This is already clear in the introductory verse 56:1: the motivation behind the invitation to do 'right and justice' is that Yahweh's salvation and righteousness will come soon.

The words of salvation in chs. 60-62 mark the centre of the book; they have numerous echoes of Deutero-Isaiah. In 59: 1-14; 63: 7-64 they are preached by popular lamentations, and between them stands a description of the intervention of Yahweh (59: 15-21; 63: 1-6). In the introductory complex chs 56-58 the Invective (56:9-57:13) is followed by an announcement of the coming of Yahweh, which echoes Deutero-Isaiah (57:14-21). Chapter 58 again begins with an accusation and admonition about fasting which leads to a popular lament in ch. 59. The closing complex, chs. 65f shows a similar construction; between two passages of accusation and admonition (65:1-16a, 66:1-24) the latter interspersed with words of salvation there is an announcement of commitment salvation (65: 16-25), which in depicted as new creation (bara, v-17, cf 41:20, 48:7). The beginning (56: 2-8) and end (66: 18-24) are connectedly the key words, Sabbath (56: 2, 4, 6, cf 66:23), house of god and holy mountain (56:5, 7 cf. 66 20),name (56: 5, cf. 66:22) and by the announcement of the addition of forgiveness to the Israelites who are brought house (56: 6-8, cf. 66: 18-21).

a) The Historical Context of the Prophet: Trito-lsaiah is of particular importance in dealing of the issue on the specific question of the nature and cause of the dissension which threatened to disrupt the life the community in the Period after the return from the exile. Isaiah 56-66 provides the main source of evidence of these internal divisions (esp. in 65-8-16, 66:5 and in chp. 57: vv-1-2 and 19-21). But to detect the nature and the depth of the problems is not an easy task because either the information is not adequate or it is ambiguous. One commonly held opinion suggests that the roots of the problem lay in a conflict of interests, together with a divergence in theological orientation, between those who, remained in the land during the period of exile and those who, having been deported to Babylon and come under powerful foreign influences. Babylonian culture and religion undoubtedly had a profound impact on those who experienced the exile, even where their response was one of rejection, not assimilation. It is generally supposed that fresh impetus to Israel's life and worship came from these returned exiles, whereas syncretistic and semi-pagan cults such as those which the pre-exilic Prophets had denounced continued to flourish among those who had stayed in the land. On this basis, 57:3-13 and 65:1-5, 11-12 have been understood as describing the debased religion of those left without adequate leadership when the elite of society were deported to Babylon.

P.D. Hanson (*The Dawn of Apocalyptic*) gives to certain extent the sociological and the nature and the causes of the dissension in the postexilic community during the time of Trito-Isaiah. Hanson seeks to elucidate the nature of the opposing factions, and the causes and subsequent development of their mutual hostility with the pervading polemical note he finds on indication of their historical setting. The roots of the conflict lay, he believes, in the opposition between-two Parties the one eager to maintain the status quo by which they had control of the temple and of the official cult, the other motivated by a sense of rejection resulting from their exclusion from Participation in worship, yet lacking the power and resources to wrest control of Zion from their opponents. The former Hanson terms the 'hierocratic Party' which consisted of a group of influential priests who had returned from Babylon and seized control of Zion; the latter Hanson describes as 'visionaries', a group composed of followers of Second Isaiah in association with the disenfranchised Levites who had been excluded by the Zadokites from participation in the service of the temple (cf. Ezek. 44:13). Hanson remarks that Trito-Isaiah is permeated deeply by Priestly concepts. For example, a recurring emphasis on God's holy mountain, Zion (66:7, 21-22; 61:7; 63:17b-19; 57:13; 65:1-10), for one of the main issues at the heart of the inner-Community struggle between visionaries and hierocrats, as Hanson sees it, was concern for the possession of Zion.

Hanson regards chs. 60-62 as the restoration programme of the visionaries, and to this same general period he assigns 57:14-19 with its joyful message of comfort and healing for the whole nation.

The sudden change of tone in 57:20-21, a passage which according to Hanson's analysis is probably a secondary insertion, is explained as a later attempt, in the light of the developing rift within the community, to modify the initial Promise of Pardon and salvation which had been addressed to the whole nation. As optimism faded and bitterness grew it was necessary that the promises of Second Isaiah should be reinterpreted if hope was to be sustained in the face of disillusionment and despair. As Hanson puts it, 'disintegrating historical circumstances prompted new modes of conceptualizing that restoration hope'. Thus expectations for the future took on a different shape, increasingly detached from the real world of politics and history; and in this way apocalyptic was born.

Hanson regards the rivalry between the two factions as the motivation of chs. 56-66 throughout. Not only is the dissension interpretation consistently as a sectarian struggle; but even the formulation of the restoration programme in 60-62 is to be understood as deliberate, opposition to the hierocratic programme in Ezekiel 40-48. For this reason Hanson rejects the widely held view that 63:7-64: 12 is an early exilic lament by the community against the external enemies who desecrated the sanctuary when Jerusalem fell in 587, and sees it as further evidence of the bitter hostility between the hierocratic party and the visionaries. It is, he believes, a lament by Levites at their exclusion from the sanctuary by Ezekiel's programme. Thus the enemies who have defiled the sanctuary (63:18) are not external ones but internal rivals'. In this context Hanson takes the threefold affirmation, 'You are our Father' (63:16, twice; 64:8), as evidence that his claim by the Levites and their associates has been rejected by the rival faction who claimed the names Abraham and Israel as their own exclusive right: (63:16), thus depriving the visionaries of their legitimate part in the covenant community. This circumstance is reflected also, he suggests, in the repeated emphasis on the new names which are bestowed on the faithful (62:4,12) who have reached the ultimate Point of disowning the traditional designation Israel.

One of the main objections to this carefully constructed hypothesis is the unfortunate ambiguity of much of the evidence. Thus in the particular instance discussed here it can equally be argued that Abraham and Israel refer not to the community but to the Patriarchs, the human 'fathers' of the nation now unable to assist the present generation in their distress, unlike God who alone 'is a living and present father' (Claus Westermann).

Third Isaiah opens with a remarkably liberal statement on membership in the Community, conferring secure status on non-Jewish adherents of the Yahweh cult and on eunuchs, permitting them to participate in the cult on condition of observing the community's covenant requirements, especially regarding the Sabbath (Isa. 56:1-8). The same broad perspective is apartment in the final section (66:18-23) dealing with proselytism, missionary preaching, the ingathering of the nations and dispersed Jews to participate in the Parousia in Jerusalem.

The nucleus of Trito-Isaianic passages, containing a compendium of the eschatological teaching of the group, is found in Isa 60-62. Like 57:14-21, they come from either the last Years of the exile or the early years after the return and betray no signs of the opposition and conflict to which these teachings were to give rise with the passing of time. They begin with an apostrophe to Jerusalem: the glory of God will appear in Zion bringing salvation to an oppressed people, those scattered abroad will return, the nations will be subject to Israel, will bring tribute and help rebuild the city, the Temple will once again be glorious and shine at the centre of the earth.

It is important to note that throughout Third Isaiah'sprophetic eschatological faith is focused on Temple and altar (eg. Isa 60:7,13; 61:6; 62:9). There is therefore no opposition in Principle between the bearers of this faith and the Temple authorities and no evidence that the former were anti-cultic. The seer who speaks for them in fact goes on to expound a teaching not unlike the Priesthood of all the faithful. The entire people will in the last days be relieved of servile labour, as are the priests, and will receive tithes from the Nations. In this way the covenant to the house of Levi will be extended to all (cf. Numb. 25:10-13).

In the last two chapters of Trito-Isaiah (65-66), there are clear indications of internal conflict in the province of Judah involving the prophetic eschatological group within which Third Isaiah originated.

b) Literary Forms and Poetic Imagery in Trito-Isaiah: Not only it is true that Trito-Isaiah used several or variety of literary forms, but these traditional forms were forced into new directions to suit the requirements of a changing historical situation. The following are the important categories of speech forms and Poetic imagery used in Trito-Isaiah.

1) Judgement Oracles:

i) Isa. 56:9-12: This passage is a masterly example of a Prophetic oracle of Judgment, comprising the two traditional elements, Pronouncement of Judgment and grounds of accusation. Its figurative language has certain reminiscences of Ezekiel's indictment of Israel's leaders (34:1-10), but its brevity is in marked contrast to Ezekiel's extended metaphor. The kaleidoscopic imagery in which the denunciation is couched reflects the multifarious sins of which the leaders are guilty. What kind of leadership is castigated is not entirely clear: both religious and political leaders may be included. 'watchman' is a term which generally signifies a prophet (Jer. 6:17; Ezek. 3:17; 33:7) whereas 'shepherd' refers frequently to political leadership (Jer. 23:1-4; Ezek. 34:1-10, especially v.4). The accusation is comprehensive. At first it is the ignorance of the watchman, their failure to realise the dangers of the situation and to alert the community to an appropriate response, which is at issue. They are quiet as sleeping dogs murmuring in their dreams (hozim, a word occurring only here which has the sense 'to talk confusedly'. But then the accusation changes. Dogs, all dogs, have ravenous, insatiable appetites, and so do the shepherds of Israel, intent on their own advantage with never a thought beyond the pleasure of the present moment as they sing their drinking songs, behaving arrogantly as if the future were at their disposal not the Lord's. The pattern of the metaphors is deliberately chiastic (placed opposite to each other): the newly coined metaphors of dumb and ravenous dogs: the former useless, the latter dangerous, serve to illuminate the conventional expressions of "Watchman' and 'shepherds', and to Provide the transition between them.

ii) Isa 58: 1-14: This passage is of particular interest both from the form-critical viewpoint and for the insight it gives into the problems and religious attitudes of the post-exilic community in Judah. Of the two traditional elements-accusation and pronouncement of judgment the former appears briefly in vv.3b-4a; the latter is entirely absent. The rest of the passage consists of a series of exhortations followed by conditional promises of blessing. It is here, in this break down of the conventional form of the judgment oracle, that the contrast with earlier prophets is most apparent.

Westermann calls this as 'symptomatic of the coming together of prophetic and liturgical speech: Following immediately on the divine authorization of the prophet as a messenger of Judgment there is a parenthetical description of the outward piety of the community (vv.2-3a), a people who lament that their practice of fasting is ineffectual and secures no response from God. It is clear from this, as well as from the language in which the promises of blessing are couched, that the community, or the section of it addressed is conscious of some kind of distress and lack of well-being, probably attributable to the disappointment of hopes raised by the promises of Second Isaiah. The responsibility is laid firmly at the community's door. Despite their outward religious observances there is only apparent, not actual, commitment to righteous action and to obedience to God's commandments (v. 2).

Westermann points out some signs of wisdom influence in this passage, there is a hint of 'the ridicule of the rationalist' in the satirical expression 'to bow down one's head like a rush' (v.5).

2) Laments: Isa. 59:1-15a; 63:7-64:12: These two laments differ considerably in their literary form, 63:7-64:12 has more traditional structure. Westermann describes it as 'probably the most powerful psalm of communal lamentation in the Bible. It follows the conventional pattern of such laments within the Psalter, consisting of the usual elements: recollection of God's past saving actions (63:7-14 cf. Ps.89); plea for help, which includes a descriptions of the distress which was the immediate cause of the lament (63:15-64:5a), and confession of sin (64:5b-7). Finally the various elements in the lament are gathered up (64:8-12), culminating in the anguished questioning of God, characteristic of the lament form: "wilt thou retrain thyself at those things, a LORD? Wilt thou keep silent, and afflict us sorely?" (64:12).

Chp. 59 is an interesting example of departure from traditional forms of lament. Many would even question whether it is appropriate to classify it as lament. The opening words introduced as they are by the particle 'behold', are to be understood as the prophet's response to an unrecorded lament by the people, perplexed by the failure of Yahweh to intervene and by his apparent disregard of their prayers. The problem, says the prophet, lies not in any limitation of Yahweh's power; it is the result of sin, their own sins. Which have raised a barrier between themselves and God. The accusation in vv.2-3 is as sharp as anything in the pre-exilic prophets (cf. Isa. 1:15); but in place of the announcement of punishment which traditionally accompanied the accusation, the direct address to the hearers soon passes over into a description of their sin and its impact heightened by the striking poetic imagery (vv.5-6). It is this descriptive aspect of the material which gives the passage something of a sermonic character since it constitutes an explanation to a despondent People rather than an accusation. The sins, referred to here are social injustices not cultic irregularities, the evils by which justice is perverted in the law courts.

Two strands seem to be inter twined, the community's lament and the prophetic voice, thus some would characterize, it as a prophetic liturgy. This chapter falls into three distinct sections: *First*, the prophet's response to a communal lament which vindicates Yahweh by way of accusing the people (vv. 1-8); *Secondly*, the ensuring lament, by or on behalf of the people, which includes confession of sin (V. 12: and unusual feature in the traditional form of judgment oracle) and admits the truth of the accusation (vv.9-15a), *Thirdly*, the assurance of God's intervention to save those who repent (vv. 15b-20; for a similarity abrupt transition to words assurance:compare Joel 2:18). Yahweh is portrayed here as the warrior God who avenges those who 'turn from transgression' (v.20; cf. 42: 13 52:10). A similar pattern of community lament followed by Yahweh's epiphany is to be found in Psalm 60. The two sections, lament (1-15a) and epiphany (15b-20) are linked together. Yahweh takes action precisely because he sees that there is no Justice (v.15 cf. vv.9 and 11). The salvation which was far from them (v.11) is seen to be at hand when he intervenes.

3) Portrayal of the Divine warrior: (Isa 59:15b-20; 63: 1-6).

There are interesting, and significant, contrasts between the portrayal of the divine warrior in these two passages. What originally concerned Yahweh's intervention against foreign enemies has now been directed against internal adversaries. In 63: 1-6, the Prophet make use of secular form familiar to his hearers - the customary summons of a watchman to an approaching stranger to identify himself - but the contest is based on the motif of the divine warrior. Yahweh is not named but the identification is clear (cf. Amos 5:17f). Fresh from his victory he announces that 'right has won the day'.

4) Oracles of both Judgment and Salvation: (Isa. 65:8-16). It is oracle both of Judgment and of salvation, addressed respectively to two opposing factions within the community. In this dual orientation it differs in a remarkable fashion from the traditional forms of pre-exilic prophecy in which the nation is treated as a corporate entity for Judgment or for salvation. In its Present form ch. 65 as a whole is symmetrical in structure: vv.l-7 consist entirely of accusation against idolaters; vv. 8-l6a set out the contrasting destiny of two disparate groups within the community, detailing the blessings in store for the one ('my servants' vv.l3-14, 'my chosen', v.15) and the sorrows which await the other; vv.16b-25 are Purely a description of blessing. These diverse sections are held together by the theme of call and response which is reiterated in vv.1,12 and 24. The central concern of Isa. ch.65 is with the deep division within the community between those who, from this perspective at any rate, one regarded as faithful worshippers of Yahweh and their opponents who are considered by them to be apostate. It is to this latter group that the oracle is addressed from v.11 onwards as a pronouncement of judgment.

c) Theology of Trito-Isaiah: The majesty and omnipotence of Yahweh, the choice of Israel to be Yahweh's People, divine anger over human sin, and the deity's determination to work the divine will in the world, all are themes found in third Isaiah connect this prophet of the restoration with the older traditions of prophecy within Israel. Following are the three major concerns of the prophet in his theology.

i) Yahweh's restoration of Jerusalem is still in the future and when it comes, it will be a day of great glory for the city and its people: Yahweh's glory will be present in the life of the city (60:1-2). The city will be a "crown of beauty" and a "royal diadem" to Yahweh (62:3). All people will respond to the magnificence of the New Jerusalem, both gentiles (62:2) and Jews still scattered abroad (60:4). Great wealth will belong to the city, which will be the place of worship for all people (60:5-7; 66:23). It will be a time of peace and concord (65:25) in which Yahweh's presence will provide all needed light (60:1a).

ii) Although Yahweh's love is universal, two groups are singled out for special treatment: the gentiles and the wicked: The Gentiles are clearly to be Participants in the glories of this new age, "Foreigners" will join themselves to Yahweh (56:6). They and "aliens" will serve Yahweh in the age to come but their menial labour is contrasted with the work of the Jews who are to be "Priests of Yahweh" and "ministers of our God" (61:5-6). As for the wicked, they are responsible for deadly of the coming of the newage (59:1-2). Yahweh, who judged this people of old will also act in judgment upon any present enemies (59:18). The prophet implores Yahweh not to allow these wicked People to delay any longer the fulfilment of the divine promises, but to institute the Judgment swift and sure ways (chp.64).

iii) The Worship of Yahweh through sacrifice and Joyful Song characterizes the life of Yahweh's People: In this new age Jerusalem will "thrill and rejoice" (60:5). The prophet rejoices over what is to come topass (61:10) as does Yahweh also (62:5). This message is consistent with the views of other restoration prophets like Haggai and Zechariah. The words of Prophet's Jubilation are seen thus: "But be glad and rejoice for ever in that which I create; for behold, I create Jerusalem a rejoicing, and her people a joy. I will rejoice in Jerusalem, and be glad in my people; no more shall be heard in it the sound of weeping and the cry of distress". (65:18-19).

iii. The Book of Jeremiah

Several complexes of texts have been combined in the book of Jeremiah but in contrast to the book of Isaiah, they have been explicitly connected with the person of the prophet Jeremiah

The main sections of the book of Jeremiahproduce the following division:

- Chapters 1-25, predominantly sayings of Jeremiah (closing note 25:13).
- Chapters 26-45, predominantly reports about Jeremiah.
- Chapters 46-51, sayings about foreign nations (closing note 51:64).
- Chapter 52 serves as an appendix to the entire book.

The collection of the sayings of Jeremiah (chs. 1 25) is a composition with many strata which was presumably based on shorter subsidiary collections. There is much to suggest that the redactional shaping took place in several phases. Some divisions can be seen within chs. l-25. First of all, chp. 1-10 clearly standout from what follows by virtue of the fact that here prophetic words with a poetic formulation are dominant (with the exception of 7:1-8:3), whereas late the prose language emerges more strongly. Moreover, in ch. 10, in the hymn (vv. 12-16) and the prayer (vv. 23-25), there are passages which serve as conclusions. A further section can be recognized at the end of ch. 6, where 6:27-30 are evidently the conclusion of chs 2-6; finally, further sub-sections are marked by 4: 4 and 9: 24 f. This produces a division into the following sections. 1; 2: 1-4, 4: 7:1-8: 3, 8: 4-9: 25, 10.

From chapter 11 on, the prose language with a Deuteronomistic stamp comes more strongly into the foreground. At the same time compositions in this language can be recognized. These can be described as stylized scenes of the proclamation of Jeremiah: 11:1-12-6; 14f; l8; 19f. They all display a similar, structure: the occasion for the proclamation - message of Judgement (word of Judgement) - persecution of the prophet - lamentation. The lamentation which always stand at the end is particularly characteristic; here the texts express thesuffering of the prophet in his office, these are usually called the confessionsof Jeremiah: 11: 18-23, 23:1-6, 15:10f, 15-21; 17:12-18; 18: 18-23, 20:7-12,14-18.

Chapters 21, 24 stand out as an independent composition. They contain sayings against the leaders. 25:1-13 form the conclusion of the collection of the sayings of Jeremiah. This section is divided according to the basic form of prophetic speech: accusation (vv. 1-7), and the announcement of Judgement (vv. 5-13), chp. 25: 15-38 deals with the judgement of Yahweh on the nations.

The collection of reports about Jeremiah (Chs. 26-45) is clearly divided into two parts, i.e., 26:35 and 36-45. As an opening to the first part (Chs. 26-35), the programmatic temple speech from 17: 1-8 is repeated in chapter 26 and expanded by the addition of a narrative (v. 7ff). Chapters 27-29 are held together by the theme of false prophets. Jeremiah's sign with the 'yoke of the kings of Babylon' (ch. 27) sparks off the controversy with the prophet

Hananiah (Ch. 28), and the false prophets also have a role in the letter of Jeremiah to the exiles (29:8f, 15, 21-23, ch. 24 ff).

The theme of the future hope began in ch. 29 is developed in chs. 30-33 (except 32 which has the character of a report) chapters 30f are often called the Book of consolation (these is a mention of a book in 30:2). They contain words of salvation, about Yahweh making new covenant with Israel. Chapter 33 also further collects the words of salvation; chapters 34f form a contrast with the words of salvation which have gone before.

The second part in 26-45 chapter section, (36-45) contains no further words of salvation to Judah or Israel, there are only two individual promises of salvation which are clearly parallel: to a Cushite court official who Jeremiah had helped (39: 15-18, cf. 38:7-13) and to Baruch (ch. 45).

Chapter 36 is a clear parallel to chapter 26, where both begin with a saying of Yahweh to Jeremiah at the time of Jehoiakim, at the same time chp. 36 is an intensification of chap. 26.

Chapter 37-44 contain a consecutive account of the fate or Jeremiah from his arrest (37:11 ff), through his liberation by the Babylonians (39:1-18) to his forced Journey to Egypt (43:5 ff). It is embedded in reports about the capture of Jerusalem by the Babylonians and its consequences. This account has been called a 'passion narrative' of Jeremiah according to Kremers.

a) The Message of Jeremiah: One of the main. objective of Jeremiah's message was to utter an explanation of the catastrophe, which will fall on Judah in 587 BC Because people have failed to comply with the law and the words of Yahweh mediated to them by the prophets (cf. 3:12ff, 11:3ff). However, Yahweh will certainly restore the fortunes of the people and gave back their land to them (29:4).

Jeremiah's message on Babylon is very positive. He warns people of Israel to subject to the Babylonian authority; (27:11). Moreover, Jeremiah sees the Babylonian authority as a legitimate monarchy on the earth established by Yahweh himself. In one of the remarkable passage, i.e., 27:4-6, Jeremiah even gives the title 'ebed' (servant) to the Babylonian King Nebuchadnezzar (Previously in other Places this word is applied only to Davidic dynasty). In the words of Klaus Koch, "Jeremiah gives the phrase (my servant) a universal connotation in a way that was unheard of for Israelite ears. It is true that Amos and Isaiah had viewed the Assyrian kings as tools of destruction instigated by Yahweh; but they did not see the foreign power as a positive ordering force". (**The Prophets**, vol. II p. 62), Everykingdom that rebels against 'Nebuchadnezzar' will be visited by Yahweh through three active powers sword, famine and pestilence. Yahweh's kingdom will extend as far as distant Elam, and will bring down evil on evil men through the agency of the Babylonian troops (44;34-39). At the same time Jeremiah points out the limitations of the Babylonian power. After seventy years (i.e., from 605 to 538

B.C.E), even this power will be shattered and the relief will come to Israel. (27:21f, 51:59f).

Jeremiah proclaims in his message that exile is not purposed for mere punishment even though it is intended to punish the sins of Judah, it is more as an opportunity to turn to God (29:10-14). This message of hope is impressively presented by Jeremiah in his preaching on the new covenant (chp. 32), also through a symbolic action by purchasing a piece of land (32:17-44). Jeremiah's basis of new covenant will be made effective by Yahweh (cf. 31:31-34; 32:37-41).

Thus starting from the saying that people's sins are cause of the events occurred in 587 B.C.E (21:5), then he moves on to say the words of assurance, hope and new creative action of God to restore his people from their misfortunes (36:3, 18:11-12; 24:6; 27:22) and in particular assures them the return to their home (31:17).[8]

iv. The Book of Ezekiel

Compared with the other prophetic books, the book of Ezekiel give the impression of being much more uniform and coherent. The main reason for this is its clear division; the book contains mainly three divisions

- The disaster for the prophets own people (Judah and Jerusalem): chapters 1-24.
- The disaster of foreign nations: chapters 25-32.
- The announcement of salvation for Israel:chapters 33-48

There is a clear chronological order followed throughout the book except at some places.

A further characteristic of the book and its distinctive language, which puts its stamp on it almost throughout; the language shows clear affinities with the 'priestly' parts of the Pentateuch, and in some respects also with deuteronomistic language.

a) Personal information: Ezekiel and his family were undoubtedly among the 8000 (approx.) exiles taken to Babylon after the siege of Jerusalem in 598 B.C. (II Kings 24:16) We are not sure of his age at the time of his call in 587 B.C., but may be 30 years (if date in 1:1 indicates prophet's age). Ezekiel was a son of Priest namely Busi (1:10. His interest in the temple, his knowledge of sacral ordinances, as well as closeness of his language to that of the code of Holiness and Priestly document provide external support to the

8 For more details on the book and the person of Jeremiah see my own book: Kondasingu Jesurathnam, *Exploring Dalit Liberative Hermeneutics in India & the World: Based on an Ancient Hebrew Prophet, Jeremiah of Anathoth* (New Delhi: Christian World Imprints, 2015).

fact that Ezekiel was a member of an influential family in Jerusalem, deported in 597 B.C.E.

From the book we can make out very little of his personal information. According to 24:14ff he was married and lost his wife by her sudden death, roughly at the time in 587 BCE when Jerusalem fell to the armies besieging it and lost its existence and honour. The situation which is recorded on three occasions, that he was sitting in his house and received a visit from the elders of Judah (8: 1), or Israel (14:1, 20:1), who expected to receive through him a word from God, giving the impression of being stereotyped as in the case of Elisha's disciples (cf. II Kings 4:38, 6:2ff). There are different opinions of the scholars who understood Ezekiel's prophecy as pathological Phenomenon. We shall consider some such opinions.

i) According to A. Klostermann, Ezek 3-24 chaps. we find Ezekiel as a diary of sick person over against which in chps 33-48, the utterances of the Person, when recovered are to be found (cf. chp.2; 3:22ff, 4:4) and in 33:21ff, form a turning point in the physical progress of the prophet, which in general is to be diagnosed as catalepsy; however, Klostermann comments that behind the sickness we must recognise an idea, implanted in his soul by God, as the effective cause.

ii) B. Baentsch: sets out "Pathological features in Israel's prophecy" and concludes that, these actions, in all their details are so precisely calculated (as in the case of Ezekiel), and directed to their purpose, that we cannot speak here of a mutual disturbance.

iii) E.C. Browne: referred the Prophet directly to the sphere of psychological illness, these traits he understands in various traits of illness which appear in the symbolic actions by Freudian categories, hut also discern directly schizophrenic features.

But also to all these proposals, Walther Zimmerli makes an observation that, there are only a few passages, in which the Prophet reveals his personal feelings, even for a moment: As a rule, his own feelings are forced into the background in the service of the high task which he fulfilled in the vigorous forms of his Prophetic office.

b) The Historical Background: Ezekiel was active during the years between 593-571, which fall in the period of the rule of Nebuchadnezzar II, the great King of Neo-Babylonian dynasty (605-562). Under Nebuchadnezzar, the contemporary Babylonian Power had once again taken control of the area of the land routes from Africa to Asia, after an interval in which Egypt, the power in the south, and sought to play a decisive role again, as it had once before in the Period of great Pharaohs of the middle and New Kingdoms.

The information given in the book of Ezekiel reflects the following important details:

It is clear that the internal strife in Jerusalem, with which King Zedekiah could not cope up with led finally to defection from Nebuchadnezzar and the withholding of tribute. On the 10th day of the 10th month of Zedekiah's ninth Year (II Kings 25:1; Eze. 24:1) Nebuchadnezzar stood at the gates of Jerusalem.

The wars surrounding the traumatic loss of Northern Kingdom under Assyria brought the Southern Kingdom of Judah into Assyrian orbit as well (cf. Isa. 6-8 chps). Its King Hezekiah had tried to revolt in 705-701, but failed; and although Judah was not wiped out completely, its next King Manasseh, remained a faithful servant of Assyria throughout his long reign.

In 605 BCE a victory over Egyptians brought the Babylonians to Power over Judah. Jehoiakim pledged loyalty to Babylon but was soon attempting to rebel and work back Judah's independence. The Prophet Jeremiah's message was lovingly carried out in opposition to this political opportunism of Jehoiakim. Jehoiakim died in the Babylonian siege, and captured, his young son Jehoiakin and in his place they named his uncle Zedekiah to rule as regent (II Kings 24:8 20). But later, when he rebelled, Nebuchadnezzar's army levelled the cities of Judah and finally burned Jerusalem to the ground, taking away whatever remained of value and exiling the rest of its leading citizens in the summer of 586 B.C.E (2 Kings 25, Jer. 52). To this kind of situation, Prophet Ezekiel brings out his message.

c) Language and Speech forms of Ezekiel: The book of Ezekiel is distinguished from other books in that it is throughout composed in the I-style, except in 1:3 and 111 24:24, Ezekiel is mentioned in the third person in a divine speech, which is introduced by the prophet in the first person (24;15,20). We shall now consider, few important speech forms used in Ezekiel: Some of the distinctive forms of speech and communication used by Ezekiel is as follows:

1) *The Visions*: The book is stamped by four great visions (1:1-3-15; 22-24; 8-11; 37:1-14; 40-48). The prophet is personally involved very deeply here. There is often mention of the hand of Yahweh which comes upon him (1:3, 3:14, 22:8, 37:1, 40:1)he falls down (1:28, 3:23, etc.), and is raised up again (2:2; 3:24) or transported elsewhere (3:12, 14 etc.) by the spirit; he has to eat the scroll of scripture (3:18), wade through water (47: 3 f), speak to dead bones (37:4 cf) etc.

2) *Signs-actions*: These are performed by the prophet himself, and the detailed interpretation followed after the action (4:1-3, 4-8, 9-17, 5:1-17, 12:1-16; 17:20, 21:11 f, 23-29; 24:15-24, 37:15-28).

3) *Metaphorical Discources*: (speeches using a figure: legal accusation, fables of animals and plants, laments for the dead) eg: Vine Ezek 15 (vv-2-5 the figure, vv-8 the interpretation): the figurative discourse is first opened up in the style of the discussion through a series of questions (vv. 2-3), to which the prophet himself, still in the figure, gives the answer which emerges with compelling force (other examples chapters 16, 23, 17, 19, 27) etc.

4) *Recognition formula*: The recurrent and stereotyped phase in Ezekiel is 'I Yahweh has spoken' with which the speech units are always concluded 5:13, 15, 17; 17:21, 24; 21:22, 37; 22:14; 24:14; 26:14; 30:12; 34:24; 36:36; 37:14) various expansions which the formula can undergo connection with the recognition formula "you will (they will) know that I (am) Yahweh" 15:17; 17:21, 37:14) IS significant, often this statement can be taken as real culmination of the divine discourse, so that it is possible to take of a genre of proof saying, which is concerned with the divine 'proof of identity'.

The message of Ezekiel present in the book can be summarised in the following important concerns:

i) *Yahweh and his appearing*: Yahweh and his action is in substance central theme of the prophetic preaching. In view of this description of the attributes of Yahweh is completely lacking except rarely (20:29, 36:20-22). Where statements about Yahweh are made the finite verb dominates. The expansion of recognition formula which as a rule sets the person Yahweh, as indicated by his name, in the centre of what is known ("know that I am Yahweh") cf. 5:13, 6:10, 17:21, 37:14 etc.

ii) *The prophet and his office*: The prophet himself and the office to which he is called gave a greatest importance to his message. However, he is addressed as "son of man", only once he is called by name (24:24) sent by Yahweh (2:3), so that Yahweh's message to the house of Israel may be given by his mouth, thus he is a prophet, thus he can be directly introduced in to the recognition formula (In 2:5; 33:33). They will know that a prophet had been in their midst.

iii) *The prophetic announcement of Woe of Israel*:

1) The announcement of judgement: This is expressed with a clear aim. eg: 6:1-7, threat of the day of Yahweh in direct address (threatens the mountains and valleys of Israel with imminent devastation by war) in 6:11-14 (5:12) the devastation is made specific by the trial of sword, famine and pestilence (as in Jer. 28:8).
2) The accusation: In this the very name "house of Israel" can be replaced by "house of rebellion", even their fathers are rebellious "up to this very day" (chapter 23).

iv) *The proclamation of Judgement against nations*: (Chapter 25-32 and also chapter 35): In this section the oracles are directed against seven foreign nations, against Egypt (29-32 chapters), against Tyre (26: 1-28:19), against Egypt, the pride of Egypt is condemned, 29:1 and 32:1 speak of pharaoh as the crocodile of the Nile which is destroyed. Against Tyre, it is described as selfish, calculating the fall of Jerusalem.

v) *The prophetic announcement of salvation for Israel*: In Chapter 34, 36-48, Yahweh's faithfulness comes out to express clearly towards the house of Israel. The new salvation which the prophet has to proclaim is especially illuminated by him from two sides:

1) The Israel of the period before judgement was shattered by its disobedience.
2) The act of renewal by Yahweh will consequently consist in his creation his people as an obedient and law-abiding people.

This new situation, which Jeremiah 31:31-34 describes as a setting of the commandments on the hearts of the people, is set out in Ezekiel l 1:191 and 36:26 as the gift of a new heart and a new spirit. The heart of stone be replaced by the heart of flesh (36:27, 37:14, 39:29). In 48: 30-35 Ezekiel describes the fact that the real salvation is seen in that Yahweh will take up his abode in the midst of the house of Israel.

Ezekiel enables the exiles, in their existing situation not to wait ideally for the fulfilment of the great promises to the house of Israel. He shows how to face up this future in immediate decisions about the specific affairs of everyday life (cf. 33: 10-20, chapters 40-48).

3.2. MINOR PROPHETS

From Hosea to Malachi are summed up as 'the Twelve Prophets'. This designation also appears in the Babylonian Talmud (Baba Bathra l4b/15a). In LXX and Vulgate the Title 'Minor Prophets' is employed, and these twelve books are always counted as one book. We shall briefly make a survey of the major concerns in each of these twelve books.

i) Hosea

Chapters 1-3 of the book are a thematic unity is which the relationship between Yahweh and Israel is described in the image of marriage and symbolically by Hosea's marriage. Chapters 4-11 are marked off as a further unit by the introductory formula. "Hear the word of Yahweh, you Israelites" (4:1) and the concluding formula 'saying of Yahweh' (11:11) chapters 12-14 is the closing section of the book with the announcement of judgement and salvation. Some important themes found is the book are as follows.

1) *Hosea's Marriage*: Chapters 1-3 deal with Hosea's Marriage. Chapter 1 reports in the form of a third-person report and chapter 3 in the form of a first-person report. Some scholars would therefore argue that two narrative texts are woven together in a single composition. In the description of Hosea's

marriage, the relationship between Yahweh and Israel is described by a picture of love and marriage.

2) <u>Hosea the Person</u>: According to 1:1, Hosea's time can be understood as like Isaiah's. The king's names Uzziah, Jotham, Ahaz and Hezekiah of Judah, and also of Jeroboam II of Israel is mentioned through Jeroboam II's reign overlaps with that of Uzziah. But some scholars argue that Hosea's activity is extended beyond the time of Jeroboam II (eg. A. Alt. saw a reference in 5:8-6:6 to the Syro-Ephraimite war, but the fall of Samaria is not presupposed). So the period of Hosea's activity is usually put between 750 and 725 BCE.

3) <u>Hosea's Proclamation about Northern Kingdom</u>: Hosea's proclamation is entirely addressed to the northern kingdom. In 1:4 the dynasty of Jehu is addressed with a recollection of the blood-guilt of Jezreel (cf. II Kings Chp 9) the capital of Samaria is mentioned (7 :1, 8:5f, 10:5, 6, 14:1) and also the cult places Bethel (10:5, 12:5, cf. 4:15, 5:8) and Gilgal (4:15, 9:15, 12:2), Judah appears as the enemy of 'Ephraim', i.e. of the Northern Kingdom (5:10, in 1:7, 5:5, 6:11 etc. there is evidence of a Judean revision)

a) The Historical Period of Hosea: No other prophet says "now" as often as Hosea (4:16; 5:37; 7:2; 8:8,10,13; 10:2,3; cf 13:13). To be sure, we possess very little biographical information about him. Yet it is possible to date his sayings with a high degree of accuracy. At the most, the exact year may be disputed, but not the decade. Hosea's initial activity coincides with the last years of Jeroboam II, Presumably at least five years before the King's death (741-46 B.C.E)- 752 at the latest. Not only is the threat in 1:4 directed at the Jehu's Dynasty, but the entire chapter is also to be dated at the time of Jeroboam II. chap. 1, which describes "how Yahweh began to speak through Hosea" already covers a period of at least five years. Chap. 2:4-17 and chap. 3:1-5 also reflect a time of political security and economic plenty. There, as in 4;1-5:7, a major concern is the flourishing cult. The great political difficulties which began with the catastrophe of the Jehu dynasty first appear in the prophet's threats (1:4; 3:4).

The second major period of Hosea's proclamation is linked with the crucial events of the Syro-Ephraimite war (5:8-11) and the subjugation by Tiglath-Pileser III of extensive territory in Israel in the year 733 (5:14; 7:8f). At that time Hosea could look back upon a long series of Palace revolts (7:7; 8:4); Political vacillation between Egypt and Assyria (7:11); Hoshea ben Elah's submission to Assyria (5:13); and Payment of heavy tribute (8:9f).

The sayings contained in chaps 9-12 are related to the quiet Period before and after the accession to the throne of Shalmaneser V in 727 B.C.E. To be sure, the mention of Shalman in 10:14 is not an allusion to Shalmaneser of Assyria, but more probably to the Moabite king Shalamanu, whom Tiglath-Pileser III named among his tribute-Paying vassals in the year 728 B.C.E. Perhaps 9:3 and probably 11:5 and 12:2 presuppose Israel's mission to Egypt in 727, during the reign of Hosea ben Elah (II Kings 17:4), the same may be said of 13:15. "where then is your king, that he may save you?" (13:10) likewise points to this final Period, When King Hoshea already had been taken captive at the beginning of Assyria's attacks. Hence, the latest group of texts which can be dated with a fair amount of certainty has its origin around 725-24, immediately preceding or at the beginning of the siege of Samaria.

b) The forms of speech used by the Prophet: A large majority of Hosea's sayings have the basic form of the **divine speech**. In these sayings Yahweh speaks in the first person. (Eg: 1:4f, 6, 9; 2: 4-24; 4: 4-9; 5:1-3, 1-7 and 8:1-12; 9: 10-13 etc.). A smaller number of sayings are clearly formulated as Prophetic speech. Here Yahweh is spoken of in the third person (3:5, 4: 1-3; 5:4-7; 9:1-9; 10:1-8; 12:3-7,13-15; 13:15-14:1-14). It should be noted that Yahweh's personal speech is found in extensive contexts, especially in sections which introduce a complex of sayings having a unified theme. However, the "disputation style", with Yahweh in the third Person, may appear in the midst of these complexes. This can result in a lively alternation from divine to prophetic speech (eg: 4:10-15; 8:11-13; 12:1-15).

Conscious of the fact that he is Yahweh's messenger, the Prophet most often utilizes the personal form divine speech; he is the announcer of God's message. Other forms of divine speech are analogous to the language of the cult: (i) Yahweh's self-introduction ("I am "Yahweh"), in connection with the Proclamation of divine law (cf: 12:9,10; 13:4); (ii) the announcement of assurance that a Prayer has been granted. (oracle of salvation) within the framework of the lamentation liturgies (6:1-3; 8:1-3; 14:5-9). Most of Hosea's Prophetic sayings are reminiscent of those speech forms which have their *Sitz im Leben* (life setting) in the legal dispute between two parties, especially when they bring their case before the elders at the city gate. This explains the connection between the prophets' accusations and the announcements of judgment. (eg: 4:1-3; 8:1-3; 13:1-3); one hardly occurs without: the other. Hosea's use of the key word **rib** ("to countered, accuse in 2:4, 4:4; law suit" 4:1,12:2-3) clearly indicate that his proclamation of the divine word is modelled after the legal procedure, in the city gate.

Three others features are prominently found in the sayings of Hosea based on the form critical analysis: (i) Words of genuine lament ant complaint may be interspersed among the threats and accusations (4:6, 5:11; 7:8f; 8:8), they attest to the compassion of Israel's God and his prophet for their People. (ii) In the book of Hosea the exhortations have their origin in the form of the "Proposal to reach a settlement" in the law suit (2:4f; 4:15; 8:5; 14:2 cf. 9:1; 10:12; 12:6) and (iii) To a lesser extent defined forms peculiar to the law teacher: didactic exhortations (5:1) and Precept (6:6; 8:6).

In addition, Hosea independently creates numerous metaphors. No other prophet – indeed, uses as man similes as Hosea does. He may take one metaphor and develop it in detail (11:1-4; 2:4-17); or more frequently he clothes the thought of each succeeding sentence in new imagery (eg: 5:11-15; 7:4-12; 13:3,15; 14:6-8). The most provocative are his similes for Yahweh and Israel. He pictures Yahweh allegorically as a husband (2: 4ff.); a father (11:1f), a Physician (14:5; 7:1; 11:3 cf. 5:13; 6:1f), as shepherd (13: 5f) and fowler (7: 12). Even Hosea uses stranger similes for Yahweh and Israel like: a lion (5:14; 3:17), a leopard (13:7) and a she-bear (13:8), as dew (14:6 cf. dawn and downpour in 6:3) and a luxuriant tree (14:9), as pus and rottenness (5:12). Corresponding to the first Yahweh similes named above, Israel appears as the wife (2:4f), then as son (11:1f) a sick person (5:13; 7:1, 9; 14:5), a herd (13:5-8), a flighty dove and other birds of the air (7:11f; 9:11); Israel is said to be like a trained (10:11) as well as a stubborn heifer (4:16), a grapevine (10:1; 14:8), the early fig (9:10), the wine of Lebanon (14:8), and the lily (14:6), the forest of Lebanon and the olive tree (14:6), a mother in labour as well as an unborn son (13:13) Israel is like a cake of bread (7:8), a slack bow (7:16), morning mist and dew (13;3a cf 6:4), chaff blown from the threshing floor, and smoke that rises from the window (13:3-6). Thus, Hosea's audience are amazed by the number and variety of metaphors he employs, he omits no sphere of life; but the imagery is drawn from the vegetable and animal world and from family life clearly predominates.

Hosea often employs parallelism in his Poetic texts, at times Hosea's enthusiastic manner of speech a step like Parallelism (eg. in 8:11: 13:6) seems to build to a climax.

Hosea makes explicit references to the traditions of early period of Israel. He mentions Jacob (12:4f, 13), the Exodus from Egypt (2:17, 11:1, 12:10, 14, 13:4) and the guidance in the wilderness (2:16f, 9:10, 13:5). It remains uncertain whether this suggests a tradition from Israel, i.e. the north. However, it is clear that Hosea stands in the context of tradition from which Deuteronomy emerged.

c) The Message of Hosea: Hosea names "Yahweh" (occurs about 45 times or more) much more often than God (elohim: occurs 26 times or more) when he specifically mentions the one he serves as messenger. For Hosea knows only the God who, since the time of Moses (12:13-14) has revealed himself in a proclamation of his law and through his liberating acts: "I am Yahweh, your God from the land of Egypt" (12:10; 13:4). Nor does Israel know another as God and saviour besides Yahweh (13:4b). Hosea is familiar with the interpretation of Yahweh's name in Exod. 3:14, as he indicates in his negation of the old covenant formula. Yahweh, the ancient God of Israel, is the God who Hosea proclaims anew.

Since this Yahweh is God not only of the past but of the present as well, the prophet can use new, extremely bold expressions in referring to him. He speaks of Yahweh, the judge of Israel, only once as "his Lord" (12:1-15).

Some of the similes used by Hosea for Yahweh sound very strange to his audience. For example, Yahweh has Hosea describe him as "pus to Ephraim" and "rottenness to the house of Judah" (5:12) or as a lion that rends and carries off his Prey, from whom none shall rescue (5:14). The prophet's language itself strikes in the hearts of his audience; the terror of Yahweh ispresently burning anger (5:10; 13:11). Subordinating all consideration of pious tradition and aesthetic sensitivities, the prophet sought to bear witness to Yahweh's awesome, overpowering strength and present action.

Hosea uses extreme imagery in his announcement of salvation. The power of God's saving deeds is elucidated by metaphors of the "dew" in I4:5-6 and of the "luxuriant fruit tree" in vv. 8-9.

Hosea talks about Yahweh as Israel's husband had its roots in the Prophet's recognition of Israel's specific guilt: the people have given themselves to "whoredom" (1:2; 2:4-7; 3:3; 4:10-18; 5:3f; 6:10; 9:1). By her cultic Practices and her dependence upon Canaanite mythology and thought, Israel has become unfaithful to Yahweh. The metaphor of the "first husband" (2:9,18 thus has the purpose of elucidating the accusation that Israel is guilty of whoredom and adultery. This metaphor also emphasizes that Yahweh is the exclusive provider of all the gifts of the arable land (2:7,10). Hosea's adaptation of the divine husband concept to Yahwism presents Yahweh as the only God and thus states Yahwism's claim of exclusiveness.

Two important observations show how Hosea's use of mythical elements is dominated by his polemic against the Baal myth, and how the myth is broken precisely 1n the marriage parable. *Firstly*, it is Yahweh who provides the gifts of the arable land and who is free to take them back again (2:10, 11, 17). Here the concept of conjugal union completely recedes and Yahweh attests that he is-in contrast to Baal-Lord over devastation and wilderness. In spite of Hosea's use of certain mythical fragments, his certitude that Yahweh alone is God disallows any suggestion of a plurality of divinities or even ofa sexually differentiated pantheon. *Secondly*, Yahweh's partner in the marriage parable is not some goddess, but historical Israel. The legal categories of covenantal thought replace the mythico-cultic fertility concepts that are rooted in the sacral marriage (cf 1:9, 2:4, 21f). This unfolding of Hosea's theology in Polemical dialogue with the cults and mythology of Canaan provides us with a fundamental example of faith's dialogue with contemporary ideology. In spite of Hosea's daring usage of certain key words from Canaanite mythology, the idea remains dominant that the Yahweh who acts in the present and future is none other than the one who has begun his covenant history with Israel at the time of her youth, with the Exodus from Egypt (2:17; 11:1; 13:4); with the making of the covenant (1:9; 6:7; 8:1); and with the gift of divine law (2:21f; 8:12;13:4f). Hosea views Israel's present and future together with her history.

It is remarkable to see how thoroughly Israel's history is embedded in Hosea's proclamation He looks back over the last decade when kings were murdered and the throne usurped (7:7; 8: 4); over the last century, with the crimes of Jehu's dynasty in 844 (1:4); on to the beginnings of Kingship under Saul, where he locates the roots of the present kingship's transgression (13:10f; 9:15). Beyond this he reaches back even more comprehensively to the Period of the conquest (2:10; 9:10; 10:11f; 11:1f; 13:5f). For Hosea the Conquest tradition is to be separated neither from the deliverance from Egypt (2:17; 11:1; 12:14; 13:4) nor from the wilderness traditions (9:10; 13:5; 2:5,16). The Period of conquest saw Israel's early encounter with the Baal cult (9:10) and with it the apostasy-determinative for Israel's present-from the God who had begun his saving history with her in Egypt and in the wilderness. Hosea's longest step basic into history takes him to the. Jacob traditions (12:4-5,713). They especially serve to lay bare Israel's present deceit against God and neighbour.

Hosea's use of traditions is more Significant than arbitrary collection of examples from the past. Three reasons for this can be identified:

i) The historical retrospect discloses early, fundamental connections within Israel's history. Her apostasy to the Baal of Peor is an abominable transgression in view of the previous election of the fathers in the wilderness (9:10). Theologically speaking, in the light of Israel's beginnings, her present transgression is revealed as transgressions against the God of love and election, against the Lord of saving history.

ii) The historical retrospect shows how God's intensive struggle with Israel reach from her past down to Hosea's present time. Yahweh's great lawsuit with his wife-turned-whore (2:4-17) and his accusing speech against the rebellious son (11:1-7) indicate how much the prophet is interested in the continuity of the defendant's Previous life.

iii) It is not accidental that Hosea gives especially close attention to various beginnings: Jehu-the first King of the Present dynasty (1:4); Gilgal and Saul the beginning of the present kingship (9:15; 13:10t); Baal-Peor-the beginning of the cult of Shamel (9:10); the wandering in the wilderness and the deliverance from Egypt -the initial saving acts of Yahweh (2:17; 9:10; 11:1; 12:10,14; 13:4-6); the Jacob story- when Israel's deceitfulness began (12:4f, 13f). Whenever Israel's beginnings are examined, her present immediately appears indeed, the present is the end of ancient saving history now has actually begun. The most impressive statement in this regard is found in the recasting of the old covenant formula as a formulae of divorce (1:9; cf. 2:4); but it is also expressed in the sayings which threaten Israel's return to Egypt, whereby the gift of the land is taken back (8:13; 9:3,6).

Hosea brings his accusation particularly against two groups within the nation: the priests and political leaders. He measures the priestly sacrifices and oracles and also the Priests activities in the festivity cult against a remarkably positive ideal of a "Knowledge of God". Thus he expects them to cultivate and use this knowledge in order to maintain People's attitude in God's saving action and justice. (4:1,6; 6:6; 13:4-6; 2:10-15,21f) He charges the Political leadership with zealous revolutionary intrigues and constant charges of direction in foreign policy which they pay out without ever seeking the will of Yahweh, the God of Israel. (5;1f,11f; 7:3-16; 8:1-4,7-10; 10:13-15; 13:10-14:1).

We find the following expression in Hosea in order to explain the rebellious attitude of Israel; Israel's "no longer knows" (2:10; 5:4; 11:3) Yahweh, "Forgets" (2:15; 4:6; 8:14; 13:6), "forsakes" (4:10) him; leaves him "to go after her lovers" (2:7,15 cf.11:2); disregards the instructions of his covenant" (6:7; 8:1); "turns to other god's" (3:1); "is unfaithful to him" (5:7;6:7); "becomes stubborn" (4:16; 9:15).

Hosea describes how God feels profound sorrow, laments the apostasy of his People; how God himself suffers under the distress their estrangement prepares them. In bringing correction on Israel numerous threats are used on "Israel to announce impending judgment". Hosea first depicted it in terms of natural catastrophes (11:5; 7:16; 8:3; 10:14f; 14:1) and then later as military catastrophes (1:5; 7:16; 8:3; 10:14f; 14:1). It is more characteristic of Hosea when he announces Yahweh personally will draw near to execute his Punishment (5:12,14: 7:12,15; 12:10; 13:7f) and that Yahweh will act not only as requite (4:9; 12:3; 9:7) but also as teacher (5:2,9 cf. 10:10). The most peculiar feature of Hosea's proclamation we find in the law suit speeches in which his God not only struggles with Israel but with himself as well; indeed, he calls his own decisions into question (2:4-17; 6:4; 11:8f). Thus according to Hosea, Yahweh's judgment in essence is his struggle for his people. In the beginning of his proclamation, Hosea's exhortations to repent become ultimatums (2:4f); later, they still appear occasionally (4:15; 8:5), though they are met with stubborn resistance (4:16), refusal (11:5b), and the complete inability to return, since the actions of the People have rendered them incapable of conversion (5:4; 7:2).

The message of salvation is also seen in the oracles of Hosea in the midst of his severe judgment speeches after Israel had broken the covenant (1:9), the new beginnings was to come only as a result of the preconditions which God himself created: in his Judgment God would block Israel's path to her idols (2:8) and bring her a new to the wilderness, the place where his saving history had begun (2:16). There Israel would turn his thoughts to Yahweh (2:9), listen to his wooing words of love (2:16f) and return to him and his goddess (3:5).

In the later part of Hosea's ministry, when it became clear that Yahweh's words of Judgment could not bring Israel to obedience God's unqualified love is expressly represented as the only precondition for healing Israel's apostasy and for giving her new life (11:8f).

ii) Joel

The character of the book of Joel is not easy to define. Two particular elements are important; on the one hand the book is marked by liturgical forms of speech (especially in 1:5-20, 2: 12-17) and on the other hand the book has largescale eschatological descriptions (especially in 2: 1-11, 3f; in English 3 counted as 2.28-32 and chapter 4 as chapter 3).

Joel is a cult prophet attached to the Temple at Jerusalem with an eschatological message. With this single difference he continues in a later period the preaching of the pre-exilic cult prophets with its propensity for proclaiming salvation for Israel and destruction for Israel's enemies.

Joel's prophecy is marked by a combination of cultic prophecy with eschatology that distinguishes him from the great pre-exilic prophets. He takes as his point of departure the economic tribulation of everyday life brought about by natural disasters, but all the while his eye is on the day of the eschatological walking. He carries out his mandate, seeking to avert economic disaster and calling upon the nation to turn to God in its distress. He demands that the leaders summon a cultic penitential assembly, with fasting and lamentation, but at the same time emphasizes the necessity for the people to turn to God with all their heart. He speaks of the universal compass of the day of Yahweh, but only in judgement upon the nations in contrast to his particularistic restriction of salvation to his own people.

a) The Date of Joel: The date of Joel is its largest introductory problem. There are four suggestions in this as proposed by scholars: First, some scholars advocate an early pre-exilic date during the reign of King Jehoshaphat (872-848 B.C.E), or possibly his grandson, King Joash (835-796 B.C.E). Arguments in favour of this period include the position of Joel in the Hebrew canon; it appears among other prophetic writings of this period. However, the order of the pre-exilic Minor Prophets is not strictly chronological, in both the Hebrew and the English versions. Also, the enemies of Israel that Joel named (Tyre, Sidon, Philistia [cf. 2 Chron. 21:16-17], Egypt [cf. 1 Kings 14:25-26], and Edom [cf. 2 Kings 8:20-22]; 3:2-7, 19) were enemies of Israel during this time. The prominence Joel gave to Judah's priests and elders rather than to her king—Joash was a boy king under the influence of Jehoiada, the high priest, early in his reign—is a further argument for this view. Second, some believe a mid-pre-exilic date of composition, probably during the reign of Joash's grandson, King Uzziah (792-740 B.C.E), fits the evidence best. Supporters of this view also claim the first two arguments cited in favour of the early preexilic view above. They argue, in addition, that the absence of references to Assyria, Babylonia, and Persia make a later date, when these nations were the major ancient Near Eastern superpowers, unlikely. Joel's reference to Greece in 3:6 may fit this period since the Ionian Greeks were at this time expanding their commercial influence in Asia Minor. Joel's reference to the Sabeans in 3:8 is appropriate for this period as well. Internal references and linguistic characteristics may also reflect Uzziah's times, and are similar to the writings of the other eighth-century prophets (i.e., Amos, Hosea, Micah, and Isaiah). However, again, much of the same evidence can fit other periods of Judah's history. Third, some interpreters opt for a late pre-exilic date. Statements in Joel could fit this period, and some of his statements are similar to those of Jeremiah and Ezekiel, and may reflect conditions before the destruction of Jerusalem, perhaps between 597 and 587 B.C.E. If true, Joel would have been a contemporary of Jeremiah, Habakkuk, and Zephaniah. Yet Joel 2:18-19 seems to imply that God had been merciful to Joel's generation, suggesting that the people had repented, but there is no record of this happening during this period. A variation of this view is that Joel wrote either just before the Assyrian invasion of 701 B.C.E or just before one of the Babylonian invasions: the 598 B.C.E invasion, or the 588 B.C.E invasion. The fourth view is that Joel wrote at a postexilic date, perhaps 515-500 B.C.E, or even as late as sometime in the 400s B.C.E. Interpreters who see Joel 3:1-2 and 17 as references to the destruction of Jerusalem and the Babylonian captivity take the references to the temple in 1:9, 13 and 2:17 as applying to the second temple (completed in 515 B.C.E). Generally, scholars who view apocalyptic writing as a late development in Judaism tend to date Joel quite late. As should be obvious from this brief review, the dating of the book rests on interpretations of various verses that are not clear. No other Old Testament book mentions Joel. Consequently, dating the book amounts to guesswork, though some writers were quite dogmatic about their convictions.

In the light of the above discussion we may suggest that the book can be dated in the mid-pre-exilic period, particularly around eighth century BCE taking into account its placement in the Hebrew canon, although it is not a strict measure to date the books of the minor prophets.

b) The Message of Joel: The Book of Joel contains a threefold vision. The first part of Joel's vision concerned a locust plague that had recently swept over the Promised Land. Joel prophesied about this plague because of the desolation that it had produced. The second part of his vision concerned a coming invasion from a foreign army in the fairly near future. He used the recent locust plague to illustrate the devastating effect of the coming military invasion. The third part of his vision concerned another coming invasion, in the far distant future, that would also be like the recent locust invasion, only worse. Joel described each of these devastations as "the day of the Lord." The term itself refers to a time when God had been or would be controlling events for Israel in an unusually direct way. It was God's day in the sense that, at those times, Yahweh was and would be especially prominent in what happened. Thus this term referred to a past "day," a near future "day," and a far distant "day," from the prophet's perspective.

The Book of Joel has two important timeless values. It illustrates the basic principles by which Yahweh governs, and it reveals the basic plan of Yahweh through the ages. It is important for us to grasp these basic principles and this basic plan, because the other prophets reveal more about them. Joel illustrates the principles by which Yahweh governs. This book does not reveal them in the sense of explaining them fully. Isaiah explains them more fully. Joel illustrates these principles briefly. Joel viewed Yahweh as enthroned in heaven, controlling affairs on earth. Joel saw God presiding patiently over all the situations through which God's people pass. He saw God pressing into God's service all the processes of nature and human activity. He also saw God achieving ultimate victory in "God's day":"the day of the Lord."God had accomplished victory by judging the people recently with a locust invasion. God would accomplish victory by disciplining God's people with an invasion from a foreign foe in the near future. And God would accomplish victory by restoring the people through a fresh outpouring of God's Spirit in the distant future. So one major lesson of this book is that God is enthroned in heaven, ruling over the affairs of humanity. A second illustration of the principles by which Yahweh governs is Joel's emphasis on grace. Grace is at the heart of God's government. Grace is the inspiration of God's government. We see this in God's appeal to the Israelites through Joel to repent, to "rend your hearts rather than your garments" (2:13a). The locust plague was a wake-up call to repent. The Israelites' repentance would affect the imminent invasion they faced. God promised judgment, but God offered mercy, if the people would repent (2:13b-14). Grace is also evident in the promise of a far-distant future outpouring of God's Spirit—in spite of the unfaithfulness of God's people. God rules with grace. God is gracious to humanity in the way God governs people. When the locust invasion swept through the land, the people bemoaned the tragedy. The locusts had so stripped the grapevines that even the drunkards could not find grapes to make wine. The people had so little grain that they could not bring offerings to the temple. They could hardly make bread to eat. They viewed the devastation as a natural disaster. Joel reminded them that the locust invasion had come by the will and hand of God. The people had forgotten God, but God wanted to get their attention, so the plague was sent. God had allowed this to happen so the people would think of God, and return to God. When the invasion happened, it was God's "day." It was God who had done this (1:1-14). Joel went on to remind the people that, because they had forgotten God, God was going to bring a worse devastation on them that would make the recent locust plague seem tame by comparison. If they turned back to God, they could avoid this worse fate, because God would be gracious to them (2:12-13).

The coming invasion, by humans rather than by locusts, would also be a day in which the Lord acted prominently. Joel even said that the Lord would lead this army of invaders (2:11). This was probably fulfilled in the Assyrian invasion of Jerusalem in 701 B.C.E. Yet in spite of future devastating judgment, God would act again, dramatically and definitely, for God's people (3:28-32). God would bring restoration and blessing to them, even after they had suffered God's chastening discipline. God would just as surely and personally do this for them as God would punish them. This, too, would be one of God's "days." And it would be the ultimate illustration of God's grace.

A second great timeless value of this book is its revelation of God's plan for Israel's future. First, there would be coming judgment that the people could affect by their repentance (2:14). Had the Israelites repented, the Assyrian and Babylonian captivities would not have overtaken them. When the Assyrians attacked Judah, the people of Judah did repent, and the Lord delivered them. But when the Babylonians attacked Judah 115 years later, the Judeans failed to repent, and suffered defeat and deportation. Joel could honestly say for God, "Return to me with all your heart" (2:12). When the people failed to repent, judgment fell upon them. Second, there would be even worse judgment in the distant future because the prophet foresaw that the people would continue to apostatize (3:1-17). This refers to the judgments on Israel during the tribulation. Yet after that, the Lord promised to restore and bless the people (2:18-32). That outpouring on Israel is still future from our position in history. Others see a double or partial fulfillment on the day of Pentecost with the church, and a future fulfillment with Israel in the Millennium. This is the viewpoint of many premillennialists. A third view is that fulfillment will only be in the Millennium, and that what Peter meant was that what happened on the day of Pentecost was similar to or like what Joel prophesied.

iii) Amos

The book of Amos gives as a very clear profile of this prophet. This may be because the book has been arranged with clear divisions with opening and closing formulae. But, on closer examination, the book reveals that it has undergone several stages of growth and redaction.

Amos comes from Tekoa (modern Khirbet Taqu'a), a village located about ten miles south of Jerusalem, on the boundary between the settled area and the steppe. He dwelt there as a shepherd (1:1) or a herdsman (7: 14), more likely an independent owner of cattle than hired shepherd.

Amos 1:1, 7:9, 10-11 indicate as the date of Amos' prophetical activity the reign of Jeroboam II in Northern Israel (786/82-753/46), which parallels the rule of Uzziah in Judah. The earthquake mentioned in 1:1 does not help us to determine the date more precisely, but the content of the prophet's words shows that Israel was then in a period of political, economic, and cultural prosperity and could point to noteworthy successes (6: 1, 13). This suggests the middle or late years of Jeroboam's reign (2 Kings 14:23-29), so that we may date Amos' ministry between 760 and 750 B.C.E.

Amos was from Judah (south), but went in to the Northern Kingdom of Israel. He first appeared probably in Samaria, the capital (3:9f, 4:1f, 6: 1f), then at the state sanctuary at Bethel, to address the multitude assembled for a festival.

a) The Time of Amos: When Amos came to the northern Kingdom of Israel to Prophecy, the King of Israel (north) was Jeroboam ben Joash (i.e., Jeroboam II). Since Jeroboam II reigned from 786-746 BCE, Amos' Prophetic activity must be dated within these limits in the middle decades of the eighth century. The title of the book in 1:1 indicates the reign of Uzziah died in 742 B.C.E.; but because he had become a leper, his son Jotham had been regent since about 750 B.C.E. If the composers of superscription reckoned Jotham's assumption of regency as the end of Uzziah's reign, it was their opinion that Amos appeared in Israel before then, the title also specifies a precise year for Amos, 'two years before the earthquake', The earthquake may have occurred about 760 BCE, if this is so Amos is placed in the fourth decade of the eighth century.

The record of Jeroboam II appears in 2 Kings 14:23-29. The account is typical of the Deuteronomistic historian's treatment of Israel's Kings in its single-minded interest, in classifying along the long list of rulers who made Israel to sin. The historian does, however, observe that Jeroboam restored the northern and southern borders of Israel east of Jordan and even concedes that Yahweh saved Israel by Jeroboam. Behind this observation there is an important point to make. Under Jeroboam II, Israel knew her best years of Prosperity and Peace. The international situation was auspicious. Assyria's power has waned under a succession of inept rulers who could only manage in defending themselves against the Kingdom of warrior until the accession of Tiglath-Pileser III (745 BCE), Syria-Palestine was free from that quarter; The Kingdom of Damascus had not yet fully recovered from her earlier defeats by Assyria and was locked in a crippling struggle with Hamath on North. Therefore at long last there was peace with Judah taking advantage of these favourable circumstances, Jeroboam had pursued a vigorous policy of expansion east of Jordan with great success. Reflections of an ebullient confidence among Israelites appear in the speeches of Amos. (6:1,8,13). Along with political success, many people were prosperous in the nation. The older homogenous economic structure of Israel gave way to sharp distinctions of wealth and privilege. The excavations at Tirzah (Tellel-Farah) uncovered evidence of social revolution that had occurred. While the city's houses in the tenth century had been uniform in size, in the eighth century by contrast there was a quarter of large, expensive houses, and one of small huddled structures (R. de vaux, *Ancient Israel*, 1961, pp.72ff.). The result was the sharp contrast between the luxury of the rich and the misery of the poor which Amos repeatedly indicts. The rich enjoyed an indolent, indulgent existence (4:1f; 6:1-6) in winter and summer houses (3:13; 6:11). The poor were a tempting target for legal and economic exploitation (2:6-8; 4:1: 5:10-12; 8:4-6). Meanwhile religion flourished in the nation. The populace thronged the shrines at festival time (4:4 f; 5:5 f) to practice and elaborate sacrificial ritual (5:21-24). Yahweh was trusted and patronized with presumptuous arrogance (5:14; 18-20; 6. 3). To such a nation Amos was commissioned to announce the word of the Lord.

b) The Forms of Speech used by Amos: It is surprising that Amos displays a wealth or rhetorical forms. We will consider few important types of speech forms under the following main categories.

1) Commission-Bound Message or Speech: When Yahweh comes to the fore in the Messenger speech, it is consistently as the first person speaker. For important types of formulae are used by the Prophet as follows:

i) The "messenger formula": which derives from the language of diplomatic exchange (cf.7: 11) is used most frequently by Amos. Eleven of his oracles contain the introductory messenger formula "Thus Yahweh had said" (*Ko amar Yahweh*: 1:1,6,13; 2:1, 6; 3:11,12; 5:3,4,16; 7:17), and five of these also show the corresponding concluding formula "Yahweh has said" (*amar Yahweh*: 1:5,8,15; 2:3; 5:17). In seven instances the messenger formula is placed at the head of the entire oracle; four times it appears only at the head of the announcement of punishment. (3: 11, 5:3,16; 7:17).

ii) The "divine oracle formula" - (Oracle/utterance of Yahweh): is found in few places: 2: l6, 3: 15; 4:3,5; 9:7a. In these places it stands at the end of an oracle, in order to distinguish it in a solemn way as a Speech of Yahweh.

iii) The "on formula": is introduced by the statement: "Yahweh has sworn by", which intensifies the usual messenger formula. Its function is related to that of the messenger formula. In two places it serves to introduce, (after a preceding accusation) the announcement of judgment as a divine oracle (4:2; 8:7); in a third place (6:8) it opens an oracle in which the announcement of punishment and the motivation are intertwined. Thus, oath formula fundamentally emphasizes the message of judgment as Yahweh's word and thereby underscores the certainty of judgment beyond any doubt.

iv) The "proclamation formula": (Hear!), it does not always immediately introduce an oracle of Yahweh (4:1, 8:4), but it is 7:16-17 shows, is tied less strictly to Yahweh's word of judgment. When the call to "hear" immediately introduces an oracle of Yahweh, the affected party is also addressed in the subsequent speech of Yahweh (3: la).

2) Free Witness-Speech: The first characteristic of this type is the absence of all framework formulas that designate Yahweh as the speaker. Three further sub-types can be classified under this section as follows:

i) Prophetic Prologue to the word of Yahweh: (Eg. 3:1 a), "Hear this Word!"; The Prophet arouses attention in preparation for the oracle of Yahweh that follows. (4:1, 5:1). In 4:1, there first follows a detailed characterization of those who are addressed and whose crimes and listed. Only after that is the word of Yahweh issued, separately introduced by the oath formula (if. 8:4-6,7). In 5:1 it becomes even clear that the call is first of all challenge to hear the Prophets own word ("Hear this word which I take up...."); the reference here is to the funerary lament in 5:2 which receives its motivation in the subsequent word of Yahweh (5:3). This combination of the proclamation formula with the prophet's own utterance corresponds to a simple form of "pedagogical introduction" of the wisdom teacher.

ii) Didactic Questions: Disputation concerning the prophet's commission can also appear in an independent sequence of oracles: 3: 3-6,8. A series of questions unfold. Each one is formulated in such a way the hearer is brought to the conviction that calamity must also be recognized as the result of Yahweh's acting (3: 6b), and the activity of the Prophet as a result of the Yahweh's speaking (3. 8b), other examples of this type can be found in 5:19 20; 6:12; 9:7.

iii) The "Woe-cries": These has a primary didactic function in a pedagogical setting. Within the clan pedagogy, the woe cries belong more to the style of basic catechetical instruction. Eg: 5: 18-20; 5: 7,10; 6: 1,3-6. Woe is constructed in series. It is always followed by a plural participle. Direct address is usually not present. Instead, deeds defined in a general way are placed under the woe. The woe-cries indicate the intensity of the situation and the grave Judgment that will be due to come upon the people.

3) Vision Reports: (7: 13; 4-6, 7-8 8: 1-3) were perhaps literary compositions from the outset, though they may have been orally transmitted to us. Everywhere in these reports prophetic 'I' is used, except in 7: 14-15, where it is Amos' autobiographical account. "Thus the Lord Yahweh showed me" are the words which introduce every vision and which are followed by mysterious voices, the voices count far more than the vision. What they say is fixed for the future. The vision, reports are developed basically as conversations evoked 1n the first pair by Amos' intercession and in the second pair by Yahweh questions. Just as the vision proper opens each resort, the words giving Yahweh's decisions always close it. Although the issue is indeed Israel's fate, not once does Israel figure in the scenes as the recipient of a message which the prophet. is being commissioned to deliver, in contrast to the situation as we find in I Kings 22:20-23; Isa 6:8-10; Jer 1:4-10 and Ezek. 2:3-3:11.

4) Other Types: In addition to the important forms of speech used by Amos as mentioned above, there are certain other types of speech forms used by Amos. We will consider few of them:

i) The "graded numerical saying": (1:3,6,13; 2:1,6) These sayings are against foreign nations focusing only one crime. He employs this sayings, not for instructional purpose but to motivate Yahweh's irrevocable announcement of punishment.

ii) In the judgment those who are indicted, a casting in Participial style is immediately apparent. The participial forms are always found in plurals. Eg: 5:18, 6:1,3-6.

iii) Antithesis occur especially as structural features of admonitory speech (5:4-5: "seek me...do not seek Bethel..!") They are widespread in the language of sapiential counselling (5:4-5).

iv) Word plays are often found in oracles of Amos. The message of "end" was impressed upon Amos himself by means of the alliteration (*Qayis*: summer fruit and *Qes*: end) other examples of this word play are: 6:1,6,7; 6:1 and 3-7.

The riches of imagery show Amos' desire to communicate clearly, a desire shaped by wisdom. The scope of his comparisons reflects the Prophets breadth of education. Certainly he knows the life of a simple shepherd and his legal obligations (3:12a), and his fear of the lion (3:4,8; 5:1a). Catching birds and other hunting experiences are familiar to him (3:5), from the vantage Point of the steppe he longs for the blessing of streams that flow perennially (5:24).

c) The Message of Amos: The first answer to the question concerning the proclamation of Amos must be, in keeping with his own perspective, that it is the message from Yahweh. For he has basically defined it as such (3:8; 7:15; 7:1-8; 8: 1-2; 9: 1-4). We can summarize the main message of Amos under the following points: each point is discussed briefly for clarification.

1) How does Amos speak of Yahweh? At the outset Amos says that Yahweh is at work with humanity. He speaks neither of Yahweh's justice or his faithfulness, nor of his covenant or his law. Nor once does Amos use any fixed expression to say that Yahweh is "Israel's God". In contrast to the listing's fullness of affirmation, the most extreme simplicity in speaking "Yahweh" is Amos' own way to express his deep emotion and reverence.

No Baal competes with Yahweh for Israel's affections as we find in the situation to be in Hosea. But neither is there a God apart from Yahweh responsible for foreign nations (1:3-8, 13-15; 2:1-3; 3:2; 9:7). Thus, Amos offers no Polemic against any cult of foreign God's. That Yahweh is the only God of Israel and of the world of nations and is not a theme of his message but its self-evident presupposition.

If Yahweh has chosen Israel before all nations-and for Amos election must be seen in connection with the giving of the land, and not with they exodus from Egypt (cf 2: 9 with 9: 7b) then this election establishes, for Amos, only the divine Judgment (3: 2). Thus, Amos is remarkably laconic (given to such a speech) and theologically independent with regard to the traditions of salvation history.

Amos often declares that Yahweh's speaking has frighteningly and powerfully overwhelmed him (3:8; 7:15). Amos presents the message of Yahweh by affirming that Yahweh himself intervenes in the situation. By using first person speech form Amos communicates the message of Yahweh thus: "I will send fire..., I will break..., I will cut off" (1:4-5,7-8,14; 2:2-3); "I will turn my hand against" (1:8); "I will wreck" (3:15); "I will pass through your midst" (5: 17b); "I will send you into exile" (5:27); I abhor..., I hate..., I will deliver up" (6:8); "I will raise up against You" (6:14) etc.

Death is brought to Israel not by Yahweh's absence, but precisely by his undesired new advent (5; 16-17). Thus Amos never speaks of Yahweh as such, but only of Yahweh's dealings with humanity, of his speaking to and through the prophet, and in all this, especially, of his advent which Israel will experience as a destructive blow.

2) The exploitation of the Poor: Amos' social criticism: In his prophecies Amos develops what the visions only suggest: the built of Israel's leaders as the reason for the downfall: the very first saying (2. 4-8) against Israel in the book gives a detailed picture of this idea:

The sale of men and women is condemned - a gross inhumanity for modern readers. In fact, the sale of men and women was permitted according to ancient oriental and Israelite law, if debts could not otherwise be paid. Amos does not oppose the existing law in principle, such as the unreasonable seizure of clothing as security, or of wine from a debtor, it was the sign of a fatal tendency in contemporary society. Under the pretext of justice, the ***derek*** (way: means the unity of a person's conduct and the course of his life) of a particular class of people is being 'turn aside'; this means meaningful living is made impossible. Amos here is concerned, not with individual events, but with their background and consequences. For his ***derek*** anthropology (and this is true of pre-exilic Israel as a whole), the ties between human beings and the God who confers salvation are inextricably linked with the economic freedom given by possession of one's own land. ***Derek*** on one's own land, given to the Patriarchs by God, counts as the precondition which makes a successful and harmonious life possible. A person has to be able to stand up straight on his own inherited ground. If he is bent down to the earth then his vital hope is extinguished. He is, for all practical purposes, dead.

In another example of Amos 4: 1-3, Amos sharply brings out his social criticism on Israel and her condition. This passage talks about a heedless, luxurious life led by an exploitative ruling class: This is the picture of the capital city i.e.: Samaria. He calls the elegant ladies 'cows'-cows of Bashan, which were a much valued breed of cattle at that time. Like replete cattle, they wilfully trample down their pastures, the lower classes of the people, on whom their existence in fact depends. Their fate will meet them on the same level. Amos may be mockingly picking up a cultic name the woman gave themselves, since they imagined themselves to be the worshippers of the mighty bull of Samaria (Hos. 8:5f), a North Israelite manifestation of Yahweh. Again Amos puts the relation between people and land in the foreground. The women will not be raped or killed, but they will be driven out of the land that nourishes them.

In 5:11f, Amos talks about the injustice m the realm of tax payment. In reality in the gateway of township of this kind - i.e., in the portico behind the one gateway in the town walls-the free, adult men of the community assembled. They alone had legal status and were empowered to take part in cultic ceremonies and to bear arms. The communal village democracy has legal and administrative competence. It decided on questions of inheritance and even pronounced judgment in the case of capital crimes. It probably also had the task of allotting to individual members of the community the taxes or compulsory labour which the state imposed on the local community. It looked after the local hilltop sanctuary; which its members visited. In spite of this democratic constitution, influential families gained the upper hand since it was they who were able to provide members for the local council. It was a great temptation to use a majority vote to distribute taxes in such a way that families which were small and economically weak bore an undue burden. This led Amos to rebuke in 5:11f.

3) Amos criticism of the cult and the search for God: In three or four sayings the prophet condemns the religious places and ceremonies of his People.When a sacrifice was offered at an Israelite sanctuary, the priest usually provided a declaratory formula. This generally declared the act to be 'well pleasing to God' and only exceptionally as 'Yahweh's abhorrence'. Amos dares to express a wholesale rejection of cultic offerings in Yahweh's name. (5:21ff):

"I hate, I despise your feasts...I have no Pleasure in your food offerings,/I will not look upon the saving offering (?) of your fatted beasts". Attending divine worship seems to be worse than questionable practices in dealings with the peasant farmers! If we know that the pre-exilic Israel was a religious and worshipping community, then what Amos was saying, if the listeners heard these words a cold shudder ran down their spines.

The sanctuaries of Bethel and Gilgal are named in horrifying terms. Amos' listeners believed that they will find Yahweh and life there. In Bethel Jacob once heard a divine voice (Gen 28: 13). At that very place, Jeroboam I set up a cult for God who "led up Israel out of the land of Egypt (1 Kings 12: 28). Gilgal was the first stage in the Promised Land, the beginning of the consummation of salvation history in the early period. It was there Joshua gave the word of Yahweh to his people. (Josh.3:10). These places are considered to be sacral than any other in the Northern Kingdom. Yet it is precisely these places which Amos declared were the breeding places of sacrilege.

What Amos attacks is not idolatrous cultic practices, or the number of altars everywhere in the country-as his contemporary Hosea does. The object of his polemic are practices which in the opinion of his listeners, were absolutely enjoyed by Yahweh on every Israelite. His listeners sought Bethel that they might live, expecting their physical existence (*chayim*) to be revitalized there, probably especially through the sacrament of the sacrificial feast (*Zebach*: 4:4; *Selem*: 5:22). Added to this was the strong thumbing of their faith; the faith that Israel would never again loose this land into which Yahweh had once led them "Yahweh is with us (5:14) was the formula coined for this. Amos turns this assurance upside down by Proclaiming the downfall of Gilgal and Bethel, Amos was forced to bring down the Pillars of traditional religion, especially Amos attacked the sacrificial meals and the sanctuaries because these the indulgent luxury of the rich was at the expense of the Poor man (cf. 6: 1-7, where an extravagant cultic celebration in Samaria is probably being castigated).

Amos also hints at alternative: a sincere search for Yahweh (5: 14f). What Amos is hinting here is not feast of jubilation but a rite of repentance, which did not require the splendour of ceremonies in Bethel and Gilgal. A rite of repentance (*som*) was an unusual ceremony. The people appeared before God with gestures of self-humiliation-torn clothes ashes in their hair, general hymns of lament-in order to hear an oracle showing that their prayers had been heard, or that collective doom had or had not averted. The prayer 'restore us' (Ps. 80: 19), belongs to this context. In Amos the search for God is bound up with the same aim. A pre-exilic Israelite was probably unable to conceive of repentance like this without some external rite. Thus Amos avoids the lofty word 'repentance', this is also indicated in the visible community relationships established by Yahweh.

4) Mispat and Sedaqa: Their reversal and Pésa: The words misphat and sedaqa is translated as, "justice and righteousness" are the Key words in the Preaching of Amos to Israel. These words occur at several places. We shall take one or two examples to express the mind of Amos in his message to Israel.

The paired concepts are used in 5:23-27. They represent the highest values of human behaviour and the human condition; and Amos can only declare that they are totally lacking at the present time. Because these values have been lost, Yahweh is incensed against Bethel and Joseph and sends an occupying power into the country. Amos' God emancipates himself from men and women and from their ritual worship.

5) The down fall of the neighbouring nations: When Yahweh wants to bring to an end the wickedness of Israel, Amos takes up all the neighbouring peoples one after another-the Philistines, the Phoenicians, the Edomites the Ammonites, Moab. A burden of rebellion has been gathered on them in the course of history, which Yahweh is no longer prepared to ignore. He will send a cleansing, destroying fire on them. All that Amos said about Israel's neighbours came to its fulfilment. All over Syria-Palestine the main cities and their places will be destroyed by fire. In the case of Ammonites, the government will be deported, and in Moab both army and government will be exterminated. The Aramean senders will be exterminated; whereas the people will be deported. The Philistines, Israel's old enemy, are to have the hardest fate. There the remnant of the people will be destroyed as well.

For Amos, the foreign nations are guilty before Yahweh because they have mistreated weaker human beings (1:3,6, 13,2:1) just as he at one time led the Philistines and the Arameans (9:76) and judged the Amorites (2:9), so he determines the future of the Arameans and the Philistines, the Moabites and the Amorites.

In describing the foreign nations; Amos' message has two important and specific elements:(i) Amos testifies that Yahweh alone is the God of Israel as well as the nations; the origin and future of both are freely determined by him; (ii) Amos equalizes nations with Israel and Israel with nations. The nations stand, just as does Israel, under Yahweh's guidance.

First of all, two cycles of speech units with uniform constructions clearly stand out: the proclamations of disaster against the nations (1:3-2:16: against: Damascus, 1:3-5, Gaza 1:6-8, Tyre 1:9f, Edom 1:11f, the Ammonites 1:13-15; Moab 2:1-3, Judah 2:4f and Israel 2:6-I6). In 3: 1-15 Amos deals with one particular issue: Yahweh will also pay special attention to the guilt of Israel, with whom he has dealt in such an exceptional way, the words of Judgement against the upper classes in the capital of Samaria are attached (3:9-11, 13-15, 4:1-3). Three admonitions appear in the following section 4:4-5:17, all of which are to do with the cult 5:18-20 talks about the day of Yahweh, 5:21-17 also talks against the way in which the cult is currently performed, an extended attack on luxurious life in Samaria followed by an announcement of judgement (6: 1-7) and two further invectives, 6:8-10 (11) and 12-14 ending again with "Yahweh, God Sabbath".

Amos ironically rejects all dependence on a faith in election (3:2) and treats with equal irony Israel's claim to be the "first of the nations" (6: 1-7). He does not even find any preference for Israel in the deliverance from Egypt, because Yahweh has guided other nations in the same fashion. Israel has deserted its God, as Amos shows above all by pointing to social and cultic sins, which constitute his major point of attack. He condemns as perverse (4:4-5, 3:4-5, 21-25) the observance of festival and sacrificial regulations he also observes that the people are filled with pride and self-confidence, eating and drinking well, and like David, babble their songs (6:1-6) a sign of then generally sinful attitude Israel will perish completely unless the repentance it has so long refused which Amos interprets as the seeking of Yahweh (5:4) and doing what is good (5:14) does not take place at the last moment. Even in this case, however, God remains completely free; Israel's repentance and return do not oblige him to forgive. All that Amos can bring himself to declare is a "perhaps" of deliverance (5:15).

iv. Obadiah

The book is the shortest prophetical writing of the Old Testament. According to the superscription (v I), the prophets message which is called "vision", the general term from the exilic period on, is directed against Edom on account of its hostile attitude towards Judah.Obadiah is composed of a variety of passages. We have the following divisions based on its stylistic characteristics; vv. 1-4, 5-7, 8-11, 12-15, 16, 17f, 19-21.

Some exegetes suggest that the date of the book ranging from ninth to the middle of the fourth century. Most scholars, however, assume that the prophet appeared in the period after the fall of Jerusalem in 587 BCE. This alone provides a reasonable occasion for the threats against Edom in vv. 16-18, because at that time Edom was ranged with the enemy and gloated over Judah's misfortune. Obadiah's word indicate that he was an eye witness to all these and preached his message soon afterwards.

a) Historical background: The Edomites were the descendants of Esau, who displaced the Horites (or Hurrians) that we read about in the Book of Genesis. The Horites and the Amorites were the original inhabitants of Palestine. During the Monarchy, David captured Edom, stationed a garrison there, and made Edom a vassal state (1 Chron. 18:12-13). Solomon later developed the port city of Ezion-geber (Elah; 1 Kings 9:26-28). Hadad, a member of the Edomite royal family, opposed Solomon and set up a government in exile in Egypt (1 Kings 11:14-17). But Judah still governed Edom during the reign of King Jehoshaphat, who posted a governor in Edom (1 Kings 22:47-48). Edom gained her freedom from Judah, in 845 B.C.E., by rebelling against Jehoram, the son of Jehoshaphat (2 Kings 8:20-22; 2 Chron. 21:8-10, 16-17). King Amaziah of Judah partially recaptured Edom between 790 and 770 B.C.E. (2 Kings 14:7). King Uzziah of Judah recaptured the port of Ezion-geber (2 Kings 14:21-22). Aram (Syria) later took back Ezion-geber from Judah (2 Kings 16:5-6). After that the Edomites revolted and attacked Judah a second time, during the reign of King Ahaz of Judah (2 Chron. 28:17). Finally, when King Nebuchadnezzar attacked Judah, the Edomites assisted the Babylonians (Ps. 137:7; Jer. 49:7-22; Ezek. 25:12-14; 35:1-15). After the Babylonian invasion of Judah—and of their former ally against Judah, Edom— the Nabatean Arabs took over the capital city of Sela (Greek:Petra) and forced the remaining Edomites into southern Judah, where they settled. The Greeks named this area "Idumea," and its inhabitants Idumeans, following Alexander the Great's conquest of Palestine in the 4th century B.C.E. After the Romans replaced the Greeks as the dominant power in Palestine, they permitted the Idumeans to enjoy some sovereignty. King Herod the Great, who was in charge of Palestine when Jesus was born, was an Idumean. The Idumeans later joined the Jews in revolting against the Romans in 68-70 C.E. Their defeat resulted in their scattering, and they ceased to exist as a people. This was the fulfillment of Obadiah's prophecy of judgment on their nation. Edom's history of antagonism against Israel was long and consistent.

b) The Message of the book: Obadiah reveals the culmination of sibling rivalry and the national antagonism that developed between the descendants of Jacob and Esau: the Israelites and the Edomites. The conflict between these two boys and their respective descendants began before they were born. The infants struggled in the womb of their mother Rebekah (Gen. 25:22). In describing this conflict, God "loved" Jacob, but God "hated" Esau (Mal. 1:2-3). The line of Esau produced the Herods. Both Jesus and the Herods were "kings of the Jews." Jesus never spoke to Herod Antipas, even when questioned by him, though He did send him a message once (Luke 13:32), illustrating the antagonism that existed between them. This antagonism consistently marked the relationship between the Edomites and the Israelites. Esau is in the foreground of the Book of Obadiah, and Jacob is in the background. Jacob and his descendants passed through suffering and chastisement, and their ultimate destiny is restoration and usefulness. Esau and his descendants were proud, rebellious, defiant, and their end was ultimate destruction. Jacob was the more unattractive personality originally, and Esau was more appealing. Yet God overruled what was natural, in order to produce what God wanted in the lives of both of these men, in view of their choices. Divine sovereignty and human choices are so intertwined that it is impossible for us to separate them. The Scriptures consistently present both as real and significant factors in the course of human affairs. Obadiah tells the story of the destruction of Edom, the nation that descended from Esau. It also shows that God will destroy all that Edom stood for and represented. "Edom" is "Esau projected into national proportions." In Obadiah, we see the essential evil of Esau, the supreme manifestation of that evil, and the inevitable result of that evil. But we also see a ray of hope even for "the mount of Esau," Mt. Seir, the most notable geographical feature in Edom, that often represents the nation of Edom in the Old Testament (by metonymy).

The essential evil of Esau and Edom was pride. This comes through in verse 3: "The arrogance of your heart has deceived you, you who live in the clefts of the rock, in the loftiness of your dwelling place, who say in your heart, who will bring me down to earth?" The Edomites lived in a rocky, reclusive region around a town that later became known as Petra: ancient Sela. The Nabateans, the Arabians who later drove the Edomites out, actually carved Petra out of solid rock. The habitation of the Edomites, who occupied this region before the Nabateans took it over, says much about them. They were self-reliant isolationists and fiercely independent. The Edomites had their idols, and they did not bow to the true and living God. The Edomites thought they were invincible. Esau had no use for the promises of God, and his descendants, too, thought they could get along quite well without God. The Edomites built their nests high, like the eagles—so high they appeared to be among the stars (v. 4). The eagle is often a picture of deity in the Bible. In the Edomites' case, they had deified themselves and made themselves their god. They thought they could protect themselves from danger and enemies by building their homes high in the cliffs of the Edom wilderness. But God said that God would bring them down (v. 4). If pride was Edom's essential sin, violence was the supreme manifestation of that sin. The Edomites not only protected themselves, but they did wrong to others, and rejoiced when they harmed others. Verses 10 and 11 say, "Because of violence to your brother Jacob you will be covered with shame and cut off forever. On the day that you stood aloof, on the day that strangers carried off his wealth, and foreigners entered his gate and cast lots for Jerusalem, you too were as one of them." When the Edomites saw their brother Israelites suffering, they not only complacently did nothing, but they even rejoiced and added to those sufferings. The Israelites represented faith in Yahweh. They stood for this ideal, though admittedly they failed to be consistent in their witness. Nevertheless, they continued to believe in God and to follow God. The Edomites' unnatural violence against the Israelites revealed their hatred for what the Israelites stood for, not just the Israelites themselves. So when the Israelites suffered, the Edomites rejoiced. Even though they were the Israelites' brothers according to the flesh, they consistently opposed them for what the Israelites stood for. For example, the Edomites refused to allow the Israelites to pass through their territory on the way to the Promised Land. The result of such godless pride, which leads to violence against the people of God, is divine retribution. The Edomites thought they were secure (v. 4), but God said that He would bring them down (v. 4). "Will I not on that day, declares the LORD, destroy wise men from Edom and understanding from the mountain of Esau? Then your mighty men will be dismayed, O Teman, in order that every one may be cut off from the mountain of Esau by slaughter" (vv. 8-9). The God, whom the Edomites thought they could disregard, would visit and destroy them. God is higher than even the eagles. God is the One who formed the mountains in which the Edomites foolishly trusted for safety. God would bring down the Edomites by overruling the plans the Edomites made. The Edomites also trusted in other nations for their security rather than in God. But the Lord would use the very objects of Edom's trust to destroy her. As usual, God would deal with Edom in poetic justice, or talionic judgment. What they had sowed they would reap (cf. Gal. 6:7-8). Esau had sowed to the flesh, and in the end the flesh became the instrument of the Edomites' destruction. God said, "As you have done, it will be done to you" (v. 15). But this prophecy does not end with promises of Edom's destruction. It ends with promises of Israel's final victory, and the vindication of Israel's God. Obadiah predicted that, first of all, despised Israel would be delivered from her proud enemy. "The house of Jacob will possess their possessions" (v. 18). "Deliverers will ascend Mount Zion to judge the mountain of Esau" (v. 21). Then "the kingdom will be the Lord's" (v. 21). This book gives us hope. God will eventually destroy all Edomite types, just as God has already destroyed the historic Edomites in fulfillment of Obadiah's prophecy.

Obadiah's message shows him to be a representative of the optimistic prophecy attacked by Jeremiah. The central message of Obadiah is not religious nationalism, but the ethical seriousness of his faith and his hope for God's compensatory justice. The expectation of just retribution, clearly stated in v.15b, run through all his sayings. It is connected with the concept of the Day of Yahweh as a day of judgement against the nations, on which Edom above all will receive its just desert. The appended promise, according to which Judah-Israel, a nation of brothers overthrown with the help of Edom, will rise again, place the book within an eschatological frame work.

v. Jonah

The book of Jonah occupied a special position within the prophetic books. It contains a prophetic narrative in which there is only one brief prophetic saying (3:4b). The name of the prophet Jonah was not only rooted in the tradition (II Kings. 14:25) but he was also assigned a particular place in the prophetic tradition.

The narrative is very clear and vivid. It is divided into two main parts with parallel constructions, both of which begin the commissioning of the prophet of preach judgement on the city of Nineveh (1:1f; 3: 1f). This is followed 1n the first part by Jonah's flight on a ship which gets into difficulties, the situation finally leads the seamen to recognize Yahweh as God (1:13-16). In parallel to this the second part reports how Jonah carries out his task and how the inhabitants of Nineveh report (3:3-10). In both the main parts there then follows a prayer by Jonah (with a similar introductory formula in 2:2 and 4:2): in 23-10 (with a narrative frame work in vv. 1, 11). There is a 'Psalm'; in 4:2f, a prayer which leads to a discussion between Yahweh and Jonah, in which Yahweh justifies his action (vv. 4-11).

a) Historicity: Since the rise of critical scholarship in the nineteenth century, many writers and teachers now believe that the events recorded in this book were not historical. They interpret this book as an allegory or as a parable. The allegorical interpretation views the book as "a complete allegory in which each feature represents an element in the historical and religious experience of the Israelites."[9] This interpretation may have arisen because "Jonah" means

9 R. K. Harrison, *Introduction to the Old Testament*, p. 911.

"dove," and the Jew had long regarded the dove as a symbol of their nation (cf. Ps. 74:19; Hos. 11:11). Jonah indisputably brought peace to violent Nineveh as a dove. Those who adopt this interpretation see the book as teaching Israel's mission and failure in being God's missionary agent to the Gentiles. Jonah's flight to Tarshish represents Israel's failure before the Exile, and the great fish symbolizes Babylon. The disgorging of Jonah stands for Israel's second chance following her restoration to the land. The parabolic interpretation also regards the book as not historical.[10] However, its advocates view it as simply a moral story designed to teach a spiritual lesson. Essentially, the lesson is that God's people should not be narrow and introverted, but outreaching and missionary in their love and concern for those outside their number who are facing God's judgment. The main argument against the book being historical is Jonah's surviving three days and nights in the fish's belly (1:17). However, various writers have documented many similar miraculous deliverances. Since such a survival is physically possible, we should not dismiss the historical view, especially since Jesus endorsed Jonah's "resurrection."

b) Genre: The book is probably a sensational didactic prophetic historical narrative in its literary genre.[11] As I mentioned before, many commentators who deny the historicity of the book regard it as a parable or allegory, and its literary tone as parody or satire.[12]

c) Purpose: The book is a revelation to God's people of God's sovereign power and loving concern for all His creatures, even cattle (4:11). This revelation came first to Jonah personally, and then through him to the Jews. It was not primarily a revelation to the Ninevites. Their responsibility was simply to repent and humble themselves. This revelation should have moved the Israelites to respond as the Assyrians did, namely: with repentance and humility. They faced similar threats, first from the Assyrians and then from the Babylonians. Jonah's lack of concern for the Ninevites contrasts with God's concern for them that was to be the pattern for His people. "The main purpose of the book is to teach Israelites that God loves other nations than their own; or, in fact, to teach us that he loves other nations than our own. In service of this purpose, Jonah stands for most Israelites— or most of us—as he represents the typical attitude people tend to have toward nations they have no reason to love themselves."[13]

---

10 Tremper Longman III and Raymond B. Dillard, *An Introduction to the Old Testament*, pp. 444-45.

11 Ernst R. Wendland, "Text Analysis and the Genre of Jonah (Part 1)," Journal of the Evangelical Theological Society 39:2 (June 1996): 191-206.

12 Leslie C. Allen, *The Books of Joel*, Obadiah, Jonah and Micah, pp. 177-181.

13 Douglas K. Stuart, *Hosea-Jonah*, p. 479.

d) Message of the Book: The Book of Jonah does not contain the record of a prophet's message as much as the record of a prophet's experience. That feature makes Jonah distinctive among the prophetic books. This prophet's experiences are what we need to look at to learn the message of this book. That is also true of the Former Prophets books: Joshua, Judges, Samuel, and Kings. They, too, teach by recording selected experiences more than prophetic oracles. There are many incidental features of this story, such as the ship, the storm, the fish, the gourd, the worm, the hot wind, and even Nineveh. They are important parts of the revelation, but they do not give us the message of the book. It is the major characters of the story that do that. The major characters are God and Jonah. God's dealings with Jonah are even more important than God's dealings with the Ninevites, from the standpoint of the book's revelation. These dealings reveal God's attitude and activity toward the nations, and toward His own people—for the nations' sake. We have here a revelation of Yahweh and a revelation of the responsibility of Yahweh's representatives. One of the characteristics that marked the Israelites was their exclusivity. During the reign of Jeroboam II, when Jonah ministered, Israel was expanding geographically. She was forming alliances with her neighboring nations. However at the same time, she was more exclusive religiously than she ever had been. The Israelites believed The major revelation of Yahweh in this book comes through in God's dealings with Nineveh and in God's dealings with Jonah. Note, first, what this book reveals about the Lord from His dealings with Nineveh. Rather than having a superior, exclusive attitude toward the Ninevites, God's attitude was compassion. We can see this attitude at the beginning of the book, when God commands Jonah to go to Nineveh. We see it again in God's patient persistence, as God brings the prodigal prophet to repentance. We see it again when God sends Jonah there a second time. The clearest revelation of God's attitude toward Nineveh, however, comes through in the last two verses of the book (4:10-11). Jonah was probably the first of the eighth-century writing prophets (ca. 780 B.C.E.). Other eighth-century prophets who ministered to the Northern Kingdom of Israel, beside Jonah, were Hosea (760 B.C.E.), who emphasized the love of God, and Amos (760 B.C.E.), who emphasized the righteousness of God. Isaiah (740 B.C.E.) stressed the holiness of God, and Micah (735 B.C.E.) the leadership of God to the residents of the Southern Kingdom of Judah. Jonah reveals the compassion of God primarily. It is an important balancing revelation among these other prophetic messages. It is God's attitude of compassion. All of God's activities in this book proceeded from this basic attitude. We might conclude that God sent Jonah to preach against Nineveh only because God was angry with it, because of its sin. Certainly it was under God's judgment for its sins, but the last verse reveals the underlying motive of God: God's compassion. Seen in this light, the troublesome statement that God changed God's mind in 3:10

becomes less problematic. The Hebrew word used here, *nacham*, carries the connotation of being relieved and comforted. We should hear God sighing in relief when we read this verse. When Nineveh repented, God saw that judgment would not be necessary, and this made God very glad. When people turn from their sin, God turns from judging them. Of course, God's judgment of sin is a manifestation of God's love, but we do not often appreciate that fact. Turning to what this book reveals about God's dealings with Jonah, we see two things.

First, God needs messengers. In one sense, God needs no one and nothing because God is self-sufficient. However in another sense, God has chosen to send God's messages through people. The New Testament expression of this truth is: "How shall they hear without a preacher?" (Rom. 10:14). God has chosen to use human messengers to carry most of His messages to other humans.

The second thing that we see, as we examine God's dealings with Jonah, is that because God needs messengers, God is persistent and patient with the messengers God selects. We see this in God not abandoning Jonah when he boarded the ship to go to Tarshish. We see it in God preparing a fish to preserve and transport him back to dry land. We see it in God re-commissioning Jonah. We see it in God providing a gourd to shelter the prophet. We see it in God's patient teaching when Jonah was burning up with heat and anger. We see it in God's attempts to bring Jonah into sympathy with God's merciful purpose. In all these instances, we see God lovingly persuading the prophet to share God's fellowship by sharing God's attitude.

To sum up: the book of Jonah is concerned with a central problem: are the announcements of Yahweh's judgement valid? Jonah knew that Yahweh is a gracious God, who repents of his announcement of Judgement (4:2), therefore he escaped so as not to be a false prophet (cf: Deut. 18:21 f). Here the view that the judgement of Yahweh proclaimed over Israel is final is rejected. In Jonah 4 we have the reason for this: human life (and even animal life) is more important to Yahweh than consistently keeping to a word of Judgement once spoken. Thus, it is also said in Ezek. 18:23, 32: Yahweh does not will the death of a sinner but that he should repent and live.

vi) Micah

The book of Micah is a complex collection of prophetic texts which has a long history behind it. It is stamped in particular by the combination of judgement of salvation which also appears in other prophetic books. Micah has come from Moresheth-gath, a small village in the hill country of Judah south west of Jerusalem. Micah was active during the time of Hezekiah (Jer 26:18), since 1:2-9 is directed against Samaria Micah's activity must have begun before the fall of Samaria in 722. His ministry, therefore lasts from around 725 sometime before 711. This makes him a younger contemporary of Isaiah; whose ministry follows chronologically that of Hosea in Israel. Therefore, Micah must have been familiar with Isaiah's utterances, two of Micah's sayings are influenced by Isaiah 1:10-15 by Isa 10:27 b-32 and 2:1-3 by Isa. 5:8-10.

Micah's writing can be examined clearly in four independent sections: 1-3. Invectives and threats against Israel and Judah: 4-5; promises: 6: 1 -7: 7; exhortations, invectives, and threats and 7: 8-20: promises.

Structurally, the book follows the two-part eschatological schemes twice repeated. First the eschatological promises in 45 were appended to Micah's invectives and threats in 1-3 producing the sequence disaster-deliverance. The same "before and after" is repeated in the sections 6:1-7:7 and 7:820, which were appended later.

a) Historical Period: The book of Micah contains sayings of several centuries even though the prophetic activity is limited to a certain Period. The book contains sayings of neo-Assyrian, neo-Babylonian as well as the sayings from a period in which an Israelite remnant in the Persian Empire was gathered together.

It is certain however, based on the majority of his sayings, Micah of Moresheth appeared in the second half of the eighth century. But the words transmitted to us in the book are related to people from the most desperate phases of history, from the second half of eighth century to around the first half of the fifth century B.C. We are however, unable to date certain original Prophecies of Micah due to some reasons; for example:

(i) In Jer. 26:18 Micah of Moresheth is mentioned only once Micah is mentioned as a prophet who appeared in the days of Hezekiah, King of Judah. Hezekiah reigned 29 years from third year of Hoshea northern King (II Kings 18:1f) thus probably from 729 to 700. "In Micah 3:12 often placed in proximity to the siege upon the city made by the Assyrian Sennacherib in the Year 701 BCE. However, in the motivation (3:9-11) for the disaster no connection with Political matters or military actions is to be recognized, as we find for eg in Isa 30:1-5; 31:1-3. Instead this text of Micah speaks only of injustice in the city (v.9), mainly rooted in the building activity. Therefore Jerusalem will become a "heap of ruins" (vv. 10-11). (ii) According to Micah 1:1, Prophet works not only under Hezekiah but also works under his two Predecessors, Jotham and Ahaz; (iii) According to 1:6-16, a different date is suggested Micah, especially in 1:6, a reference is made against Samaria which was under siege for three years (725-722 B.C).

In light of those considerations, we can say 722 B.C. is the *terminus ad quem* for the entire text in 1:6-16 originally from Micah.

The texts contained in the book of Micah extend far beyond the final quotation of Micah 3:12 in Jer. 26:17-19 already indicates. The historical background of all the prophecies contained in the book of Micah comprehends, therefore a span of time of about three hundred years.

b) The Language of Micah:

1) Style: Micah carefully follows the order of events and with a lively interest, notes their details and features. Even when Micah uses parallelism, he moves quickly from fact to fact. He sometimes emphasizes the climax of a speech by using alliteration. eg: 1:16 "Make large your baldness like a buzzard (vulture)..."

Micah's passionate accusations can also be expressed crudely and dramatically. For eg: what the construction workers must suffer in Jerusalem he portrays with metaphors borrowed from the butcher shop. What the farmer in the Shephelah routinely does only to his cattle the leaders in the capital city do to human beings "remove the hide" - "break the bones" - "devour their flesh" (3:2f,10). Micah's usage becomes lively by this frequent use of quotations (cf. 2:3 f; 2: 1 f): "we are completely ruined; our fields are divided". We always find in Micah the forms of direct address (2nd Person Plu. cf. 2:3b-4a, 8-10, 3:12a). Questions also promote his contact with his audience; he formulates questions with his audience's quotations (2:7a, 3:11a). Questions he himself poses (2:7b), counter questions to the authorities (3:1b).

2) Genre: Three important genres are Prominent in Micah's Speech:

i) The **judgment speeches:** found in 1:6f, 2:2-4; 3:1-4; 8,9-12 They all exhibit a taunt form, usually of two Parts, in which the accusation, as a rule, Precedes (2:11f; 3:1-3,5,9-11), and is often more detailed than, the announcement of disaster (2:3f; 3:4,6-7, 12). The announcement of disaster, usually attached to the announcement by **laken** ("therefore" -2:3; 3:6-12 except 3:4 where **'az** "then' is used) is the proof of guilt which provides the motivation for divine announcement. Only in 1:6,7b is the announcement followed by the accusation with a "because" or "for" clause gives the motivation for divine punishment. The simple form of two-part judgment speech accords with the manner method of the elders who, sitting in the legal gate of the villages, made their indictments, brought attention to legal infringements, and explained their legal decisions.

This parallels describe our attention, because Micah usually introduces the Punishment as the direct consequence of the guilt (a wisdom connection) to which he has pointed, without presenting the punishment as though it were brought on by the special direction of Yahweh (cf. 3:4,6,12) only one saying is given with messenger formula (2:3a).

ii) By contrast, the judgment speech in 2:1-4 exhibits an element that is central to the **funerary lament**. Sentences of the accusations are introduced with the use cry from the death lament. The woe cry belongs to the mourning ceremonies of the clan, and thus Micah as clean elder would be familiar with it. In 1:8-16, many other elements of the mourning rites (weeping, rolling in the dust, lamentation, shaving the head bald in vv. 8,10,11) devastating war and capitulation (vv.11-15), also symbolic action of "barefoot and naked".

The summons to lament do not speak of the guilt of Judah or Jerusalem, where the reports of disaster led to serious actions besides mourning rites, nevertheless at no point do they summon the people to pray to repent, or some act of worship, Micah is in no way connected with cultic functions, he speaks in 'a religious' manner, this too is true in the light too of his office as an elder from Judah.

iii) The **disputation speech:** Probably belongs as well to the rhetorical forms of the elders at the city gate: the form occurs in 2:6-11. It begins with a quotation of Micah's opponents, who register their protest (v.6) and then asks questions (v.7a), a reply is then given, which, formulated as direct address (2nd Person), immediately shifts from a general accusation (v.7a) reply is than given, which formulated as direct address (2nd person), immediately shifts from a general accusation (v. 8a) to concrete reproaches (vv. 8b-10) Micah's rejection of his opponents concludes with a sarcastic picture of the kind of accommodating prophet desired by the people (v 11), Yahweh is mentioned once by the protesters (v. 7a). The alteration between direct address (2nd person), and report (3rd person) reflects the course of, disputation speech: at first, in the style of a report (3rd Person v.6a). Micah quotes his opponents (probably before the assembly before the city gate), next, in the course of indictment he addresses them directly (2n Person vv. 11) refers to them as "this people over there" as he hands them over to the assembly for sentencing.

c) Message of Micah: The heart and the centre of Micah's message can be stated briefly: Yahweh is bringing inexorable doom on Samaria, Jerusalem and the cities of Judah. The guilt for this rests with the authorities and the leading citizens, such as Judges, Prophets, and Priests.

Prophet is concerned about his home town. Village after village is exposed to the doom (2: 1-11) but at the same time Micah is concerned about Jerusalem (3:1-12).

What is the origin of the approaching disaster? While the destructive elements are clearly scotched out, all of which point to military conquest, nevertheless "the conquest" (l;15a) is not mentioned by name. "Assyria" is mentioned in 5;5b (6b) by a late of voice. The Prophet expresses that Yahweh as the author of imminent catastrophe (1:12b, 2:3). For Micah, Samaria will be demolished (1-6), Jerusalem will be completely destroyed, and even the temple mount will become a wilderness (3:12), the present authorities become enslaved, losing their property (2:3f), the children of the people will be carried into exile (1:16), there are also hints of military occupation and flight (1:15).

Motivation for the disaster: it is Yahweh's judgment that terrifies Micah (2:3), the guilty are not the individual members but "Jacob" and Israel, with its wickedness and sin i.e., the same entity for which he holds the heads and leaders of Jerusalem responsible, according to 3:1,19. Micah places the guilty before a court of justice which is not ministered in the gate of the village;

rather, it is Yahweh who, comprehensively and conclusively executes justice over Judah and Jerusalem.

If more precisely we ask to whom in particular Micah accuses in his judgment speeches, then clearly it is not the people of Judah and Jerusalem as a whole; rather, it is exclusively the leaders in positions of responsibility; the authorities (2:1b), especially the heads, overseers, judges, priests and prophets in Jerusalem (3:1,5,9,11).

Why does he accuse them of guilt? Because they transgress against one people whom Micah considers himself so responsible-a responsibility which they are supposed to carry out. What for Micah is the decisive criterion of his accusation? Justice (mishpat) i.e. the orders and institutions of justice which guide and orient Israel, and to which the heads and judges of Jerusalem should equally consider themselves obligated but which they abhor (cf. 3:1b, ab with 3:8a). Accordingly, Micah can formulate his accusation against the leading circles in general terms: "They hate the good and love the evil" (3:2a) or "They twist all that is straight". When Micah expresses himself in concrete terms, he appreciates catchwords for guilt from Israel's legal tradition: "covet", "role", "Oppress" (2:2 cf. Exod. 20:17a, b; Lev. 19:13 etc.).

Micah's message turns out to be powerful and distinct in his own context. He had first-hand experience with the social evils he attacks, especially the Jerusalem - based dissolution of ancient agrarian law in favour of large, property owners. The violence of his attacks and the bitterness of his threats, which go beyond What is usually found in prophecy, are explained by his sympathy with the sufferings of the peasants and his contempt for the professional cult prophets, who say what the rich want them to sayfor financial gain. He gives a more basic reason in his description of his mission (3:8). With power, justice, and might he is to confront and are therefore protected against any disaster. To the claim to be, God's people he replies (2:6-8) tersely and caustically, "you are anything but 'my people!'" His only message, therefore, can be inescapably destruction.

vii. Nahum

The superscription of the book of Nahum tells us only that he comes from Elkosh, but the location of this town, which tradition places near Nineveh as well as in Judea and Galilee, is completely unknown.

At first sight, two passages clearly stand out in the book of Nahum: an introductory psalm (132-8) and an announcement of disaster for Nineveh (2:4. 3:19) consisting of several strophes. There is a dispute about the relationship of these and about how the intervening verses 1:9-2:3 are to be understood. Without doubt the Psalm (1:2-8) offers an interpretation of the books as a whole: Yahweh is the penal and gracious God (1:2-3a); because he is creator and Lord of the World (vv. 3b-5) no one can resist him (v.6) and whereas he is a refuge for those who trust in him (v.7), he is making an end for his adversaries (v.8). The section 1:9 2:3 is also governed by the contrast between danger from enemies and preservation by Yahweh. The next section 2:4; 3: 19, is directed as a whole against Nineveh, which is explicitly mentioned in 2:9-3:7. It is clearly divided into three sub-sections(i) In 2:4-14 there is the dramatic portrayal of the conquest of Nineveh by an uncanny enemy who is not mentioned by name; after a taunt song (vv. 12 f) the conclusion is made up of Yahweh's threat 'Behold I will . . .' (2:14). (ii) 3:1-7 begins with a 'woe' on the 'blood city' and continues to description of the annihilation. (iii) In 3:8-19 Nineveh is compared with the city No-Amon (=Thebes) which also had to fall, again there is a taunt-song at the end (vv. 18 f).

a) Historical Background: There are two specific historical events mentioned in the book. The first (in chronological order) is the sack of the Egyptian city of Thebes, called **No'amon** in 3:8, by Esarhaddon, King of Assyria. He brought it under Assyrian control in 670 BCE but finally captured it in 661 BCE. The other is the fall of Nineveh in 612 BCE to Cyaxares, the Mede, in alliance with the Babylonians after a siege of three months. We might suppose from this that we are able to pinpoint Nahum somewhere in the period between 661 and 612, as it is done by many scholars: but two difficulties because of this: (i) it is by no means clear when a Prophet is referring to a past event and when he is Predicting something yet to happen in the future. That is because of the rhetorical device known to Hebraists as the **prophetic perfect** (i.e., explaining a past event as though it happened at Present). This Partly explains why commentators have been divided in their opinions as to whether Nahum is predicting the fall of Nineveh, or is describing something which had already taken Place: (ii) the 'historical' references in the prophetic books is that they may have had at the time the original Prophet used them, or acquainted latter among those who Passed on his words, a symbolic meaning (eg. Babylon in the first chapter of the book of Revelation as equal to Rome). It is quite possible that the book of Nahum uses 'Nineveh' in such a way and, if that were so, we could no, more 'date' it by the fall of historical city of Nineveh than we could date the author of 'Revelation' by the fall of the historical city of Babylon.

However, it is safe to assume that there was a Prophet Nahum somewhere behind the Present book, and that he lived in the time of Assyrian domination over Judah and much of the ancient Near East, probably towards the time of the decline and fall of that empire. Micah lived in the shadow of cast by the rise of Assyrian power, Manasseh as the King of Judah (647-642 B.C.E) was a vassal of Assyria throughout his reign. The great Assyrian King Ashurbanipal (668-627 BCE) as the King who sacked Thebes in 661 (Nah. 3:8). But by the end of his reign Assyria was already being menaced by the combined threat of the Medes and the Babylonians. Soon after Ashurbanipal's death these inflicted a defeat on the Assyrians just outside Babylon in 626 B.C.E. In 614 the capital city of Asshur fell of Cyaxares the Mede, and two years later Cyaxares and Nabopolassar of Babylon took Nineveh. So, if Micah may be said to have witnessed the dawn of the Assyrian empire, Nahum celebrated its sunset.

b) The Poetic Style of Nahum: The prophet expresses his ideas in vigorous, imaginative, lively poetry which makes it something of a literary masterpiece. The oppressor nation is a lion in its den (2:11ff) or again a Prostitute (3:4), the shock of Yahweh's judgment produces the staggering and helplessness of drunkenness (3:11). Similes: God's victims are swept away like stubble before God's wrath which burns; like fire (1:12), the cries of the captive women sound like the moaning of doves (2:7,8). The city is like a Pool of water evaporating in the sun (2:8) cf. 3:15, 3:16. The literary device of the rhetorical question sharpens the irony: 1:6; 2:11 et. al. In 1:6 "who can stand before his indignation?"; 2:11 "Where is the lion's den?"; 3: 8: "Are you better than No-Amon?".

c) The Message of Nahum: According to this prophet, Yahweh is the champion of the outraged and helpless and "will by no means justify the guilty" (1:3). In the final analysis, the threat against Nineveh does not stem from Personal hatred of the human author or some historical event in the seventh century B.C.E, but from the nature of God who is jealous for the righteous, wrathful towards his enemies, and claims dominion over the world. The vision of Nahum renders intelligible this imminent sovereignty of Israel's God over the history of nations. In the words of B.S. Childs this idea is further captured strongly "What nation can withstand the God who overcame the Primordial Chaos" (**OT Introduction**p. 444). The prophetic message is the defeat of Nineveh (Assyrians) is a sign of the victory of God and the basis for hope that his power and justice will ultimately conquer all evil.The book of Nahum it is made clear from the beginning that Nineveh is simply, the representative and example of the powers opposed to Yahweh and that none of these powers can withstand him since he is creating of the world (1:3b-6).

viii. Habakkuk

He is referred as a professional prophet with a message against foreign nation. He was probably associated with Jerusalem temple, where he actively sought to receive a vision (2:1), proclaimed the instruction that he received (2:4), and wrote it upon a tablet (2:2).

The division of the book is clear: a lament by the prophet is twice (1:2-4, 12-17) followed by a divine answer (1:5-11, 2:1-5), the second answer (1:5-11, 21:1-5) is followed by a series of woes (2:6-20) concluded by a Psalm (ch. 3), which is provided with an introduction of its own (v.1) and a closing note about the musical way in which it is to be performed (v. 19b).

The sayings in 1:2-2:5 seem to more on two different levels. The prophet complains about violence and the decline of justice among his own people (1:24). However, instead of announcing the hoped for help the divine answer (vv. 5-11) forecasts the attack of the hostile people (according to v.6 the Babylonians) which will exercise its own right (v. 7) and practiced violence (v.9). In the renewed lamentation (vv. 12-17) the speech about the people destined by Yahweh for judgement (v. 12b) is combined with a lamentation over injustice (v.13b).W. Rudolph, refers the speech about the unrighteous who swallow up the righteous (v. 13) to be Babylonians, they are summoned by Yahweh to punish the unrighteous and now themselves prove to be unrighteous. So the seemed lament is an 'accusation' (2: lb) and the criticism of the conduct of the Babylonians who have arrogantly exceeded the task set them (vv. 15:17 is understandable in this context. Yahweh's second answer (2:15) must similarly be understood in that light against present appearances the prophet is told in a future-oriented 'vision' that in the end the righteous person who has so far kept faith will live (v.4). While the violent ruler who exceeds himself will perish (v.5). In chapter 3 then prophet I describes the present historical occasion points to an eschatological theophany of Yahweh.

a) The Historical Context: Habakkuk's message fits historically in the context of the fall of Nineveh (612 BCE) and emergence of Babylon as the Neo-Babylonian Kingdom (605 BCE) mentioned in 1:6. Habakkuk witnessed significant shifts as the death of Josiah brought an end to the era of reform and Judah rapidly lost her independence. She would only dance to the Piping of the international powers around her. Jehoiakim, a selfish, tyrannical, and godless King, took over following the brief reign of Jehoahaz (in 609 BCE).

Habakkuk cried out against the violence he witnessed (1:2), he spoke God's word in a crisis situation from an increased lawlessness and injustice in Judah (vv.2-5). After Josiah's sudden death. (609 BCE) and the rise of Babylon in 605 BCE. Assyria and Egypt had been defeated by Babylon at Carchemish, and Judah's days were numbered.

b) Literary forms in Habakkuk: The book of Habakkuk has two Prophetic laments (1: 2-4, 12-17) in which the prophet questions Yahweh's righteousness. The Lord responds with oracles of Judgment (vv. 5-11; 2:1-4). The dialogue between God and the prophet ends (2:5) only to be followed by a taunt, comprising five "woes" (vv. 6-20). The connection between the dialogues (1:2-2:5) and the taunt is left for the reader to apprehend, but this ambiguity and the terse poetic style encourage the reader to listen closely to his speech, to God's speech to the Prophet, and to the prophet's speech against Babylon.

The third chapter is set apart with its own introduction, "A Prayer of Habakkuk the Prophet" (3:1), and with its musical notation (see v.1 on

Shigionoth, v.1 "For the director of Music. On my stringed instrument," v.19). This chapter consists of several genres (hymn, lament, and thanksgiving).

c) The Message of Habakkuk: Habakkuk deals with the moral questions of God's raising up the Babylonians. The Assyrians had been cruel, Nineveh had been destroyed in 612 B.C.E, just as Nahum had Prophesized, and the last vestiges of Assyrian power were to come to an end at Carchemish (605 BC). Assyria, "the rod of God's anger", had fallen prey to its own Pride, but they wondered God could use Babylon to inflict Judgment on Judah when their cruelty and pagan way further destroyed God's Kingdom? The questions of Habakkuk encouraged godly to develop an experiential faith (the righteous will live by his faith", Hab 2:4) and to submit to God's rule, who freely uses crooked instruments in the establishment of his kingdom. To focus sharply on the message of Habakkuk, two important issues can be brought out here.

1) God's freedom and Righteousness in Judgment: Habakkuk charged the Lord with being unfair using the form of a Prophetic complaint (1:2-4). How could the Lord permit the country of Judah to continue breaking his covenant? Idolatry, immorality, and corruption were so Prevalent that God's Kingdom was "Paralyzed" (v.4). The wicked has overtaken the righteous in number. The days were so harsh that the godly were considered accused, whereas the wicked prospered. The Lord's response (vv. 5-11) was not completely to Habakkuk's liking, but violence of the Babylonians. "Like" would be overcome by "like" but for Habakkuk, the point is how can Babylon might accomplish God's purpose?

Habakkuk's second complaint (1:12-17) was twofold. *Firstly*, he charged Judah with destroying the foundations of God's Kingdom by reverting justice and righteousness. *Second*, he lamented God's response, fearing that in his freedom, all his righteousness might be uprooted from the land and result in absolute anarchy (v.17). "living by faith" is the key expression of Habakkuk, the lord revealed to the Prophet that his righteous Kingdom will be established in the end (2:2,14, 2:3 et. al.).

2) The final triumph of God's righteousness: The book of Habakkuk challenges the righteous to discern God's will in adverse times and calls for perseverance while awaiting the establishment of God's righteous Kingdom. The Last chapter is in the form of a liturgy with a Prophetic Prayer (3:1-19) to be sung. By means of a regular liturgical use, the people of God encourage one another meditate on God's Past acts and to hope for the glorious and victorious future to which Habakkuk has borne witness. Habakkuk's contribution to the prophetic wisdom is seen here; meditate on acts of God in the past; pray in present crisis; live in fidelity to Yahweh; rejoice in the future deliverance. These are perspectives for living with a vision according to the prophet Habakkuk.

Like Nahum, Habakkuk is a cult prophet. To him Judah is the "righteous" (2:4) to whom he promises aid rather than demanding humility and repentance.

He sees God's righteousness not as a demand placed upon his people but as a contrast to the wicked empire. Habakkuk shares the true prophetical awareness of the majesty of God, who intervenes on behalf of those who are unjustly treated, possesses power over all the nations, raises them up or brings them low, and uses them as instruments of his will. These insights bring him finally to demand the confident endurance of the faithful, contrary to all appearances.

ix. Zephaniah

The book of Zephaniah seems more coherent and more of a unity than the Prophetic books which immediately precede it. The picture in the book can be understood in three thematic and focal points: First: invective against Judah and Jerusalem predominates (1:2-2:3). This section is stamped by mention of the day of Yahweh (1:7, 14 etc.) Judgements on other nations begin in 2:4, Second: sayings against Jerusalem in 3:1-7, with a concluding saying against the nations (3:8), Third; the words of salvation (3:9-20), first for the nations (vv. 91f), then for Jerusalem and Israel.

The composition of the book has been worked out in many ways by means of keywords and word repetition, through which connections within the book have been brought out: the often and varied mention of the day of Yahweh (1:7, 14), day of wrath of Yahweh (1:15, 18, 2:23), the day of distress, of oppression, of darkness, and so on. (1:14-16); day of sacrifice (1:5); day on which Yahweh raise himself up (3:8); seeking Yahweh (1:6, 2:3); accepting instruction (3:2-7); worshipping (1:5, 2:11); fearing (3:7, 15, 16); visiting (1:8, 9, 12; 2:7; 3:7), remnant (2:7, 9, 3:12, 13). This shows that on many occasions the choice of word has determined the composition.

The superscription dates the book during the reign of Josiah (639-609). The contents of the book reveal that the Deuteronormic reformation had not yet, taken place: alien Gods are still worshipped in Jerusalem (1:4-5). Zephaniah; ministry can be placed around 639 B.C.E.

a) Zephaniah's Period and Person: According to Zeph 1:4, the period of the Prophet was stated to be a time of syncretism. Both in Judah and Jerusalem people practiced the Canaanite cult of Baal, Assyria's religion of Astral mythology (or star worship of the cult of god Moloch or Milcom) which originated among the Ammonites. The prophetic critique aims at those cults that were undermining the pure monotheism of worship of Yahweh, had to the conclusion that Josiah's reform of the cult had not yet taken place. We are thus at a Period Preceding the Deuteronomistic reform of 622 B.C.E. According to 1:8, the "phrase" "kings sons" may means Josiah's childhood (II Kings 21:1). On the basis of 2:13-15, a reference to Nineveh indicates, perhaps we are at a date before 612 B.C.E. since the fall of Nineveh had yet taken place.

From these reference points we are led to conclude finally that Zephaniah must have made his appearance after the period of the dark reigns of Manasseh

(687-642 B.C.E.) and Amon 642-641 B.C.E. (see 2 Kings 21 and 2 Chronicles chap. 33). After almost a half century prophetic silence, among as a group of new witnesses we find Zephaniah in the last decades of the seventh century along the side of the prophets Nahum, Jeremiah and Habakkuk, according to this calculation, Zephaniah came to the fore in 639 B.C.E in the first half of Josiah's reign in Judah, and served Primarily in Jerusalem.

The name Zephaniah means: "the lord has hidden" or "the lord has caused to be hidden". This name was, common in Israel (eg: Jer 29:29; Zech. 6:10,14). the authors intention in tracing the prophet's family three generations beyond his father remains a mystery; perhaps it is to show that the prophet comes from royal family, therefore King Hezekiah was his great-grand father, but his father Cushi, a foreigner.

The circumstances of prophet's life are completely unknown, he knows well about the capital city and its, leaders. He gives precise topographical descriptions of Jerusalem, royal Palace (1:8-9), a temple mount and its neighboured (1:10-11), old city (1:12-13), new city (1:10-11) Zephaniah is a relentless critic of his age. He knows well the leading strata of society and castigates them severely: the royal court (1:8-9), the priesthood (1:4, 3:4) the judges and officials (3:3), the merchants and financiers (1:11).

Zephaniah is well acquainted with the works of 8th century prredecessors. eg: The Day of Yahweh (Zeph 1:7-13, 14-18, cf. Amos 5:18-20, Isa 2:4ff). Zephaniah contributes to Israel's rich literary heritage. The book, mainly Poetic, open with a dramatic judgment oracle on all creation (1: 2-3) and on Judah (vv. 4-9) Zephaniah graphically develops the Day of the Lord in the imagery of War, theophany, and judgment (vv.14-18). He combines a universal message (vv.2-3; 2:4-15; 3:6-8) and a Particularistic Judgment on Judah (1:4-6; 3:1-4). The Prophets directs style employs poetic device of parallelism, word play, repetition, assonance and metaphor. The prophetic speech forms reflects a paucity of extended descriptions or a creative use of prophetic heritage. Zephaniah communicates his message in a straight forward manner.

b) The Theology of Zephaniah: Zephaniah's theology is placed right in the midst of his own historical situation. Following are the important concerns in his message.

1) A righteous God is offended by human sin: Zephaniah talks about the heterodox syncretism which Manasseh had imposed upon Judah and which was still a feature of life during Josiah's Youth comes in; Yet it is wrong to think that Zephaniah is only concerned about cultic matters. **mishapt** ("commands"), **tsedheq** ("righteousness") and **'anawah** ("humility") are identified as the ideals by which the saved remnant is to be identified (2:3). This is in accord with the character of Yahweh who is righteous (**tsadiq**) and who each morning, "shows forth his **mishpat**" ("Justice", 3:5), In his description of ideal society which Yahweh will create beyond the judgment,

there will be a universal, acknowledgement of Yahweh's rule (3:9) and life will be characterized by humility, integrity, and truthfulness (3:12-13). It is the current absence of these qualities which angers and offends Yahweh.

2) Yahweh will destroy, all creation: Even though Zephaniah's primary concern is with Judah, Yahweh Judgment will extend to all creation. Foreign nations will be destroyed because of their godlessness (2:5-15), all living creatures will cease to exist. (l:2-3).

The phrase "the day of Yahweh" is frequently used by Zephaniah in his theology (1:7,10,12, 2:2; 3:8;,9,11,16). In some places, it seems, as with Amos, that the Day of Yahweh is near at hand (1:14), whereas at other times it seems to be somewhere in the distance (3:8).

The main emphasis of Zephaniah is that the total destruction of life upon earth has spoken forcefully to the people of God in times of great, disaster, such as during the Middle Ages when war, famine, and disease frequently wiped out entire populations. Similar thing is going to happen in Judah according to Zephaniah.

3) A remnant of the Jerusalem community will be restored to its land and will preside over a renewed humankind: The idea of remnant who may be saved is suggested in 2:3 where those who are righteous and humble may perhaps be hidden from Yahweh's wrath on the awful day. It is referred again in 2:7,9 where the remnant is depicted as inheriting the lands of Judah's evil neighbours after the Judgment has taken place. In 3:9-20, it is stated that remnant will preside over a humankind which acknowledges Yahweh (vss. 9-10). This remnant will dwell in safety and in a golden age will be admired by all the people of the earth (3:20).

More generally we may say that Zephaniah followed in the footsteps of Isaiah, Amos and Micah, in particular developing and elaborating the interpretation of the Day of Yahweh put forward by the first two. Yahweh's terrible Judgement will overwhelm the sinful ruling class of Judah and Jerusalem along with other nations. If, however, the people make use of the time remaining to recall the commandments of Yahweh, if they repent and turn to righteousness and humility, a portion of Israel will be spared, like the remnant of an army that escapes after a bloody defeat; as in the days of their fathers, they will dwell humble and lowly, but faithful, upon mount Zion, will act righteously, and live in peace.

c) Postexilic Prophecy: (Trito-Isaiah, Haggai, Zechariah and Malachi):

General context of postexilic prophecy: A great deal of misunderstanding has arisen from the common assumption that for all practical purposes prophecy came to an end with the Babylonian exile. But this is not true at least four of the prophets whom we are going to consider belong to the postexilic period.

In order to understand how prophecy functioned and in what ways it was different from earlier forms we must first take stock of the quite different political situation in which the province of Judah found itself after the transition from Babylonian to Persian rule.

Jerusalem and the surrounding area of Judah (Yehud) formed one of several Provinces, together with Syria, Samaria, Megiddo and others, under the jurisdiction of the local satrap, probably resident in Damascus. Under Persian rule these provinces enjoyed a fair degree of autonomy, issuing their own coinage, policing their own territory, and collecting tribute and taxes. In keeping with the Policy of the Persian rulers, in this respect much more enlightened than that of their predecessors, the juridicial status of local political entities was generally respected. Judah's was one of several provinces the status of which was determined by its Temple and the cult carried on there. It was the policy of the central Government to sponsor subsidize and, where necessary, restore such local cults. So, for example: the founder of the Achaemendid Empire claimed to have restored the Marduk cult in Babylon after the neglect that it had suffered under the last Babylonian King, Nabonidus. Later Darius reproving the satrap Gadatas for imposing tribute on the shrine of Apollo in Magnesia. It is therefore possible that the same King should have subsidized the rebuilding of the Yahweh Temple in Jerusalem (Ezra 6:8).

In keeping with this Policy, local law codes remained in force and were backed by the coercive power of the central government. Darius, mandated a codification of ancient Egyptian laws and enjoined their observance, and in the same spirit a later King commissioned Ezra to enforce 'the law of the God of heaven' among Jews in the Trans-Euphrates satrapy (Ezra 7:14, 25-26). Much of the legislation in the Pentateuch formed the civil constitution of the Jerusalemite temple community backed by the authority of the imperial governments. This too must have been extended to the Jewish community.

The province of Judah therefore, can be described as a temple community not unlike others in the Persian Empire (for example, in some of the Greek cities along the Ionian seaboard) The Temples were not just places of sacrifices and prayer, they served as administrative centres with their own bureaucracies issued loans, controlled colleges of scholars and scribes, apart from butchers, bakers, keepers of sacrificial herds, and the like. Supreme authority over this organisation was, of course, vested in the monarch. It is with in this capacity, Cyrus restored the Jerusalem Temple, formerly a dynastic Temple. An important reminder of this status was the requirement that prayers for the well-being of the imperial family be incorporated into the daily liturgy (Ezra 6:10).

Royal authority was normally exercised through officials and commissioners appointed by the central government whose primary concern was to oversee the financial management of this complex operation and ensure Political stability. Expediency and good sense would occasionally dictate the appointment of local People to discharge these functions. Cyrus, for example, appointed a Lydian to oversee the Sardis treasury, while under Darius a Davidite, Zerubbabel, was sent out as governor of Yehud. Under normal circumstances, however, the day-to-day task of administration develop on the Priesthood.

This last point is particularly important for understanding the situation in Jerusalem and Judah after the return. The authority of the priesthood is not only confined to the Temple but even to the civic field. The priesthood, wielded enormous Power not only in the religious sphere (the cult being the Primary and indispensable means of salvation) but also economically and politically.

Right from the beginning of the period basic issue was that of qualification for membership in the Jerusalem Temple Community. This matter could not be decided purely on grounds of national identity in view of the changes in the political history of the country from time to time. Other factors entered into play including, for the first time, laws governing ritual purity (eg. Hag. 2:10-14). It is therefore no surprise to find disagreement on the status of specific categories of People, including those who had defiled themselves with idolatry, resident aliens (*gerim*) and eunuchs, with respect to this last category, for example, Isa. 56:3-5 expresses an inclusive attitude quite at variance with the Deuteronomic law (Deut 23:1). For the same reason, marriage with women outside the group became increasingly problematic and emerged as a major issue at the time of Ezra and Nehemiah.

One of the major issue of the post-exilic community was not the conflict confined to repatriates versus natives, but was going on in the **golah** group itself (the ones who claim to be in direct line of succession to the old Israel). One of the major issues was control of the cult and the status of Temple Personnel. Some of them who claimed priestly lineage but who could not substantiate their claim were excluded "until there should be a priest to consult "Urim and Thummim" (Ezra 2:59-63). These were members of priestly groups that had settled in Babylon. More significant, however, are the indications of conflict within the ranks of the priesthood that led to the emergence of a second order of clergy. Such a distinction was unknown during the time of the monarchy and is attested only in the very latest editorial stratum of Deuteronomy (27:14).

The incidents that happen following this, we shall discuss on particular events in relation to the prophecies of each prophet at relevant places. One thing seems to be clear from the foregoing discussion on the postexilic historical situation, i.e., the context is so complex that we can see the concerns raised by the prophets of this are very crucial and vital.

x. Trito-Isaiah

The Theophany which Deutero-Isaiah had painted in such glowing colours failed to materialize. Cyrus was not converted. And in Jerusalem restoration measures soon came to a halt because of an extremely uncertain Political and economic situation. Israel's fate had taken a new turn; but it certainly did not mean an eschatological revolution: Deutero-Isaiah had overcome the discouragement of the people for a time; but it can be no surprise to discover that this discouragement now made itself felt once more.

The last ten chapters of the book of Isaiah (56-66) tell us about this. The language is so closely; reminiscent of Deutero-Isaiah that he had continually been taken to be their author. But the conditions underlying these writings are completely different, pointing to the Palestinian homeland and not to the **golah** (the dispersed community).

a) The Historical Context of the Prophet: Trito-Isaiah is of particular importance in dealing of the issue on the specific question of the nature and cause of the dissension which threatened to disrupt the life the community in the period after the return from the exile. Isaiah 56-66 provides the main source of evidence of these internal divisions (esp. in 65-8-16, 66:5 and in chp. 57: vv-1-2 and 19-21). But to detect the nature and the depth of the Problems is not an easy task because either the information is not adequate or it is ambiguous. One commonly held opinion suggests that the roots of the problem lay in a conflict of interests, together with a divergence in theological orientation, between those who, remained in the land during the period of exile and those who, having been deported to Babylon and come under Powerful foreign influences. Babylonian culture and religion undoubtedly had a profound impact on those who experienced the exile, even where their response was one of rejection, not assimilation. It is generally supposed that fresh impetus to Israel's life and worship came from these returned exiles, whereas 5 syncretistic and semi-Pagan cults such as those which the Pre-exilic Prophets had denounced continued to flourish among those who had stayed in the land. On this basis, 57:3-13 and 65:1-5, 11-12 have been understood as describing the debased religion of those left without adequate leadership when the elite of society were deported to Babylon.

P.D. Hanson (*The Dawn of Apocalyptic*) gives to certain extent the sociological and the nature and the causes of the dissension in the postexilic community during the time of Trito-Isaiah. Hanson seeks to elucidate the nature of the opposing factions, and the causes and subsequent development of their mutual hostility with the pervading polemical note he finds on indication of their historical setting. The roots of the conflict lay, he believes, in the opposition between-two parties the one eager to maintain the status quo by which they had control of the temple and of the official cult, the other motivated by a sense of rejection resulting from their exclusion from participation in worship, yet lacking the Power and resources to wrest control of Zion from their opponents. The former Hanson terms the 'hierocratic Party' which consisted of a group of influential Priests who had returned from Babylon and seized control of Zion;

the latter Hanson describes as 'visionaries', a group composed of followers of Second Isaiah in association with the disenfranchised Levites who had been excluded by the Zadokites from participation in the service of the temple (cf. Ezek. 44:13). Hanson remarks that Trito-Isaiah is permeated deeply by priestly concepts. For example, a recurring emphasis on God's holy mountain, Zion (66:7, 21-22; 61:7; 63:17b-19; 57:13; 65:1-10), for one of the main issues at the heart of the inner-community struggle between visionaries and hierocrats, as Hanson sees it, was concern for the possession of Zion.

Hanson regards chs. 60-62 as the restoration programme of the visionaries, and to this same general period he assigns 57:14-19 with its joyful message of comfort and healing for the whole nation.

The sudden change of tone in 57:20-21, a passage which according to Hanson's analysis is probably a secondary insertion, is explained as a later attempt, in the light of the developing rift within the community, to modify the initial promise of pardon and salvation which had been addressed to the whole nation. As optimism faded and bitterness grew it was necessary that the promises of Second Isaiah should be reinterpreted if hope was to be sustained in the face of disillusionment and despair. As Hanson puts it, 'disintegrating historical circumstances prompted new modes of conceptualizing that restoration hope'. Thus expectations for the future took on a different shape, increasingly detached from the real world of Politics and history; and in this way apocalyptic was born.

Hanson regards the rivalry between the two factions as the motivation of chs. 56-66 throughout. Not only is the dissension interpretation consistently as a sectarian struggle; but even the formulation of the restoration programme in 60-62 is to be understood as deliberate, opposition to the hierocratic programme in Ezekiel 40-48. For this reason Hanson rejects the widely held view that 63:7-64: 12 is an early exilic lament by the community against the external enemies who desecrated the sanctuary when Jerusalem fell in 587, and sees it as further evidence of the bitter hostility between the hierocratic Party and the visionaries. It is, he believes, a lament by Levites at their exclusion from the sanctuary by Ezekiel's programme. Thus the enemies who have defiled the sanctuary (63:18) are not external ones but internal rivals'. In this context Hanson takes the threefold affirmation, 'You are our Father' (63:16, twice; 64:8), as evidence that his claim by the Levites and their associates has been rejected by the rival faction who claimed the names Abraham and Israel as their own exclusive right: (63:16), thus depriving the visionaries of their legitimate part in the covenant community. This circumstance is reflected also, he suggests, in the repeated emphasis on the new names which are bestowed on the faithful (62:4,12) who have reached the ultimate point of disowning the traditional designation Israel.

One of the main objections to this carefully constructed hypothesis is the unfortunate ambiguity of much of the evidence. Thus, in the particular instance discussed here it can equally be argued that Abraham and Israel refer not to the community but to the patriarchs, the human 'fathers' of the nation now unable to assist the present generation in their distress, unlike God who alone 'is a living and present father' (Claus Westermann).

Third Isaiah opens with a remarkably liberal statement on membership in the Community, conferring secure status on non-Jewish adherents of the Yahweh cult and on eunuchs, permitting them to participate in the cult on condition of observing the community's covenant requirements, especially regarding the Sabbath (Isa. 56:1-8). The same broad perspective is apartment in the final section (66:18-23) dealing with proselytism, missionary preaching, the ingathering of the nations and dispersed Jews to Participate in the Parousia in Jerusalem.

The nucleus of Trito-Isaianic passages, containing a compendium of the eschatological teaching of the group, is found in Isa 60-62. Like 57:14-21, they come from either the last years of the exile or the early Years after the return and betray no signs of the opposition and conflict to which these teachings were to give rise with the Passing of time. They begin with an apostrophe to Jerusalem: the glory of God will appear in Zion bringing salvation to an oppressed people, those scattered abroad will return, the nations will be subject to Israel, will bring tribute and help rebuild the city, the Temple will once again be glorious and shine at the centre of the earth.

It is important to note that throughout Third Isaiah, prophetic eschatological faith is focused on Temple and altar (eg. Isa 60:7,13; 61:6; 62:9). There is therefore no opposition in principle between the bearers of this faith and the Temple authorities and no evidence that the former were anti-cultic. The seer who speaks for them in fact goes on to expound a teaching not unlike the Priesthood of all the faithful. The entire people will in the last days be relieved of servile labour, as are the priests, and will receive tithes from the Nations. In this way the covenant to the house of Levi will be extended to all (cf. Numb. 25:10-13).

In the last two chapters of Trito-Isaiah (65-66), there are clear indications of internal conflict in the province of Judah involving the prophetic eschatological group within which Third Isaiah originated.

b) Literary Forms and Poetic Imagery in Trito-Isaiah: Not only it is true that Trito-Isaiah used several or variety of literary forms, but these traditional forms were forced into new directions to suit the requirements of a changing historical situation. The following are the important categories of speech forms and Poetic imagery used in Trito-Isaiah.

1) Judgement Oracles:

i) Isa. 56:9-12: This passage is a masterly example of a Prophetic oracle of judgment, comprising the two traditional elements, pronouncement of judgment and grounds of accusation. Its figurative language has certain reminiscences of Ezekiel's indictment of Israel's leaders (34:1-10), but its brevity is in marked contrast to Ezekiel's extended metaphor. The kaleidoscopic imagery in which the denunciation is couched reflects the multifarious sins of which the leaders are guilty. What kind of leadership is castigated is not entirely clear: both religious and Political leaders may be included. 'watchman' is a term which generally signifies a prophet (Jer. 6:17; Ezek. 3:17; 33:7) whereas 'shepherd' refers frequently to Political leadership (Jer. 23:1-4; Ezek. 34:1-10, especially v.4). The accusation is comprehensive. At first it is the ignorance of the watchman, their failure to realise the dangers of the situation and to alert the community to an appropriate response, which is at issue. They are quiet as sleeping dogs murmuring in their dreams (*hozim*, a word occurring only here which has the sense 'to talk confusedly'. But then the accusation changes. Dogs, all dogs, have ravenous, insatiable appetites, and so do the shepherds of Israel, intent on their own advantage with never a thought beyond the pleasure of the present moment as they sing their drinking songs, behaving arrogantly as if the future were at their disposal not the Lord's The pattern of the metaphors is deliberately chiastic (placed opposite to each other): the newly coined metaphors of dumb and ravenous dogs: the former useless, the latter dangerous, serve to illuminate the conventional expressions of 'watchman' and 'shepherds', and to Provide the transition between them.

ii) Isa 58: 1-14: This passage is of particular interest both from the form-critical viewpoint and for the insight it gives into the problems and religious attitudes of the post-exilic community in Judah. Of the two traditional elements-accusation and pronouncement of judgment the former appears briefly in vv.3b-4a; the latter is entirely absent. Rest of the passage consists of a series of exhortations followed by conditional promises of blessing. It is here, in this break down of the conventional form of the judgment oracle, that the contrast with earlier prophets is most apparent.

Westermann calls this as 'symptomatic of the coming together of Prophetic and liturgical speech: Following immediately on the divine authorization of the prophet as a messenger of judgment there is a parenthetical description of the outward piety of the community (vv.2-3a), a people who lament that their practice of fasting is ineffectual and secures no response from God. It is clear from this, as well as from the language in which the promises of blessing are couched, that the community, or the section of it addressed is conscious of some kind of distress and lack of well-being, probably attributable to the disappointment of hopes raised by the promises of Second Isaiah. The responsibility is laid firmly at the community's door. Despite their outward religious observances there is only apparent, not actual, commitment to righteous action and to obedience to God's Commandments (v. 2).

Westermann points out some signs of wisdom influence in this passage, there is a hint of 'the ridicule of the rationalist' in the satirical expression 'to bow down one's head like a rush' (v.5).

2) Laments: Isa. 59:1-15a; 63:7-64:12: These two laments differ considerably in their literary form, 63:7-64:12 has more traditional structure. Westermann describes it as probably the most powerful psalm of communal lamentation in the Bible. It follows the conventional pattern of such laments within the Psalter, consisting of the usual elements: recollection of God's past saving actions (63:7-14 cf. Ps.89); plea for help, which includes a descriptions of the distress which was the immediate cause of the lament (63:15-64:5a), and confession of sin (64:5b-7). Finally the various elements in the lament are gathered up (64:8-12), culminating in the anguished questioning of God, characteristic of the lament form: "Wilt thou retrain thyself at those things, a LORD? Wilt thou keep silent, and afflict us sorely?" (64:12).

Chp. 59 is an interesting example of departure from traditional forms of lament. Many would even question whether it is appropriate to classify it as lament. The opening words introduced as they are by the Particle 'behold', are to be understood as the prophet's response to an unrecorded lament by the people, perplexed by the failure of Yahweh to intervene and by his apparent disregard of their Prayers. The problem, says the prophet, lies not in any limitation of Yahweh's power; It is the result of sin, their own sins which have raised a barrier between themselves and God. The accusation in vv.2-3 is as sharp as anything in the pre-exilic prophets (cf. Isa. 1:15); but in Place of the announcement of punishment which traditionally accompanied the accusation, the direct address to the hearers soon passes over into a description of their sin, its impact heightened by the striking poetic imagery (vv.5-6). It is this descriptive aspect of the material which gives the passage something of a sermonic character since it constitutes an explanation to a despondent people rather than an accusation. The sins, referred to here are social injustices not cultic irregularities, the evils by which justice is perverted in the law courts.

Two strands seem to be inter twined, the community's lament and the prophetic voice, thus some would characterize, it as a prophetic liturgy. This chapter falls into three distinct sections: *First*, the prophet's response to a communal lament which vindicates Yahweh by way of accusing the people (vv. 1-8); *Secondly*, the ensuring lament, by or on behalf of the people, which includes confession of sin (V. 12: and unusual feature in the traditional form of judgment oracle) and admits the truth of the accusation (vv.9-15a), *Thirdly*, the assurance of God's intervention to save those who repent (vv. 15b-20; for a similarity abrupt transition to words assurance compare Joel 2:18). Yahweh is portrayed here as the warrior God who avenges those who 'turn from transgression' (v.20; cf. 42: 13 52:10). A similar pattern of community lament followed by Yahweh's epiphany is to be found in Psalm 60. The two sections, lament (1-15a) and epiphany (15b-20) are linked together. Yahweh takes action precisely because he sees that there is no justice (v.15 cf. vv.9 and 11). The salvation which was far from them (v.11) is seen to be at hand when he intervenes.

3) Portrayal of the Divine Warrior: (Isa 59:15b-20; 63: 1-6).

There are interesting, and significant, contrasts between the potrayal of the divine warrior in these two passages. What originally concerned Yahweh's intervention against foreign enemies has now been directed against internal adversaries. In 63: 1-6, the prophet make use of secular form familiar to his hearers - the customary summons of a watchman to an approaching stranger to identify himself - but the contest is based on the motif of the divine warrior. Yahweh is not named but the identification1 clear (cf. 5:17-). Fresh from his victory he announces that 'right has won the day'.

4) Oracles of both Judgment and Salvation: (Isa. 65:8-16). It is oracle both of Judgment and of salvation, addressed respectively to two opposing factions within the community. In this dual orientation it differs in a remarkable fashion from the traditional forms of pre-exilic prophecy in which the nation is treated as a corporate entity for Judgment or for salvation. In its Present form ch.65 as a whole is symmetrical in structure: vv.l-7 consist entirely of accusation against idolaters; vv. 8-l6a set out the contrasting destiny of two disparate groups within the community, detailing the blessings in store for the one ('my servants' vv.l3-14, 'my chosen', v.15) and the sorrows which await the other; vv.16b-25 are Purely a description of blessing. These diverse sections are held together by the theme of call and response which is reiterated in vv.1,12 and 24. The central concern of Isa. ch.65 is with the deep division within the community between those who, from this Perspective at any rate, one regarded as faithful worshippers of Yahweh and their opponents who are considered by them to be apostate. It is to this latter group that the oracle is addressed from v.11 onwards as a pronouncement of judgment.

c) Theology of Trito-Isaiah: The majesty and omnipotence of Yahweh, the choice of Israel to be Yahweh's people, divine anger over human sin, and the deity's determination to work the divine will in the world, all are themes found in third Isaiah connect this prophet of the restoration with the older traditions of prophecy within Israel. Following are the three major concerns of the prophet in his theology.

i) Yahweh's restoration of Jerusalem is still in the future and when it comes, it will be a day of great glory for the city and its people: Yahweh's glory will be present in the life of the city (60:1-2). The city will be a "crown of beauty" and a "royal diadem" to Yahweh (62:3). All people will respond to the magnificence of the New Jerusalem, both gentiles (62:2) and Jews still scattered abroad (60:4). Great wealth will belong to the city, which will be the Place of worship for all People (60:5-7; 66:23). It will be a time of Peace and concord (65:25) in which Yahweh's presence will provide all needed light (60:1a).

ii) Although, Yahweh's love is universal, two groups are singled out for special treatment: the gentiles and the wicked: The Gentiles are clearly to be Participants in the glories of this new age, "Foreigners" will join themselves to Yahweh (56:6). They and "aliens" will serve Yahweh in the age to come but their menial labour is contrasted with the work of the Jews who are to be "Priests of Yahweh" and "ministers of our God" (61:5-6). As for the wicked, they are responsible for deadly of the coming of the newage (59:1-2)- Yahweh, who judged this people of old will also act in judgment upon any present enemies (59:18). The prophet implores Yahweh not to allow these wicked people to delay any longer the fulfilment of the divine promises, but to institute the Judgment swift and sure ways (chp. 64).

iii) The Worship of Yahweh through sacrifice and Joyful Song characterizes the life of Yahweh's People: In this new age Jerusalem will "thrill and rejoice" (60:5). The prophet rejoices over what is to come Pass (61:10) as does Yahweh also (62:5). This message is consistent with the views of other restoration prophets like Haggai and Zechariah. The words of prophet's jubilation are seen thus: "But be glad and rejoice for ever in that which I create; for behold, I create Jerusalem a rejoicing, and her people a joy. I will rejoice in Jerusalem, and be glad in my people; no more shall be heard in it the sound of weeping and the cry of distress". (65:18-19).

xi. Haggai

The book of Haggai marks the; beginning of the group of three postexilic prophets in the book of twelve prophets. The first, two, Haggai and Zechariah, areassociated by exactdating with the rebuilding of the temple in the years after 520 B.C.E.

The book is divided into four sections by the dates it contains. Chapter 1, 2:1-9; vv. 10-19; vv. 20-29. The introductory dating in 1:1, 2:1, 10, 20 are all associated with the word event formula as "the word of Yahweh came through Haggai".The dominant them here is the rebuilding of the temple. The arrangement of the book first of all brings out the role of the prophet Haggai in the resumption of work on the temple: the first section (ch. 1) reports how his admonitory sermon (vv. 4-8, 9-11 are expansions at the same theme) marks his audience hearken to the voice of Yahweh and fear him (v.12). He "arouses" their "Spirit" by Yahweh's promise mat he will be with them (v. 13), and so they begin work.

In the second section (2:1-91, Zerubbabel, Joshua and the people are summoned, in view of the sorry state of the new building (v.3) to be strong and set to work (v.4 cf. I chron. 22:11-16, 28:10, 20) because Yahweh will be with them (v.5). This is followed by an eschatological proclamation of salvation about the glory of the new temple (vv. 6-9) in which Yahweh will give salvation.

A new theme emerges in the third section (2:10-19). The prophet is charged to give a Priestly Torah (or) the question whether cultic impurity is contagious (vv. 11-13). V. 14 gives the interpretation 'this people' is unclean. This is often related to the Samaritans. From the day of the laying of the foundation stone of the new temple onwards Yahweh will not only give the fertility which he has so far withheld (cf. 1:6, 9-11), but with his good pleasure in the temple (1:8) with salvation (2:9) and blessing (2: 19b), the impurity will also cease.

In the fourth section (2:20-23), the eschatological trend of the book reaches its climax. The eschatological phenomena which have been foretold (2:6ff) will begin (vv. 21f), and Zerubbabel will be Yahweh's chosen king of salvation (v.23). This is the expression of a clear messianic expectation which is connected with the person of Zerubbabel.

a) The Historical Setting: During the years from 558 to 529 BCE, Cyrus, King of Anshan, engaged in a series of conquests. The Babylonian Empire: Which had up to that time controlled the Tigris-Euphrates basin, often called Mesopotamia, was overthrown, and Babylon itself captured a new Power was established, now generally known as the Persian Empire, whose western boundaries extended into modern Turkey and reached to the borders of Egypt. Prophet Haggai, Zechariah l-8, come from this Period when Persian rule was first being established in Syria-Palestine.

Persian rule was to last for some two hundred years, until the conquest of Alexander the Great about 330 BCE; yet our knowledge both of the Persian Empire in general and its impact in Syria-Palestine in Particular remains very limited. The Old Testament is one of the chief source of information. Yet in comparison with Babylonian and earlier periods the information is very scarce in this period. Nor is there from Persian sources anything comparable to the wealth of Assyrian and Babylonian inscriptional material (The most important exception to this is the 'Cyrus Cylinder', which relates to the conquest of Babylon).

From the various Old Testament sources a very different Picture emerges. Cyrus himself is described in the book of Isaiah as 'the shepherd' and the 'anointed' of Yahweh the God Israel (Isa. 44:28; 45:1); much of the book of Ezra is given over to an account of the favourable treatment of the Jews be Persian rulers; both the story of Esther and the episode of Daniel in the lion's den (Dan.6) picture Persian emperor's in highly favourable terms. The books is dated by the years of the reign of the Persian Emperor Darius, as if his rule were Part of the divine ordering of affairs. It is striking that in Haggai (1:1,15) Darius is simply called 'the King'.

The general historical setting of Haggai is established beyond doubt. He lived and proclaimed the word of Yahweh at time when Persian rule in Palestine was being established, and Haggai is in no way opposed to the establishment of Persian rule. When we come to look at the historical situation in greater detail, however, certain problems arise.

Cyrus, the founder of Persian Empire, died in 529 BCE and was succeeded by his son Cambyses (529-522). Under his rule Persian power was extended to the borders of Egypt. In 525 in his attempt to invade Egypt died in 525 BCE, Precipitated a series of riots which put the whole empire under pressure for more than a Year. Eventually Darius I Hystaspes established himself as King (522-486) and as already pointed out, Haggai's activity is dated in this Period.

Some of the events that happened during this period are related to the Prophet Haggai. For instance, the alleged 'disappearance' of Zerubbabel, during Darius' period, permission was available for the rebuilding of the temple in Jerusalem (cf. Ezra chps. 5-6). Haggai summoned the people to work on the temple reconstruction (1:1-2:9 and 2:15-19).

But an historical difficulty arises in the construction of the temple if we compare Haggai's account with that of Ezra's. According to Ezra. 3, a Start on the work of rebuilding had already been made in 538, immediately Upon the first return of exiles from Babylon; yet Hag. 1:4,9 speak of 'the house', that is, the temple lying in ruins. Apparently, according to this, no work of rebuilding had yet been done. It would obviously be possible to construct some kind of harmonization of the two accounts: One might argue that work done nearly twenty years before Haggai's time and then neglected would be in ruins. Whether or not some preliminary work on the temple had been done, there was still much to be achieved, and this was a major focus of Haggai's prophetic words.

b) Haggai's Message in his context: In Haggai's time the generation that had known of a living temple in which God's glory manifested had now effectively passed away (2:3), and they found it possible to survive without a temple (or at least without a properly restored temple). This attitude seems to Haggai to reflect a perverted sense of priorities. Now a more ambitions work of rebuilding could be embarked upon; that such a plan was possible seems to have been common ground between Haggai and his hearers (1:2). Haggai supposed that all other blessings would automatically follow upon Proper attention to the temple. Just as current troubles were due to its neglect (2:15-17), so future blessings could be guaranteed if rebuilding was taken seriously in hand (2:18f). Haggai's intention is not simple rebuilding of the temple, as Ackroyd had rightly pointed out that 'the failure to rebuild is much more than a matter of reconstruction of a building. It is reordering of a Temple so that it is a fit place for worship. Rebuilding is therefore linked to the condition of the People for the service of God". (**Exile and Restoration**, p. 156).

Thus there is another wider concern here based on 2:1-9, that God is assuring the people of his lasting presence with them, a presence which is recalled in the past history of his dealings with them ('the promise that I made you when you came out of Egypt'), which is assured as present reality ('My spirit abides among you; fear not'), and which is promised as a sign of future glory ('I will shake all nations, so that the treasures of all nations shall come in').

A restored community would need effective leaders, both political and religious; and this supplies the context for the concern shown by Haggai for Zerubbabel and Joshua. There is no suggestion that Haggai simply had, in mind a return to pre-exilic days with the Davidic monarchy in control of an independent nation-state. A dual leadership of the community's efforts was needed. The words which Haggai proclaims to Zerubbabel, the ruling governor, are just as high-flown as the expectation of the period of blessing which is to ensure immediately after the reopening of the Temple. He designates him as nothing less than the ruler over the whole world. Yahweh will soon shake the universe so that the thrones of the ruling Princes will topple and a struggle of each against all will break out on earth. Then Zerubbabel will be the signet ring on the hand of God, the ring which God will use to stamp his will to peace into the very earth itself (Hag. 2:20-23). However, Haggai does not usually confine what he says solely to the governor. He also addresses the high priest, Joshua (1:1-2:2).

Haggai's preaching is outwardly influenced by the fact that he appeared at the time of crisis for the new PersianEmpire. This must have aroused hope in Judah that Yahweh would finally bring about the long-awaited transformation of all things and inaugurate the age of eschatological salvation, exercising dominion over the world through his Davidic representative. Haggai proclaims that the future holds only blessings-and expects, upon completion of the building, a convulsion that will shake all nature and all nations, as the transition is completed and the time of salvation truly begins

xii. Zechariah

The book of Zechariah is the within the book of the twelve prophets to contain a collection with clearly divergent parts. The dating in 1:7; 7:1 closely connect the first part (chs. 1-8) with the book of Haggai and the rebuilding of the temple. The second part (chapter 9-14) is not included in the dating. It is clearly divided from the first part by the title *massa*, 'saying' in 9:1 and 12:1 and at the same time is further subdivided. These chapters (9-14) are often called 'Deutero-Zechariah' although they do not have so clear a profile as Deutero-

Isaiah'. Occasionally this designation is limited to chapters 9-11, and chapters 12-14 are known as 'Trito-Zechariah'.

The first part (chapter 1-8) is divided into three equal sections by the dating 1:1-6 is prefaced to the whole section as an introduction, a call to conversion (v.3) which refers to the example of the 'fathers'. This example is initially negative, because they did not listen to the words of the 'former prophets' (v.4f) and then positive, because they repented after the accomplishment of what the prophets had foretold. The post-exilic community is to learn its lesson from these experiences of the fathers.

The second most extensive section (1:7-6:15) contains a series of visions which are usually called 'Night Visions' (cf. 1:8, 4:1). The eight successive accounts of visions reveal a very marked basic pattern; they have partly been expanded by further sayings of Yahweh. The visions are evidently composed as a consecutive cycle. This becomes clear if we look at the section about the high priest Joshua in chapter 3 as an independent tradition. The remaining seven visions are a self-contained composition with a symmetrical construction. At the centre is the fourth (in the present collection the fifth) vision (4. 1-14) of the lampstand and the two olive trees, i.e. the anointed, framed by a pair of visions which depict the outward, political liberation of Jerusalem (2:1-5, 5-9) liberation from sins (5:14, 5-11), at the beginning and end there are two more visions which announce the intervention of Yahweh in the history of the world (1:8-15) and finally set it in motion. Everything happens for the sake of Jerusalem (1:12, 14 cf. 16f).

The third section (chapters 7f) contain a collection of Prophetic sayings which is again dominated by the reciprocal relationship of Judgement and salvation. The starting point is a question about the fast day in commemoration of the destruction of the temple (7:13; cf. II Kings 25: 8). The question is first of all answered with criticism of the practice of fasting (7:4-7), the gist is continued only in 8:16f: The enquires are to do what the former prophets said, bring truth and right to fulfilment in their midst; then the fast days will become days of Joy (8: 18f. Two groups of texts are to be found in this frame work: 7:8-14 a survey of history which depicts judgement as a consequence of disobedience to the words of'former prophets' (v. 12, cf. v 7) 8: 1-15 words of salvation for Jerusalem.vv. 1-5 are words of salvation for Jerusalem: w. 6-8 words of salvation for the Diaspora; vv. 9-13 words of salvation in connection with the building of the temples vv. 14-15 are words of salvation for Jerusalem vv. 68 words of salvation for the Diaspora vv. 9-13 words of salvation in connection with the building of the temple's vv. 14-15 words of salvation for Jerusalem and Judah. In chapter 8: 20-23 it is said that Jerusalem and Judah will be the eschatological centre of the world of nations.

The second part of the book Zechariah (Chapters 9-14) contains quite a variety of passages, the relationship between which is not parts, recognize. First of all, there is a clear sub division into two parts, each of which is introduced by the title *massa*, saying (chapter 9-11; 12-14).

Chapters 9f begin and end with sayings against foreign in nations (9:1-8, 10:11b-12) and other important concerns dealt here are: Yahweh's victorious epiphany (10:11a), home coming of the northern kingdom from exile (9:11f, 10:6-10). The key word shepherd (10: 2b, 3a) also provides a connection with chapter 11; the shepherd allegory (11:4-7).

In chapters 12f, 12:2-13 begins a consecutive section which is shaped by the frequently recurring phrase, "On that day (it will come about)" (12:3, 4, 6, 8, 9, 11; 13: l, 2, 3). Here Jerusalem is in the centre of discussion, withstanding the assaults of the enemy (12:2-8), after which it is purified (vv. 9-14). Chapter 14 contains a great eschatological description of the struggle for Jerusalem, and this chapter takes up the theme of the pilgrimage of the nations to Zion, with which the first part of the book of Zechariah ends (8:20-23).B.S.Childs says that the addition of chapters 9-14 has given the book of Zechariah a new eschatological dimension which goes far beyond the framework of chapters 1-8.

a) Literary Form of Zechariah: The book of Zechariah is "the obscurest and longest of the twelve Prophets", but its complexity is in Proportion to the significance of the message. Baldwin comments that it is a mosaic written by an "artist adding colourful, windows with their symbolism, gaiety and light". The book is largely prosaic with poetic sections (chaps. 9-10). It contains a mosaic of hortatory oracles (1:2-6; 10:1-2), Visions (1:7-6:8), symbolism (6:9-15), Prophetic judgment oracles (9:1-8; 12:2-8), liturgy (9:9-10), salvation oracles (vv. 11-13; l3:1-6,7-9) taunt song (11:1-3) narrative (vv. 4-17), and apocalyptic. The presence of visions, symbolism, and eschatological imagery classify Zechariah as a Prophetic apocalyptic writing.

The first eight chapters are united by a dating formula (1:1-7; 7:1), common formula. The lack of dating, the variety of thematic content in the chapters 9-14, and the absence of the messenger formula have led scholars to Posit that another Prophet (Deutero-Zechariah), whose concern was, more with the restoration of the Davidic dynasty and the Kingdom of God than the temple; Accepting the division between chapters 1-8 and 9-14, Childs argues in favour of a relationship between the two sections. According to him the second section expands, develops and sharpens the theological Pattern of the "end time", which emerges from chapters 1-8. The book thus seeks to explain that notwithstanding the return from exile, the full experience of redemption still lies in the future.

Zechariah in all its diversity contributes to a vision of (1) The New Jerusalem (2:5; 9:8; 14:1): (2) The grandeur of fulfilment (1:17; 4:10; 8:6-15; 9:12); (3) The removal of evil and God's judgment on the nations

(1:15,21; 6:1-8; 9:1-8; 12:1-9; 14:1-15); (4) The Participation of Jews and Gentiles in the mercies of God (2:11; 8:7-8,22; 10:9-10; 14:16); (5) the cleansing, consecration and empowering by the spirit of restoration (4:6; 5:4; 12:10; 13:13); and (6) The humble and glorious messianic figure (3:8; 4:6; 9:9).

b) The Message of Zechariah:

i) The Age of responsibility: Zechariah's prophecy complements that of 'Haggai. He too, was concerned with the completion of the Temple and with the renewal of spiritual life. Haggai emphasized the responsibility of the 'people in view of the dawning of the new age. Zechariah urged the postexilic community not to repeat the mistakes of their ancestors, but instead to devote themselves to God (1:1-6) and to trust him in Working out his promised deliverance. Like Haggai, he attached great importance to the future of the temple and Davidic dynasty. But he focused on the presence of God with his people, and in this regard comes closer to Ezekiel. So P.D. Hanson writes "Zechariah sees his nation at the point in history Prophesied by Ezekiel when Yahweh would return to Zion to dwell in the midst his People"! (**Dawn of the Apocalyptic**, p.249).

Zechariah provided a theological perspective on covenant life with its blessings and threats. He exhorted the people to remember that the prophecies of exile had become a reality (1:6; 7:7-14). Fearing the recurrence of God's judgment, Zechariah encouraged the new generation to reflect on the past. They must not repeat the mistakes of their forerunner who had been led into exile and alienation and had received the curse of God (1:5-6; 7:14). The lessons from the past explain that the Former (pre-exilic) Prophets had called in vain for repentance (1:4; 7:6-7), that their ancestors had failed to respond (1:4; 7:11-12), that they had angered the LORD (1:2; 7:12), that he had stopped listening to their prayers and appeals to his Covenant love (7:13), and that he had unleashed his curse on them.

ii) The Present reality of Restoration: Zechariah went beyond the past to a reflection on the situation and opportunity at hand. He inspired the People of God to see how the prophetic word regarding restoration was being fulfilled in their generation. Though the fulfilment seemed distant, God encouraged the new community with visions (1;7-6:8) that gave them a perspective on the progressive fulfilment of the Prophetic Oracles.

The eight visions may be organised structurally as four parallel Visions:

A. Vision of the nations at rest, 1:7-17; B. Vision of judgment on the nations, 1:18-21; C. Vision of Zion; 2:1-13; D. Vision of the new age; forgiveness and Peace, 3:1-10; D'. Vision of the new age; messianic ministry; 4:1-13; C'. Vision of the removal of evil; 5:1-4, B'. Vision of Judgment on Babylon: 5:5-11; A'. Vision of the spirit at rest, 6:1-8.

These eight night visions portray what God was doing for his people. Through the interpretation of the angelic intermediary, the prophet explains what he sees. The visions, are given for the purpose of comfort and the godly might know that the Lord was zealously working out all aspects of redemption. This redemption consists of the vengeance on God's enemies the vindication and glorification of his cleansed and holy people, and the consequent glorious established of his holy rule (1:13-15).

The night visions may be viewed as a set of a stained glass windows placed opposite each other: The first and the last, the second and the seventh, the third and the sixth, and finally the fourth and the fifth. The central visions (four and five) focus on the form of symmetry. All aspects of restoration are rooted in the hope of God's presence, and presence of God is at the same time the goal of restoration.

iii) The Era of Restoration: fulfilment of the Promises: Zechariah confirmed the promises concerning the people, the land, and the presence of the land in blessing, Protection, peace, the spiritual metamorphosis (forgiveness cleansing, and holiness), the inclusion of the nations, and renewal of creation.

The presence of Yahweh in blessing and protection is the present guarantee of the restoration as well as the hope of the transformation to come. The focus of the promise is the return of God's presence symbolized, by the temple People (1:16). His presence will assure the covenant relationship, symbolized in the names associated with the city of God. "Then Jerusalem will be called the city of Truth, and the mountain of the LORD Almighty will be called the Holy Mountain" (8:3). Yahweh's presence was experienced in the postexilic community, as God affirmed: "Now I have determined to do good again to Jerusalem and Judah. Do not be afraid" (8:15). The LORD promised to remove their fear and to give them reasons to rejoice in his goodness. (2:10-11).

The LORD was present in blessing (8: 12-14), in protection, and keeping watch over his people (vv. 12-14; 9:8). Though they might suffer adversity, he is with them as their God, for they are his precious people (9:8-16; 14:3-7,9). The LORD is kind and the people make up his kingdom on earth. He gives them the peace that the preexilic prophets had proclaimed: "In that day each of you will invite his neighbour to sit under his vine and fig tree", declares the LORD Almighty". (3:10). God's peace will be extended to all the nations, as envisioned in God's covenant with David (9:10; see P8. 72:8-11).

The people of the LORD will increase in number as Jews and Gentiles together will seek shelter in Zion (3:10; 8:20-23). Zion, the city of God, denotes here, God's blessings and Protection that come from God's Presence with his People (see. Ps. 46). Yahweh declares that he is zealous for his people, and his zeal comes to concrete expression in the restoration of the people to the land and cities (1:17), in the Joy and prosperity of his people (8:4-6), and in the honour his children will enjoy instead of shame (9:16-17). No one will be permitted to hurt God's people, without hurting himself (10:4-12). Yahweh reassures the people and the godly from the nations that he will be zealous in working out the restoration of his children (1:14; 8:12). They constitute the new community, composed of people who have been cleansed and forgiven by "the blood of my covenant" grace; but the LORD delights in children who are zealous for the LORD, God's Kingdom and his worship. They will enter into the fullness of the covenant privileges (8:20-23; 14:20-21).

The land is intimately connected with the restoration of the people of God. God will grant God's blessing on the land by giving rain and increasing the crops (10:10). In the vision of new creation, the prophet affirms the hope of the cooperation of creation with the redeemed because of God's kingship, symbolized by light and water (14:6-11). God will establish his Kingship "over the whole earth" (14:9).

The benefits of God's rule confirm the promises of all the covenants. Zechariah used promise and covenant language to assure them that the LORD is faithful in the progress of fulfilments. However, God also expects his people to be involved. Involvement in Zechariah's time pertaining the temple of God, which was still not complete (8:9-10). This involvement also Pertains to God's concern for the justice on earth. Wicked and selfish people (i.e., covenant breakers) have no place in the eschatological kingdom (13:2). Covenant keepers establish the kingdom of God by living in accordance with the principles of God's rule of justice, righteousness, and love (8:16-22; see 7: 9) The LORD promises to bless God's people in proportion to their commitment to God's Kingdom.

iv) The Humble and Glorious Messiah: In the visions of Zechariah portrayed the harmonious relationship between the high Priest and the Branch, the Davidic descendant. The Branch will foster the worship of God and bring in an era of peace and prosperity. He appears both humble and glorious. He is humble in his entrance (9:9). The prophet also intimates that this Messiah is to suffer as the smitten shepherd (11:7-14; 13:7-9). But this humble Messiah is powerful enough to bring to his people full deliverance from Suffering, to be God's means of grace and purification, and to bring the gift of the spirit of restoration to all who mourn over his being pierced (12:10-13:1). He is the Priest King who serves "the LORD of all the earth" (14:14) and rules over all who believe on him, Jews and Gentiles (8:20-23), The Presence of God will be evident: "The house of David will be like God, like the Angel of the LORD going before them" (12-8). In the end, the Messiah will vindicate the saints and judge the unbelieving nations: "On that day his feet will stand on the Mount of Olives,...Then the LORD my God will come, and all the holy ones with him" (14:4-5). On that glorious day the LORD and creator of humankind will transform everything (14:6-8) and grant his blessing on the new community, which may share in this transformed and holy world (14:20-21).

xiii. Malachi

The transition from the book of Zechariah to Malachi is surprising. After the eschatological battle over Jerusalem (Zech. 14), there is new again a discussion of the problems of everyday life.

We have a very clearly defined units in the book of Malachi. E. Pfeiffer had defined six units of the book of comparison with Isa. 40:27-31 and Amos 5:18-20. These six united are to be understood in three stages. (a) an initial statement is made (b) the partner in the discussion objects (c) the statement is substantiated in detail and necessary conclusion is drawn. The six units are to be seen as follows:

1) 1:2-5 discusses the demonstration of Yahweh's love for Israel (Jacob) which has been preserved, while the related nation of Edom (Esau) must perish.

2) 1:6-2:9 accuses the priests of offering inferior sacrifices and threatens them with a curse if they persist.

3) 2: 10-16 reproves the men who wantonly commit adultery and divorce their wives.

4) 2:17-3:5 addresses itself to doubts concerning God's righteous retaliation, pointing to the immanent day of judgement.

5) 3:6-12 blames the current calamity, a bad harvest due to drought and locusts, on a withholding of tithes from the Temple, and promises rich blessings if the people will return to Yahweh.

6) 3:13 - 4:3, once more attacks those who doubt, explaining that on the day of Judgement those fear Yahweh will receive God's reward, while the wicked will be destroyed.

a) Date of the Prophet: There is generally agreed date emerged regarding Malachi. the first half of the fifth century B.C.E, after the establishment of the Second Temple in 515 and before the reforms of Nehemiah began about 445 (If the traditional dating of Ezra, 458, is accepted, this would make the conventional dating of Malachi is still more precise). The grounds for this judgment are mainly twofold: first the reference to the 'governor' (1:8) clearly implies that **Peha** (governor) appointed by the Persian authorities, rather than a native king is in a position of responsibility and this implies the second rather than the first temple period. (the word **Peha**, governor, is that used of Zerubbabel in Haggai and also of Nehemiah (5: 14, 12: 26). Secondly it is commonly held that a more Precise identification within the Persian Period can be made on the basis of the various abuses listed in Malachi: The implication is that the reforms of Ezra and Nehemiah had not yet taken Place. This is thought to point to period after the first enthusiasm for Temple building had worn off and before the reforms which led to a purification of the cultus. Sometimes the attempt is made to provide external support for this dating by reference to the history of Edom. (cf. Mal. 1:2-6). But two points are supposed to be noted here:

First: It is far from certain whether the references to Edom should be taken as historical or whether Edom represents here the typical enemy. Edom is in fact portrayed as such in a great variety of material in the Old Testament, from the Jacob-Esau stories in Genesis through Amos, Jeremiah and Obadiah down to Malachi, but it would be precarious indeed to attempt precise historical reconstruction of the underlying situations behind each of these prophetic condemnations. In other words, Mal: 1:2-6 may reflect a literary continuum as much as an historical comment.

Second: We need to be aware of the gaps in our historical knowledge. In the Second Temple period in particular these are far too great for detailed reconstruction to be legitimate. Book of Ezra and Nehemiah each claiming to made reforms in the returnees of the exile, but even their precise dates cannot be given accurately. Most of the dates are based on the superscriptions, as in the case of book of Malachi, which are considered to be later additions, therefore the living prophetic traditions cannot be pinned down to precise points in time. Our conclusion with regard to the date of the prophet Malachi therefore be that he is to be placed within the Persian period, sometime between 515 and 330 B.C.E, but that greater precision than that is scarcely available.

Very often Malachi's words are linked with the theme of Deuteronomic writings. J.M.P. Smith, for instance in 1912 noted in particular that the reference to the priest as bound by the covenant with Levi (2:4,8) and use of such expressions as 'the law of my servant Moses', 'Horeb' and 'all Israel" (4:4) all Point to a links with Deuteronomy rather than with the Priestly Code. This may also have some bearing on date, in so far as reference to an Aaronic Priesthood and to the holy mountain as Sinai increasingly became the norm; but a greater significance of this kind of usage lies in the fact that Malachi appears to have been attempting to apply the particular emphases of the Deuteronomists in the circumstances of his own day. R.L. Smith pointed out that Malachi uses the themes characteristic those of Deuteronomy. Smith refers in Particular to 'Love' 'fear', and 'faithfulness' as being especially noteworthy in this regard.

b) Form and Message of Malachi: Malachi seems to have been deliberately adapted to the substance of the message he has to give. The form, is unique in a prophetic book in that it consists of an exchange of a series of questions and answers between the prophet and his hearers. This form is found elsewhere as one element in a prophetic collection (eg, in Hag 1:4ff; 2:3ft) but nowhere else is it carried through as here so as to cover virtually the whole book, and nowhere else are the supposed answers of those accused set out in the detail given in Malachi, which is interspersed with phrases such as 'You say', introducing the answers to the prophetic accusations. Such a form probably has a legal background, with charges being made, answers being put forward, and these in their turn being dismissed as inadequate, Malachi has some elements in common with the **rib pattern**, particularly in the accusatory material of 1:6-2:9, but it would be impossible to reconstruct anything like a complete' 'law suit' from Malachi.

Malachi is overwhelmingly concerned with religious matters, with the Priesthood and the Temple, and with the proper way in which God should be worshipped. He also sees this responsibility laid on the religious leaders, on whom he is very much severe than on the community at large. The priests in particular are harshly condemned (1:6-2:9).

Malachi's words of judgment expressions bring out a strongly positive aspect of God's power. Thus in 1:5, the initial condemnation of Edom, which is in some respects very negative and harsh, reaches its climax in an assertion of Yahweh's supernatural power. 1:11, is most difficult verse to interpret. Some would interpret. It as (based on Christian liturgy), the 'pure offering to which it refers being interpreted as being in some way 'fulfilled by the Christian Eucharist. But this is hardly accepted as the intention of the author. Another possibility is that the reference here might be to the Jews living away from Jerusalem, in the Diaspora. This is the interpretation accepted by the most Jewish commentators, also by J. Blenkinsopp (**A history of Prophecy in Israel**, p.240f). But perhaps the most likely interpretation, is provided by the clue given by Mason, that the phrase 'from the rising of the sun to its setting' is virtually identical with Ps.50:1b. In that Psalm, as in this verse, the lord's universal power is proclaimed, and the efficacy of animal sacrifice rejected. In Malachi 1:11 the sacrifices referred are not those of animals. It seems therefore that we May legitimately see here a proclamation of the Lord's universal power, perhaps set over against excessive claims made on behalf of the sacrificial system of the Jerusalem temple as being the only assured way to divine favour. If so, Malachi would have anticipated some of the bitter disputes concerning the status of the Jerusalem cult which characterized post biblical Judaism and can still be traced in the New Testament.

The section 3:13-4:6, characteristic warning of judgement for the wicked, but the last part (4:1-4) stand somewhat apart. Some would regard it as a later addition, though the continued Deuteronomistic links (eg. The use of 'Horeb' in 4:4) certainly supply a measure of continuity with what has preceded. Some suggestions are worth considering in this regard:

i) The reference in 4:4 to 'the law of my servant Moses, the statues and ordinances that I commanded him', is surely, intentionally reminiscent of Deuteronomy. Even in Deuteronomy the information is given as a looking back upon what God had done for his people at Horeb, with the intention of emphasizing the continued importance of the commands made there for a later generation. Here in Malachi at even later time than Deuteronomy we find it strongly emphasized that those laws are still operative despite all the changes that have taken place in the life of the community.

ii) The form of this reference strongly suggests that the 'law' has now reached a fixed and effectively final shape; it can in effect be appealed to as 'Scripture'. The community that is to 'remember' this law is now the community which is bound to God by a Holy book as well as by the sacrifice of the temple. And it is now 'Israel' in the sense of a religious grouping not of a nation-state.

iii) The second appendix (4:5-6) has little connection with the first and may have come from another hand. It is in effect an explanatory note on 3:1, elaborating on the identity of the promised messenger, the link between the two passages perhaps being provided by the reference to 'Horeb', the name given to Sinai in Deuteronomy and the mountain to which Elijah fled according to I Kings 19. The first appendix (4:1-3) looked back this one (4:5-6) looks forward. It is the first example known to us of the Working out of a role for Elijah in God's future plans.

iv) This section relates to the way in which it rounds off the whole prophetic collection. In Malachi's time the Jews had been home from exile in Babylon about one hundred Years They were cured of their idolatry, but had returned to then former state of indifference and spiritual lethargy. The Priests had been lax and degenerate, sacrifices were inferior tithes and offerings were neglected, divorce and mixed marriage were common (3:9-11).

Still chafing under a foreign yoke, the promises by the prophet concerning Israel's glorious future yet unrealised, many in the nation had begun to ask whether or not God loves Israel (1:2). What had become of divine Justice (2:17)? Was it profitable to serve God any longer (3:11-15)? They complained that as God's chosen people they were left in a low estate while the wicked heathen prospered. If God still loved them, where is the promise of the Messiah and His universal Kingdom? And where is Justice? "Everyone that does evil is good in the sight of Yahweh, and he delights in them … where is the God of justice?" they cried. Again others lamented, "It is vain to serve God; and what profit is it that we have kept his charge, and that we have walked mournfully before Yahweh of hosts? And now we call the proud happy; Yea, they that work wickedness are built up; yes, they tempt God and escape", Many, therefore, in the face disappointments, the lack of Prosperity, and unscrupulous nobles and Priests, turned to sin, religious indifference and scepticism. Thus the Jews, impatiently awaited Messiah. Malachi assured them that God would surely come, but God's sudden appearance would only issue, judgment for them unless they repented and rendered faithful obedience (chaps. 34). In this regard we can see how the prophet Malachi Places considerable emphasis on the "day of the Lord". Six times prophet announces its approach (1:11 (implied); 3:2,17; 4:1,3,5).

The book addresses its message to a community whose eschatological expectations, aroused by Haggai and Zechariah, have not been fulfilled, and whose deep disappointment finds expression in difference and neglect of the cult 111 this situation the prophet assures those who doubt that the coming final judgement is inescapable. The important thing for the people 13 to prepare for the day of eschaton, by fulfilling their cultic and moral obligations and for the community to remain pure. The prophet also demands humble veneration of God, who is a great king, feared by the nations (1:14), whose name is great throughout the world, and to whom pure offerings are made (1:11) Man's duty is to return uprightly to Yahweh (3: 7) and accept with all his heart obligation to obey Yahweh's will.

4. THE WRITINGS

The third part of the Hebrew canon contains the 'writings' (*Ketubim*), It contains writings of very different character, the common feature of which is essentially that they have not been incorporated in one of the two other parts of the canon. It too was open for a long time, as is clear from the divergent order in the Septuagint. We shall summarise and review the contents of the books of Writings in the following pages.

4.1. The Book of Psalms

The book of Psalms (*tehellim*, 'songs of praise') consists of a collection of psalms of very different periods of the history of Israel. Many of them originally had particular functions in public worship in the temple in Jerusalem (eg. Hymns of different kinds, popular lamentations, royal Psalms), others accompanied the cultic acts of individual Israelites (individual lamentations and thanksgiving); yet others are to be regarded more as religious poems without a particular place in the cult (eg. individual hymns, wisdom Psalms). On the basis of the form critical analysis, A.A. Anderson classifies four types of Psalms His classification is based on Hermann Gunkel.

a) The Praises of God

These are the responses of the worship or cultic community to what God has done. This category is further divided into three sub types:

1) Hymns of Descriptive Praise: These are praises of Yahweh for what Yahweh has done in nature and history. God is spoken in third person. This type of Psalms hasthree-part structure: Introduction (exhortation to praise); mainsection (grounds for exhortation often begins with "because" or "for"); Conclusion (re-echoes introductory formula, occasionally ends with prayer or wish). In the descriptive praise psalms three further types are recognized (i) Praises of God in general (eg. 114, 136); (ii) Praises celebrating kingship of Yahweh (Mowinckel calls them as enthronement psalms). For eg 47, 93, 96-99

(may be 95 and 100); (iii) Songs of Zion (indirect praises of God) (48, 76, 84, 87, 122 and possibly 46 & 132): these are praises of God, praising Temple or Holy city, there is lack of hymnic introduction.

2) *Declarative Praises of the Individual (Individual songs of thanksgiving)*: 2-10, 18, 32, 34, 92, 116, 118, 138. These Psalms usually have three-part structure: (i) Introduction: invocation of Yahweh's name (hymnic additions and the declaration of intent are seen here); (ii) The main section: The account of distress experienced (9:3ff) and the divine deliverance are made clear; (iii) conclusion (ps. 9:9-20); often ends with an invitation to praise. The cultic occasion of these Psalms may have been the sacrifice of thanks-giving.

3) *Declarative Praises of the people: (National songs of thanksgiving)*: Eg. Ps. 124 (Gunkel includes 66: 8-12, 67, 124, 129). These Psalms declare God's doing either for self or for nation.

b) Laments

Almost one third of the Psalms come from this category. These are basically responses of the human beings in their afflictions: It has two main parts: (i) Introduction: Invocation of Yahweh's name and call for help; (ii) Main section: It has number of elements, but the order of these elements may Vary Description of distress (P5. 5) or misfortune, prayer and cry for help and deliverance, motivation for appealing to Yahweh, confession of sin or protestation of sin (Job), wishes and curses (Ps. 137), a vow to praise God. Often Lamentation changes from supplication to thanksgiving due to a priestly oracle promising deliverance. These laments are further divided into three major types as follows:

1) *Laments of Individual*: Eg. PS. 3, 5, 6, 7, 17, 22, 25, 109, 130, 141, 143, et. al. These are the most often recognized by content not by type. In this way they are further sub-divided into. (i) Prayer of unjustly accused person: 7, 17,26, 35, 57, 69 perhaps these psalms are recited by / for the accused person in the sanctuary in order to obtain a favourable divine Judgement. (ii) Psalms of penitence: 6, 32, 38, 51, 102, 130, 143.

2) *Laments of the Nation*: The background of these psalms is national disaster effecting the entire nation, a day of fasting prayer would then be held; perhaps these psalms are used on fixed days of prayer and penitence or as part of the annual rituals. cf. Zech. 7th chap. Eg. Pss. 60, 74, 79, 80, 83, 90, 124, 134 (?),144 (?).

3) *Psalms of Confidence*: These are individual psalms which emphasize certain aspects of the lamentation. Even though the content is confidence: still there containsa motif of lamentation thus they are put under this category Eg. Ps. 125, a collective song of Trust.

c) Royal Psalms

(2, 18, 20, 21, 45, 72, 101, 110, 132 sometimes other psalms like 28, 61,63& 89 are also included). These are basically the psalms of which deal with the relationship between God and king. These psalms presents the theology of kingship: king is depicted as God's adopted son, vice-gerent of God, king also represents people before God; king is also Yahweh's anointed. Most of the royal Psalms are coming from pre-exilic period, some psalms are possibly from post-exilic messianic following the pattern of royal psalms. These psalms are used it coronation of king in Ps. 45:6, the king is addressed as the representative of god; Ps. 45 is used at the wedding ceremony of the king.

d) Minor Types

These psalms have no clear structure, they are linked and identified by common content or aim. They are: (i) Entrance liturgies, used by the pilgrims wishing to enter the temple eg. 15, 24; (ii) Wisdom Psalms: these psalms express the idea of reminiscent of wisdom literature in subject matter, style and language eg. Pss. 1, 32, 73, 112, 127, 128, 133. The common wisdom phrase used in these psalms in "Blessed is the man"; (iii) Prophetic psalms or liturgics (oracular Psalm): In some cases, only a part of the psalm is involved eg. Pss. 2, 12, 50, 62, 75, 81, 82, 85, 95, 1'10; (iv) Sacred legends: Pss. 78, 105, 106, (also Ps. 46); (V) Pilgrimage songs: Pss. 84, 122 (Zion psalm); (vi) Mixed poems: Ps 119.

e) The Composition of the book of Psalms

The book of Psalms is called collection of collections because several smaller collections are put together and the Psalter having achieved its final process through a long and complicated process. Examples are as follows to this evidence:

i) Doublets: Ps.14 is equal to Ps. 53 and Psalm 40:13-17 is equal to 70:1-5
ii) Triplets: Ps.108 is equal to 57:1-11 plus 60:5-12
iii) In Ps. 72 at its end prayers of David are ended, but Psalm 86 again has a title as prayer of David.
iv) The titles (superscriptions) given to the Psalms are not uniformly divided. Ps.1-89 most of the Psalms have titles, Whereas Psalms 90-150 only a few Psalms given titles.

In the following pages we shall treat the book of Psalms based on some sub-topics, except the theme of literary types which was already dealt earlier.

a) *Main divisions and doxologies:* The Psalms may be divided into smaller or larger collections on the basis chiefly of the superscriptions and secondarily of shared key words (like the literary types: enthronement (royal) Psalms, the hallelujah Psalms and so on). Four times always at the end/conclusion of a sub collection (at the end of Ps. 41, 72, 89,106) there is a doxology, "Blessed be the Lord …" These make it possible, at least in retrospect to regard the Psalter as like the Pentateuch in as much as it comprises five books. Psalm 150 may be regarded as a concluding hymn for the entire Psalter. Conversely the invitatory call to salvation in Ps.1 and Ps.2, a royal Psalm that it probably interpreted eschatologically, is prefixed to the first book of the Psalter, which contains the extensive and relatively ancient Davidic Psalter (Ps.3-14). Before we move on to discuss the possible process of compilation of the entire Psalter in five major steps, we shall present the picture of the use of divine name in different sub-sections of the Psalter:

Psalms	God (Elohim)	The LORD (Yahweh)
1-41	15	278 (Yahwistic Psalter)
42-83	201 (Elohistic Psalter)	44
84-89	7	31
90-150	9	339 (prefers to use the name Yahweh)

The process of compilation presented below is only a hypothetical picture, which may be subjected to several modifications.

First Stage: Small collection of Psalms was initiated at individual sanctuaries as follows:

(i) First Davidic Psalter: 3-41
(ii) Korahite Psalter: 42-49, 84-85, 87-88
(iii) Asaphite Psalter: 73-83 plus 50
(iv) Second Davidic Psalter: 51-7l plus 72

Second Stage: During this stage, smaller collections are combined to make larger ones. During this stage, the major Elohistic Psalter was formed by combining

(i) The Korahite Psalter: 42-49
(ii) The Asaphite Psalter: 73-83 plus 50
(iii) The second Davidic Psalter: 51-71 and 72, thus make a collection of Ps.42-83. In this stage, the divine name Yahweh is changed into Elohim. The first Davidic Psalter was untouched during this stage rather it existed separately.

Third Stage: In this step, the combined Elohistic Psalter in the previous stage has now been taken into it: The First Davidic Psalter i.e; 3-41 to make it as one block Ps. 3-89 and with addition at the introduction of Psalm 2 plus Ps. 84-89 added at the end, thus we now have a collection of Ps. 2-89 completed in this stage.

Fourth Stage: The Compilation of Ps. 2-89 happened in the previous stage has now been further enlarged by the addition of other blocks of Psalms of different origin coming from different dates. They include the following:

(i) Songs of Ascents: 120-134

(ii) Hallelujah Psalms: 146-150

Those collections were added along with other minor gaps being filled with the addition of Psalm 1 at some point of time and it served as introduction to the entire Psalter.

Fifth Stage: In this final stage, the entire collection occurred in all the previous four stages have now been divided into the five books as we have in the final form. They are as follows: 1-41; 42-72; 73-89; 90-106; 107-150. Moreover, during this stage, doxologies were added to the each of 4 major divisions at their end. They include the following: 41:13; 72:18-19; 89:52; 106:48 and Psalm 150 is considered as doxology to the fifth division and also as a concluding doxology to the entire Psalter.

b) Closure and Compilation: Even after the above mentioned hypothetical five stage process of compilation, the entire collection was not closed all of a sudden. For instance, LXX has Psalm 151 (probably this is because of counting one Psalm into two). Psalm 151 is also found, in Qumran Cave 11 as 11 Q Heb Ps.151. Many scholars would argue that the Psalter was closed in third century C.E. Moreover, this scroll contains only 41 biblical psalms. Based on all these observations scholars like J.A. Sanders argue that, there was an open-ended Psalter in the first century A.D. But there are some scholars who argue that, the Psalm scroll discovered in cave IV of Qumran is not to be identified with Psalm scroll proper! Another compounded problem along with this is, we can hardly date any psalm with precision. Psalm 137 may be dated during the time of Babylonian exile in 587 B.C.E and several other psalms are generally dated as post-exile and there are few pre-exilicpsalms as well, but on the whole they can't be accurately dated since most of them are meant for liturgical usage.

c) Canonization of the book of Psalms: The position of the Psalter in the Hebrew Canon presents a perplexing picture in the various areas of text tradition. The familiar printed edition in most cases place the Psalter at the head of the Kethubim thus follow the tradition of the Jews of central Europe. The order varies between Psalms – Job – Proverbs and Psalms – Proverbs – Job. But we go back to the earliest time in the canon tradition that is still recognizable today, we find that the order is extraordinarily various. In the Palestinian text tradition, Chronicles seem to have stood at the head of Kethubim. Witnesses are Codex L, Michael Ben Uzziel, and the manuscripts of the Masora of Palestine. The Spanish "Jews follow this tradition, that is, in which the Psalter appears in the second place in the Kethubim. Still other principles of arrangement are operative among the Jews of Eastern dispersion.

From Talmud (Baba Bathra 14b) we learn that, also the book of Ruth, among others, was w place directly before the Psalter. Obviously the ancestry of the Psalmist David was especially to be emphasized.

In the canon of the Masoretic Text (MT), the book of the Psalms, Job and Proverbs form a characteristic group with in Kethubim. A Peculiar accent system is used exclusively in these books. Special characteristic of this system is that in addition to the **'atnah**. We also find the **'oleh we yored**. While the **'atnah** appears as the divider between verses only in shorter sentences, the **'oleh we yored** serves as the chief divider in longer sentence structure. The 150 Psalms of the Psalter have different numbers in Greek (LXX) and in the Hebrew text (called Masoretic Text - MT). The following chart displays this point clearly:

MT	GREEK	MT	GREEK
Ps. 1-8	1-8	116:10-19	115
Ps. 9-10	9	117-146	116-145
Ps. 11-113	10-112	147:1-11	146
Ps. 114-115	113	147:12-20	147
Ps. 116-1-9	114	148-150	148-150

According to this chart, Greek contrasts Ps. 9 and 10, and latter also Ps. 114 and 115, into one Psalm each. In addition, at the end Greek also preserves an additional Psalm 151, in which I Samuel 16: 1-14 and I Samuel chapter 17 are freely used. But already in the oldest tradition this additional product is consistently labeled as "Supernumerary". Psalm 151 is an example of the later offshoots of Psalm writing as we see it in the non-canonical collections of the thanksgiving humans from Qumran such as the "Psalms of Solomon" and the "Odes of Solomon". As mentioned earlier, the open-ended nature of Psalter is highly probably, only at the late date, the compilation has been concluded.

d) Superscription's and titles to the individual Psalms: Before we go into the consideration of individual titles and superscriptions we shall note the types of titles or categories of superscriptions as proposed by Sigmund Mowinckel. There are four categories as follows:

1) Titles that comprise technical designations of psalms, including mizmor, mikhtam, maskil, tephillah and Shir hamma alath.

2) Titles pointing to the purpose of the psalms such as thanksgiving etc., hazkir, yedhuthun and leannoth.

3) Titles of cultic origin, which, according to Mowinckel, include the bulk of psalms such as the "Choirmaster" collection, these titles mentioning melodies and perhaps the obscure title muthlabben (Ps.9)

4) Titles containing specific musical references such as neghinoth, selah, haggayon, nehilogh etc...

The presence of superscriptions fall all except thirty-four Psalms (Ps. 1-2, 10, 33, 43, 71, 91, 93-97, 89, 104-107, 111-119, 135-137 and 146-150) poses certain difficulties of historicity and interpretation. Some of the allusions purporting to relate to King David, for example, follow a tradition that is at variance with Samuel. Thus in Ps. 34, the king before whom David simulated madness was named Abimelech, where as in I Sam. 21:10ff, he was named Achish. Again the title of Psalm 56 seems to imply that David was captured by the Philistines and brought to Gath where as in I Sam. 21:10, David is indicated to have fled there on his own initiative.

It seems probable that in at least some instances the titles were the result of editorial activity that may well have been intended to preserve some historical tradition with respect to specific compositions, or to perpetuate a certain familiar usage, whether in connection with origin, character, music, or liturgical function of the psalm.

The superscriptions of thirteen psalms support to preserve the historical traditions relating to the life of David, in terms of which the particular psalms were composed.

(a) Ps. 3 cf. II Sam. 15:1-18:33; (b) Ps. 7: Cush of Benjamin is nowhere mentioned in the OT accounts of the life of David; (c) Ps. 18 cf. I Sam. 19:1ff, 24:1f, 26; II Sam. 5:17f, 8:1f, 10:1f, 15:1-18:33; 21:15f; (d) Ps. 34 cf. I Sam. 21:10f, but perhaps this Psalm refers to another occasion of simulated madness than that which occurred in the presence of Achish and which is not recorded in the OT; (e) Ps. 51 cf. II Sam. 11:1f; (f) Ps. 52 cf. I Sam. 22:6f; (g) Ps. 54 cf. I Sam. 23:14f; (h) Ps. 56- This may preserved in different traditions from that in I Sam. 21:10ff, 22:1, 27:1ff, regarding the reasons why David went to Gath. (i) Ps. 57 cf. I Sam. 22:1f, 24:1f; (i) Ps. 59 cf. I Sam. 19:8f; (k) Ps. 60 cf. II Sam. 8:3f, 10:15f; (l) Ps. 63 cf. I Sam 24:1f, II Sam 15:1f; (m) Ps.142 cf. I Sam. 22:1 (24:1). It may well be that in at least some of the foregoing instances the titles were added by an editor who was aware of circumstances under which "the particular compositions of the Psalm in Question. Some specific terms related to superscription are as follows:

(i) Alanioth - is rare occurring only in Ps. 46, I Chronicles 15:20 and as a final word of Ps. 48. It's association with the Hebrew noun almah might indicate that it was meant of designate a tune for female voices.

(ii) Names of melodies appear to be reflected by several titles: "Do not destroy" - "Altaschith" - Ps. 57-59, 75, cf. Isa. 65:8; "The hind of the Dawn" (Ps. 22); "Lilies", "Shoshannim" (Ps. 45, 69, 80). "The lily of the Testimony", "Shushan-eduth" (Ps.60); Uncertain in this regard are: Gittith" (Ps. 8, 81, 84), which may be (following LXX) a vintage-tune associated with the word git meaning "wine press" (cf. Joel 4:13) or may refer to Philistine (Gath) musical instrument.

(iii) Mahalath: (Ps. 53, 88), which may have been a tune named after a woman (cf. Gen. 28:9, II Chro. 11:18).

(iv) Mahalath Leannoth: (Ps. 88) - which also may have been dedicated to some female, although leannoth may mean "for affection" or for singing.

(v) Muth-labben: means "die for the son"? May be it is an obscure expression in the title of Ps. 9, may be a corruption of almot or alternatively, the name of a tune.

(vi) Musical instruments may be referred to under the named Nehiloth (Ps. 5) which occurs only here in the Old Testament, consequently obscure meaning and Sheminith (Ps. 6,12) - but "Sheminith" seems to refer to an "octave" and its only other occurrence is I Chro. 15:21, it is of doubtful meaning.

(vii) Stringed instrument: (in Ps. 4, 6, 54, 55, 67, and 76), 4 of these contain the term "mizmor", pointing clearly to instrumental accompaniment of singers.

(viii) Choirmaster: (in vulgate: "in finem", "to the chief musician"), appears to be reasonably assured in the light of the evidence furnished by I Chr. 15:21 (The verb seems to imply the rendering of Music and not "smoothing the countenance of Yahweh) and it may be that the Psalms to which this designation was attached had been taken from a collection belonging to an unknown presenter, or perhaps dedicated to him. Jeduthun, the name of a Levitical choir leader in the Solomonic period (II Chr. 5:12cf. II Chr. 35:15 as the name of the sun in Josiah's time), and also the cognomen of Levite in the time of Nehemiah (Neh. 11:17), appeared in the titles of three Psalms (39, 62, 77), and may have had some significance in connection with choral work, but this also is uncertain.

(ix) Individuals or guilds of singer appeared under various designations, one of the more common being Asaph (Ps. 50, 78-83). A prominent court-musician in the time of David bore this name (I Chr. 6:39; 15:17), and it may well be that the "sons of Asaph" in the period of Nehemiah (Neh. 7:44) were members of a musical guild that went back to the days of David and the monarchy. Asaph, in the Psalter could refer either to guild, to some member of it, or to their collection of religious poetry.

(x) Ethan, the Ezrahite: (Ps. 89) cf. I Chr. 6:44. In I Kings 4:31 Ethan is a Hebrew sage and He-man, the Ezrahite (Ps. 88 cf. I Chr. 6:33), enshrined the native Canaanite tradition of music and psalmody.

(xi) Sons of Korah: (Ps. 42, 44-49, 84-85, 88-89), may imply the existence of another musical guild whose traditional origins probably reached back to Korah, the great-grandson of Levi (Num. 16:17; I Chr. 6:31 cf. II Chron. 20:19).

(xii) Maskil: occurred in 13 titles (Ps. 32, 42, 44, 45, 52-55, 74, 78, 88-89, 142) has been interpreted to mean a "didactic" or "meditative" Psalm. The root idea of the verb appears to be that of "Prudence" or "insight" (cf. Amos

5:13), and since maskil is causative in force it might imply the conveying of insight.

(xiii) Mikhtam: is a matter of debate for several years. It occurs in six Psalms (16, 56-60), not to be translated as "golden" as done by the Authorized Version. Sigmund Mowinckel proposes that on the books of Assyrian term Ka-ta-mu, "to even", the word is related to the atoning or expiatory functions or associates of the Psalms concerned (but Mowinckel's idea has not been furnished with much of evidence).

(xiv) Shiggayon: (found in Ps.7 only cf. Habakkuk 3:1), may be related to Akkadian shegu or lamentation Psalm, but the actual meaning is not known.

e) Cultic setting of the Psalms (Book of Psalms as Hymn book of the second temple): Both ancient writers and critical scholars of 19th and early 20th century tended to regard the psalms as providing evidence of private, individual devotion in Israel. Ancient authorities were, of course, bound by the traditional psalm headings; but earlier critical scholars, though rejecting the originality of these superscriptions, were still inclined to see the psalms as individual compositions, reflecting particular historical circumstances. Even Hermann Gunkel, who played a significant role in the form critical analysis of the Psalter, failed to attain a complete cultic understanding of the Psalms. While he rightly saw that Psalmography must go back to pre-exilic times and that some of our psalms date from that period, he believed that the majority of our extant psalms are post exilic, spiritualized imitations of the earlier cultic psalms, and that they are derived from small, more or less private conveticles of pious laymen. He supposed that the many references to cultic matters in the Psalter were only metaphorical.

As a result of the work of Mowinckel, however, this view is no longer generally accepted. The psalms are littered with cultic allusions, which only make sense of they were used in public worship in the temple in Jerusalem. For example, references to the temple include Ps. 23:6; 26:8; 27:4; 63:2; 96:6; 122:1, and Psalms 24, 6, 118 and 132 make allusion to cultic processions, while similarly Ps. 48. 12 alludes to the perambulation around the walls of Mount Zion. References to sacrifices of various kinds are found, e.g. sacrif1ces generally (Ps. 4:5; 27:6), burnt offering (Ps. 20:3), a covenant sacrifice (Ps. 50:5), and a free will offering (Ps. 54:6). Mention is also made of dancing (Ps. 30:11; 87:7; 149:3; 150:4), singing (Ps. 9:11, 30:4; 33:2; 47:6-7) and various kinds of musical instruments (Ps. 33:2, 47:5; 81:2; 98:6; 150:5).

Support for the cultic interpretation of the Psalms may be found in Mishnah and other rabbinic sources, which stipulate various cultic occasions for the use of psalms. Some of the psalm headings also attest liturgical-usage, though they also contain some uncertainties. When we come to the late period, we actually find psalms composed in non-cultic, pious circles, specifically the psalms of Solomon and the Qumran Hodayoth (Thanksgiving Psalms). These differ markedly from our Old Testament psalms in various ways, and their non-cultic orientation highlights all the more the cultic nature of the biblical psalms.

E.S. Gerstenberger has argued that the great majority of the psalms derive not from the Jerusalem temple, but primarily from small-group local community worship, mainly the synagogue of the post-exilic period. However, the grounds for this theory are not convincing, we know nothing about synagogue worship in the Persian period - it is not even certain that synagogues existed there and Gerstenberger gives insufficient weight to the indications of a temple cult origin as well as to evidence that a very large number of psalms are pre-exilic. It should also be noted that some scholars who accept a temple setting for Psalms generally make an exception of the wisdom and Torah psalms, locating them in a school context, but even this is somewhat doubtful.

As a book of cultic songs the Psalter has sometimes been referred in the past as 'The hymn book of the second temple' i.e.: of the postexilic period. This is fair enough, provided that we remember that a considerable part of it was also the 'hymn book' of the first temple. i.e.: of the pre-exilic period. On broader terms we can say that there appears to be pre-dominance of the pre-exilic Psalms in the first two thirds of the Psalter and the post-exilic psalms in the last third. It was fashionable at the end of 19th and early part of 20th century to regard most Psalms as late (For instance, B. Duhm, could regard the exilic Psalm 137 as the earliest Psalm), it later became generally recognized that there are a large number of pre-exilic Psalms (a trend carried to extremes by I. Engnell who regarded Ps. 137 as the latest). Although, some would argue for Psalms as predominantly post-exilic (e.g. Gerstenberger, O. Loretz), most would now recognize that there are in fact a large number of both pre and post-exilic Psalms.

f) The Role of Psalms in the community: Some psalms take on the nature of prayer and relate private thoughts, while others take on the nature of prayer and relate public attitudes. Personal laments contain intimate descriptions of the psalmists 'suffering, voicing the sufferers' private fears of pain and death. Such open confession offers therapeutic benefit, as does the occasional confession of sin which appears in various types of psalms. In the following lines we will briefly discuss on the relationship between psalms and their use in the community.

1) Personal confession: The laments provide a format for the expression of "improper" reactions to suffering and struggle. Psalmists, like Job, frequently overself the limits of propriety based on Israel's standards as well as our own. In the framework of a lament the worshipper can voice strong expressions of God's unfairness and capriciousness. The worshipper does not fear reprisal, since the questionable attitudes remain incidental to the greater purpose of the lament. The lament achieves its purpose by festering confidence in God's eventual deliverance. Whether the worshipper intends to describe suffering to obtain forgiveness, or to release pent-up anger, the psalmist always directs the confessions of the Psalms of God.

2) Community unity and stability: The use of psalms to release detrimental emotions also relates the place of the psalms maintaining the unity and stability of the community. The psalms absorb tensions including: (i) Contrasting feelings (in a single person), (ii) Attitudes and words unacceptable in other contexts, and (iii) God's disposition toward his people. The community gained solidarity when Psalms served as acceptable outlets for potentially damaging attitudes. Psalms provided an outlet for the individual's admixture of joy and grief, depression and confidence. They allowed that person to voice the deepest emotions in the strongest terms even when the emotions and their expressions were not socially acceptable (for example, the claim in Psalm 44 that God had wrongly punished his obedient people, or the desire to break vengeance on innocent babes in Ps. 137).

Apart from the release valve for tension, the psalms also added to the stability of the community by identifying common foes and suggesting common goals. Common goals relate these two tasks. The identification of the type of behaviour acceptable to God differentiated the community of Israel from the wicked or proud. The psalms present widely varied portraits of God, Israel, the ideal community as a nationalistic consolidation of the nation to the ideal community as a peaceful conglomeration of all peoples, and from the world as the setting for incessant pain to the world as the medium for God's lavish blessing. These perspectives added to the unity and stability of second temple Judaism due to their eclecticism. The psalms as a whole show eclecticism rather than exclusivism. They tend to promote the broadest range of response to history rather than limiting the worshiper to a narrow band of propriety.

3) Medium of Instruction: When psalms serve as a medium for instruction, traits of both eclecticism and exclusivity become important. The tension between God as an avenger and God as the redeemer of Israel remains. Each aspect provides insight into important dimensions of theology. God is depicted both as the avenger of the righteous and showing his covenant love. Moreover, God is depicted as creator and elector. The presentation of God's work in history creates a sense of identity as well as providing theological insight for the individual believer and the community.

The wisdom psalms (the most notable tools for instruction in the Psalter) reveal this same dual identity. Torah psalms such as 1, 19, 119 encourage devotion to God and draw attention of religious duty. The reflection they engender compares to that recommended by the Shema (Deut. 6:4-9). Maintaining a relationship with God and fellow worshippers of God involves constant meditation on the meanings and ramifications of the commitment. The wisdom Psalms, including Torah psalms and others, concentrate on a single dynamic simply in terms of the "righteous" and the "wicked". To the contemporary ethics these decision making. On the other hand, their usefulness as basic resources for moral instruction appears clearly. All moral responsibility depends on the primary categories, "good" and "bad". This provides a foundation for the more sophisticated reflections urged in the Torah psalms.

4) Reconstituting reality: In contrast to the earthly concerns of the wisdom psalms, the laments especially express the aim of reconstituting reality. This involves a denial of current negative experiences and a reimagining of the present. Laments base those attitudes on trust in Yahweh's activity in the future. From this perspective, the poetry of the psalms aims to reconstitute present experience. As ritual documents, the psalms enable hope amid hopelessness and justice amid injustice. A similar phenomenon occurs in the hymns (especially Zion songs) in their anticipation of an era under God's complete control. Such psalms provided opportunity for worshippers whose current experience offered no encouragement to live in the future. They understand goals of faith as achieved in spite of situations to the contrary in the here and now.

This special philosophy of time occurs when words serve as the medium for faith. The psalms attempt to express transcendent experience with finite communication. The Hebrew psalmists continually stretch language out of a constant preference for God's sovereignty. Since these poems actually made God present, they also worked as effective agents to bring change to the worshipper's experience. The laments often called God to earth, which makes anything possible. So, the poetry actually changed the face of God, linking its effect directly to his identity.

g) The Theology of Psalms

Whenever Israel experienced the saving acts of Yahweh, they did not keep silent: not only did she repeatedly take up her pen to recall those acts of Yahweh in a wholly personal way she offered praise to him, and asked him questions, and complained to him about all her sufferings, for Yahweh had pot chosen his people as a mere dumb object of his will 1n history, but for converse with him. The answer of Israel's which we gather for the most part form the Psalter, is theologically a subject in itself. In the following pages we shall take up the issues in the theology of psalms.

a) Yahweh, the God of Israel: In the Psalter, we find not a theoretical monotheism but a practical monotheism is stressed. Israel is to worship only Yahweh cf. the echo of the beginning of the Decalogue in Ps. 81:9-10: "There shall be no strange god among you; you shall not bow down to a foreign god.

I am the Lord your God, who brought you up out of the land of Egypt". This is not the same as saying that other gods do not exist. However, the post-exilic passages about the idols of the nations in Ps. 115:4-8 and 135:15-18 clearly do reflect a belief in absolute monotheism. When the existence of other gods is not denied it is Yahweh's incomparability and superiority which are emphasized, for example Psalm 95:3: "For the Lord is a great God, and a great king above all gods", Ps.97:7 "... all gods bow down before him". Furthermore, the understanding of God of Israel, Yahweh is presented in the psalms under various sub-headings as follows:

i) Yahweh the creator and the Lord of History: Yahweh's creation of the world is a recurrent theme in the psalms. Quite often it is associated with Yahweh's conflict with the chaos waters or dragon, which preceded the effective work of creation. Sometimes this event is appealed to in laments as a reminder of Yahweh's past triumphs (cf. Ps. 74:12-l7; 89:9-13), and here the dragon is referred to, named either as Leviathan or Rahab. More commonly we hear of the sea or waters subdued at creation (cf. Ps. 65:6-7; 93:3-4; 104:5-9); in Ps. 33:67 a demythologization has taken place in so far as the conflict with the waters appears to have become simply a job of work, as in Genesis l. In Ps. 29:3,10 God's supremacy over the waters is a sign of his effective lordship over the creation. This was the theme associated with Yahweh's kingship at the feast of Tabernacles. One of the passages cited, Ps.104:5-9, forms part of a larger whole extolling Yahweh's Lordship over creation. This psalm also shows evidence of dependence on Pharaoh Akhenaten's hymn to the sun, and in turn seems to be one of the sources underlying Genesis 1, where the order of creation is strikingly similar.

The splendour of the universe was held to declare the glory of God. As Psalm 19 declares, in words made famous by Haydn's splendid composition: "The heavens are telling the glory of God; and the firmament proclaims his handiwork". In other places in the psalms the various parts of creation are exhorted to praise Yahweh (Ps.96:11ff; 98:7f). It is in the hymns in the Psalter that Yahweh's creation of the world is characteristically alluded to.

The revelation of Yahweh as the God of universe is manifested in the history of his chosen people. The historical psalms, which deal with the beginnings and early events of Israel's existence, tell of this. The great deeds of Yahweh are that to which Israel is constantly relating itself in the Psalms and on which Israel's life is based. In all these testimonies to history there is no doubt even for a moment that God's people are not relying on themselves, on their faith, on their accomplishments, but on Yahweh alone; this history is not a dumb and anonymous history of fated course of events. Rather, God personally drew near to this history of his with Israel in word that he addressed to Israel, and; he chose her to be his partner in conversation. Just as Yahweh's choice of Israel was the creative expression of his unrestricted sovereignty, so

Israel's history was dependent on God's intervention an activity, which always made it possible for Israel to confront the moment and move forward. Thus it is one of the deepest mysteries of Israel's history that the presuppositions of the existence of God's people and of their course of life are based on the theme of "creation" this is expressed most clearly in the confession, "our help is in the name of the Lord, who made heaven and earth" (Ps.124:8; 121 :2; 115:15).

As mentioned above, in innumerable hymns and historical psalms in the Psalter the deeds of Yahweh in history and creation are recited and praised in close connection with each other. Psalm 136 is the clearest example of this. Creation is seen as a work of Yahweh in history, as the first, basic deed which brought into being the area of God's activity, of his choice of Israel and his establishing the covenant, of his leading and speaking with the people, and finally and above all Yahweh's coming to the peoples of the earth.

Israel knew Yahweh as creator, not in the numinous manifestations of nature or in cosmogonic myths, but only in that he himself manifested and communicated his name, and in the history of his speaking to his people and his saving them. "O Lord, our Lord, how majestic is thy name in all the earth!" (Ps. 8: 1). "The north and the south, thou hast created them; Tabor and Hermon joyously praise thy name" (Ps. 89:12). The creator God, to whom the OT and especially the Psalter give testimony and honour is not just any supreme being, but the Lord of Israel's history, Yahweh, who has revealed himself and made himself known in the history of his deeds and self-disclosures. In their encounter with the cosmogonic myths of the religions of Israel's neighbours, Israel perceived and experienced the creative power has been specifically encountered in election and deliverance. This is clearly shown in Ps. 89. The statements about creation in this psalm is Polemical, confessional, and doxological. But this psalm shows the soteriological understanding of creation, i.e.: the relation of creation and salvation history to each other, is also found in Isa.40-55 and Ps. 74:12-17.

In the history of Yahweh's acts Israel experienced the absolute sovereignty of God, a sovereignty never in doubt, never involved in process of development. Yahweh's superiority in all activity and his power as the cause of everything, necessarily had its effect on creation theology. The Old Testament knows nothing of any theogonic speculations that precede the act of creation. "Before the mountains were brought forth, or even thou hast founded the earth and the world, from everlasting to everlasting thou are God" (Ps. 90:2)

ii) Yahweh's attributes and the Presence: One image employed of Yahweh in the psalms is that king (e.g. Ps. 24:7-10; 29:10; 48:2; 74:12; 93:3; 96:10; 97:6; 99:1). This epithet too was borrowed from the Canaanites. Some passages associate Yahweh's kingship with the victory over the chaos waters (cf. Ps. 29:10; 74:12ff; 93:1ff), which clearly derives ultimately from the Canaanite god Baal, whose victory over the god yam (sea) formed the basis of his kingship, as it is known from the myth preserved in the Ugaritic texts. The Old Testament on a number of occasions connects Yahweh's kingship with his creation of the world (cf. Ps. 74:12ff; 93:1ff; 95:3f; 96:10). As king, Yahweh was envisaged as enthroned on the cherubim in the Holy of Holies of the Jerusalem temple (Ps. 80:1), and the gods formed as it were his heavenly court (Ps. 29:1, 82:1,6; 89:5-7). It should be noted that the images of Yahweh as shepherd (cf. Ps. 23:1ff; 80:1) and judge (e.g. Ps. 82:1; 96:13) are alternative ways of referring to his kingship.

Another way in which Yahweh's greatness is indicated in the psalms is by referring to him as the Most High (Hebrew: **'elyon**, cf. Ps. 46:4; 47:2; 82:6; 87:5; 97:9). Yahweh in the psalms is presented as a holy God. On a number of occasions, he is called the Holy one of Israel (Ps. 71:22; 78:41; 89:18). Another term used remarkably frequently of Yahweh in the Psalms is the Hebrew word **chesed**. Altogether it occurs there over one hundred times. It is variously translated as steadfast love, mercy, loyalty, or loving kindness etc. and denotes Yahweh's characteristic attitude towards the Israelites, both collectively and individually. Psalmists repeatedly (25:6; 31:16) and it is constantly given as a reason for praising him (cf. Psalms 117; 136). Because of his loving kindness Yahweh is a God who delivers his people, both individually and collectively. The verb **yasa'** ('save') is used in the imperative form in lament Psalms in appeals to the deity (e.g. Ps. 7:1; 22:21; 28:9). Sometimes the verb "redeem" is used in connection with God, also the rood **go'el** (redeemer) was a kinsman who redeemed a relative from slavery (Lev. 25: 47-55), bought back their lost land (Lev. 25:23-34) or undertook marriage to a female relative so as to remove her widowhood (Ruth 4). As employed of God, therefore, the term had warm personal overtones. Various terms are used to give expression to the psalmist's confidence in Yahweh. For example, God is spoken of as a rock (Heb. *sela'* or *sur*, e.g. Ps. 18:2; 31:2-3), or fortress (e.g. Ps. 94:22; 14:42) am as one under whose wings one shelters (e.g. Ps. 17:8; 63:7).

The Hebrews conceived of Yahweh as both transcendent and immanent, and this is reflected in the Psalter. He is regarded as dwelling at once in heaven and in the temple on Mount Zion cf. Ps. 11:4, "The Lord is in his holy temple the Lord's throne is in heaven........" Yahweh's presence was associated with Mt. Zion from the time of David, when he brought up the sacred Ark into Jerusalem (II Sam. 6), and with the temple in Jerusalem from the time of Solomon, when the Ark was taken up into that sanctuary. Ps. 132 indicates a repeated cultic bringing up of the Ark into the sanctuary at the feast of Tabernacles (cf. Ps. 24:7-10; 47:5, 68:1, 18). It should be noted that the Psalter suggests that God's presence was particularly apprehended in the course of worship in the temple (cf. Pss. 23:5-6; 27:4; 42:1-2; 84:1-7,10). Isaiah's majestic vision of God in Isa.6, which contains echoes of Psalm 99, was experienced in the temple. Ps.139 adequately declares, it is impossible to escape from God's presence.

b) The Sanctuary and Its worship: In the sanctuary in Jerusalem Israel gathered as a worshipping community. In the following pages we shall consider the following things: certain concepts, expressions, and statements that are related to worship will be examined. Then the Zion theology is examined and presented followed by actual cultic practices involved in a theology of worship.

i) The Sanctuary: The starting point must be the name of the city of God, Jerusalem. Psalm 125:2 describes its location: "The mountain, are round about Jerusalem". This mountain that surround the "city of David", situated on the southeast elevation of the later city of Jerusalem are higher than Mount Zion, the highest elevation of the city of God "Jerusalem" is the first of all the name of the city which functioned as the "property of the crown" of Davidic dynasty and as the royal capital of Judah. In the Psalms there are references to the destruction of this city and to its rebuilding (Ps. 79:1-3; 51:18). But Jerusalem is also and especially the designation of the central sanctuary of the Israelite tribes (Ps. 122:3-4). In its "midst" is the "house of the Lord" (Ps. 116:10). From his temple Yahweh shows his power over Jerusalem (Ps. 68:29). In other words, the city of Jerusalem lies within the sphere of the glory and might of the sanctuary. Thus "Jerusalem" can be used as a synonym for "Zion" (Ps. 102:21; 135:21) and also as a designation for the place where Yahweh dwells (Ps. 135:21).

The distinctive designation of the Jerusalem sanctuary, however, is the name Zion. It is found predominantly in the form of "mount Zion" (Ps. 48:2,11; 74:2; 78:68; 125:1; plurals Ps. 133:3). From Zion, God "shines forth", his theophany is manifest, help comes for the oppressed (Ps.14:7; 20:2; 53:6), and Yahweh's blessings goes forth (Ps. 128:5; 134:3). On Zion, Israel's songs of praise ring out (Ps. 65:1; 147:12).

As the mount of Yahweh, Zion is Yahweh's holy mountain (Ps. 2:6; 3:5; 15:1; 43:3; 48:1; 87:1; 99:9), the "holy place" of the holy God (Ps. 24:3), the place where he is present and where he has "holy habitation" (Ps. 68:5, 76:2). On this "holy mountain" the temple stands, the house of Yahweh. The one praying in Ps. 5:8 proclaims, "I......will enter thy house, I will worship toward thy holy temple". The worshipping community bows down before the temple, addressing its prayers to the house of Yahweh (Ps. 138:2), because in the temple, in the inner sanctuary Yahweh is present, "dwells", is "enthroned". Therefore, in prayer one's hands are raised towards the "most holy sanctuary" (Ps. 28:2). Temple and inner sanctuary are the "holy place". There Yahweh communicates his word (Ps. 60:6; 108:7), and from there come help and comfort for those who are oppressed and needy (Ps.20:2). The concept of the sanctuary includes the gates of the holy area (Ps. 9:14; 87:2; 100:4; 118:19-20; 122:2) and the outer courts, and on the festival days participates in the cultic Observances entered the temple itself.

The Jerusalem sanctuary on Mount Zion was in pre-exilic times the sacred hill of the original Canaanite inhabitants, the Jebusites. The question of now cultic traditions of this Jebusite sanctuary were carried over into Zion theology of the Old Testament will be taken up later, but now we will consider another question: how Israel's sanctuary received its legitimation i.e. how Mount Zion became the central sanctuary to which the tubes of Israel, in accordance with the ordinance, were to make their pilgrimage (Ps. 122:4). In order to answer this question which is complex in nature we need to trace out some more history.

The first temple that can be identified in early Israelite times is in the Sanctuary at Shiloh. The destruction of this sanctuary sent shock waves through following centuries and had its echo in the Psalter as well (Jer. 7:12; 26:9; Ps.78:60). The function and meaning of the Ark of Yahweh are attested to in a tradition that served as the **hieros logos** ("sacral tradition") of the Jerusalem sanctuary, where the ark was kept. Ark was considered not only as the throne of God (I Sam.4:4; II Sam. 6:2) who in the cult was honoured as present; it was also carried into battle as the palladium of the "holy war" (I Sam. 4:3). The army welcomed this sign of Yahweh's presence with a great shout of joy (I Sam. 4:5). Where ever the Ark made its appearance it was received with fear and joy. (I Sam. 6:13; II Sam.6:9). Burnt offerings and sacrifices were presented before it (I Sam. 6:14ff). Following this Philistines captured the Ark and in the same hurry sent it back to Israel.

After David had conquered the Jebusite city of Jerusalem, the perished Shiloh cult began to be renewed in the city of Jerusalem. The king rescued the holiest of ancient Israelite objects from its obscurity in Kirathjearim and brought it to Jerusalem. This procedure was of decisive significance (Ps. 132:5ff). By virtue of the presence of the Ark in the city of David, Jerusalem was raised to the rank of Israelite cultic center. In this way traditions and institutions of ancient Israel were transferred to Zion sanctuary. Jerusalem was now the chosen place (Ps. 78:68; 87:1; 132:13). The hieros logos ("sacral tradition") of the Ark narrative thus clearly intends to announce that the history of worship in Jerusalem is a continuation of the Shiloh tradition, the previous site of the Ark.

The warlike concepts of Yahweh, "mighty in battle" which are connected with the Ark are clearly seen in Psalm 24:7-10. In Jerusalem the "shepherd of Israel" (Ps. 80:1) "dwells" and "is enthroned upon the cherubim", and he comes to be designated by and honoured with the titles "king", "judge", "mighty God", and "creator". He dwells on Zion (Ps. 9:11; 132:13-14), and his throne is in heaven (Ps. 11:4; 103:19; 123:1).

Some of the statements in the Psalms are worth examining at this point: Joy and praise of God in the sanctuary have a tendency to permeate and fill all of life: "So I will bless thee as long as I live" (Ps. 63:4). The statement, "I shall dwell in the house of the Lord forever" (RSV. margin, "as long as I Live" Ps. 23:6), is not a mere confession of faith uttered by the Levites, but an expression of the longing of all those who have "tested" and "seen" the blessing bestowed by the holy place (Ps. 34:8), "Blessed are those who dwell in thy house, ever singing thy praise" (Ps. 84:4). However, it would be erroneous to ascribe this exaltation and ecstasy to the influence of the holy precincts themselves. The life that is exalting and enabling, filling and fulfilling, which the ancient Israelites experienced in the sanctuary, is life that comes from Yahweh, the God of life: "For with thee is the fountain of life; in thy light do we see light" (Ps. 36:9). This is a key verse for our understanding of Israel's cultic life. Fulfilled life (in the sanctuary) is not the result of some magic power, but the result of the power of the divine presence, the gift of God's steadfast love; it is blessing and shalom received from him.

ii) The Zion Theology: In the same Psalms which contain a detail portrayal of the sanctuary on Zion, or Jerusalem, the city of God, we find also a remarkable Zion theology. The primary passages in this regard are "Songs of Zion", Pss. 46-48 and 76 as "eschatological concepts" and consequently he "eschatologized" his overall explanation of these psalms. But we are not sure of the history of the transmission of the traditions related/connected to these psalms.

In Ps. 48:2, the location of Jerusalem is described as Mount Zion in the far north. The Concepts, Mount Zion and north here mean: the clue is given in Isa. 14:13-14. This text contains taunt song described against the king of Babylon. He himself speaks with arrogance and hubris: "I will ascend to heaven, above the stars of God, I will set my throne on high, I will sit on the mount of assembly in the far north; I will ascend above the heights of the clouds, I will make myself like the Most High", even though this song was composed quite lately, it shows that Mount (Zaphon) was a mountain of the gods, soaring into the heavens, above clouds and stars. This sacred mountain was the throne of "God Most High" and the place of the "assembly" of the gods. It is now possible to identify Mount "Zaphon" and to locate it topographically.

As the dwelling and throne of "God Most High" the "mountain in the North", Mount Zaphor, was the center of the universe, the navel of the world. As Zaphon, Zion can be termed ("Joy of all the earth" - Ps. 48:2). The majesty of the place where Yahweh sits enthroned shines out into all the world. Everywhere the beauty and splendour of the mountain of God are spoken of (Lam.2:15). The spender of paradise came to be associated with the concept of Mountain Zaphon, and a great wealth of cultic and mythological concepts was transferred to Jerusalem, the city of God, and to Mount Zion. Yet all these concepts are merely the glorification of Yahweh, the God of Israel, or of the place where he is present.

The statement in Ps. 46:4, "There is a river whose streams make glad the city of God" is merely an embellishment in reference to Zion, but the context shows clearly that the concept of the primeval ocean, which is found also in against, also echoes here, so that we are reminded of the powers of chaos (v.5). All the metaphors and allusions are in the service of the declaration concerning the superior power of Israel's God, the protective might of the one who is enthroned on Zion and who intervenes for his people (Ps. 46:1,3,7,11). This enunciates a further theme of the Zion theology. Enemies threaten the city of God (Pss. 46:6; 48:4; 76:5-6). In Ps. 46:3 the tumultuous, chaotic primeval floods, aroused by an earthquake, threaten the mountains symbols of all that is fived and permanent. This cosmic motif probably represents the original from the threat (cf. Ps. 93:3-4). In Ps. 46:6 the destructive powers of chaos make their appearance in a "historicized" form: "The nations rage, the kingdoms totter". It is noteworthy that these enemy's powers are characterized as "kingdoms" (Ps. 46:6), "princes" (Ps. 76:12), or "kings" (Pss. 48:4; 76:12). The city of God is surrounded by hostile armies (Pss. 2:2a; 48:4ff.). The foes threaten and roar like "many waters" (Isa. 17:12f; Job 6:23). Obviously, the myth of the raging of the chaotic primeval waters has been applied specifically to Jerusalem in a historicized, political form, from which all mythological concepts and events have been eliminated. It is unlikely that this involves the cultic dramatization of a battle, as proposed by Mowinckel, rather these are ancient cultic traditions that are appropriated by Israel, given new form, and stripped of their mythological significance. It is highly significant that the historicizing of the cosmic struggle against chaos first took place during the transmission of the material in Israel.

When the foes attack, it is shown that the city of God is unconquerable. This is supported by several factors. Jerusalem is the city of God (Pss. 46:49; 48:1b; 87:3). Here is found the "holy habitation" of the Most High (Pss. 46:4b; 76:2; 87:5). The city of God is situated on Yahweh's "holy mountain" (Pss. 48:2; 87:1). On the summit of "Mount Zaphon", which reaches into the heavens (Ps. 48: 2). But the decisive reason for the invincibility of the city of God is the fact that Yahweh is "in the midst of her" (Pss. 46:5; 48:3). This is no area of taboo protected by Magic, rather, "the Lord of hosts is with us, the God of Jacob is our refuge" (Ps. 46:7,11). The theme of the invincibility of Jerusalem seems to rest on a very Old tradition (II Sam. 5:6). It was a firm certainty that Zion "cannot be moved", but "abides forever" (Ps. 125:1; Isa. 26:1). When the foes attack they will be beaten back and destroyed (Ps. 76:36; 48:5,6; Isa. 17:13-14; 24:21; 29:8). Yahweh himself shatters his foe with his thunder (Ps. 46:6), with his rebuke (Ps. 76:6; Isa.17:13), and with the "terror" of God (Ps. 46:8; Isa. 17:14). He destroys their weapons (Ps. 46:9; 76:3-6). A careful analysis of all those factors shows that on the one hand, such motifs as the "rebuke" had their origin in the stream of pre-Israelite mythological tradition, which assumed historicized form in Jerusalem. In the unconquerable city of God, Yahweh confronts his enemies as the creator God who "rebuked" the primeval waters (cf. Isa. 17:13; Ps.76:6). On the other hand, the ancient Israelite traditions of holy war can be clearly recognized (Ps. 46). Two streams of traditions merged.

Jerusalem, the city of God, is the abode of peace. In her the shalom of Yahweh reigns. In the Psalms the concept shalom is used in four distinct meanings. *First*, the people pray for hope for, and await shalom for the land and for the whole earth. It will be manifested in the form of fruitfulness and undisturbed growth, prosperity, and life (Pss. 72:3,7; 85:11; 147:14). *Second*, Israel prays for, hopes for, and awaits shalom for the whole nation (Pss. 29:11; 85:8; 125:5; 128:6). *Third*, shalom is the basic theme involved in the activity of the king (Ps. 72:3-7), *Fourth*, Shalom is a distinctive force that is available to the city of Jerusalem (Ps. 122:6f). The people should pray for the shalom of Jerusalem. The object for which they should pray is made explicit in Ps. 122:7, "Peace be within your walls, and security within your towers".

In summary, we can say that the themes and motifs of the Zion theology have given us a profile of the cultic traditions of Jerusalem.

iii) Worship in Jerusalem: The pilgrimage to Zion sanctuary was described one of the key elements of worship in Jerusalem. The clans and families travelled to Jerusalem, the mountain of Yahweh, with glad songs and the sound of flutes (Isa. 3 0:29). This arrival is described in Ps. 122:2, "our feet have been standing within your gates, O Jerusalem!" who was worthy to pass through the gates which in Ps. 118:19 are called "gates of righteousness", "He who walks blamelessly and does what is right, and speaks the truth from his heart....." (Ps. 15:2 cf. Ps. 24:3-4). In the "gate liturgies" the conditions for and mission are made known to those who are arriving to take part in worship. The marks of the "righteous" are proclaimed in the "gates of righteousness". This was a liturgical act, in which the Torah was recited. Based on Ps. 5 it is possible to understand that anyone who was unjustly accused and wanted to appeal sacral justice in the holy precincts had to undergo a preliminary examination at the gate. No one who was boastful or an evildoer was permitted to come into the presence of Yahweh (Ps. 5:4-6). If the initial questioning was decided according to "righteousness", then the accused was granted permission, but since he had not yet been declared innocent he would affirm, "But I through the abundance of thy steadfast love will enter thy house. I will worship toward thy holy temple in the fear of thee" (Ps. 5:7). The "gates of righteousness" were opened to those who were righteous (Ps.118:19). And they entered into the sanctuary (Ps. 118:20).

Immediately following the entrance ceremony of the "gate liturgy" in Ps. 24:1-6 we find the description of the entrance of Yahweh into the sanctuary

(Ps. 24:7-10). It is evident that these two events were directly connected. These were the events of the first day of a festival, perhaps the feast of Tabernacles.

Ps. 95:6 contains the cultic cry, "O come, let us worship and bow down, let us kneel before the Lord, our maker". The verb "let us worship" is significant here. It denotes bowing before Yahweh, falling down and praying "towards thy holy temple" (Ps. 5:7). The goal of the procession of Yahweh and the cultic community was the great act of bowing down in the outer court of the temple before the divine king (Ps. 100:4). The community that was gathered there worshipped Yahweh "at his foot stool" (Ps. 99:5) and praised, lauded, and honoured him. In this act of worship, the noble appellations of Israel's God were spoken - "Kind", "Almighty God", "Creator", and "Judge". Here music of worship was performed (Ps. 150). Israel came into the presence of Yahweh in order to praise him and give him thanks (Ps. 100:47). The worship of God at the festival began with the call, "serve the Lord with gladness! come into his presence with singing!" (Ps. 100:2). Thus, worship in Israel was characterized by joy. To serve God means in cultic terms to come before his face, to praise him, laud him, and honour him (Ps. 95:1-6). In the spirit of the universal nature of the appellations of Yahweh, Israel's adoration knowns no bounds. All peoples, the whole of creation, heaven and earth, join in the praise of the divine king and creator (Ps. 96; 97:6-9; 98:7-9; 99:1-5; 100:1). The praise of God knows no limits of time. All the Psalms are characterized by continual, never ending adoration. Even during the night, Praise rises up (Ps. 134; 8:3; Isa. 30:29). We shall now turn to another aspect of Jerusalem worship i.e., the sacrifice under separate sub-heading.

c) Sacrifice in the Psalms: The presentation of the sacrifice has constituted a special theme in the cultic life of Jerusalem. But it is surprising that only a little about it is mentioned. It is appropriate to begin with the general understanding of sacrifice in the OT before dealing in particular to the Psalter.

The first type of sacrifice offered in the OT is usually called, **Zebah**, which etymologically means a "slaughtering" - But it is not the mere fact that the slaughtered animal is vital, but the fact that a common eating of the flesh of the slaughtered animal establishes community. Simply by the fact that they together eat the meat of the sacrifice, those who share in the meal become a community. The meaning, purpose, and effect of the Zebah is the establishment of community among those who share in it. This human community is constituted by the basic community of the people with Yahweh, who is present as a participant in the meal. The fellowship formed creates not union; it creates an offensive and defensive alliance; there is a reciprocal acknowledgment ("I will be your God, and you shall be my people" Jer. 7:23; "our God" - Ps. 95:7; 'thy people' - 79:13), one stands up for other, those involved live together in a relationship of mutual trust and faith.

The other type of sacrifice is the gift offering. This gift offering (**minhah**) signifies something that is "offered" or "presented". In a secular context is denotes a gift that is intended to win a favour (Gen. 32:13-21; 43:11). Someone gives a gift to another person to show his respect for the other person. It is entirely his own affair and done of his own free will.

Third type of sacrifice mentioned in the Old Testament is **'olah**, usually translated "burnt offering", and in fact the gift presented as an 'olah was usually to be consumed by fire. The smoke that ascended to heaven accompanied the homage, praise, petitions, and laments of the giver. The 'olah like minhah, was designated for the exclusive use of Yahweh. In every case the shared offering and the gift offering are two totally different types of sacrifice. In the gift offering, man disposes of something which belongs to him for one reason or another. He gives. He surrenders his gift completely. He surrenders it by destroying it in the fire. He surrenders it because he seeks God's face. His forgiveness, His favour, His good will. In the gift offering he does not seek God's fellowship. The gift offering does not establish a relationship; it underlines in fact the distance between the two. It is an act of homage, a token of respect, submission and surrender to him who receives the gift.

The Psalter makes frequent references to the types of sacrifices mentioned above at several places. Zebah for instance offers in Ps. 4:5; 27:6; 54:6; 116:17, the 'olah alluded in Pss. 20:3; 66:13,25. The Psalter also mentions the thank offering (**toda** Pss. 56:12; 100; 107:22; 116:17), the free will offering (Ps. 54:6), minhah (Pss. 20:3; 86:8). In spite of these occurrences, the Psalter does not offer any proper theological explanation of the meaning of sacrifice. However, it does contain some interesting 'anti-sacrificial' passages, Ps. 40:6; 50:8-15; 51:116f to which may be added Pss. 69:30f and 141:2. Anti-sacrificial passages are also found elsewhere in the Old Testament, especially in the prophets (cf. I Sam. 15:22; Isa. 1:11f; Jer. 6:20; 7:21f; Hosea 6:6; Amos 5:21f; Micah 6:6f; Prov. 21:3). In all the instances mentioned above in the Psalter, the rejection or opposition is not to sacrifice per se, but an affirmation that ethical righteousness and obedience to God are more important than sacrifices - cf. Pss. 50:8-l5; 69:30f. What is reprieved is that kind of notion that Yahweh is dependent on sacrifices for food and drink (cf. Ps. 50:12-13, also the idea of feeding the deity with sacrificial meat to give strength is an idea of Canaanite sacrificial practice).

d) Psalms and the kingship: Several songs in the Psalter celebrate the king. In the royal Psalms, the central figure is King (Pss. 2:6; 20:8; 21:1,7; 45:1: 61:6; 63:11; 72:1; 89:18. A distinctive feature is the use of the term "anointed" for the king of Israel: Pss. 2:2; 20:7; 84:9; 89:38,51; 132:10. The king is Yahweh's anointed: Pss. 2:2; 20:7; 84:9; 89:38,51; 132:10. Psalm 89:20 even declares that Yahweh himself has anointed him with the holy oil (cf. Ps. 45:7). W.H. Schmidt rightly observes that, the anointing was not the essential part of coronation ritual, but from time to time it was practiced in Egypt, Syria and even in Hittite context whenever the officials are installed. In Babylon it was believed that the Kingship came down from heaven in mystical prehistory. But in Israel, it is quite different. It is not possible to speak of kingship as such. The striking historical aspect of kingship in Israel is that Israel established this in situation only late in its history. In the Psalms, what is said of the king always involves the name David. David is the first one to be chosen (Pss. 89:3,20,35; 132:1,10,17; 144: 10). The kings in Jerusalem (Ps. 144:10) are the "seed" the descendants of David, and therefore the heirs of the promise given through Nathan (II Sam.7), which promised David and his family an everlasting kingdom.

King is called "Son of God", a foreign religious influence in Israel brought in to the divine choice of king in Israel in a demythologized form. In Ps. 2:7 the ruler is declared to be the son of Yahweh. In the act of coronation, the ruler is called to Yahweh's side and is invited to take his place, "sit at my right hand" (Ps. 110:1), he can be called "the man of thy right hand" (Ps. 80:18). As the one enthroned at the right hand of God, the ruler shares in Yahweh's dignity and power as "highest" and can be acclaimed as "the highest of the kings of the earth" (Ps.89:27). Many of these expressions are in the background of ancient near Eastern court style. Filled with awe, a cultic speaker calls the king "my Lord" (Ps. 110:1), accords to him the divine designation "shield" (Pss. 84:9-11; 89:18) and even addressed him as "god" (Ps. 45: 6). But this reading of "God" is disputed because of the reason that, "it is beyond doubt that the Jerusalem monarchy, and even more, the monarchy in the states of Israel and Judah, was never regarded as divine" suggests Martin Noth. Furthermore, Noth translates the word "God" as "Thy throne is (like) that of God, enduring for ever and ever" (Ps. 45:6). This idea is to be firmly maintained because in Israel the king was not regarded as equal to God, and thus was never consciously addressed in theological terms as "God".

It is beyond doubt that in Israel's worship the king was not the object of veneration. Not even rudiments can be found of any veneration offered to him. At the same time the reigning king in Jerusalem exercised cultic functions. According to Ps. 110:4 the office of Priest was conferred on him. The kings were responsible for performing mediatorial functions, such as offering prayer for all cultic institutions in royal sanctuary in Jerusalem (I Kings 8:22-26), blessing the assembled people of the nation (I Kings 8:14), and on special occasions, offering sacrifices (I Kings 8:62-63). In spite of all this the role of king was limited only to a practical affair as the Priests in Israel grew more steadily.

The king of Israel received royal charisma and concrete commission from Yahweh. Prayers are offered to the king that would receive the gift of rendering justice to his people (Ps. 72:1). It was his commission to judge the people in righteousness, but above all to be the advocate and support of the weak and oppressed (Ps. 72:2, 4, 12ff). As the one who defended the divine will for justice against men of violence, the king was to carry out the office of judge - on behalf of those to whom justice had been denied. He loved righteousness and hated wickedness (Ps. 45:7). He was to intervene for the oppressed when there was no longer any other voice raised on their behalf. In Jerusalem there were "thrones for judgement … the thrones of the house of David" (Ps122:5).

It is probably noteworthy in Israel is the twofold basic relationship of the royal office of judge in Jerusalem. *First*, the kings who pronounce judgement on Zion are successors of an ancient Israelite in situation, which was embodied in the office of "Judge of Israel". This "Judge of Israel" had the responsibility to know and explicate the law and to give information about it, to watch over its observance, and to be responsible for its application to new situations and thus see to it that it has further developed and validated. When the monarchy became established in Israel, the old system confronted a crisis. There is no doubt that the Davidic kings rendered the final verdict in legal cases and in the framework of their royal charisma and commission continued the old tradition and institution. (cf. II Sam. 15:1-6; I Kings 3:16-28; Jer. 21:12; Isa. 16:5; 11:3). *Second*, the judicial activity of the kings in Jerusalem is to be seen in its consistent reference to Yahweh, the God of righteousness and justice. Righteousness and justice proceed himself fully to the righteous will of God. As "righteous" (said) he stands in a right relationship to his God, a relationship in which Yahweh's own righteousness and his own justice will be able to find expression.

The influence of the monarchy operating under the authority of Yahweh went beyond the sphere of justice and the pronouncement of verdicts. I involved shalom of the land and the people. Life, bounteous harvest, good fortune and blessing in boundless measure - these are the expectations connected with Yahweh's presence with his king (Ps. 72:3) and they are not to be thought of as due to the immanent power of a "divine monarchy".

Furthermore, the charisma and commission of the king is characterized by war and conquests of all foes by the king. Yahweh himself arms his anointed when he goes to war against the foes of his people (Ps. 18:39). God intervenes for his king and aids him (Pss. 2:5; 8-9; 21:8-9; 110:2-3; 144:1-2). With the help of Yahweh, the king defeats and destroys all his enemies. They are made a stool for his feet (Ps. 110:1).

In the post-exilic period, when there was no longer an Israelite king on the throne, the royal Psalms were interpreted in an eschatological sense as referring to an ideal future ruler - whom we should call Messiah - though the OT itself employs this term only of the current King.

e) The Psalms in the New Testament: In the New Testament the word "Psalm" is found seven times and the verb *psallmein*, "to sing praise" four times. Some references are not clearly identified, but some are identified clearly. We shall make a general survey of these occurrences to begin with and then talk about their significance in this section. While studying this theme three things in specific should be kept in mind. There are: First, the context of each psalm quotation is to be investigated to; determine the intention of its kerygma. This includes a precise determination of the place of the quotation in this specific context. Second, from the New Testament context we should identify the purpose for which the Psalm has been quoted. Then we must identify the kerygmatic scope of meaning which the Old Testament text has helped to advance. Third, we should also reflect on the character which the NT context has given to the quotation in its relationship to the way the text was understood in the Old Testament.

(i) New Testament References to the Psalms: While in Judaism the Torah is at the center of worship and life, in the early church the prophetic writings and the Psalms took on special importance. The Septuagint, the Greek translation of the OT, served as the primary source for quotations.

In Luke 20:42 and Acts 1:20 the Psalter is called "the book of Psalms". Luke 24:44 identifies a Psalm quotation as found "in the Psalms". In Acts 13:33; Ps. 2:7 is quoted with the identification "in the second Psalm". Other readings of this text (The Nestle-Aland Greek Testament) identify it as being the "first" Psalm. The term "Psalm" is also found in I Cor. 14:26. Perhaps this quotation refers to three types of Psalm poetry which were inspired by the Psalms of the OT and influenced by its language: *First*, the Jewish psalmody which is accessible in the remarkable example of the **Hodayoth** ("Thanksgiving Psalm") of Qumran; *Second*, the Jewish-Christian Psalmody which is seen in Luke l:46:55, 68-79; 2:29-35; *Third*, the Christian psalmody which permeates the book of Revelation (Rev. 5:9-10; 11:17-18; 12:10-12; 19:6-8). The criterion of it is appropriate to use in worship is the (**oikodome**), the edification of the church.

Ephesians 5:19-20 and Col. 3:16 also refer to Psalms that were sung by the early Christians or used in their prayers. The worshippers are exhorted to "be filled with the Spirit, addressing one another in Psalms and hymns and spiritual songs, singing and making melody to the Lord with all your heart" (Eph. 5:19-20). In these texts the purpose of using Psalms is kerygmatic in function. Even though Psalms are directed to God in petition, adoration, thanks, and song, they are also intended to speak to those hearers who are the same time singing and praying.

(ii) Psalms of special significance: It is clear that in early Christianity several Old Testament Psalms were extremely important. They were quoted again and again as "star witnesses" in the proclamation that the promises of God had been fulfilled. These are Psalm 2; 22; 69; 110; 118. It seems appropriate to begin with Psalm 2 and 110, two "royal Psalms", because these two songs stand at the center of the messianic message of the NT and are used as witnesses to the messiahship of Jesus of Nazareth.

Psalm 2 is quoted often in the NT, especially in the synoptic Gospels in connection with the baptism of Jesus and his transfiguration (Matt. 3:17; 17:5; Mark 9:7; Luke 3:22; 9:35). II Peter 1:17 also cites it in reference to the transfiguration. Psalm 2 is also quoted in Acts (4:25f; 13:33), in the letter to the Hebrews (1:5; 5:5; 7:28), and in Revelation (2:26f; 6:15; 11:15,18;17:18; 19:19). Two themes are stressed in these quotation in the New Testament: divine sonship (based on Ps. 2:7) and the rebellion and defeat of the hostile nations (Ps. 2:1-2, 8-9). Since particular attention has been paid to me witness to divine sonship, and the motif of the nation derives its significance in connection with the often-quoted saying in Ps. 2:7, it is appropriate to begin with the saying.

In LXX. the Hebrew text is translated by the words: "You are my son, today I have begotten you" - Ps. 2:7, It should be borne in mind that what God says, transmitted by a prophet, had its Sitz-im-Leben in the royal ritual of the enthronement (or annual festival) of the king of Jerusalem, and that the testimony given "today" is to be understood as an act of adoption, and thus as a legal act. The ruler was installed by Yahweh as his "son", that is, as the representative of divine power and majesty. Thus the adoption took on the meaning of a choosing of the king. The chosen ("anointed") is placed at Yahweh's side as the one nearest to him, as the "heir" of the realm of divine glory (Ps. 2:8-9).

We need to ask the question: How the word "today" in Ps. 2:7 was understood in the early Christian kerygma, that is, in terms of what event the elevation to divine sonship in the OT passage was understood in the New Testament. Four possibilities can be discerned in the text. *First*, the "today" is the event of baptism of Jesus. *Second*, in the miracle of transfiguration Jesus was declared to be the "son of God". *Third*, Jesus became the "Son of God" by his resurrection from the dead, *Fourth*, the ascension in to God's heavenly world elevated the one who was humbled to be God's son.

In addition to these Christological interpretations of Ps. 2:7, the early church drew attention to the relevance of two other themes in Ps. 2 for the decisive divine statement: *First*, threats against "God's anointed" by the hostile nations, and Second, the triumph over these nations and their rulers by the sound of God, who had been installed as heir and emperor. The first of these themes is developed in Ps. 1-2 and is cited in Acts 4:25-26. When the apostle Peter and John were released often their interrogation and went back to their supporters, they reported about being brought to trial before the elders and chief Priests. The community responded with the praise and adoration of God. In this context they are referred to Ps. 2:1-2, as translated in LXX. In v.24 they praised the creator and Lord of heaven and earth and in vv.25f., with the quotation from Psalm 2, they praised the Lord of the nations. Still, the situation described in Ps. 2:1-2 of a worldwide revolution of the "kings of the earth" and the "rulers" is not applied directly to the legal accusations that Peter and John had faced, but the judicial procedure against "thy holy servant Jesus, who thou didst anoint" (v.27). Herod, Pilate, and the Gentiles are named. It is remarkable how immediately the application is drawn to the trial of Jesus. In this context, and in illustration of this scene, Ps. 2:1-2 is quoted. That means that it is against Jesus as the Christ that the power of the Gentile world rose in rebellion, and not have been crucified. In vain they dared to seek to dethrone "God's anointed". But if this is a repetition of threat of a worldwide revolt against God and his anointed, then the community can, in the light of the Christ event and thus in the assurance that the enemy has already been defeated pray that God will hear and rescue them out of their present perils. What they are experiencing are in reality nothing but rearguard actions. For in the trials of Jesus the fate of the nations and their rulers has already been decided. Psalm 2 as here been fulfilled as a whole. Psalm 2:1-4 is seen in the light of the eschatological enthronement of Jesus Christ. With the crucifixion, opposition and accusations have resulted in an event that was in accord with will of God, and which attained its goal in the exaltation of Christ and the defeat of the hostile forces. Jesus is the "servant of God" (Isa. 52:13ff), who astonished the nations and closed the mouths of kings (Isa. 52:15). "God was with him" (Acts 10:38). He raised him from the dead (Acts 3:26) and glorified him (Acts 3:13). Every uprising of the nations has been brought to an end in this eschatological event, an event foreshadowed in the Old Testament. The promise made implicitly in Ps. 2:1-2 is recognized as a promise in its explicitly manifested fulfillment and is proclaimed as having attained its goal. The promise of God given to David and his dynasty, with all the events involved in its accomplishment, has been fulfilled in Jesus the Messiah. From now on the hostile powers that confront the Christian community can accomplish nothing that is not the will of God. This will, was accomplished in the crucifixion. Who are attacking their uprising will therefore never achieve its purpose. Moreover, the quotation of Ps. 2:1-2 was made a part of a prayer of the community in the early church, as a promise in the context of the Davidic history (Acts 4:25), in the context of the promises given to David, to which the Messiah's community could appeal in a situation of concrete peril.

(iii) Other Psalm Texts cited or quoted: In the pericope of the "wise men from the East" (Matt. 2:1-18) the fulfillment of a prophecy found in Ps. 72:10,15 and Isa. 60: 6 is described Three things are significant in Matt. 2:11. *First*, the structure of the passage with the use Of the OT materials; *Second*, the enhancing of the statements about the "wise men" by the use of Psalm 72 and its words about "kings" that come from afar, which had effects on the tradition of the church; and *Third*, the messianic understanding of the entire pericope - it is God's Messiah who is being adored. Other examples are: In the account of the temptation (Matt. 4:1-11; Luke 4:1-13) the use of the OT is quite different. Psalm 91:11-12 is quoted by the tempter (Matt. 4:6; Luke 4:10-11). Here scripture is used as a kind of lively affirmation of one's own commitment and faith to God Matt. 5:4 'Blessed are those who mourn for they shall be comforted", reminds the hearer of Psalm 126:5-6, "May those who sow in tears reap with shouts of Joy!" and also of Isa. 61:2; The Beatitude in Matt 5:8 draws on the phraseology of the Psalm that speak of a "pure heart" (Ps. 24:4; 51:10; 73:1). The recasting of the concept is interesting. According to Ps. 24:4 those who have a "pure heart" will be permitted to enter the sanctuary (Ps. 24:4), while in Matt. 5:8 the eschatological vision of God will be fulfilled of the promise. Thus the NT makes explicit in eschatological terms the old cultic formula "to see the face of God", which in the psalms means to enter into the sanctuary, the place where Yahweh is present.

4.2. The Book of Proverbs

The Hebrew word for the proverbs is <u>*mashal*</u> which means likeness or similarity, therefore it means a proverb, or a saying; the book belongs to the general class of wisdom literature of Job, Proverbs and Ecclesiastes. The book is written to serve the purpose of education, for rulers for good and profitable behaviour.

Rabbinic Judaism ascribed the book of Solomon, the wise king who authored Proverbs and songs (I Kings 4:32) Individual collections within the Proverbs are ascribed to Solomon (cf. 10:1 and 10:25) but there are also other origins stated in 22:17, 24:23, 30:1, 3.11:1 possibly some individual Proverbs go back to the time of Solomon.

a) Authorship, Date and Composition: Although certain features of the book associate the name "Solomon" with discrete units, other names also occur in connection with specific sections of the book. Some textual units lack any name whatever. Furthermore, the superscriptions may derive from a time later than the actual composition of the sayings. Within a given collection The Book therefore takes the shape of an anthology, its individual components coming from various periods of Israel. At least two and probably three, short sections contain from non-Israelite sources, making the anthology truly international. There are at least seven individual collections discerned in the book of Proverbs. We shall briefly present them as follows:

First: Chapters 1-9, titled as the Proverbs of Solomon, appears to be latest collection of the entire book, this collection is predominantly a hortatory (sermonic) section, the most and highly developed literary form in the entire book in comparison with other sections. Within this block, 1:1-6 serves as a prologue to the entire book and was possibly inserted as a final redaction. The personification of wisdom in this section could have been influenced from Egypt and may not be from the Greek influence. The basic and ideal theme of this sections is: the first principle knowledge (wisdom) is to hold the Lord in awe (1:7 and 9:10). The warnings against strange women and the personification of wisdom amounts for the dating of this section in the Post-exilic period (but it 15 only a probable conclusion).

Second: 10:1-22:16, titled as the "Proverbs of Solomon." Thig section, on the basis of form and content be divided into two sections; (i) **Chapters 10-15**; consists of proverbs in antithetic parallelism contrasting wise/righteous with fools/evil doers. Repetition of some sayings (cf. 10:1=15-20; 10:2=11:4; 13:14=14:27) with the replacement of "the teachings of the wise" by the phrase, "the fear of the LORD", This fact indicates of a process of gradual accumulation; (ii) **16:1-22:16**: contains antithetic, synthetic and synonymous parallelism in equal shares (for the explanation of these terms see the section before on the characteristic features of Hebrews Poetry). Proverbs about the king are found here: Moreover, concern for trade and legal problems points to an upper class background in the capital city during monarchy. In chapters 10-15, Yahweh is the guarantor of the moral ordering of the world and in 16:1-22:16, Yahweh is the Sovereign ruler and the creator of the world; collection of independent proverbs in this section at times is the distinctive feature, found mostly in prose as well.

Third: 22:17-24:22 titled as the "sayings of the wise". These have units with more than two lines. Here in this section antithetic parallelism disappears (thus it is argued that it is form critically later than second section). One of the interesting feature found in this section is that, there is a parallel between Prov. 22:17-23:1 and to that of Egyptian "Instruction of Amen-em-opet", both in form and content, the resemblances are found. The Egyptian Amen-em-opet is dated from 13th-12th century B.C.E. Out of thirty precepts in this section of Prov.24:17-24:22, nine of the first ten have exact parallels to that of Egyptian Amen-em-opet. This leads us to think that perhaps a Hebrew sage/scribe may have modelled his work in proverbs on the basis of Amen-em-opet; since 23:12-24:22 contains "parental instruction", this and 22:17-23:11 may have come from the monarchic period.

Fourth: 24:23-34 is a small appendix to the previous section, titled as a "further sayings of the wise". This section contains sayings against corruption in courts (24:23b) against flaunting evil as good (24:24-26), on one's domestic priorities (24:27) against false witness (24:28), against the law of retaliation (24:29), and one longer passage, which might be titled the wisdom work ethic (24:30-34). The longer passages of this type in the book of Proverbs seem to be example of the teacher's exposition of shorter wisdom sayings. The present one may be a parable or the teacher's personal reminiscence. This theme appeared earlier in 6:6-11 where the conclusion is almost identical (cf. 6:10-11/24:33-34).

Fifth: 25-29 chapters titled as the "Hezekiah's collection", perhaps these were also collected from the time of Solomon (Prov. 29:27), but edited later by Hezekiah's men. It may be that already existing Solomonic proverbs are collected by Hezekiah's time. Chapters 25-27 has four lines in English text and two lines in Hebrew text. The tone here is more secular and less moralizing then section two; Yahweh is mentioned only once in this section (25:22), righteous and wicked are contrasted only once. Chapters 28-29, in this block parallelism dominates, religious faith as the door to wisdom is asserted again. In this entire section (25-29 chaps) court played an important role, thus lead some scholars to develop a court wisdom genre.

Sixth: Chapter 30, titled as sayings of Agur. The frame work of this section is vv.1-14 and v. 32-33 and in between section vv.15-31 are the numerical proverbs, which has some similarities within the Ugaritic literature. The name Agur son of Jakeh is found in south Arabic inscriptions. The Septuagint translator translated Agur as a verb means "fear", moreover the arrangement of chapters is also different than the Masoretic Text (In LXX, the arrangement of Prov.22:17-31:31 is as follows: 22:17-24:22; 30:1-14; 24:23-34; 30:15-33; 31:1-9; 25:1-29:27; 31:10-31).

Seventh: Chapter 31, it contains two further divisions vv. 1-9 are the words of Lemuel, King of Massa (perhaps Massa, name of Kingdom in North-West Arabia (cf. Gen. 25: 14), nomadic or semi-nomadic wisdom is prevalent here; thus an inclusion of foreign material in the book of Proverbs may have taken place, vv.1-9 are the words of Lemuel, King of Massa, with which his mother instructed him. Other references have been made to the teaching of the mother and its importance (Prov. 1:8; 5:20) and even when only the father's instruction is mentioned, the mother's may be included. The content of this discourse is an appropriate conclusion for a book largely written by a King and collected by one. It focuses, not upon the privileges of Kingship but upon the responsibilities of the office.

The second section of chapter 31 is vv.10-31, the words in praise of virtuous wife. it is an acrostic open, each new verse begins with a different letter of the Hebrew alphabet in sequence. This extended poem on the significance of the mother and wife balances out the social spectrum of the book of Proverbs very well. In the previous section (vv. 1-9) mother's teaching and in here the mention of a virtuous woman is an indication of the fact of the transmission of teaching of wisdom and the positive and affirmative role played by the women and also it indicates the matriarchal collection of material in the bible. Claudia Camp undertook an extensive study on the wisdom in the feminine in the book of Proverbs made more observations in-depth like the one mentioned above. Regarding this section C. Hassel Bullock writes positively as follows: "And lest the male-dominated language of the book appear to excuse the women of society from religious obligations, this poem puts the joyful yoke of religious observance upon women, too" (C.H. Bullock, **An Introduction to the OT Poetic Books** (Revised and expanded edition), Chicago: Moody Press, 1988, p.177).

There are several problems in the exact dating of the individual components of the book. However, following suggestions can be made regarding the composition date of collections in the book. Chapters 1-24 have a framing device and cyclic composition, whereas 25-31 chapters are an additive technique. Chapters 1-9 combine two elemental or core blocks (2-4, the personal acquisition of wisdom, and 5-7 ethical advice, mostly about sex). A speech in first person (1:20-33 and 8:1-36) and a framing ring (the prologue 1:27 and the final contrasting "allegory" about wisdom and folly, 9:1-18), enclose the two kernel blocks, chapter 10 serves as an entrance way into the following collections, and chapter 15 functions as a second theological focus. Within chapters 10-15 only 14:7 uses the style of instruction, but in 26:1-22; 16 it occurs frequently (16:3; 18:22; 19:l8,20,27; 20:16; 22:6,10). Chapters 25-27 appear to be more empirical and general, whereas 28-29 contain a pronounced theological bent. A plait pattern is discernible in chapter 29, a linking of a verse with the one after its immediate sequel (land 3; 2 and 4; 7 and 9; 12 and 14; 15 and l7; 19 and 21; 20 and 22).

In the sections mentioned earlier (seven sections or collections) sections two, three and five are to be Pre-exilic and sections four, six and seven cannot be dated accurately. Section one in the Present form is to be dated as post-exilic document, probably added to the final redaction of the book.

b) Canonicity: Sparse information on the disposition of the book of Proverbs in the canonization process is found in the Babylonian Talmud (**Shabbath** 30b). A question revolved around the alleged contradiction between Proverbs 26:4 and 26:5. "Do not answer a fool according to his folly......Answer a fool according to his folly" (KJV "as his folly deserves"). The rabbinic resolution was to view the first as a reference to matters of the law and the second to secular affairs. The doubts about the book were dispelled early in Post-exilic time, and Proverbs exercised a pervasive influence upon Judaism and early Christianity.

c) Some literary genres found in the book of Proverbs: Already in our discussion earlier we have considered several literary types of wisdom and their significance in general. Here we shall once again pick up few genres in relation to the book of Proverbs;

1) Allegory: (with metaphor as a devise in allegory) E.g. Prov. 5:15-23 (also ct. Amen-em-opet VI:1-10)

2) Sayings: It has three sub-divisions as follows: (i) **Numerical sayings**; (Prov.30:18-19; 6:16-19) here there an attempt made to systematize to order things of knowledge acquired by human beings; (ii) **Experiential sayings** (or observational sayings) conclusions are to be drawn by the reader E.g. Prov.

11:24 and 18:26. In 11:24, the famous saying goes as follows: "One man pretends to be rich, yet has nothing, another pretends to be poor, yet has great wealth", (iii) **didactic (learned) sayings**. It is something that goes beyond a mere statement about reality. It is characterized in one's attitude and conduct. E.g. Prov. 14:31: one's relation to God is defined in terms of one's treatment of the poor (cf. Prov. 19:17; 22:22-23). It also has an artistic way of saying (15:23; 25:11; 26:25 cf.).

3) Wisdom teaching: It is a systematic teaching about a specific topic, its Sitz-im-Leben is the context of education (school) E.g. Prov. 1-9 chapters contain many such teachings.

4) The Hymn: It occurs in the cosmic transcendence of wisdom, also in the sphere of creation (especially Prov. 8:22ff). The Poetic description and language is of high literary master piece type.

5) Beatitude: The Sitz-im-Leben of it is official cult E.g. Prov. 3:13; 8:32-34; 16:20 et.al.

6) Popular Proverb: It is in a didactic form E.g. Prov. 1:17; 11:2; 13:3 etc.

7) Command and Prohibitions: Supported by the genre of instruction. E.g. Prov. 8:33; 16:3; 16:20. These also contain motive clauses like: "because", "lest" etc. Here the teacher is engaged in persuading and convincing his disciples/students. In these sayings usually the following elements are found:(i) Call, (ii) notice, (iii) exhortation, (iv) consequence.

d) Theological view Point: The book of Proverbs affirms the fact that wisdom is not primarily human achievement, yet through instruction and self-discipline it can achieved. All young men and women can receive wisdom by preparing themselves to receive it as a gift from God (Prov. 2:1-8), and for those who receive it, wisdom becomes a guide in their life. It is also stressed clearly that the fear of the Lord is the basic foundation of wisdom (cf. Prov. 1:1-5,7 and chapter 2). Wisdom is the understanding of the way of god life for human beings and of its dynamic relationship to the right order established by God as the Creator (cf. chapter 8 of the Proverbs). It is remarkable to note that the book does not mention any cultic obligation (except very rarely in 3:9-10). This is further exemplified in the contrast set between righteous and wicked, the point made here is this:it is not to be seen in the cultic regulations, nor in the law, but quality of life exhibited as a wise person is far more vital than any ritual/cultic obligation. The most important theological contribution of the book is found in chapter 8 where wisdom is seen in its nature and its origin is the cosmic principle and power. This way wisdom serves as an effective link between God and human beings.

The book of proverbs presents the picture that wisdom is not primarily human achievement, yet through instruction and self-discipline, every one may receive wisdom. God gives the wisdom as a gift (prov. 2:1-8) and for those who receive it, wisdom becomes a guide in their life. Fear of the Lord is the basic foundation of wisdom (1 :1-5, 7, chapter 2). Wisdom is the understanding of the way of good life for human beings, and of its dynamic relationship to the right order established by God as the creator (Prov. Chapter 8). Wisdom is seen as a primordial principle which emanated from God and thus God is seen as the source and beginning of wisdom.

4.3. The book of Job

The book of Job discusses the problem of suffering of the righteous, and the problem of theodicy i.e. justice of God. There is a truth of presupposition of the wisdom presented in the book i.e. the world is governed in a rational way by divine wisdom. However, the book doesn't sustain this presupposition. There is no logical and consistent reply given to Job's question in the book. His questions are apt resolved in rational sphere, but are resolved in faith i.e., in the realm of faith.

a) Title, nature and place of the book in Canon: The book of Job, like the books of Joshua and Ruth, bears the name of its hero. The Hebrew form of the name' **Iyyob** was represented in Greek by **Iob**, and then through Latin came the English form Job. Some have connected the meaning of the name with the root'**yb** to yield the meaning 'the hated one' or 'the persecuted one' or 'the hater' or even 'the aggressor.' Others have looked to the Arabic'**wb** for the meaning, and have suggested 'the persistent one'. It is improbable we should seek a meaning appropriate to the story, and the name may have been taken over by the author from the tradition on which he based his book.

The book discusses on the problems of suffering of the righteous, the problem of theodicy i.e. Justice of God. There is a truth in the presupposition of the wisdom i.e. the world is governed in a rational way by divine wisdom. However, the book doesn't sustain this presupposition throughout. Moreover, there is no logical and consistent reply given to Job's question/s in the book. His questions are not resolved in a rational sphere, but are resolved in faith (i.e. in the realm of faith).

In the Hebrew canon the book belongs to the third division, the Kethubim, which contains also Psalms, Proverbs, Ruth, the Song of Songs, Ecclesiastes, Lamentations, Esther, Daniel, Ezra, Nehemiah, 1 and 2 Chronicles. In some manuscripts, Job follows Psalms and Proverbs and in some it stands between them. In Syriac it stands between Deuteronomy and Joshua, doubtless coming to the fact that the scene of the book is set in patriarchal age.

In Greek manuscripts, the prophetical books were transferred from the second division of the Hebrew canon to follow the three 'poetical' books, Job, Psalms and proverbs (these three not always in the same order), and Daniel was placed among the prophetical books, while the other books of the Kethubim were distributed, similarly the manuscripts of vulgate vary, while following the same general principle as the Greek and the English order follows what had become the prevailing order of Vulgate.

b) Date and Authorship: The book of Job has been attributed to the widest variety of dates, ranging from the Patriarchal age-due to the fact that the scene in set in that age-to the second or first century BCE. Even within the present century dates from the time of Solomon to the Hasmonean period have been suggested. Most recent scholars argue that in its original form, the book was of post-exilic origin, and the secondary parts of later composition. Reference has made earlier to the book of some similarities with the Deuteronomic doctrine of the rigid correlation of desert and fortune on the national scale. It is generally accepted that the Deuteronomic school flourished in the seventh century BCE and that Deuteronomic history embodied in the former prophets was composed in the seventh and sixth centuries. It was probably under the influence of the application of this principle to the individual that the hard doctrine of Job's friends became accepted in certain circles. Based on these observations, scholars date the book not earlier that 500 BCE and more probably later. The substantial Aramaic colouring of the language also some would like date it in the early fifth century.

Concerning the author of the book we know nothing apart from this book and only speculations are possible in this regard. J.P. Nash thought that the author was a disciple of Deutero-Isaiah, but without any evidence. Humbert thought that the book was composed in Egypt and E. Dhorme stresses the author's acquaintance with Egypt. F.H. Foster thought the book had been translated from an Arabic original, and Pfeiffer thinks the author was an Edomite.

It is hard to think that he was not an Israelite. That there is no reference to the land or cultus of Israel is not surprising, since the scene is set in the Patriarchal age and the person who figure in the books do not appear to be themselves Jews. The original tradition on which the book is based was probably a non-Israelite story, which the author adapted for his purpose. He was certainly a monotheist and a worshipper of Yahweh, and if he was influence by Deuteronomic and post-Deuteronomic theory, it is hard to think to him as anything but a Jew.

c) Content and Structure: The book of Job consists of a narrative, framework and a poetic core. The prose section is divided into a prologue (1:1-2:13) and an epilogue (42:7-17), the poetry is embedded between these two together prose and poetry examine the possibility of being good without thought of either reward or punishment and explore the nature of innocent suffering, whether or not it exists, how one ought to act in the presence of misery and why such injustice occurs. The prose framework deals with loss and eventual restoration without so much as a raised voice and in its simplicity embraces and makes possible the eruption of volcanic emotions in the poetry.

Emphasizing the historical gap between the time of the hero and the subsequent narrating of the events, the narrative sets the action in (pre) patriarchal times. Job's possessions, like those of the patriarchs, consist of cattle and servants, not only his three friends but also his enemies (nomadic Sabeans and Chaldeans) come from the greater environment associated with Abraham's wanderings; The monetary unit (42:11) belongs to that ancient era (cf. Gen. 33:19); Job's life span exceeds that of the patriarchs and the sacrifice of animals corresponds to the practice prior to official priests. The name Job recalls a folk hero associated in Ezek. 14:14, 20 with Noah and Daniel, probably the Daniel of Canaanite epic texts. Although the meaning of Job's name is uncertain, similar forms are attested from early times in Egypt and Mesopotamia with the meanings "where is the divine father?" and "Inveterate Foe/Hated one", In accord with the universality typical of early wisdom, the hero seems to have been an Edomite (only a Probability), famous for the wisdom of its inhabitants and setting in the land of UZ echoes the noun "counsel" (42:1-6).

The action of the prologue (l:1-2:3) alternates between earth and heaven, the events of the latter hidden from Job. The hero, perfect outwardly and inwardly according to irrefutable testimony (1:3,8) enjoys the fruits of virtue-until God directs the adversary's attention to him, eliciting suspicion of Job's motive for being good and provoking a test to determine the truth. Calamity befalls Job without warning. Having lost his children and possessions, Job blesses the Lord as source of good and ill. (1:21). A second heavenly scene ensues, with God's "I told you so" and the adversary's insistence that the real test must touch the actual person (2:3-5). God accepts once more, insisting that Job's life must not be taken. The facial scene depicts a surely afflicted Job, but one restrains his integrity despite his wife's urging to curse God and die (2:9-10). This time Job's confession takes interrogative form, but he does not curse God. Having heard of Job's misfortune, three of Job's friends, Eliphaz, Bildad, and Zophar, journey from their homes in Tennan, Shuah and Naaman respectively to offer comfort in adversity.

The conversation in the form of a poetic dialogue consist of three distinct units: Job versus Eliphaz, Bildad and Zophar (chaps.3-37), and God's lectures to Job (38:1-42:6, with brief responses by Job in 40:3-5 and 42:1-6).

The epilogue (42:7-17) ties up all loose ends, having repented, of what. is unclear, Job intercedes on behalf of the three friends, at whom God is angry because they did not speak truth about God as Job did. A temporal connection between prayer and restoration occurs, and Job returns to his previous state, with one bonus: his three daughters losses unsurpassed beauty, besides an inheritance. Seven times the verb "blessed" occurs in the story (1:5,10,11,21; 2:5,9; 42:12), alternating between the meanings "curse" and "bless" except the last two which are reversed.

Few elements of laments can be found in the book which contains: petition, wish, motivation and a vocal of trust. In chapters 3 and 30 of the book, there is a threefold articulation of lament is visible.

First: the lament is directed to God: *Second*, self-lament and *Third*, a lament about enemies E.g. chapters 3: Job cursing his birth, in vv.3 and 10 of chapter 3, the lament is directed against enemies, v.11: is a self-lament and v.23: is a lament to God; again vv.24-26: self-lament chapters 29-31 genuine or true lament. In chapter 29 we find Job's retrospective look on his earlier fortune. Chapter 31 is understood as an oath of clearance or assertion of innocence. In chapter 30 the lament is threefold as mentioned above: to God, to self and against enemy.

Claus Westermann is the one who strongly argues for the elements of laments present in the book. He writes thus; "At the base of my investigation lies the simple recognition that in the Old Testament, human suffering has its own peculiar language and that one can understand the structure of the book of Job (based on content as well) if one has first understood this language, namely, the language of lamentation. As lamentation, which is suffering expressed in speech, gets developed along the three axes which determine human existence in general-the self in isolation, the self over against other human beings, and the self over against God's-so the poet of the Book Job presents the suffering of Job through three representations of this threefold aspect of human existence: Job himself, the friends of Job who become his enemies, and God. This basic recognition, garnered from the structure of lamentation, provides the key that unlocks the meaning of the entire book of Job. Not only those parts which contain Job's laments, but also the whole polarity of lamentation and praise out of which the dramatic dialogue arises" (Quotation taken from Claus Westermann, **The Structure of the book of Job**, p.vii).

Another element in the lamentation in the book of Job is wishes and Petitions in the speeches of Job are identified by Claus Westermann. There are four such elements as follows:

First: The wish to die (3:11-13, 21-22; 6:8-20; 7:15 an echo of this wish occurs in 10:18b-19).

Second: The wish that God would leave Job alone, due to the reason that Job might be able to breathe freely (7:10b; 10:20b) or so that human kind might be able to breath freely (14:6, 13-15).

Third: The wish that Job's cause might be heard and that he might find an advocate despite his death (16:18-22; 17:3; 19:23.24).

Fourth: The wish to encounter God (23:3-12; 31:35-37 the summoning of God). Petition or something like petition intrinsically belong to the lament.

In two important parts, the book of Job's content can be neatly grasped:

First: The speeches of Job: First speech begins with an apology and later contains a personal defence. Second speech begins with concurrence, no attack on the friend and in third speech, Job occupies his friends' provocative intervention on God's behalf.

Second: The speeches of God: God's answer to Job is in the form of disputation (although other varieties of forms are proposed) speech. Job's final lament ends with summoning God to a law suit, couched in die form of a wish that God would answer him. The wish is fulfilled for Job. To be sure, this answer does not correspond to what Job has expected. In this answer Job neither learns the indictment against him (31:35)-and there by the reason for God's terrible anger against him-nor finds either the advocate or the vindication for which, despite all appearances on the contrary, he had been waiting (16:19-21; 19:25). But none of that alters the basic fact that God does answer him.

God's answer to Job puts **one** question to Job: who are you? (38:2) God pushes Job to the spot where Job can experience and receive the assurance of God, the intervention of God on his behalf. The question is developed from 38:12 to 41:34. If one transposes it from direct top indirect discourse it reveals itself for what it really is; Praise of God the creator. Along with disputation, praise of the creator is a motif which ties together all three characters in the drama. The whole divine speech is segmented in accord with the Psalmic motif; Praise of the creator-praise of the Lord of history. Peculiarity and uniqueness of God's speech is not its content, but rather in transformation.

Further to this God's answer Job's answer is seen in two parts. *First*: an act of silence which precedes the answer itself (42:2-6). *Second*: 42:5 contains 'solution' to the 'problem' of Job. Job now knows of God, not just one aspect of God's activity-what Job has recognized and whom he has seen remains concealed. Confession of Job concludes the drama.

d) The Structure of the book: As we have noted above the general content of the book, the book can also be systematically divided into following units on the basis of its arrangement. Three major parts with several sub divisions in part two can be seen as follows:

i) Prologue (chapters 1-2): Prose-Divine name Yahweh used. Suffering is presented as a test of a person's righteousness. A righteous person lives righteously not for the sake of reward but for the sake of the relationship with Yahweh, which endures in adversity as well as in property.

ii) Speeches (3:1-42:6) Poetry. Divine name Elshaddai or Eloah used (except for whirlwind speeches 38:1-42:6)

a) Chaps. 3-27: Triple exchange of speeches, beginning with Job's cause on the day on which he was born (ch.3).

Job 3	12-14	21
Elephaz 4-5	15	22
Job 6 - 7	16-17	23-24
Bildad 8	18	25

Job 9 - 10	19	26-27
Zophar 11	20	missing

View of suffering: suffering results from sin. Since Job is suffering, Job must be a sinner.

b) Chaps. 28: Independent poem on wisdom. It may be a latter addition to the work. Describes the search for wisdom, reading its climax in 28:28 "Behold, the fear of the Lord (not Yahweh), that is wisdom: end to depart from evil is understanding".

c) Chaps. 29-31: Job summarizes his position 29; his former happy position 30; his recent hopeless lot 31; his oath of clearance (sometimes called as "the sermon on the Mount of the Old Testament") ending with a challenge to God to answer him (31:35-37).

d) Chaps 32-37: Speeches of Elihu, argues that suffering has disciplinary value. Sees Job's suffering as the result of his self-righteousness (34:5-9), humility would bring God's blessing (36:8-12). Points out that if there were a mediator who suffers a ransom, humans would be able to pray to God and be accepted and come into the divine presence with joy (33:23-30).

e) 38:1-42:6: The speeches of the LORD (Yahweh) from the whirlwind with Job's replies. The LORD reminds Job that there are many things in creation that he does not understand. In 40:8, Yahweh reveals Job's true sin. Job, is insisting on his own righteousness, has questioned the justice and goodness of God; he has set himself up as a judge of God. Job is not vindicated, but he is accepted by the creator. The creator has entered into communion with him. This is the answer to Job's need (42:5). The just live, not by their own righteousness, but by faith. It is emphasized here that God's ways are not transparent to humans. What is questioned here is the legalistic application of the understanding of the cosmic order found in wisdom thought (and in the Deuteronomistic theology).

iii) Epilogue: (42:7-17) Prose. Divine name Yahweh used. Job prays on behalf of his friends, who have not spoken of God what is right (vv.7-9), Job's fortunes are restored with double restoration of goods, new children born (vv. 10-17). The view of suffering here is that the suffering of the righteous and the prosperity of the wicked are temporary, and both will pass away, leading to times of just punishment and reward.

e) Theological view point: The book of Job represents a response to the time of crisis. It is believed that the story was orally circulated and is reworked by the narrator (there is an opinion that perhaps the book was originally written and then translated into Hebrew?). Following are the important observations to summarize the theological view of the book.

First, the narrator wanted to stress that God is creator and also wanted to reemphasize God as provider or sustainer or God as immanent judge of his people.

Second, In this book we mostly find that there is a shift from communitarian concept of Israel to individualistic view (piety).

Third, Emphasis on God's transcendence and not insisting on God's immanence.

Fourth, Yahweh as the Lord over cosmic order; the design of God is not governed by a necessary law of reward and retribution; God's wisdom is of a higher order and remains a mystery.

H.G. Reventlow made the following observation on the theology of the book Job. The book presents the problem of crisis of wisdom, between deed and consequence (cf. Klaus Koch's view; God, one who is involve in the human affairs of deed and consequence, not an automatic connection is operative). Similar type of crisis in wisdom is also found in Akkadian literature such as: The prayer of righteous sufferer, from Egyptian context, a man's dialogue with his own soul as to the merits of suicide as a way of escape from the miseries of life (ANET, pp.405ff) and another narrative which narrates a man's bold and persistent appeal against social injustice until his wrong were righted (ANET, pp.407ff). In Babylonian literature we do find a parallel to Job's such as: 'A pessimistic Dialogue between a master and his servant' (W.G. Lambert, **Babylonian Wisdom Literature** 1960, pp.139ff), "the Babylonian Job" (Lambert pp.21ff). God's answer to Job in 38:1ff reveals that God's act of creation human's existence is a short one and human wisdom also has limits. In reply to God's speech Job's silence is maintained because no answer will suffice. 42:5 is the key verse to the entire book, that is, the realm of faith is important, repentance is only the answer. Human wisdom can't comprehend the whole. Before the eyes of God human beings are in any case the sinners, God's wisdom is a mystery, which no one can understand (seems to be a paradoxical answer). Norman C. Habel writes: "In a world where paradox and in congruity are integral to its design, there is no simplistic answer to the problem of innocent suffering. The baby eagle survives because another young creature dies. God does not eliminate the forces of chaos, the role of Death, or the presence of the wicked. They operate within the eternal constraints of his design, light is balanced by darkness. Each night the wicked function, but with each dawn they are exposed and contained (38:12-15). No mechanical law of reward and retribution operates in this design. The "wasted wasteland" is as much God's concern as the rain that breaks the drought (38:26-27, 37-38). For there is a celebrative aspect to the world which puts all structural and function features into perspective. In his design there is a measure of the cosmic with the controlled, the bizarre with the beautiful, the serendipitous (something happening you don't expect) with the serious. Yahweh challenges Job to show the discernment necessary to keep this paradoxical world in balance. From these parallels in the natural world Job is left to draw the necessary conclusion relevant to his personal world. Job's complaint that the innocent sufferer unjustly is never refuted. It stands side by side with the answers of Yahweh as part of the paradox of that design. Yahweh's theophanic appearance honors Job; his speech challenges Job; his enigmatic design throws Job back into a bewildering world of wonder. In that world Job reluctantly foregoes his demand for litigation" (question taken from Norman C. Habel, **The Book of Job** (OT Library), London, SCM press, pp.534-35).

James A. Sanders (**Torah and Canon** pp. 104-108) has taken to pen out few remarks recently in his what is called a recent and fresh approach, to the book of Job. He writes thus: "The question which the Book of Job passes is how to relate, the mosaic prophetic theology of the God of Israel as a nation to the situation of Israel's dispersion, where covenant responsibility has dramatically shifted to the individual wherever he might be. The answer it offers is that the theology of the new Israel in the Diaspora, nascent Judaism, should emphasize God's transcendence a simply not insist so much on his immanence. God should be seen primarily as a creator God and less as the intruder in history who rules by his judgments... For (the Job poet) it was better to let God be God the creator, a little distant, a bit aloof, and not accountable to man for the vagaries of history and nature or a burden, to theologians to explain it all and "plead the case for God" (Job 13:8).

According to Mitchell (**The Book of Job**, San Francisco: North Point Press, 1987), the voice in the whirlwind ushers Job into a new dimension of reality where his eyes light up with joy inspired by the dance of death and life. Engulfed in primary energy, Job recognizes the triviality of his quest for justice, but J.L. Crenshaw contents that besides Mitchell's insights into the language of the biblical masterpiece, he misses its pathos. Divine perfidy and human suffering ought to evoke a loud outcry that can be heard above Job's enforced silence.

We also find some more important theological ideas in the book (i) the narrator wants to stress that God is creator and provider or sustainer (ii) Yahweh is depicted as the Lord of the entire cosmos: The design of God is not governed by a necessary law of reward and retribution, God's wisdom is of a higher order and remains a mystery. (iii) The book concludes with the presupposition that suffering of the righteous and the prosperity of the wicked are temporary. Both will pass away, leading to the times of just punishment and reward.

4.4. Ecclesiastes

Ecclesiastes, like Job, questions the justice of life's retribution, such discussions seem as much a part of the wisdom pursuit as the corresponding endorsement of the rigid view of retribution in Proverbs. The book presents two opposing approaches to life. These exhibit no obvious connection with other Hebrew wisdom. Other wisdom books assume life's meaningfulness. The Hebrew author of Ecclesiastes called Qoheleth "the Preacher" or "Preacher", sees things from a different perspective. Qoheleth's claim that life is empty (for example 1:2-11) apparently runs counter to the books advice to fear God and enjoy life (for example 2:24-25). The memes themselves offer less difficulty than the apparent contradiction. Wisdom occasionally offer opposing truths, but it does so with proper acknowledgment and consistent advice. In the following pages we shall focus our attention on the study of the book of Ecclesiastes by paying particular attention to the following issues: The Title, authorship, date and place of authorship, background of the Qoheletlh's wisdom, content and place of the book in canon and the message of the book.

a) Title: The Hebrew word used is Qoheleth (Qal feminine singular of **Qahal** means to assemble). This means, collector or the leader of the assembly, the word is put in the feminine because it describes an office or activity. In LXX (Greek), the title given is **Ekklesiastes** translated as "a member of the assembly". In vulgate, the term "cocionator" is used to means "Preacher". Identification of Qoheleth with Solomon was deliberate because of the tradition of issuing wisdom teaching as the King's teaching (as in Egyptian "royal instructions"). This fictitious royal authorship doesn't influence the book after chapter 2 (4:13-14; 7:19; 8:2-5; 10:16-17 presupposes the point of view of a King's subject not the king himself).

b) Date, author and Place of authorship: The book contains full of Aramaisms, using Persian loan words (for e.g. **pardes** translated as "park" in 2:5, **pithgam** translated as "decree" in 8:11). The book reflects Hellenistic ideas such as the cyclic nature of time (1:9-10) rather than Hebraic linear view of time, this is the reason the date for the book is suggested as 3rd century BC. According to Whybry, it is most likely the time during Ptolemy II Philadelphus reign (286-246 BCE) may have been written (during this King's reign LXX was translated and he advocated the religion of tolerance, thus Greek influence in the writing is natural to expect). This reign of Ptolemy II was also a time of peace and prosperity. Zenon Archives in Egypt reflects a political situation of economic prosperity in upper class of Jewish society in about 250 BCE. According Stephen de Jong this date is probable because to him it was a time of prosperity, peace, efficient administration and economic boom. It was a time of great ambition and optimism. This is the time 'the preacher' proclaims his message thus middle of third century BCE may be the probable date.

The book usually seen as the work of one author. The superscription 1:1 and epilogue 12:9-14 are considered redactional 12:12-14 of the book in particular looked upon by many scholars as an attempt to criticize the book from a mere "orthodox" point of view, and to reinterpret it. Some would accept the epilogue as the work of Qoheleth himself (It is best "fear God and keep his commandments, for this is the duty of the whole man" 12:13). According to H.G. Reventlow, it seems that is, this idea is much against the tone of Qoheleth on the whole, because Qoheleth is against traditional understanding of wisdom cf. chapter 3 in this regard and other passages as well. Qoheleth is not a nick name for Solomon and that the author sought to inform us of that by means of the enigmatic name that he chose and the unusual phrase "king in Jerusalem". Nevertheless, he assumed the personality of Solomon as a literary device to convey his ideas. According to Robert Gordis (**Koheleth-The Man and His world**, Texts and studies of the Jewish Theological Seminary of America. vol. 19. 2nd enlarged edition, New York: Bloch, 1955, p. 194) "The book of Koheleth is not a Pseudepigraph, which the author seeks to attribute to Solomon, like "the wisdom of Solomon". He impersonates Solomon only in the opening section because he wishes to prove that both wisdom and pleasure are worthless as goods in life (1:16-18; 2:1-12) and Solomon had the reputation of possessing both in superlative degree".

The book was probably originated in Jerusalem, Alexandria, Jewish circles in Phoenicia have also been suggested.

c) Place of the book in canon: Ecclesiastes occurs among "writings" the third part of Hebrew Bible. It is one among five books of megilloth which was read during the feast of tabernacles. The fourth position of the book in the megilloth was may be due to the fourth festival, the feast of Tabernacles in the calendar of the synagogue. Fragments of Qoheleth have been found out in the fourth cave of Qumran (5:13-17; 6:3-8; 7:7-9 for instance, one single manuscript of Qoheleth was found at Qumran dated in the middle of 2nd century BCE). The Synod of Jamnia (approx. 100 CE) included the book in the list of holy scriptures, the school of Shammai questioned the canonical value of Ecclesiastes but the school of gate; accepted it. It is generally held that the book gained the canonical status because it was attributed to Solomon, but this generalization may not be true because even other "Pseudepigrapha" in the name of Solomon like, Wisdom of Solomon or the Odes of Solomon could not get canonical status. However, the book's inclusion in the canon is justified based on the words found in the epilogue (12:9-14) which removes the stings of skepticism and advocates traditional beliefs of the book towards the end.

d) The background of the Preacher's wisdom: It is observed that wisdom in Israel was not an isolated phenomenon but had developed through the same phases as its West Asian neighbors. The fact that the empire of Ptolamies were dominating at the time of Qoheleth, the Greek influence on the book, no doubt, was found. Aristotelian, Stoic and Epicurean Philosophies seem to have been directly influenced in the book of Qoheleth. Many scholars dismiss the book as parallel with Greek literature, not from one period and from one philosophical system, could be claimed as a whole makes the basis of Qoheleth's teaching. In the Hellenistic Period, certain terms are introduced to serve as intermediaries between God and human beings such as: the name, the word, wisdom and spirit. Numerous angles and archangels made their appearance in Greek literature (thus the development of angelology in several places of the intertestamental literature are seen). The influence is clearly seen in the book of Tobit (ca. 200 BCE). In the midst of such a tremendous influence of Greek philosophies, the book of Ecclesiastes still holds to the idea of remoteness of God.

There are more similarities in some Mesopotamian texts with Qoheleth's ideas. For instance, in Gilgamesh epic, Gilgamesh was advised to enjoy wife, fine cloths and tasty food. This may be similar to Qoheleth's idea of advising to eat, drink and enjoy. Themes such as, death and memory of ones name after death are also dealt in Gilgamesh epic. In another document namely, "I will praise the Lord of wisdom" has similarities with Qoheleth who holds that divine laws are not known to human beings and they are hidden (3:11; 8:12-14 and 8:17).

"Babylonian Theodicy" and "The dialogue between Master and His slave" also have some similarities with Qoheleth (although these are more nearly paralleled to Job). According to Loretz, there are similarities between Mesopotamian literature and Qoheleth with regard to the concept of theodicy, retribution and so on. But Loretz feels the difficulty is no one is able to explain how these types of literature reached Qoheleth.

The late Egyptian texts like: papyrus Insigner and "the instructions of Onkshashongy" refer to the hiddenness of God and similar fate explained in Qoheleth. "The dialogue of a Man with his soul" remains Qoheleth's preoccupation with death. The protest against the traditional (old) wisdom and its values which are not valid practically is opposed by the Teaching of Anii. According to the story, Anii's father forces him to obey the old (traditional) wisdom, but he protests against it. As all the neighbours of Israel has some similarities to the Qoheleth's made of thinking, it is possible to say, it is not that they are depending on each other in writing their material (although that factor cannot be ruled out) but all of them are simply independent expressions of a widespread human mood.

Qoheleth's relationship with other Old Testament traditions reveal some important points too. Archie Lee has worked on the comparative traditions between Qoheleth and the book of Job. He has taken the issue of divine retribution and limit of wisdom. He opines that Qoheleth is a "critique of foundation" in Hebrew wisdom tradition. He further contends that both Job and Qoheleth call into question the doctrine of retribution and the foundation of wisdom heritage itself. Qoheleth talks on retribution but comes out with a negative result. But Job's discussion on reiteration is resolved finally in the realm of faith. It capitulates wisdom of God is higher than the human wisdom.

R. N. Whybray has dealt more extensively with the question of relationship between Qoheleth and the Old Testament tradition in general. According to him Qoheleth has both traditional and anti-traditional materials. Moreover, the anti-tradition materials in Qoheleth have their counterparts throughout OT material even from the earlier times. Further, Whybray thinks that like all other OT texts, Qoheleth believes there is one God who created the world (3:1) and has sovereign power over it (3:14; 6:10; 7:13; 9:1 and 11:15). Whybray cites J.L. Crenshaw who has referred God as an "oppressive presence" by quoting the story of sacrifice of Isaac (Gen. 22) Where God is indifferent to the torment which he is inflicting on his faithful servant Abraham. In another example of Qoheleth 6:7-8, in v. 7 it is written: "All human toil is for the mouth, yet the appetite is not satisfied" is a traditional wisdom saying like any other wisdom observation. However, v. 8 reads thus "For what advantage have the wise over fools? And what do the poor who know how to conduct themselves before the living?". This saying is clearly the expression that may be termed as anti-traditional material, which is the innovation (contribution) of Qoheleth himself. Thus Qoheleth while affirming the old traditional concepts of wisdom radically questions them too.

e) Literary Form and Structure of the book: Some of the literary forms found in the book are common to other parts of OT and to wisdom literature, while some forms are special to Qoheleth himself.

(i) Synonymous couplets: Here the second line echoes the first line Eg. 1:15,18; 7:7; 10:8,9,18; 11:4.

(ii) Antithetical couplets: Two opposites are contradicted with implicit approval of one of them Eg. 2:14; 7:14.

(iii) Non parallel couplets: Two lines of which the second line completes the thought of the first. Sometimes it is also called as Synthetic parallelism Eg. 4:5; 10:3,5.

(iv) Couplets declaring A to be preferable to B: The so called better sayings these are common in wisdom thinking, more special to Qoheleth's thinking. Eg. 4:6,13; 6:9; 7:2,5; 9:17.

(v) Metaphor: This form is a force comparison of image and reality, found usually in proverbial and other old wisdom materials Eg. 7:26.

(vi) Parable: The preacher uses small stories for teaching to express an idea that wisdom is useless. Eg. 9:13-15.

(vii) The Rhetorical Question: The question presupposes the answer Eg. 8:4.

(viii) Allegory: Translates every picture into reality, a series of metaphors appear in the form of allegory in 12:3-4.

(ix) Malediction and benediction: is also juxtaposed in 10:16-17.

Concerning the integrity of the book, Crenshaw raises four important concerns as follows:

First, the author writes the bulk of the book, with editorial glosses entered in the book at a later stage.

Second, the author cites traditional wisdom and refutes it.

Third, the author enters into a dialogue with an interpreter be it real or imagined figure.

Fourth, the book reflects a single author's changing view points over the years, as well as life's ambiguities, thus we have varied opinions and thought forms with a single writing.

Several scholars proposed several structural arrangements for the book of Ecclesiastes, but the structure proposed by Sphinx and Skehan seems to be better. It is as follows:

(a) Introduction: 1:1-11 (Prologue)

I. Qoheleth's investigation of life. 1:12-6:9

A. Double introduction 1:12-15, 16-18

B. Study of pleasure seeking 2:1-11

C. Study of wisdom and folly 2:12-17

D. Study of the fruits of toil 2:18-6:9

II. Qoheleth's conclusion 6:10-11:6

A. Introduction 6:10-12

B. A man cannot find what is good for him to do; critique on traditional wisdom; on the day of prosperity and adversity 7:1-14

a. on justice and wickedness 7:15-24

b. on women and folly 7:25-29

c. on the wise man and the king 8:1-17

C. Man does not know what will come after him 9:1-11:6

a. He (man) knows he will die, the dead know nothing 9:1-6

b. There is no knowledge in Sheol 9:7-10

c. Man does not know what will happen 9:13-10:15

d. He does not know what evil will come 10:16-11:2

e. He does not know what good will come 11:3-6

D. The joy of Youth and Old age 11:7-12:8

f) Conclusion 12:9-14 (Epilogue)

i) Content and the message of the book: The book of Ecclesiastes contains reflections, confessions, proverbs and meditations of various kind. All these center around one problem i.e. the problem of death. Everything is "Vanity of vanities" (1:2) better translated (based on the Hebrew word **Hebel**) as "nothing but vanity". Even wisdom, the divine cosmic power which rules the universe is justice and in vain (1:18). Pleasure, works, riches, fame all likewise are vain, for all leads to death "A living dog is better than a dead lion" (9:4b).

However, Qoheleth doesn't affirm atheism either theoretically or practically. He affirms the power of God over against the weakness of human beings. God's purposes endure, even if human hope and glory crumble to dust.

Most important to Qoheleth's vocabulary is **Hebel** (as mentioned above), which is translated differently as follows; futility, absurdity, nothingness etc. According to Whybray, this word may not have negative connotation, but it means more than a 'mystery' or 'impermanence'. To enjoy is God's gift, take life as it comes and enjoy because, we can't change the fate which God has chosen for us and we can't know what God has instore for us. Wisdom is gift, but there is a wide gap between God and human beings and human beings are kept ignorant (same as Job at this point), every human action is futile because God holds the card and death cancels everything.

Qoheleth taught by means of various literary types that earlier optimistic claims about wisdom's power to secure one's existence have no validity. No discernible principle of order governs the universe, rewarding virtue and punishing evil. The creator, distant and uninvolved, acts as judge only (if at all) in extreme cases of flagrant afferent (for example, reneging on religious vows). Death cancels all imagined gains, rendering life under sun absurd. Therefore, the best policy is to enjoy one's life (see above for the same idea) with one's wife, together with good food and drink, during youth for old age and death will soon put an end to this "relative" good. In short, Qoheleth examined all of life and discovered no absolute good that would survive death's effect. He then proceeded to report this discovery and to counsel young people on the best option in the light of stark reality. It follows that Qoheleth bears witness to an intellectual crisis in ancient Israel, at least in the circles among whom he taught.

All that is mentioned above can be recaptured under the five-point structure (i) Death cancels everything (2:17); (ii) Wisdom can't achieve its goal (3:11); (iii) God is unknowable to human beings (3:15); (iv) World is crooked (v) Pleasure commend itself.

4.5. The Book of Ruth

The book of Ruth is seen as a perfect example of an art of story-telling. According to the Talmudic tradition Samuel was considered as the author of the books of Judges, Ruth and Samuel. E.F. Campbell proposes that the book was composed by the Hebrew singers, but finally elevated to prose style, but there is no evidence to substantiate this thesis. The book was named after its main character which is understandable as the entire story rests on the character and significance of a Moabite woman who takes a leading role. Thus, the book also constructs the events and characters surrounding her.

a) Place of the book in the Canon: Since the book is associated with the feast of Weeks, which is directly connected with the feast of wheat harvest and the forerunner of the feast of Pentecost, the book is placed first among Megilloth but in some manuscripts it is placed as a second book.

b) Authorship, Date and Composition: In the Rabbinic tradition, Samuel is considered as the author of the book according to Baba Bathra 14b. While some scholars support this view other scholars argue for a postexilic date since the book is concerned with the mixed marriage and use of Aramaisms. Perhaps we may conclude that book can generally be dated in the postexilic period with the possibility of the inclusion of earlier material as well. Moreover the book may have been written by someone familiar with royal house matters around 450-250 BCE.

c) Form of speech used in the book: Perhaps the book is simple and easy to follow as it contains one single form used. The story is well described with well-developed plot and with a clear climax. Scholars generally agree that this story is put in the form of novella. The story is a typical example of how a country side carries out the story-telling method and thus it is perfectly crafted for the sake of listening audience.

d) Content and Theology of the book: Perhaps many historical circumstances are reflected in the story of Ruth: Levirate marriage (ch. 4), Israelite Burial practices (1:17), threshing floor, the gate etc. some names like Ruth, Naomi, Boaz etc. are appeared to be Hebrew proper names, at the end of the Canaanite or at the beginning of the Israelite period. May be we can suppose that the names are basic means to fix events and narratives. Ruth may be told in the form of a story set in history.

Chapter 1 depicts the picture that blessing and affliction comes from God, a parallel is drawn between human achievement and what is expected by God. Chapter 2 mentions Yahweh's acts indirectly. Yahweh is understood as the faithful God who bestows his mercy on his children. Chapter 3 captures the idea that it is Yahweh who changes misfortune and suffering in to a future hope thus we see that Naomi is not let without redeemer. In chapter 4:1-17b it is understood that humans collaborate with Yahweh, and Yahweh is the one who resolves crisis and there is a limit for human achievement. 4:17c-22 depicts the visible proof of continued blessing of Yahweh, single and individual family has been extended further.

In the book of Ruth, we find God's providence is not seen directly implied. Prayers (1:8-9, 2:12, 19-20, 3:9-10 etc.) are indicated how God led people faithfully. God's plans in the lives of the people are secretly at work. cf. 1:6, 9, 2:12, 3:10. Just as Yahweh is faithful to his people regarding his covenant promise people also need to exercise their responsibility to one another. The terms "covenant brother" (2:1), "covenant-circle" (3:2) attest to this fact, one should have responsibility towards his neighbour, then God rewards (4:1 1-17). The book begins with a complaint (1:3) against God, but it ends with a joy and celebration of God's grace (4:14-17). By including Ruth in the genealogy of David the status of Ruth is elevated by God. Although, Ruth being a Moabite woman God treats everyone equal without any disparity. Thus the universal salvific plan of God by treating all the nations and people equally is demonstrated by the book of Ruth.

4.6. The book of Esther

The book of Esther faced considerable problems in its orientation. This is because of the fact that no mention of God's name in the book (although it is intended for the salvation of the people). Moreover, this is the only book absent from Qumran scrolls, no allusions to this book are made in the New Testament, and very few church fathers made reference to this book. Just like Ruth thus book is also named after the main character and all other events surrounding that character. The word Esther is derived from Persian word means *star*. The Hebrew name of Esther is *Hadhassah* means *myrtle*.

a) Place of the book in the Canon: In the Hebrew Bible the book of Esther is placed between Ecclesiastes and Daniel. But in the LXX it is placed just after 2 Esdras (Ezra-Nehemiah) and just before Judith. In Vulgate Esther placed between Judith and Job. In the Protestant English versions Esther is placed between Nehemiah and Job. This wide variation indicates that the place of the book in the canon was widely debated and it was only at a later time the book was accepted into the canon. No direct reference to God in the book and no Persian reference to the names Vashti and Esther makes the book to be more complicated. Even the reformer Martin Luther opposed the book to be included in the Hebrew canon. Esther is the only book that is not included in the Dead Sea Scrolls.

b) Authorship and the date of composition: According to Baba Bathra 15a the book of Esther was written by the men of great Synagogue. According to Josephus (Antiquities 11:6:1) Mordecai was considered to be the original author of the book of Esther. Internal evidence suggests (10:2) that the book is written after the death of Ahasuerus (Xerxes), but all this information cannot decide the exact date and place of writing of the book. Some scholars argue that the book may have been written before 330 BCE as there are no traces of any Greek influence in the book.

Although the book's content reflects the time of Persian period, some scholars are of the view that the events in the book may even go beyond Persian period. One can also find very little information about the Persian period and related events in the book. Based on the above discussion the book's date may be placed broadly between 300-100 BCE.

Some would argue that perhaps the book may have been written by a non-Jew since the author has not used God's name Moreover, Jews are referred in third person, and the festival of Purim which is important for a non-Jew. The book of Esther is often understood as a wisdom book because the idea of impersonal, remoteness of God is seen in it. Moreover, God is understood as supernatural, and the absence of divine name. The wisdom idea is further stamped in the book that successes and failures are attributed only to the human actions.

c) Importance of the Festival of Purim: The book of Esther along with its description on Purim, probably originated in the (Jewish dispersion to the east, and was taken over only at a later date, on the basis of the linguistic data, the book cannot be dated much before 300. B.C.E. Some would rightly argue that the purpose of the book is to recognize the importance and celebration of the Festival of Purim. The book of Esther as we know talks about Haman's plot to kill the Jews and to destroy them altogether. But after Esther's intervention the tables are turned and Haman was punished for his plot against Jews. Consequently the Jews celebrated the victory in the form of Purim Festival. But contrary to this idea we may note that Purim was first mentioned between 100-50 BCE in 2 Maccabees 15:36 where it is called "Mordecai's Day" (14th day of Adar)and is associated with "Nicanor's Day" (13th day of Adar) when Jews celebrated a Maccabean victory over the Syrians. So, the debate on Purim continues without any conclusive evidence.

d) Literary Formin the book: The book of Esther has described many things that cannot be realistically viewed. Such things cannot be historically viable. Six months of feasting (1:4), beauty contest preparation for a year (2:12), the height of Haman's gallows (5:14), many people killed by the Jews (9:16) are some of the impossible things to have happened. We can also note some real historical problems in the book. According to Herodotus Xerxes's queen was Amestris (neither Vashti nor Esther); also Herodotus is of the view that there are twenty satrapies in the Persian Empire not 127 provinces as mentioned in the book of Esther (1:1; 8:9).[14] On this basis we may argue that the book of Esther is not a historical record but a fictional story. The only exception to this view may be the historical figure of King Ahasuerus though the identity of this King as a King of Persia is still debated.

e) Structure of the book: It is generally argued that the book of Esther is brilliantly written story that has a chiastic structure by which we can see the sleepless night of the king becomes a pivotal point. The chiastic structure is seen as follows:[15]

A Opening and background (Chapter 1)
B The king's first decree (chapters 2-3)
C The clash between Haman and Mordecai (chapters 4-5)

14 For more detailed discussion on this and related issues see, Mervin Breneman, "Ezra, Nehemiah, Esther," in *The New American Commentary,* Volume 10 (Nashville: Broadman & Holman, 1993), p. 280.

15 The above chiastic structure of the book of Esther is adapted from Ibid, p. 288.

D "on that night the king could not sleep" (6:1)
C' Mordecai's triumph over Haman (chapters 6-7)
B' The king's second decree (chapters 8-9)
A' Epilogue (chapter 10)

f) Main focus of the book: Inspite of the fact that no divine name is mentioned in the book, there is a strong motif of deliverance of God'speople, there is a strong belief in the province of God and ultimately God's people are saved. God very much operates from behind the scene. People are expected to be loyal to God and also people should be loyal to their socio-religious heritage with their allegiance to a foreign king. This idea also clearly reflects the real situation of diaspora setting. Moreover the book talks about the self-sacrifice of Esther for her own people at the expense of her own life and safety. There is an overwhelming opinion that the book depicts the importance of fasting, sackcloth, ashes etc in order to talk about the religious piety of Jewish community. But the author is so careful not to highlight that aspect in order to maintain the secular character of the book in the context of Diaspora.

4.7. The Book of Lamentations

Psalms shows the clearest similarities of the Book of Lamentations. In fact, Lamentations contains five or more Psalms, conforming to the patterns followed in the Psalter. Appropriate to the title of the work, the entire book consists of Psalms, of distress. The book of Lamentations, like the Torah and Psalms, neatly divides into five units corresponding to the chapter divisions. Within each of the first four chapters, succeeding lines begin with successive letters of the Hebrew alphabet. All poems in this book relate in theme to the fall of Jerusalem in 586 B.C.E and the subsequent Babylonian exile. In the following pages, we shall make a brief survey on the issues like Title, place of the book in the canon, date, authorship, form and structure, content and main theological message of the book.

a) Title: Original Hebrew title of the book is **Qinoth**, "dirges" or "laments", according to Rabbinic tradition. But now it is titled as 'Ekah', "Alas, how....." based on the first word of the text. LXX uses the threnoi means "lamentations", followed by Vulgate and modern translations. In LXX, Vulgate and modern translations, the book appears after Jeremiah. The superscription in LXX B (Codex Vaticanus) specifically connects the book with Jeremiah (by the words: "Jeremiah had wept and lamented"); this usage is followed by other versions. Probably due to II Chr. 35:25, which speaks of Jeremiah composing a funeral lament for king Josiah on the latter's death. This is not, however, the content of lamentations, which speak of the destruction of Jerusalem.

b) Place of the book in Canon: This is one of the five books of Megilloth and in the Hebrew Canon it is placed in the eleven books of the third part of the Hebrew bible namely **Kethubim**. In Rabbinic bible the book is arranged as per the order of the festival which each of the five books of megilloth is read: Song of Songs (Passover), Ruth (Pentecost or weeks), Lamentations (9th of the month Ab), Ecclesiastes (The feast of Tabernacles) and Esther (the festival of Purim). Codes Leningradensis and Biblia Hebraica Stuttgartensia (BHS), the book is arranged according to the chronological order: Ruth (in the time of Judges), Song of Songs (in the young age of king Solomon), Ecclesiastes (in the old age of king Solomon), Lamentations (during the time of the fall of Jerusalem). In LXX and Vulgate as already been mentioned, the book is placed after Jeremiah due to the assumption that in II Chronicles 35:25. There is Jeremiah's funeral lament after the death of king Josiah, but as already stated that is not what the book is concerned about.

c) Date: Traditionally, the book is dated soon after the Babylonian exile somewhere around 586 BCE; thus the statements reflect no hope situation (Lam. 2:15a). Based on the order of the content we do have the following suggestions: According to W. Rudolph, chapter 1 is perhaps written after 597 BC because it does not speak about destruction but only about famine and chapter 3 is considered to be the latest because the destruction is described more vividly than chapter 2 (but no strong evidence to prove this point). W. Fuerst contends that, not all chapters in this book are written at the same time, but D.R. Hillers is of the opinion that all the chapters are written and composed at the same time.

d) Authorship: Rabbinic tradition, LXX, Syriac, Targum and Christian tradition attributed the authorship of the Lamentations to Jeremiah till 18th century C.E. But in 1712, Vander Hardt challenged Jeremiah's authorship to Lamentations by saying that chapter was written by Shadrach Daniel. Ibn Ezra later on did not deny Jeremiah's authorship, but rejected the view that it is the scroll burnt by king Jehoiakim. Moreover, in the Masoretic Text, no clue is given in the title as to say that the book is written by Jeremiah. Those who strongly argue for the Jeremiah's authorship of this book also furnish the following clues: II Chro. 35:25, Jeremiah laments for the king Josiah and in 9:1 of Jeremiah, Jeremiah weeps, perhaps lamentations 4:20 may have been referred to Josiah. If the book of Lamentations is an integral part of the book of Jeremiah why then is it separated from the latter? the reasons given to this question are: Lamentations 4:20 has a definite reference to king Zedekiah (but Jeremiah was perhaps against royal theology?); the other clues are in Lam 1:10, Jeremiah was against the temple and 2:9 there are no visions given to the prophet is in time with Jeremiah's thinking. There are other suggestions for the authorship of the book suggested by other scholars: According to F.M. Cross and N.K. Gottwald, the author of the book was a cult prophet, lay person in the royal court or even the probable idea that the book is written by many authors. The reasons for this is: in chapter 1 Hebrew ayin comes before Pe; in chapter

3 and 4 Pe comes before ayin and other reason is that chapters 1, 2, 4 are individual laments, but chapter 5 is a communal lament. Probably a redactor at a later stage compiled all these individual parts into a single unit.

e) Form and Structure: Chapter 1-4 are composed in third person in form and content. Usually the book is called acrostic poem with Qinah (used in laments, especially in funerary laments like Amos 5:1ff with 3+4 meter in Hebrew throughout) meter. The questions why this poem is acrostic? Four reasons are furnished by N. K. Gottwald as follows: (i) belief in magical power of writing, (ii) exhibit artistic form, (iii) form by which merismus (wholeness of beginning and end) is achieved, (iv) format by which mnemonic expressions (boundless grief is expressed). The other form is found in its Chiastic Structure: Chapter I: a generalizing summary; Chapter 2: Vivid description; Chapter 3: intensified acrostic structure; Chapter 4: Vivid description; Chapter 5: Generalizing summary. The center this five-chapter structure is Chapter 3:31, 32, 33 with the theme of "assurance" in the midst of trouble.

The genre contains mixed and varied forms. On the whole the Poem contains individual and communal laments. Chapters 1, 2, 4 are individual laments and funeral dirge; Chapter 5 is a communal lament. Chapter 3 contains a mixture of genre: vv.19-24 and 54-58 thanksgiving words; vv. 25-39: wisdom song; Chapter 4:21-22 contains mixed oracles of salvation and judgement. i.e., salvation for Zion and Judgement on Edom. 5:19 is a hymnic speech. In general, on the whole the meter of this poem is 3+2 (Qinah meter), but 4+2 (in chapter 5) and 2+2 is also present at certain places. The city of Zion is personified as virgin at least 25 times in the poem. Let us talk more on the acrostic structure of the Poem in the following lines.

Several features of this acrostic poem of Lamentations make the series unique. *First*, Lamentations concentrates on a single disaster, the fall of Jerusalem in 586 B.C.E along with subsequent hardships. *Second*, the book views the disaster three perspectives, including complaints from individuals, the community as a whole, and Jerusalem itself. *Third*, Lamentations shows signs of thematic development from poem to poem. *Fourth*, the acrostic structure of the units show four variations in type in five chapters. All these unique features combine to indicate that Lamentations, unlike the Psalms, comprised a single carefully constructed unit.

The acrostic structure presents obvious evidence of the book's careful design. All five of the poems contain a number of lines divisible by twenty-two (the number of letters in the Hebrew alphabet). The lines of chapter 1 and 2 follows an AXX, BXX pattern. Chapter 3 follows an AAA and BBB pattern. Chapter 4 follows an AX, BX pattern. Chapter 5 can be designated X, X with no acrostic pattern. English translations however, indicate none of these patterns. Two features of this acrostic organization reveal a concern for the development of the book as a whole. *First*, the numbers of lines per chapter decrease from the beginning to end. Such a design may mimic the 3+2 pattern of Qinah rhythm. *Second*, the acrostic pattern reaches its climax with Chapter 3. Chapter 3 possesses three lines in succession beginning with each letter of the Hebrew alphabet. Only Chapter 3 exhibits this threefold acrostic structure. This represents the apex of the 'exiles' complaint. The third chapter deserves special attention for this reason. The following Table explains the Acrostic form in the book of Lamentations. (Table is adapted from Donald K. Berry, **An Introduction to wisdom and poetry of the OT**, Nashville: Broad man & Holman publishers, 1995, P. 413-415).

Chapter	Number of Verses	Acrostic Structure
1	66	First letter of the first time of triple lines forms acrostic
2	66	First letter of first line of triple lines forms acrostic
3	66	First letter of all triple lines form acrostic
4	44	First letter of first line of double lines forms acrostic
5	22	No acrostic form

The table below again shows a sense of varieties of types of units with combinations employed in the chapters. These varieties show the depth of the sense of grief and problem expressed.

1	Report of suffering and grief	(throughout)
2	Corporate confessions of sin	3:40-42
3	Account of the fall as a divine operation	2:1-9
4	Call for help	1:22; 2:20
5	Call for lamentation	2:18-19
6	Statement of trust	3:22-29
7	Remembrance of better fortunes	4:7
8	Imprecations against enemies	4:21-22

f) Content: The contents are also based on the form already described in our previous section. We shall deal with the content in this section according to each chapter.

Chapter 1: divides into four main parts A communal lament.
vv.1-11: lament over the overthrow of the city, personified as a woman, the daughter of Zion, who speaks in 9c and 11c.
vv.12-16: the personified city laments (note v.13).
v.17: a transition which says Zion has none to comfort her; the Lord has sent the enemies.
vv.18-22: Zion again laments, calling on the Lord to hear her and deal with the enemy as He has dealt with her.
To be dated in 597, after the first deportation (according to W. Rudolph) or after 586 BCE.

Chapter 2: a communal lament which describes vividly the fact that Yahweh became like an enemy to destroy Jerusalem. The concrete details suggest that it was composed soon after the disaster of 586.

Chapter 3:
vv.1-18: the confession of suffering of an individual.
vv.19-24: a confession of trust in Yahweh.
vv.25-33: instruction, in the Spirit of wisdom, to wait for the help of the Lord. Note vv.31-33, which are at the center of this chapter (and the book).
vv.34-39: Voice the doubt which afflict the people; refutes them.
vv.40-41: call to common prayer.
vv.42-47: prayer in the form of a communal lament.
vv.48-66: an individual lamentation.
This poem appears to be a liturgy of lament, which seems to presuppose a cultic memorial celebration at the ruins of the temple (suggested by Zech.7:1ff and 8:18ft).

Chapter 4:
vv.1-16: descriptive lamentation over the misery of the people of Jerusalem; it is emphasized that the distress is Yahweh's punishment for sin.
vv.17-20: lamentation in 1st person plural, pointing a vivid picture of the destruction of the city. Note v.20, describing the taking of King Zedekiah: this is an excellent summary of the Theology of kingship which gave rise to the messianic hope ("anointed" meshiah).
v.21: Punishment of Edom in the form (Gattung) of a salvation saying, Ironic.
v.22a: a salvation saying for Zion. Compare with Isaiah 40:1-2, unique in lament.
v.22 b: A threat saying for Edom.
Like Chapter 2, this must be dated soon after 586 B.C.

Chapter 5: A classic form of communal lament.
v.1: Introduction, with invocation of Yahweh and the call for help.
vv.2-28: the prayer and cry for help and deliverance.

All five of these poems witness to the crisis of faith in Jerusalem after its fall. The Royal-Zion theology of Judah stated that Jerusalem would not fall; the Davidic dynasty would not end. The songs lead the community from doubt and disappear to a lamentation and intercession. (Chapters 1-3); to the thought that Zion's suffering has redeemed its guilt (4:22a); to prayer before God.

In addition to these insights, it is interesting to note that in Chapter 4: there is a formula that presents the contrast between former glory and present shame in a "once.....now" format. The following table lists major examples from Chapter 1, adapted from D.K. Berry, **An Introduction to poetic and wisdom literature of the OT**, P.416.

Once	Now	Verse
Full of people	A widow	1
Princes	Vassal	1
Many lovers	No comforter	2
Many friends	All enemies	2
Festivals	Mourning	4
Foes	Masters	5
Majesty	Rules displaced	6
Precious things	Afflictions and wandering	7
Pure sanctuary	Filled with Gentiles	10
Treasures	Starving	11
Lovers	Liars	19
The "once…now" scheme	Also appears in 4:1-2 and 5:1-18	

g) Theology: The point discussed throughout the poem is concerning the destruction of the city, temple and the aftermath of the destruction of Jerusalem in 587 B.C.E. The destruction on the whole is seen as a horrible scene, but there is a realization that the punishment is deserved because of their sin (the realization is on the part of the people concerning their sin). Even the prophets and the Priests share the blame rather than people only (2:14; 4:13). There are also some references to the traditions which have been broken and this make the people very difficult to pray for Yahweh.

Another significant contribution of the book of Lamentations is concerning its reference to the Royal Zion Theology. Two things in particular are said about this. *First*, the reference to Zion past (2:15). All who pass by clap their hand by looking at the present pathetic condition of Jerusalem by passing comments on her. Is this the city that once called the perfection of beauty, the joy of the whole earth? According to 4:12 the inhabitants of the world not believed that enemy could enter into the gates of Jerusalem; even it is mentioned in 2:4f that Jerusalem is visible. *Second*, reference to the royal past is made. According to 4:20 the anointed one of the Lord is taken away, O King. The sins of Judah were too much that the unconditional promise to Zion was written off, therefore turn to God (3:40). But there is a feeling that the punishment given to them is well deserved for what they have done but at times felt that it is too much, therefore, there is a shift in emphasis in chapter 3:31,33. God will not cast off his people forever, God doesn't afflict his chosen ones willingly. To have faith means it is waiting for Yahweh. The basic deuternomic idea that punishment is the result of sin is applicable here although this view is dominant in the entire book.

The content of the book also relates to an annual commemoration of the fall of Jerusalem. The present day of fasting known as the ninth of Ab May have originated in such responses during the exile. These laments evolved into the current text which is mere a record of the depth of suffering than a conventional lament. These chapters survive as reminders to future generations of the absolute desperation of times.

4.8. The Song of Songs

The book takes its name from its first two words: **sirhassirim** (Song of Songs). In Greek the title is: **asma asmator**; Vulgate gives the title: **Cantium Canticorum**. The periphrastic superlative is intended to suggest that the book is "the most beautiful (or best) Song of Solomon", who is reputed to have written 1500 songs (as mentioned in I Kings 4:32). The association of this book with Solomon is probably the real reason why the book became part of the Canon; its canonical status dates back to before the so-called Synod or Jamnia (ca, AD. 100), nor was it questioned at that time. Subsequently during the second century, doubts arose as to the propriety of its inclusion, but these were put to rest by the statement of Mishna Yadayim 3.5. Evidence for the use of the book as the festival scroll for Passover dates from the eighth century. Thus, this is regarded one among the five books of Megilloth. In the following pages we shall focus our attention on this book by dealing with the issues like: the structure, form and in relation to the sitz-im-leben of the book as proposed by several scholars. Also brief consideration on the points like: authorship, date, place in the canon, interpretation and purpose.

a) Structure: There has been always a question raised concerning the structure of this book: Is it a loose connection of individual poem? Or unified compositions of five to eight poems (longer ones), with the integrity of the theme and the unity of action? N. K. Gottwald identities unity and context through the repetition of figures of speech. For instance, in 2:15 there is a description of vineyard and in 5:1 and 8:13 there is also description of garden. Both these descriptions are compared to women in 1:1-3 to chapter 8, Then there is a possibility that it may contain an inclusion. Rolf Rendtoff finds a structure or frame work of 1:2-6 and 8:8-14. It contains the following elements in a chiastic construction: *First*, declaration of love by the woman for her beloved with the invitation "Draw me alter you, let us make haste" (1:2-4); this is matched by the conversation of the lovers at the end (8:13f) which in turn leads up to the woman's invitation, "Make haste my beloved". *Second*, the depicted as the vineyard. *Third*, associated with second, the speech of her welcoming her beloved. This framework is anchored to the center of the composition by the invitation of the man of his betrothed "come with me, my bride" (4:8), which corresponds to the invitations of the woman at the beginning and at the end.

One basic dividing line is provided by the woman's appeal to the "daughters of Jerusalem". It has a twofold function in the composition. On the one-hand the phrase, 'I adjure you, daughters of Jerusalem', used four times (2:7; 3:5; 5:8; 8:4), each time marks a conclusion, so that the whole collection with in the frame work is divided into four sections, 1:7-2:7 contains three conversations between the lovers (1:7f; 9-17, 2:1-3) and a final description of the love scene with words of the woman (2:4-7) which ends with the appeal to the 'daughters of Jerusalem' 2:8-3:5 contain only words or songs of the woman; here 2:8f and 17 correspond, and in 3:1-5 again, to conclude with, there is the description of a love scene which ends with the appeal to the 'Daughters of Jerusalem'. 3:6-5:1 begin with the description of a splendid procession of king Solomon (3:6-11) and are followed with words of the man: first of all, a description of the beloved (4:1-7) and then further discourses and songs to the 'bride' (**kalla**, the Hebrew word only here in 4:8-12; 5:1), which ends with a conversation (4:16-5th chapter). The section 5:2-8 serves as a transition: this time the concluding love scene does not take place, so that the appeal to the 'daughters of Jerusalem' (5:8) is at the same time an introduction to a conversation with a double question-and-answer play (5:9-16; 6:1-3). 6:4-7:10 contain descriptions of the beloved and love songs by the man (6:4-7,8-10,11f; 7:2-6,7-10); in 7:11 the woman again speaks until the concluding love scene in 8:1-4, which again ends with an appeal to the 'daughters of Jerusalem'.

Between the lost love some (8:1-4) and the final part of the framework (8:8-14) there is a concluding conversation between the lovers (vv.5-7) which contains emphatic, reflective sayings about love ('Love is strong as death', v.6). This forms the climax of the love conversations and songs.

The structure of the Song of Songs can be presented as follows: However, this is not an exclusive structure in itself. There can be modifications and variations possible. 1:2-6: Invitation to set out, vineyard metaphor, brothers (v.5- Daughters of Jerusalem).

I : 7-2:7	
1 : 7f	
9 - 17	Conversation of the lovers
2 : 1-3	**Love Scene** ('I adjure you, daughters of Jerusalem')
2 : 4-7	
II. 2 : 8-3 : 5	
2:8-14	
15	Songs of the woman
16f	**Love Scene** ('I adjure you, daughters of Jerusalem')
3:1-5	
III. 3 : 6-5:1	
3:6-11	Splendid procession of King Solomon (vv. 10f. 'Daughters of Jerusalem Zion)
4:17	
4:8	(Invitation to set out)
9-11	
4:12-15	Song of the man
4:16-5:1	
Interlude 5:2-6:3	
5:2-8	Delayed love scene ('I adjure you, daughters of Jerusalem')
9-16	Conversations with the 'daughters of Jerusalem'
6:1-3	
IV. 6:4-8:4	
6:4-7	
8-10	
11f & 7:1f	Songs of the man
7:2-6	
7-10	
11-14	
8:1-4	Invitation to the beloved Love Scene ('I adjure you. daughters of Jerusalem')
8:5-7	Concluding conversation of the lovers
('Love is a strong as death')	
8:8-14	Brothers, vineyard metaphor, invitation to set out.

There are others who comment on the structure by saying that the song cannot comprise a drama in the proper sense, due to the lack of plot. Other features associated with drama (characters, scenes, settings, action) occur frequently. However, on the basis of the vocabulary and the content of the images, the sentiment expressed in 8:6 identifies the theme: "Love is strong as death". Emphasis throughout the work is on the exclusive devotion of the couple to one another. Love remains in spite of interference (2:2), separation (5:6), and beating (5:7). Not only does it endure, but its intensity never diminishes. Instead, its depth may actually increase from beginning to end. This tenure development offers the nearest thing to plot, making the drama something of a dramatic illustration of the moral expressed in 8:6. Based on the thematic or formal units in the Song of Songs, the following structure is proposed by D.K. Berry, **An Introduction to Poetic and Wisdom Literature of the OT**, 1995, p.386.

1:2-4	Love
1:5-8	Pastoral images
1:9-17	Royal luxury
2:1-7	Pastoral images
2:8-17	Pastoral images
3:1-5	Night / sleep
3:6-11	Royal references
4:1-5:1	Pastoral / garden imagery
5:2-8	Report of events (linked to 5:9-6:3 by question in 5:9)
5:9-6:3	Questions (5:9; 6:1)
6:4-10	Pastoral images (linked to 5:9-6:3 by question in 6:10)
6:11-14	Pastoral images, "looking"
7:1-9	Pastoral images, beauty
7:10-8:4	Pastoral images
8:5	(Isolated Questions)
8:6-7	Strength of love
8:6-10	Breasts / Building imagery
8:11-12	Vineyard / Solomon
8:13	(Isolated Statement)
8:14	(Isolated Statement)

b) Form and Sitz-im-Leben: It has been recognized that the form of this book is love poetry but with different genre like: Song of yearning for love, Songs of admiration of the beloved (Therefore we find some words like: boasts, teases (teasing), descriptive forms of the physical love experiences. This type of form is found in the Arabian Poetic expression which are called

Wasfs. The **Wasf** describes the beauty of the spouse's (or lover's) body. It typically surveys the subject's appearance from feet to head or head to feet: vv.1-5 of chapter 4 review the appearance of her upper torso involving images listed in the following chart. This table / chart is adapted from D.K. Berry, **An Introduction to Poetic and Wisdom Literature of the OT**, 1995, p.393.

Chapter 4:1-3 of Song of Songs

Verse 1	Eyes	Doves
Verse 1	Hair	Flocks of Goats
Verse 2	Teeth	Twins of washed sheep
Verse 3	Lips	Crimson Thread
Verse 3	Cheeks	Pomegranate halves
Verse 4	Neck	Tower of David
Verse 5	Breasts	Twin fawns

There are similar examples too we find in the Egyptian love songs, (cf. also 6:4-9). Others call the expression of love poetry in the song as Travesties, here the lover is portrayed in a role above or below in the social ladder. For example: Lover is either portrayed as a king or as a shepherd. All these elements are combined and woven together in the entire poem, perhaps sung at the wedding ceremony in Palestine. Related to the question of form, the sitz-im-leben is very vital question we shall now discuss in brief. There are at least four important proposals in this regard made by different scholars.

First, According to J.G. Wetzstein, (1873), who was an anthropologist contended that the song was a marriage song, resembling Palestinian wedding customs. But this view is very old and is also disputed by the scholars because of the reason that, not all the songs in the book are marriage songs, some are Wasfs, not at all connected with any marriage occasion.

Second, According to Ewald (1826) who proposed dramatic theory in which he said that the Song of Songs is a plot of the drama. The "Shulamite" woman was brought before the king to be with him, but she remains faithful to her lover, who is a shepherd. But Rolf Rendtroff refutes this idea and calls it as a woman's song; the woman has the first and last words and also plays a dominant role in other respects. Her conversation partners are always the 'daughters of Jerusalem'. Her beloved, who also speaks often (mostly indirectly with in one of the woman's discourses 2: 10-14; 5:2), is described as a herdsman (1:7; 2:16 etc.) who comes from out on the mountains (2:8,17 etc.). He is contrasted with king Solomon, on whom the woman looks from afar with the 'daughters of Jerusalem' (3:6-11) and chose many wives (6:8) and rich vineyards (8:11) only serve as a contrast to her beloved (6:9; 8:12). Moreover, Rendtorff says that it is not a plot, nor is it a drama.

Third, Meek and Miller suggests that it is a cultic drama like in the pattern of cult of dying and rising of Tammuz / Ishtari (Haller and Schmoekel also subscribe to this View). Ishtar looks for Tammuz but he is dead. This cultic drama (in the cultus) is enacted by a priest (Tammuz) and a priestess (Ishtar), representing divine marriage (as in Babylon) and at the end heavens are opened and rain comes (resembles fertility cult). But scholars strongly object to these view found in the book, rather Song of Songs speaks more of a longing, physical and emotional love is more indicated rather than love in marriage.

Fourth, N.K. Gottwald raises the question, where is the class of origin of such a literature? Indeed, this was not originated in the context of Patriarchy. This poem speaks about woman: 2:10-14, 5:2ff etc. Then is a collection of such poems found in the Egyptian upper class, Gottwald supposes that it may be the same in the case of Israel with only the difference that like what we described in the form of Travesties, may be lower class is playing a role like an upper class here in this poem.

c) Authorship, Date and Place in the Canon: Traditionally it is believed to be written by Solomon (cf. I Kings 4:29-32 – because Solomon wrote many songs), but the superscription (1:1) may be a later addition, the lover of the girl is considered to be the king (1:4,12 due to the presence of the phrase: "king has brought me"). According to Baba Bathra 15.a, Hezekiah and his scribes may have written this song like many other songs, so also the Proverbs (Prov. 25:1ff). Some would strongly argue for the wisdom influence in the song. According to 30:19, there is an idea that, the way of the man is with woman, Song of Song: also illustrates this point very well throughout.

Concerning the date of the book, the final redaction (not actual composition) of it may have taken place after the time of Solomon, most probably the date goes back to the Post-exilic times, even as late as third century B.C. This conclusion drawn based on the image of words of Post-exilic times in the book. For instance, usage of Persian word like "Parotes" means "Orchard" in 4:13; Greek or Iranian loan word like apriyon means "chariot" in 3:9 is used; the prefix **Seh** is used instead of **'aser** (which is normally used in other poetic texts), Moreover, several words are related to Aramaic.

The words like daughters of Jerusalem, Sharon (2:1), Hermon (4:8), Carmel (7:5) etc. indicate that this book was probably had its origin in Palestine.

The book's inclusion in the Canon is due to the reason of Solomonic authorship. For Jews this book means God's love for Israel, for Roman church Jesus' love for Mother is the theme to which the book is compared with. For Christian tradition this book is interpreted in terms of God's love for the church (the community of believers).

d) Interpretation and Purpose: From the early church father's time onwards, it was an allegorical interpretation of the text that was dominant regarding this poem.

A broad tradition of Jewish and Christian exegetes answer the question, how did a collection of love songs come to be in the canon of Holy Scripture? By saying that, by means of an allegorical interpretation. "may contend that the texts do not deal with the love between man and woman but with that between God and Israel or between Christ and the Church. However, it is by no means certain that this allegorical interpretation antedated the incorporation of the work into canon. Sharp criticism from Rabbi Akiba (c. AD 50-135) is reported of those who sing the Song of Songs in the taverns, so this evidently happened at that time. The Mishnah (Tractate Yadayim III. 5) hands down a rabbinic discussion about the sanctuary (i.e. the canonicity) of the Song of Songs (and Koheleth), here again Rabbi Akiba declares against those who challenge them. "All scripture is holy, but the Song of Songs is most holy".

Another leading interpretation on the Song of Songs is called Dramatic interpretation proposed by Milton, Origen and later developed by Selitzch in the 19th century. According to this interpretation, two twin characters are found in this song: Solomon and Shulamite girl i.e. "Solomon takes her from her village and eventually marries her". Another suggestion in the same ground is made by Ewald: Solomon, Shulamite girl and shepherd lover are the main characters in the drama. However, "she (the girl) remains true (to her lover) despite the King's desperate efforts to win her". According to Wetzstein, the Song of Songs is in the form of Nuptial songs, used in the marriage with so plain and erotic meaning.

The main purpose of the book is to serve as an object lesson, an extended mashal. The Song illustrates rich wonders of human love, provides a wholesome balance between the extremities i.e. asceticism and too much romantic outlook. Love is pure than our own thinking, and it is a deeply felt expression. The Song in its literal sense viewed as a celebration of love between man and woman, but more than that, the elevation of a love so genuine at it cannot be purchased with royal enticements. It is like divine love, given freely and unmeritoriously.

4.9. The Book of Daniel

Before we dwell on the details of the book of Daniel we shall briefly state the importance of the apocalyptic literature and its significance. The word "Apocalyptic" is derived from the Greek word *apocalypsis* meaning *revelation*. It is loosely used in a broader sense of the revelation of hidden things or even 'secret' things. It has a unique genre and has subgenre within itself. Accoding to John Collins the apocalyptic literature can broadly be classified into two groups: first, the "historical" Apcalypses such as the book of Daniel, Book of Dreams and Apocalypse of Weeks in 1 Enoch, Jubilees, 4 Ezra and 2 Baruch.

Second, otherworldly journeys such as Book of the Watchers, Astronomical Book, Similitudes (all in 1 Enoch), 2 Enoch, 3 Baruch, Testament of Abraham, Apocalypse of Abraham, Apocalypse of Zephaniah, and Testament of Levi 2-5.[16]

The book of Daniel is one of the most important yet disputed books is the Old Testament. The book is placed in the Hebrew canon in the writings, before Ezra-Nehemiah and Chronicles whereas the Septuagint places it at the end of the series of Major Prophets i.e., after Ezekiel. The book is named after the prominent character of the book called Daniel. In Hebrew the word "Daniel" means God is my judge or God has judged.Daniel is counted among wisest men in Ezek 28:3. The name Daniel is mentioned along with Noah and Job in Ezek 14:14 and 20.

a) Place of the book in the canon: In Septuagint and Vulgate the book is placed among Major Prophets including in the English translations just after the book of Ezekiel. The Gospel of Mathew accepted Daniel as prophet (Matt 24:15) and Josephus too accepted this view (Antiquities X:11:7). The Essenes in the Qumran community placed Daniel as one of the prophetic books. However the Hebrew canon placed it among the Writings since the book was lately accepted into the canon. While there are 12 accepted chapters in the book by the Hebrew canon, the Roman Catholic canon following the Greek translation includes another four passages like: The Prayer of Azariah, the song of the three young men chapter 3, the stories of Susanna and of Bel and Dragon. It looks like the additional four chapters in the Roman Catholic canon has taken place after the closure of Hebrew canon.

b) Date of composition and the author/genre of the book: Like any other apocalyptic literature the pseudonymity of the composition of the book of Daniel is obvious. It was generally proposed as written during sixth century, some scholars rejected this proposal and instead it is now argued for the Maccabean period in the second century, particulary during the persecution of the Greek ruler Antiochus Epiphanes.

The book is divided into two major parts: chapters 1-6 contain a series of stories of Jewish exile in the sixth century in Babylon and Daniel is presented as a wiseman in that context. Daniel may have recorded the main story found in the book although it is highly disputed opinion. The second section of chapters 7-12 we have an apocalyptic visions most likely reflecting the Jewish persecution during the Greek period. One of the main reasons for a heavy dispute in the authorship of Daniel is because of its bilingual nature: written in Hebrew as well as in Aramaic. Chapters 1:1-24a and chapters 8-12 are written in Hebrew, chapters 2:4b-7:28 are written in Aramaic. In order to solve this

16 John J. Collins, *Daniel with an Introduction to Apocalyptic Literature* (Grand Rapids: William B. Eerdmans, 1984), pp. 6, 14.

complex issue some would argue that in chapter 8-12 we see an expanded version of Hebrew revelations to the original Aramaic document. But it is not an easy matter to be resolved in such a simplistic manner. Probably several people would have been involved in editing the manuscript and finally we have a complex document with bilingual presentation.

The book also occupies a special position in terms of genre. At first glance the book seems to be divided into two parts, which have quite different character Chapter 1-6 contain narratives about Daniel and his friends, and chapters 7-12 contain visions. But this division contrasts with another dividing lines based on the use of two languages. The back begins in Hebrew, changes into Aramaic in 2:4 in the middle of the narrative and returns to Hebrew at the beginning of chapter 8.

c) Content of the book: The book as we pointed earlier has two major sections. Chapters 1-6 are considered to be the tales of wise Heroes. Chapter 1 seems as an introduction to this section. The names of the Heroes are given in both Hebrew and Chaldean language. The Kings mentioned in these stories are: Nebuchadnezzar chapters 2, 3, 4, Belshazzar (5, 7, 8), Darius (6, 9) and Cyrus (6:29, 10:1). There is also a common theme between chapter 2-7 of the book, these chapters 3-6 seems to four metals and four beasts. Then chapters 3-6 seems to be a separate section and small unit within 1-6 chapters. Chapter 3 talks about the story of golden image but ultimately victory can be claimed only in the name of Yahweh. Chapter 6 depicts the plot of Daniel's friends but here too Yahweh gives victory to Daniel through deliverance.

Chapter 7-12 contains the Apocalyptic visions; four such visions are explained. First, the vision of the Beasts from the Sea and "Son of Man" (7: 1-28): This vision is introduced by an introductory formula, "I was seeing", "behold". The word "little horn" a secondary addition. The phrases: "Ancient of Days" and "Son of Man" are also seen as later reactional material. This portion is using the genre of symbolic dream vision, throne scene, judgement scene and verses 23-25 are called exeventu prochecy. The intension of this vision is to give comfort at the time of persecution, the persecuted Jews are confronted by means of the supernatural forces and looking unto heaven for the resolution of the conflict: Second, the vision of the Ram and the He-goat (8: 1-27). This vision is connected with the first one. It is presented in the form of a symbolic dream vision. Ram and He-goat are interpreted as Kings of Media, Persia and Greece. He goat's first horn is interpreted as Alexander the great, and four horns may refer to the four military generals of Alexander. Little horn is interpreted as Antiochus IV Epiphanes. The intention of this vision is to explain the fact that the career of Antiochus IV Epiphanes is conformed to the pattern of Lucifer. This little horn will be broken by the human revolt in the later days (perhaps an allusion to the Maccabean revolt). Third, the interpretation of Jeremiah's prophecy (9: 1-27): The vision of presented in the form of Angelic discourse and Epiphany. The setting of the story is in the first year of Darius' reign but the events in it like the disruption of sacrificial cult, abomination of desolation in the temple reflects Antiochus IV, Epiphanes, desecration of the temple, and probably this chapter is composed shortly after this event in 167 B.C.E or early 166 B.C.E. The intention of this vision is to give an assurance to the persecuted Jews, their time of trial is coming to an end. Fourth the Angel's revelation (10:1-12:13). The content here is when Antiochus IV Epiphanes magnified himself against God, the great crisis occurred in the life in the nation, but this crisis is resolved in eschatological conclusion. It is presented as a historical apocalypse in the form of Epiphany (cf: Revelation 1:13-15). The form also conforms to the genre of Angelic discourse and exeventu regnal prophecy. The setting of the vision dated to Cyrus, but actual setting is in chapter 11, which is Antiochus IV Epiphanes. This indicates perhaps chapters 10-12 are written between 167 and 164 BC. The intention of this vision is to console and exhort the persecuted Jews, even the hope of resurrection is given to this end (chapter 12).

d) Theological focus: Rainer Stahl states that there are four important theological observations we can make regarding the purpose of Daniel 7-12 chapters: (i) God's Justice is executed at the time of injustice; because, God the giver of eternal life. (ii) Be not anxious about wrong things of this world because such acts will have an end. (iii) In out every day endeavours we need to work with on what is possible. (iv) God is with us in suffering: An experience of power of God can be seen even in adverse situations.

On the whole the book affirms the sovereignty of God of Israel in the midst of other gods in the courts of the earthly kings like Nebuchadnezzar, Belshazzar, and Darius. At the same time the book of Daniel is written to protect the righteous ones, though persecuted at present would one day be honoured and rewarded.

4.10. Ezra-Nehemiah

The books of Ezra-Nehemiah are the only narrative account of the time after the Babylonian exile to have been handed down in the Old Testament. Both the books are regarded as one single manuscript as it is also supported by many ancient Hebrew and Greek Manuscripts along with the Hebrew Bible. Some would regard the books of Ezra Nehemiah as part of the Chronicles on the basis of Ezra l: l-3a almost synonymous with II Chronicles 36:22. However it is only an exception to the introductory verse, their content is almost independent of the books of Chronicles, therefore it is better to treat them separately.

The Babylonian Talmud (Baba Bathra 15.a) and Jewish historian Josephus considers the books of Ezra-Nehemiah as one book. The Bomberg Bible of AD. 1525 has divided both books into two. But the Hebrew Bible

(Masoretic Text) places the Masoretic notes of Ezra Nehemiah at the end of Nehemiah rather than after each book, thus considering both the books as one.

a) Authorship and date of composition: Jewish tradition suggests that Ezra wrote his book (Baba Bathra 15a). Although Ezra's authorship was agreed for some time it was proposed that both Ezra-Nehemiah and the book of Chronicles are written by the same author for the reason suggested above based on 2 Chronicles 36:22. Brevard S. Childs is of the view that "A large number of scholars would assign the present shape of Ezra-Nehemiah to the editorial work of the Chronicler, who used sources such as letters, royal decrees, lists, and genealogies to continue the history which has begun in Chronicles."[17] Several dates for composition of the book have been suggested. The dates vary from 330, 400-300 and 250 BCE. But since the books cover over a long period of history there is a possibility to suggest a date of composition between 350-250 BCE.

The books are composed from different independent sources put together. At first both Ezra and Nehemiah memoirs are brought together (Ezra 7-10, Neh. 1-7, 7 12: 31 34 and 13:4-3l). In the second stage, Nehemiah, chapter 8-10 are added to the previous section. This section contains: Proclamation of the law confession, renewal of the commitment to covenant. This seems to be the bale idea to this material; in the third stage Ezra 1-6 has joined to complete the process of composition.

The books also contain a clear structure on the basis of the content. It has three major sections and some sub-sections:

A. Potentially (objectives defined): decree to build the house of God (Ezra l: 1.4).
B. Process of actualization: According to the decree of Cyrus the temple was built (Ezra 1:5 Neh. 712).
    a. Introduction: Prophetic Summons (Ezra 1: 5-6).
    b. First movement: Returnees built altar and temple according to the decree of Torah (1:7 6:19).
    c. Second movement: Ezra and the exiles build the community according to Torah (Ezra 7:1 10:14).
    d. Third movement: Nehemiah and the Judeans build the wall (Neh. 1:1 7: 5).
    e. Recapitulation: List of Returnees (Neh. 7:6 22).
C. Success (objective reached): Community dedicates the house of God according to Torah (Neh. 8:1 13:31).

(The above structure is adapted from Tamara C. Eshkenazi, "The structure of Ezra Nehemiah and the integrity of the book", JBL, 107, 1988, pp. 641-656).

---

17 Brevard S. Childs, *Introduction to the Old Testament as Scripture* (Phildelphia: Fortress Press, 1980), p. 628.

b) Theological focus: The books consists of major theological points and we shall briefly summarize them as follows:

1) The books develop idea of history of salvation, there is a tendency of 21 How of historical continuum all events took before the exile are brought together in the sense that the history continues from those past events until now. After the fall of Judah, politically people of Israel felt insignificant and they had the problem of identity crisis. Israel lost her hope of continuity. In this situation of crisis Ezra-Nehemiah's presentation of ideas in the books address to the situation. Two particular points to be noticed clearly: (i) Rebuilding of the temple is seen as an important institutional continuity (i.e. rebuilding the temple at its Original site (Ezra 6:7). Even the temple vessels, personnel and cultic practices are same as earlier times (Ezra 3:3-6, 10-11, Neh 8: 13 18 etc.) Even the genealogical purity of the people is to be maintained, as a mark of their continuity from the past (Ezra 2, Neh 7) (ii) The idea of typology is also seen in the description of Ezra Nehemiah's words. They recall the significance of earlier historical traditions of Israel. For instance, Ezra Nehemiah used extensively the Babylonian exile and Exodus traditions and connect both of these. The people who now returned from Babylonian exile are the same people who were brought out of the land of Egypt (Eg. Exodus 33:1 Ezra 3:8, 17 and Neh 9:8).

2) Ezra-Nehemiah affirms that God is to act through a Persian Monarch, Cyrus, in order bring restoration to his people. Nation and people are therefore subjected to this king (Ezra 5:14).

3) The law book read by Ezra in 7:2 sometimes identified with the Pentateuch, although this is not true. In order to maintain the purity of the community the observation of law codes is very important. If the community fail to follow the precepts of the Lord they will face serious consequences (Ezra 9:1, Neh 8:1318).

4) Temple occupies the main place in the discussions of Ezra-Nehemiah. The rebuilding and repair of broken walls of the Jerusalem was successfully completed by Nehemiah and his associates despite some hurdles. At the end dedication of the temple with celebration was carried out. Thus the temple becomes a center of their life in the community 9Ezra 6:16ff).

5) Use of scripture occupies a prominent place in the books of Ezra-Nehemiah. Some portions of the Law of Moses were read out to the people in public followed by the celebration of the festival of Sukkot (Booths) in Neh 8. It was clear that Ezra and Nehemiah wanted the community of returnees along with others to strictly adhere to the Law of Moses so that they live as God's covenant community.

4.11. The Books of Chronicles

a) Title: The two books of Chronicles form a single work with the Hebrew title: *diber hayyamin* which means "the words of the days." LXX divided the book into two and gives the title: *paraleipomena* which means "things omitted/passed over," and Jerome interpreted the Hebrew title as *verba dierum.*

b) Place of the book in the canon and its authorship: Although, Chronicles is not listed among the disputed books in terms of finding its place in the canon, it was not really given importance due to its dependence on other books like Genesis, Samuel and Kings. Moreover, the content of the book is not appealing to the readers since it has lot of genealogical lists, other ritual matters concerning Jerusalem Temple. However, we cannot rate the book and its material as secondary since all of the content is of immense value and importance in terms of the history and theology of the Kingdoms of Israel and Judah. We can also see the new perspective as a historian-theologian seems to be the author of the book of Chronicles. Most scholars agree that Ezra may be the probable author of the book but there is a strong suggestion that Chronicles may have been written by an anonymous author called Chronicler.

c) Date of composition: Based on the language and tone of the book it may have been composed during the time of Ezra and thus book may be dated in the latter half of the fifth century BCE, probably between 450-425. Others suggest that the book may be dated in the Persian period and even pushed forward to Greek period. But pushing it so far to date it is not justified so it can be conveniently placed in the period between 350-300 BCE. However, great caution must be exercised with this kind of precise dating of the book.

d) Content of the book: Surprisingly, the last book of the Hebrew canon contains a second account of the history of the period of the monarchy, beginning with the death of Saul (I Chr. 10) and ending with the Babylonian exile (II Chron. 36: 17 ff). However, we can immediately see a fundamental difference from the account in Samuel and kings. Chronicles contains only a history of Davidic monarchy. Only in the circumstances of his death Saul was mentioned (I Chron. 10; cf: I Sam 31). The books of Chronicles mainly based their material from the Deuteronomistic History as found in the books of Samuel and kings. However, certain places in the Chronicles certain alterations were made deliberately. Therefore, a comparison of the two accounts gives us important insights into the purpose of Chronicles.

The book begins with a large-scale genealogy (I Chron 19), which begins from Adam (1:1) to the return from the Babylonian exile (9: 1ft). This genealogical section utilizes some texts from Genesis, it leads from Adam to Abraham (1:1-27 cf. Gen. 5:10 f) and his sons and to the twelve sons of 'Israel' i.e. Jacob, (1:28-22). Then follows the genealogy of Judah down to David and his king (2:3-17) and further branches of Judah (2:18-55; 4:1-23). The other Israelites tribal genealogies, particularly the tribe of Levi is given (5:27-6:6). 8:33-40 presents Genealogy of Saul, again repeated in 9:35-44 after the insertion of a loss of those who returned from exile (9:1b-34). In all these list stress is laid on the genealogy of David and the Levites.

The history of David (I Chron. 10:29) begins with the account of the death of Saul (ch. 10). The death of Saul warns and depicts how due to the "faithlessness" of Saul the whole kingdom posed problems. The beginning of David's reign is made impressive (chs. 11:16). The chronicles, does not mention David's temporary rule over Judah but, diverging from his source, simply has 'all Israel' make David King (11:1 cf: II Sam 1:5).

In chapters 17-29 which is mainly devoted to the theme of the future building of the temple, Chronicles avoids all features which might disturb the picture of David and Solomon. For instance, David's adultery with Bathsheba and the subsequent judgement of Nathan and the rebellions against David are not mentioned (the whole succession narrative is passed over).

II Chronicles 1-9 presents details on the building of the temple prepared for by David, now taken over by Solomon. The description of the splendour and the riches of the temple even surpass the description in I kings 6-8. In building the temple Solomon is given a very high position, at the same time there is a constant stress that he (Solomon) reaped the fruits of David's preparation (II Chron. 2:6,13,16, 3:1; 5:1; 6:3-11).

Chapters 10-36 of II Chronicles completes the entire history of Judah after Solomon until its Babylonian exile. Here too chronicles sometimesliterally repeats kings accounts, and sometimes deliberately alters to suit his purpose.

e) Theological focus: Chronicle's purpose in the presentation of his material differ widely than other sources of monarchic history. Chronicles stresses and vindicates Jerusalem and its temple as the sole legitimate place for worship of Yahweh. However, chronicles also consider northern Israel as part of the kingdom. Indeed, the chronicles continues to see 'Israel' as a unity which embraces all twelve tribes.

Chronicler asserts that God is active in the history of his people, who personally intervenes to help them. He is the God of the fathers, God of the people of Israel (I Cho. 22:20) Chronicler follows the Deuteronomistic theology of retribution that obedience beings blessing and disobedience results in punishment, but chronicler departs from the mechanical understanding of this concept (cf. II chronicles 16:7 10; 20:20).

For Chronicles the entire nation is important including North and South. On several occasions this was clearly articulated: "Then all Israel gathered together to David at Hebron" (2 Chron 11:1); "David and all Israel marched to Jerusalem" (1 Chron 11:4); "So David assembled all Israel from the Shihor of Egypt to Lebo-hamath, to bring the ark of God from Kiriath-jearim"

(1 Chron 13:5); "Rehoboam went to Shechem, for all Israel had come to Shechem to make him King" (2 Chron 10:1); "Then Abijah stood on the slope of Mount Zemaraim that is in the hill country of Ephraim, and said, 'Listen to me, Jeroboam and all Israel! Do you not know that the Lord God of Israel gave the kingship over Israel forever to David and his sons by a covenant of salt?" (2 Chron 13:4-5). Thus, the entire Israel was included in the plan of God as one single nation and one people with one temple at Jerusalem.

Importance is given to the Temple at Jerusalem and its worship and all other aspects like Temple singers, personnel, and the entire cultic regulations of the Temple. Several reference can be cited in this regard: 2 Chron 13:10-12; 36; 29:22; 7:8-10; 30:21-26.

For Chronicler Davidic dynasty and kingship is given more prominence than the other kingships citing the reason that God entered a special covenant with David and this kingship was ordained by God (1 Chron 10:14; 17:13; 28:5; 29:23; 2 Chron 13:8).

Chronicler puts major emphasis on the ideas of retribution and repentance by suggesting that obedience leads to blessing and disobedience to punishment (1 Chron 10:13-14; 2 Chron 12:5-12). The Chronicler affirms that those who seek the Lord will receive help and those who forsake God will be rejected (1 Chron 28:9; 29:1-9; 2 Chron 15:17; 34:31).

Given the time in which Chronicles was written where there were divisions and conflicts within the Jewish community the books put more emphasis on the unity of all people as one nation with one God, one ideology, one temple, one covenant obligated to live under God's sovereign rule.

5. Post-Biblical Jewish Writings and Canonization

5.1. What is Talmud: The word "Talmud" is a Hebrew word meaning "learning, instruction." The Talmud is a central text of mainstream Judaism and consists primarily of discussions and commentary on Jewish history, law (especially its practical application to life), customs and culture. The Talmud consists of what are known as the Gemara and the Mishnah.

In addition to the inspired written Hebrew scriptures, which Christians call the Old Testament, Judaism has an "Oral Torah" which is a tradition explaining what these scriptures mean and how to interpret them and apply the laws. Orthodox Jews believe God taught this Oral Torah to Moses, and to others, down to the present day. This tradition was maintained only in oral form until about the 2nd century A.D., when the oral law was compiled and written down in a document called the Mishnah. Over the next few centuries, additional commentaries elaborating on the Mishnah were written down in Jerusalem and Babylon. These additional commentaries are known as the **Gemara**. The Gemara and the Mishnah together are known as the Talmud. This was completed in the 5th century A.D.

There are actually two Talmuds: **the Jerusalem Talmud and the Babylonian Talmud**. The Babylonian Talmud is more comprehensive, and is the one most people mean if they just say "the Talmud" without specifying which one. The Talmud is not easy to read. There are often gaps in the reasoning where it is assumed that you already know what they are talking about, and concepts are often expressed in a sort of shorthand. Biblical verses that support a teaching are often referenced by only two or three words. The Talmud preserves a variety of views on every issue and does not always clearly identify which view is the accepted one.

Christianity does not consider the Talmud to be inspired in the same sense that the 66 books of the biblical canon are "God breathed" (2 Timothy 3:16). While some of the teachings from the Talmud may be "compatible" with biblical teachings, the same can be said for many different writings from many different religions. For the Christian, the study of the Talmud can be a great way to learn more about Jewish tradition, history, and interpretation, but the Talmud is not to considered the authoritative Word of God.

The **Talmud** (/ˈtɑːmʊd, -məd, ˈtæl-/; Hebrew: תַּלְמוּד *talmūd* "instruction, learning", from a root *lmd* "teach, study") is a central text of Rabbinic Judaism. It is also traditionally referred to as ***Shas*** (ש״ס), a Hebrew abbreviation of *shisha sedarim*, the "six orders". The term "Talmud" normally refers to the collection of writings named specifically the Babylonian Talmud, although there is also an earlier collection known as the Jerusalem Talmud, or Palestinian Talmud. When referring to post-biblical periods, namely those of the creation of the Talmud, the Talmudic academies and the Babylonian exilarchate, Jewish sources use the term "Babylonia" from a strictly Jewish point of view,[1] still using this name after it had become obsolete in geopolitical terms.

The Talmud has two components: the Mishnah (Hebrew: משנה, c. 200 CE), a written compendium of Rabbinic Judaism›s Oral Torah (Talmud translates literally as "instruction" in Hebrew); and the Gemara (c. 500 CE), an elucidation of the Mishnah and related Tannaitic writings that often ventures onto other subjects and expounds broadly on the Hebrew Bible. The term "Talmud" may refer to either the Gemara alone, or the Mishnah and Gemara together.

The entire Talmud consists of 63 tractates, and in standard print is over 6,200 pages long. It is written in Tannaitic Hebrew and Aramaic, and contains the teachings and opinions of thousands of pre-Christian Era rabbis on a variety of subjects, including Halakha (law), Jewish ethics, philosophy, customs, history, lore and many other topics. The Talmud is the basis for all codes of Jewish law, and is widely quoted in rabbinic literature.

5.2. What is The **Mishnah** or **Mishna** (/ˈmɪʃnə/; Hebrew: מִשְׁנָה, "study by repetition"), from the verb *shanah* שנה, or "to study and review", also "secondary," is the first major written redaction of the Jewish oral traditions known as the "Oral Torah". It is also the first major work of Rabbinic literature. The earliest known copy of the Mishnah has additions, and is contained within a book featuring commentary that was printed in Naples Italy during the late 15th century.

The Mishnah was redacted by Rabbi Yehudah HaNasi before his death around 217 CE, in a time when, according to the Talmud, the persecution of the Jews and the passage of time raised the possibility that the details of the oral traditions of the Pharisees from the Second Temple period (536 BCE – 70 CE) would be forgotten. The majority of the Mishnah is written in Mishnaic Hebrew, while some parts are Aramaic.

The Mishnah consists of six orders (*sedarim*, singular *seder* סדר), each containing 7–12 tractates (*masechtot*, singular *masechet* מסכת; lit. "web"), 63 in total, and further subdivided into chapters and paragraphs or verses.

The word *Mishnah* can also indicate a single paragraph or a verse of the work itself, i.e. the smallest unit of structure in the Mishnah. For this reason the whole work is sometimes called by the plural, *Mishnayot*.

5.3. What is Midrash: In Judaism, the ***Midrash*** (/ˈmɪdrɑːʃ/;[1] Hebrew: מדרש; plural *midrashim*) is the body of exegesis of Torah texts along with homiletic stories as taught by Chazal (Rabbinical Jewish sages of the post-Temple era) that provide an intrinsic analysis to passages in the Tanakh.

Midrash is a method of interpreting biblical stories that goes beyond simple distillation of religious, legal, or moral teachings. It fills in gaps left in the biblical narrative regarding events and personalities that are only hinted at. The purpose of midrash was to resolve problems in the interpretation of difficult passages of the text of the Hebrew Bible, using Rabbinic principles of hermeneutics and philology to align them with the religious and ethical values of religious teachers.

According to the PaRDeS approaches to exegesis, interpretation of Biblical texts in Judaism is realized through *peshat* (literal or plain meaning, lit. "plain" or "simple"), *remez* (deep meaning, lit. "hints"), *derash* (comparative meaning, from Hebrew *darash*—"to inquire" or "to seek") and *sod* (hidden meaning or philosophy, lit. "secret" or "mystery"). The Midrash concentrates somewhat on *remez* but mostly on *derash* (Some thinkers divide PaRDeS into pshat, remez, *din* (law) and sod. In this understanding, midrash aggada deals with remez and midrash halakha deals with din).

Many different exegetical methods are employed to derive deeper meaning from a text. This is not limited to the traditional thirteen textual tools attributed to the Tanna Rabbi Ishmael, which are used in the interpretation of *halakha* (Jewish law). Presence of apparently superfluous words or letters, chronology of events, parallel narratives or other textual anomalies are often a springboard for interpretation of segments of Biblical text. In many cases, a dialogue is expanded manifold: handfuls of lines in the Biblical narrative may become long philosophical discussions. It is unclear whether the midrash assumes these dialogues took place in reality or if this refers only to subtext or religious implication.

Many midrashim start off with a seemingly unrelated sentence from the Biblical books of Psalms, Proverbs or the Prophets. This sentence later turns out to metaphorically reflect the content of the rabbinical interpretation offered. This strategy is used particularly in a subgenre of midrash known as the *petikhta*.

Some Midrash discussions are highly metaphorical, and many Jewish authors stress that they are not intended to be taken literally. Rather, other midrashic sources may sometimes serve as a key to particularly esoteric discussions. Later authors maintain that this was done to make this material less accessible to the casual reader and prevent its abuse by detractors.

5.4. What is Halakah: The name "*Halakha*" is derived from the Hebrew *helekh* (הָלַךְ) meaning "behavior" (in a different pronunciation, "halakh" - "to walk" or "to go"). Taken literally, therefore, "*halakha*" translates as "the way to behave" rather than "law". "*Halakha*" is used to refer to the corpus of rabbinic legal texts, or to the overall system of religious law.

Halakha is often contrasted with *Aggadah* ("the telling"), the diverse corpus of rabbinic exegetical, narrative, philosophical, mystical and other "non-legal" texts. At the same time, since writers of *Halakha* may draw upon the aggadic and even mystical literature, there is a dynamic interchange between the genres. *Halakha* also does not include the parts of the Torah not related to commandments.

Halakha constitutes the practical application of the 613 *mitzvot* ("commandments", singular *mitzvah*) in the Torah, as developed through discussion and debate in the classical rabbinic literature, especially the Mishnah and the Talmud (the "Oral law") and as codified in the Mishneh Torah ("A repetition of the Torah") or Shulchan Aruch ("Code of Law").

The *Halakha* is a comprehensive guide to all aspects of human life, both corporeal and spiritual. Its laws, guidelines, and opinions cover a vast range of situations and principles, in the attempt to realize what is implied by the central Biblical commandment to "be holy as I your God am holy". They cover what are claimed to be better ways for a Jew to live, based on what is not stated, but has been derived from the Hebrew Bible ("Torah").

Because *Halakha* is developed and applied by various Halakhic authorities rather than one sole "official voice", different individuals and communities may well have different answers to Halakhic questions. Controversies lend rabbinic literature much of its creative and intellectual appeal. With few exceptions, controversies are not settled through authoritative structures because during the Diaspora (age and place of exile) Jews have lacked a single judicial hierarchy or appellate review process for *Halakha*. Instead, Jews interested in observing *Halakha* typically choose to follow specific rabbis or affiliate with a more tightly structured community.

Halakha has been developed and pored over throughout the generations since before 500 BCE, in a constantly expanding collection of religious literature initially consolidated in the Talmud. First and foremost, it forms a body of intricate judicial (rabbinical) opinions, legislation, customs, and recommendations, many of them passed down over the centuries, and an assortment of ingrained behaviours, relayed to successive generations from the moment a child begins to speak. It is also the subject of intense study in *yeshivas*; see Torah study.

5.5. What is Haggadah: *Not to be confused with Aggadah.* Illuminated Haggadah (14th century) plural: **Haggadot**) is a Jewish text that sets forth the order of the Passover Seder. Reading the Haggadah at the Seder table is a fulfillment of the Scriptural commandment to each Jew to "tell your son" of the Jewish liberation from slavery in Egypt as described in the Book of Exodus in the Torah ("And thou shalt tell thy son in that day, saying: It is because of that which the LORD did for me when I came forth out of Egypt." Ex. 13:8).

Sephardi and Mizrahi Jews also apply the term *Haggadah* to the service itself, as it constitutes the act of "telling your son."

5.6. Aggadah (Aramaic אֲגָדָה: "tales, lore"; pl. *aggadot* or (Ashkenazi) *aggados*; also known as *aggad* or *aggadh* or *agâdâ*) refers to non-legalistic exegetical texts in the classical rabbinic literature of Judaism, particularly as recorded in the Talmud and Midrash. In general, Aggadah is a compendium of rabbinic texts that incorporates folklore, historical anecdotes, moral exhortations, and practical advice in various spheres, from business to medicine.

In terms of etymology, the cognate Hebrew: הַגָּדָה means "telling", while the Aramaic root אגד (as well as נגד from which אגדה may arise) has the dual implication of "expanding" / "drawing out" and "binding" / "drawing in".[1] Correspondingly, the Aggadah may be seen as those teachings which communicate Rabbinic traditions to the reader, simultaneously expanding their understanding of the text, while strengthening their religious experience and spiritual connection.[2] The root also has the meaning "flow",[3] and here relates to the transmission of ideas.

5.7. Canons of the Hebrew Bible

The word canon comes from a Greek word that means "standard" or "measurement." It simply refers to the list of writings that are considered authoritative within a religious group.

There was no "official" canon for either Judaism or Christianity until tensions between the two traditions forced official lists to be made. The Jewish canon is usually associated with the Council of Jamnia around AD 90, while the Christian canon was not defined until the fourth century and could still be debated in both Eastern Orthodoxy and Protestantism as late as the 16th century.

The word ‘canon’ is derived from the Greek word kanon, which means ‘measuring stick’, it also means a curtain rod, and a stick kept for drawing a straight line. Later it came to be used to refer to corpus of scriptural writings which is considered as authentic and inspired by God. Books which are not considered as authoritative are often called ‘non canonical’ or extra canonical?

According to Josephus, the canon is a divinely inspired writing, fixed in numbers originating within a limited period of time, with an established text.

It is impossible to say exactly when the individual stages of the collection and formation of the canon came to a conclusion. However, we have some important indications. Thus the author of Chronicles had access to the books of Samuel and Kings in essentially their present form. Moreover, for the genealogy in I Chron. 1-9 he used traditions from Genesis and other books of the Pentateuch. Towards the end of the first century CE Josephus speaks of twenty-two books (contra Apionem 1, 7f). About the same time IV Ezra speaks of twenty-four books (14:44-46), here both represent different ways of counting the books of the Hebrew canon (in English it reckoned to be thirty-nine).

One of the most important insights in canon is that the shaping of the biblical books in their present form is usually not the result of chance or of thoughtless and uncomprehending redaction, as was often supposed by earlier historical-critical exegesis, but that quite deliberate forces of shaping were at work which were often important testimonies to the history of Israelite and Jewish religion.

We must take into account the possibility that it was not make chance which led to the present form of the canon rather the form often canon is to be understood as an expression of particular religious and theological developments and decisions. Some scholars further elaborate these points: Wanders has pointed out that the canon is the form in which particular traditions were laid down as building and that this expresses the self-understanding of the community which made this assertion. J. Blenkinsopp further developed these ideas. He showed that there exists a reciprocal relationship between prophecy and Torah and showed that the authority of the canon depends essentially on its prophetic character, but that here there is a transformation in the understanding of prophecy which makes Moses the central figure. The tensions between Torah and prophecy is kept alive: by the eschatological shaping of post-exile prophecy this is mentioned in the imminent ‘Day of Yahweh’ (Malachi 3:22-24).

Generally, for the Old Testament books the Christian tradition simply accepted the Jewish collection of books that were considered authoritative by their use in the community. However, since the Jewish canon was not officially set, some books were in use within Judaism that had not yet reached the status of being authoritative. That fact allowed different branches of the Christian church to take slightly different views of some of these books, primarily those that dated to the intertestamental period of the first three centuries BCE. For example, some writings were accepted in the Western Church that were not as readily accepted in the Eastern churches (see further below).

The Christian churches tended to follow the arrangement of Old Testament books within the third century BCE Greek translation of the Hebrew Scriptures, the Septuagint. These were basically arranged topically, with the so-called "**law**" books first, followed by **historical** books, and ending with the **prophetic collection**. This arrangement fit well with the categorical thinking influenced by Greek philosophy, and also fit theologically with the role of prophets as understood in the early Church. Ending the Old Testament canon with the prophets, understood as predictors of the future, set the backdrop for the New Testament writings.

However, the Jewish tradition chose a more theological organization for the Old Testament canon. There is debate as to whether this was the retention of an older arrangement or was a deliberate attempt to distance itself from the Christian canon. In any case, the arrangement reflected the relative status of the three major divisions of the Hebrew canon. **The Torah** was the primary foundation of the community. **The Prophets** both Former Prophets (Joshua, Judges, Samuel, Kings) and Latter Prophets (Isaiah, Jeremiah, Ezekiel, the Book of the Twelve), were the practical outworking of those foundational tenets. **The Writings** were the reflective and liturgical dimensions of the tradition. This difference in approaches to the canon explains the different order of books between the Jewish and Christian versions of the Hebrew Bible.

In the Jewish canon, the books of The Torah have different names than in the Christian canons, taken from the first Hebrew words of the book: *Berishit* ("in beginning"), *Shemot* ("names"), *Vayikra* ("and he called"), *Bemidbar* ("in the wilderness"), and *Debarim* ("words"). The Christian names of the books are from the titles in the second century Greek translation, the Septuagint.

During the 200 years before the birth of Jesus and into the first centuries of the Christian era, in both Judaism and Christianity there were a great number of writings circulating within the various communities in addition to what we think of as the biblical books. Generally in Judaism, in spite of some other writings appearing in the third century BCE Greek translation (Septuagint) only the books that had gained authoritative status prior to the third century BCE were accepted as part of the Jewish canon. This left out most of the apocalyptic works that flourished from 200 BCE to the first century AD. An exception to this may be the Book of Daniel, which some scholars date to around 165 BCE, a product of the Maccabean Wars.

However since there was as yet no official New Testament canon, the early Christian churches were more open to these newer writings. Many were widely circulated and read in churches throughout both western and eastern areas of the Church. Over time, various Christian communities and traditions came to acknowledge some of these as authoritative.

Many of these writings were included in the lists of authoritative books in various places in both Eastern and Western churches as early as the fourth and fifth centuries. Yet they were not officially recognized by Roman Catholics until the 15th century **(Council of Florence, 1431-1449)** nor by Eastern Orthodoxy until the 17th century **(Council of Jerusalem, 1672)**. These authoritative books that are not a part of the Hebrew Old Testament are sometimes referred to as **Deuterocanonical** or a "second canon." This distinguishes them from the books that are shared by both Catholic/Eastern and Protestant traditions, sometimes referred to as Proto-canonical Books ("first canon").

There were also other mostly Christian writings, although considered helpful in some way that were not considered authoritative for doctrine. These "helpful" but not authoritative books are often referred to as the **Apocrypha**. However, since this term is used in various ways in different church traditions it is somewhat ambiguous.

Other writings, many of which claimed authority by linking to some prominent figure of the past, such as ***The Gospel of Thomas***, are called **Pseudepigrapha** by Protestants ("false writings," referring to the inauthentic connection to some authority figure). However, these books are also called the **Apocrypha** by Catholics ("hidden things"). The Pseudepigrapha were never accepted as authoritative by the larger Church. However, the New Testament Book of Jude references both *The Assumption of Moses* (Jude 9) and *The Book of Enoch* (Jude 14-15). Some scholars argue that influences from these and other pseudepigraphic writings can be discerned in both New Testament Gospels and Epistles.

During the Protestant Reformation in the 16th century, some of the Reformers rejected these Deuterocanonical books, both on historical and theological grounds. They accepted only those Old Testament books that were included in the Hebrew Bible, so the Deuterocanonical books are not generally included in the Protestant canon. However, in some Protestant traditions, such as Anglicans, the Deuterocanonical books are still included and are used in the cycle of lectionary readings for worship.

Some Protestants, following Martin Luther, have tended to refer to the Deuterocanonical books as the Apocrypha. In some circles, this took on strongly pejorative connotations implying "suspect" or "of questionable origin." However, in many cases Apocrypha was simply a designation for the Deuterocanonical books, and the terms were used interchangeably. These "apocryphal" books were included with the 1611 *Authorized Version* (*King*

James Version) yet were gradually eliminated from most Protestant Bibles beginning around the middle of the 17th century.

Several New Testament books were challenged by some of the Reformers, such as Hebrews and the book of James, but they were eventually fully accepted. The New Testament canon is virtually identical in all branches of Christianity.

These differences in the Old Testament canon between Christian traditions should not obscure the fact that the canon of the Old Testament is very similar for both Christians and Jews, as well as for different groups within Christianity. It is helpful to understand the differences and the reasons for them. But there probably should be more attention paid to the similarities, and the implications that has for understanding the Bible as Scripture for the Church.

Deuterocanonical books are in *italics*

Jewish	Catholic	Orthodox*	Protestant
Torah	**Pentateuch**	**Pentateuch**	**Pentateuch**
Genesis Exodus Leviticus Numbers Deuteronomy	Genesis Exodus Leviticus Numbers Deuteronomy	Genesis Exodus Leviticus Numbers Deuteronomy	Genesis Exodus Leviticus Numbers Deuteronomy
Prophets (Former)	**Historical Books**	**Historical Books**	**Historical Books**
Joshua Judges 1-2 Samuel (1-2 Kings) **1** 1-2 Kings (3-4 Kings)	Joshua Judges Ruth 1-2 Samuel (1-2 Kings) **1** 1-2 Kings (3-4 Kings) 1-2 Chronicles 1 Esdras (Ezra, 2 Esdras) **3** 2 Esdras (Nehemiah) *Tobit* *Judith*	Joshua Judges Ruth 1-2 Samuel (1-2 Kings) **1** 1-2 Kings (3-4 Kings) 1-2 Chronicles *1 Esdras (Greek Ezra)* **2** 2 Esdras (1 Esdras, Ezra) **3** 2 Esdras (Nehemiah) *Tobit* *Judith*	Joshua Judges Ruth 1-2 Samuel (1-2 Kings) **1** 1-2 Kings (3-4 Kings) 1-2 Chronicles Ezra (1 Esdras, 2 Esdras) **3** Nehemiah (2 Esdras)
	Esther *(with additions* **4***)* 1-2 Maccabees	Esther *(with additions* **4***)* 1-2 Maccabees 3-4 Maccabees	Esther

Prophets (Latter)			
Isaiah Jeremiah Ezekiel Book of the Twelve 5			
The Writings	**Wisdom Books**	**Wisdom Books**	**Poetic Books**
Psalms Proverbs Job Song of Songs 7 Ruth Lamentations Ecclesiastes Esther Daniel Ezra Nehemiah 1-2 Chronicles	Job Psalms Proverbs Ecclesiastes Song of Songs 7 *Wisdom of Solomon* *Ecclesiasticus (Sirach)* 8	Job Psalms [*Odes* 6] Proverbs Ecclesiastes Song of Songs 7 *Wisdom of Solomon* *Sirach (Ecclesiasticus)* 8	Job Psalms Proverbs Ecclesiastes Song of Songs 7
	Prophets	Prophets	Prophets
	Isaiah Jeremiah Lamentations *Baruch* 9 Ezekiel Daniel (*with additions*) 10 The Twelve 5	Isaiah Jeremiah Lamentations *Baruch* 9 *The Letter of Jeremiah* 9 Ezekiel Daniel (*with additions*) 10 The Twelve 5	Isaiah Jeremiah Lamentations Ezekiel Daniel The Twelve 5

*There are several branches of the Eastern Orthodox tradition that have minor differences in their canons of Scripture.

1 In the Greek tradition (the Septuagint and some modern traditions that follow the Eastern church tradition), 1 and 2 Samuel are combined with the books of Kings, known as 1-4 Kings or 1-4 Kingdoms. In most Protestant canons of the Western Church, the books are known as 1-2 Samuel (1-2 Kings) and 1-2 Kings (3-4 Kings).

2 *1 Esdras* in the Eastern canon is a Greek version of the book of Ezra that contains 99 additional verses not included in the Hebrew version. It is accepted as canonical by the Eastern Orthodox tradition.

3. The books of Ezra and Nehemiah were originally combined into a single book. The combined book, Ezra-Nehemiah, was sometimes referred to as Esdras (Heb: Ezra, Gk: Esdras) but called 1 Esdras in the early Greek translations to distinguish it from another book from the same period (containing 2 Chron 35-36, Neh 7:38-8:12, plus other material not found in the Old Testament) that was also known as Esdras. While this second book was sometimes also called 1 Esdras it later came to be known as 2 Esdras. Still a third pseudepigraphic book of apocalyptic visions entitled Esdras was circulated a little later and was also known as 2 Esdras. After Ezra-Nehemiah was split into two books, Ezra was known as 1 Esdras, Nehemiah as 2 Esdras, the expanded OT version book as 3 Esdras, and the apocalyptic book as 4 Esdras. In the Eastern canon, Ezra and Nehemiah are still combined as one book called 2 Esdras.

<table>
<tr><th>Protestant</th><th>Catholic</th><th>Eastern</th></tr>
<tr><td></td><td></td><td>1 Esdras
(Greek Ezra)</td></tr>
<tr><td>Ezra</td><td>1 Esdras</td><td rowspan="2">2 Esdras</td></tr>
<tr><td>Nehemiah</td><td>2 Esdras</td></tr>
</table>

4. The Book of Esther in the Catholic and Eastern canons adds 103 verses that are not in the Hebrew version or the Protestant canon.

5. The Book of the Twelve contains the remaining 12 prophetic books: Hosea, Joel, Amos, Obadiah, Jonah, Micah, Nahum, Habakkuk, Zephaniah, Haggai, Zechariah, Malachi. These are sometimes called the Minor Prophets in Christian tradition due to their shorter length, while the longer prophetic books are called the Major Prophets.

6. *The Book of Odes* is a collection of fifteen songs or prayers from both the Old Testament (for example, *First Ode of Moses*, Ex 15:1-19; *Prayer of Habakkuk*, Hab 3:2-19), and the New Testament (*Magnificat*, Lk 1:46-55; *Nunc Dimittis*, Lk 2:29-32). It also contains material from various Deuterocanonical writings (Prayer of Azariah, Deuterocanonical Daniel 3:26-45; *Song of the Three Hebrew Youths*, Deuterocanonical Daniel 3:52-88), as well as *Canticle of the Early Morning*, composed from various passages in both Testaments. While it appears in some manuscripts it is not considered canonical by Orthodox traditions. It is usually published as an appendix to the Psalter.

7. Song of Songs is also known as Song of Solomon.

8. Also known as the *Wisdom of Jesus ben Sira*.

9. In the Roman Catholic canon, *Baruch* includes *The Letter of Jeremiah*; in the Eastern Orthodox canon *The Letter of Jeremiah* is a separate book. Neither are present in the Jewish or Protestant canons.

10. Catholic and Eastern canons include Deuterocanonical material in Daniel that is not present in the Jewish or Protestant canons: *The Prayer of Azariah*, *Song of the Three Hebrew Youths*, *Susanna*, and *Bel and the Dragon*.

The first is what scholars call **The Hebrew Canon** or the **Palestinian Canon** (i.e, the one from Jamnia around 90/95 CE). This first canon contains 24 books in the Old Testament. It appears as a reaction to the fall of Jerusalem in 70 CE and responds to the rising Christian movement by "closing of the ranks" in the Jewish community (Pelikan 47). Christians later took the 24—book model and altered it—chopping the collection into 39 books in several ways--such as cutting Samuel into 1st and 2nd Samuel, or dividing the book of minor prophets into twelve separate books). Hebrew scribes prefer in general to classify the Hebrew Canon into three sections (1) The **Torah** (the Law), (2), the **Nebhi'im** (the Prophets), and (3) the **Kethubi'im** (the Writings.) A quick chart illustrates the distinctions here. Protestant Christians divide the Hebrew Canon instead into five groupings: Law, History, Poetry and Wisdom, and the Prophets, a quite different *schemata*.

The **Alexandrian Canon** arose in Alexandria, Egypt, where many Jews resided during the Greek period (c. 330-30 BCE). It was probably about this time that the Jewish tradition developed the idea of an immortal soul. Previously, older books of the Bible often stressed *sheol* ("the grave"), and did not dwell on a potential afterlife. This material doctrine reflected a more traditional religious perspective that persisted even unto the time of Christ, where we still find the Sadducees embracing the older beliefs. Initially, the Alexandrian Jews accepted the Torah (Law) and the Prophets. However, they gradually expanded the canon to include fifteen extra writings. Modern Protestants typically reject these additional books as being apocryphal. The Alexandrian Canon powerfully influenced the medieval/patristic scholar Saint Jerome, who in the late fourth and early fifth century of this era translated the Greek Septuagint (a Greek translation of the Hebrew Bible according to the Alexandrian Canon) into the Latin Vulgate, adding to it the New Testament.

The **Apocrypha** includes fifteen books–1, 2 Esdras; Tobit; Judith; the additions to the Book of Esther; The Wisdom of Solomon; Ecclesiasticus of the Wisdom of Jesus the Son of Sirach; the Letter of Jeremiah; the Prayer of Azariah and the song of the Three Young Men; Susanna; Bel and the Dragon; the Prayer of Manasseh; and 1, 2 Maccabees. These were a standard parat of the Bible until Protestant groups rejected them–and this rejection did not take place until the 16th and 17th centuries. Even editors as late as Martin Luther and the original 1611 King James translation included the Apocrypha, and the Catholic Church still retains them, as witnessed by the contents of any Douay-Rheims Bible from a Catholic bookstore.

The **Pseudepigrapha** (Greek, "false writings") are a collection of writings composed between 200 BCE and 200 CE. They include a number of apocalypses, legendary histories, psalms, and wisdom writings. Often they are attributed to ancient figures such as Adam, Moses, Isaiah, and so on. None of these writings is currently held as canonical by any orthodox Jews or Christians (though the texts may be reverenced in the Coptic church and other groups with more unorthodox beliefs).

The **Dead Sea Scrolls**: These writings were discovered in 1947 near Qumran, a community not far from Jericho located near the Dead Sea. They contain fragments and (in some cases) complete scrolls of every book in the Old Testament except the Book of Esther. Additionally, they contain a number of non-canonical Jewish writings. Essenes, a separatist Jewish sect, wrote the Dead Sea Scrolls, hid them in sealed clay jars, and deposited the containers in caves so they would survive the destruction of Qumran when the Roman army attacked in A. D. 68. (The Romans were *en route* to destroy Jerusalem during the Jewish-Roman War, and stopped briefly to demolish the Essene community.) With the exception of a short fragment from Proverbs, the Dead Sea Scrolls are the oldest biblical manuscripts available as physical artifacts.

The Process of Canonization: Yarbrough describes the process of Hebrew (Old Testament) Canonization as occurring in three stages, but Metzger and Coogan break the canonization of early Christian (New Testament) texts into four stages. Let us deal with the Hebrew Bible first.

(1) The Torah (Law), the first five books of the Old Testament, appeared as a collection possibly as early as the Babylonian captivity. It was probably accepted as authoritative sometime after the Babylonian exile, perhaps during the time of Ezra (5th century BCE). For the Sadducees and the Samaritans, the canonization process stopped here. They argued that none of the later additions to the Hebrew Bible were legitimate.

(2) The **Prophets**, for the Hebrew editors, existed as a collection by at least the second century BCE. The apocryphal book of Ecclesiasticus, the Wisdom of Jesus, the Son of Sirach, had a prologue attached to the work. Sirach's grandson probably did this about 132 BCE. He refers to the "the law and the prophets" and the "others" or the "other books." (See "Prologue,"*Sirach*, RSV Apocrypha, p. 128). This is the earliest evidence we have that the first two parts of the Old Testament Canon had been linked together and anthologized and that the first half of the Canon was on its way to becoming accepted as authoritative.

(3) The **Writings** are the third division of the Hebrew Canon. By the time of Jesus and the early church, we can see the Jews accepted them as authoritative. Luke 24:44 and Matthew 23:35 contain statements strongly indicating the authors already had some vague idea of an authoritative collection--one covering the range from Genesis to Chronicles, the entire range of Old Testament Scripture. Hence, the Old Testament or the Hebrew Bible had gained recognition as official by 90 CE, and it would receive official sanction in the Council of Jamnia.

Selected Bibliography

Achtmeir, Paul J., *Inspiration and Authority: Nature and Function of Christian Scripture.* Peabody: Hendrickson, 1999.

Ackroyd, P. R., *The People of the Old Testament.* Bangalore: United Theological College, 1987.

Ahlström, G. W., *Who were the Israelites?* Winona Lake: Eisenbrauns, 1986.

________., *The History of Ancient Palestine from the Paleolithic Period to Alexander's Conquest.* Sheffiled: Sheffield Academic Press, 1993.

Albertz, Rainer., *A History of Israelite Religion in the Old Testament Period.* Vol. 1. Kentucky: Westminster Press, 1992.

Anderson, A.A., *The Book of Psalms: New Century Bible.* Vol.1 & 2. London: Oliphants, 1972.

Anderson, B. W., *Understanding the Old Testament.* New York: Prentice Hall, 1959.

Anderson, B. W. *Creation Versus Chaos*. New York: Association Press, 1967.

Anderson, G. W., *A Critical Introduction to the Old Testament.* London: Gerald Duckworth, 1979.

Auld, A. G., *Amos.* OT Guide. Sheffield: JSOT Press, 1986.

Aune, D. E., *Prophecy in Early Christianity and the Ancient Mediterranean World.* Grand Rapids: Eerdmans, 1985.

Banks, Diane. *Writing the History of Israel*. New York: T & T Clark, 2006.

Barton J., *Holy Writings, Sacred Texts: The Canon in Early Christianity.* Louisville: Westminster John Knox Press, 1997.

Bergant, Dianne, *Israel's Wisdom Literature: A Liberation-critical Reading.* Minneapolis: Fortress Press, 1997.

Berry, D. K., *An Introduction to Wisdom and Poetry of the Old Testament.* Nashville: Broadman & Holman, 1995.

Birch, Bruce C., *et al., A Theological Introduction to the Old Testament.* Nashville: Abingdon Press, 2005. Second Edition.

Blenkinsopp, Joseph. *The Pentateuch: An Introduction to the First Five Books of the Bible*. New York: Double-day, 1992.

Blenkinsopp, Joseph., *A History of Prophecy in Israel.* Philadelphia: Westminster John Knox Press, 1996.

Blenkinsopp, Joseph., *Wisdom and Law in the Old Testament: The Ordering of Life in Israel and Early Judaism.* Oxford: Oxford University Press, 1995.

Bright, John, *The History of the Israel*. Philadelphia: Westminster Press, 1981. Third Edition.

Brown, William P., *Character in Crisis: A Fresh Approach to Wisdom Literature of Old Testament.* Grand Rapids: Eerdmans, 1996.

Brueggemann, W. and H.W. Wolff, *The Vitality of Old Testament Traditions*. Atlanta: John Knox Press, 1982 (2nd Edition).

Ceresko, Anthony R., *The Old Testament: A Liberation Perspective*. Mumbai: St. Paul's, 2009. Revised Edition.

Childs, Brevard S., *Introduction to the Old Testament as Scripture*. Philadelphia: Fortress Press, 1980. Second Print.

Childs, B.S. *Exodus*. London: SCM Press, 1974.

Clements, R. E., *Prophecy and Covenant.* London: SCM Press, 1965.

_____________., *Prophecy and Tradition.* London: Basil Blackwell, 1975.

Clifford, Richard, J., *Wisdom Literature*. Nashville: Abingdon Press, 1998.

Clines, D. J. A., *He, We and They A Literary Approach to Isaiah 53.* Sheffield: JSOT Press, 1983. JSOT Supplement Series 1.

Coggins, Richard., Anthony Phillips and Michael Knibb (eds)., *Israel's Prophetic Tradition; Essays in honour of Peter Ackroyd.* Cambridge: Cambridge University Press, 1981.

Coggins, R. J., *Haggai. Zechariah, Malachi.* OT Guides. Sheffield: JSOT Press, 1987.

Collins, John J., *Daniel with an Introduction to Apocalyptic Literature*. Grand Rapids: Wm. B. Eerdmans, 1984.

Coogan, Michael D., *The Old Testament: A Historical and Literary Introduction to the Hebrew Scriptures*. Oxford: Oxford University Press, 2006.

Craigie, Peter., *The Old Testament: Its Background, Growth and Content.* Nashville: Abingdon Press, 1986.

Crenshaw, James L., *Ecclesiastes.* London: SCM Press, 1988.

Crenshaw, J. L., *Old Testament Wisdom: An Introduction.* Atlanta: John Knox Press, 1981.

Crenshaw, J. L., *Ecclesiastes: A Commentary.* Old Testament Library. London: SCM Press, 1988.

Crenshaw, J. L., *Urgent Advice and Probing Questions.* Mercer: Mercer University Press, 1995.

Davies, E. V., *Prophecy and Ethics: Isaiah and the Ethical Traditions of Israel.* Sheffield: JSOT Press, 1981. JSOT Supplement 16.

Davis, Ellen F., *Getting Involved with God: Rediscovering the Old Testament.* Cambridge, Massachusetts: Cowley, 2001.

Davis, Ellen F., *Proverbs, Ecclesiastes and the Song of Songs.* Louisville: Westminster John Knox Press, 2000.

Day, John, *Psalms: OT Study Guides.* Sheffield: JSOT Press, 1993. Reprint Edition.

Dell, Katharine J., *Book of Job as Skeptical Literature.* Berlin: Walter De Gruyter, 1991.

Dever, William G. *Who Were the Early Israelites and Where Did they Come From?* Grand Rapids: Wm. B. Eerdmans, 2003.

Eissefeldt, O., *The Old Testament: An Introduction.* San Francisco: Harper, 1965.

Ellison, H. L., *Men Spoke from God.* Milton Keynes: Paternoster, 1973.

Esler, Philip, ed., *Ancient Israel: The Old Testament and in its Social Context.* Minneapolis: Fortress Press, 2005.

Fohrer, Georg., *Introduction to the Old Testament.* London: SPCK, 1976.

Fox, M. V., *A Time to Tear Down and a Time to Build Up: A Re-reading of Ecclesiastes.* Grand Rapids: William B. Eerdmans, 1999.

Garbini, G., *History and Ideology, in Ancient Israel*, Trans. J. Bowden, New York: Crossroads, 1988.

Goldingay, John., *God's Prophets God's Servant: A Study of Jeremiah and Isaiah 40-55.* Milton Keynes: Paternoster Press, 1984.

Gottwald, Norman K., *The Hebrew Bible: A Socio-Literary Introduction.* Philadelphia: Fortress Press, 1987. Reprint Edition.

___________., *The Hebrew Bible in its Social Word and Ours.* Atlanta: Scholars Press, 1993.

Gowan, Donald. E., *Theology in Exodus.* Louisville: Westminster John Knox Press, 2005.

Gowan, Donald E., *Theology of the Prophetic Books: The Death and Resurrection of Israel.* Louisville: Westminster John Knox, 1998.

Grabbe, Lester L., *Priests, Prophets, Diviners and Sages: A Socio-Historical Study of Religious Specialists in Ancient Israel.* Valley Forge, PA: Trinity Press International, 1995.

Gunkel, Hermann., *Psalms: A Form-Critical Introduction.* E.T. Thomas M. Horner, Philadelphia: Fortress Press, 1963.

Habel, Norman C., *The Book of Job: Old Testament Library.* London: SCM Press, 1985.

Hanson, Paul D., *The Dawn of the Apocalyptic.* Philadelphia: Fortress Press, 1975.

Harrison, R. K., *Introduction to the Old Testament.* Peabody, Massachusetts: Hendrickson Publishers, 2016. Revised Edition.

Hartman, Louis F, and Alexander A. Di Lella., *The Book of Daniel: The Anchor Bible*. Vol. 23. Garden City, New York: Doubleday & Co, 1977.

Heaton, E. W., *The Old Testament Prophets.* London: Dalton, Longman & Todd, 1977.

Horsley, Richard., *Scribes, Visionaries, and the Politics of the Second Temple Judea*. Louisville: WJK Press, 2007.

Jesurathnam, K., "A Dalit interpretation of Wisdom Literature with special reference to the underprivileged groups in the Hebrew society: A Mission perspective," Peniel Jesudason Rufus Rajkumar, Joseph Prabhakar Dayam and I. P. Asheervadham (eds), *Mission at and from the Margins: Patterns, Protogonists and Perspectives* (Oxford: Regnum Books International, 2014), pp. 179-199.

Jesurathnam, K., Abraham Saggu and Hranagthan Chhungi (eds)., *Liberation Hermeneutics in the Indian Interpretation of the Bible*. Bangalore/ Thiruvalla: Society for Biblical Studies in India/Christava Sahitya Samithi, 2012.

Johnson, A. R., *The Cultic Prophet in Ancient Israel.* Cardiff: University of Wales Press, 1962.

Johnstone, W. *Exodus* (Old Testament Guides). Sheffield: JSOT Press, 1990. Reprint, 1995.

Kaiser, Otto., *Introduction to the Old Testament*. Translated by John Sturdy. Oxford: Basil Blackwell. 1975.

Knight, G. F. A., *Deutero-Isaiah: A Theological Commentary on Isaiah 40-55.* Nashville: Abingdon Press, 1985.

Koch, Klaus., *The Prophets: The Assyrian Period.* Vol. I. Philadelphia: Fortress Press, 1982.

______________., *The Prophets: The Babylonian and Persian Periods.* Vol. II. London: SCM Press, 1983.

Kraus, Hans, J., *Psalms 1-59: A Commentary.* Vol. I. Trans. Hilton C. Oswald. Minneapolis: Augsburg, 1988.

______., *Psalms 60-150; A Commentary*. Vol. II. Trans H. C. Oswald. Minneapolis: Augsburg, I989.

______., *Theology of Psalms.* Trans. Keith Crim. Minneapolis: Augsburg Publishing House, 1986.

Laffey, Alice., *The Pentateuch: A Liberation-Critical Reading*. Minneapolis: Fortress Press, 1998.

Lemche, Niels Peter., *Early Israel: Anthropological and Historical Studies on the Israelite State before the Monarchy.* Leiden: E. J. Brill, 1985.

_________., *Ancient Israel: A New History of Israelite Society*. Sheffield: JSOT Press, 1988.

_________., *The Israelites in History and Tradition*. Louisville: WJK Press, 1998.

Lindblom, J., *Prophecy in Ancient Israel.* London: Basil Black Well, 1963.

Luke, K., *TPI Companion to the Bible: Bible in General & Old Testament.* Vol. 1. Bangalore: Theological Publications in India, 1987.

Mckane, W., *Proverbs: A New Approach*. London, SCM Press, 1970.

Melugin, R. F., *The Formation of Isaiah 40-55.* Berlin: Walter de Gruyter, 1976.

Menezes, Rui De., *The Cultural Context of the Old Testament*. Bangalore: Theological Publications in India, 2005.

Miller, Patrick D., *Interpreting the Psalms*. Philadelphia: Fortress Press, 1986.

Murphy, Roland E., *Wisdom Literature: Job, Proverbs, Ruth, Canticles, Ecclesiastes and Esther*. Grand Rapids: Eerdmans, 1983. Reprint Edition.

Nickelsburg, George W. E., *Jewish Literature between the Bible and the Mishnah.* Philadelphia: Fortress Press, 1981.

Noth, Martin., *The History of Israel*. London: SCM Press, 1983. Revised Edition.

Noth, Martin., *A History of Pentateuchal Traditions*. New Jersey, Englewood Cliffs, 1972.

Perdue, Leo G., *Sword and the Stylus: An Introduction to Wisdom in the Age of Empires.* Grand Rapids: Abingdon Press, 2008.

Prichard, J. B. (ed)., *Ancient Near Eastern Texts Relating to the Old Testament.* Princeton: Princeton University Press, 1969. Third Edition.

Ramsey, George W., *The Quest for the Historical Israel*. Atlanta: Westminster John Knox Press, 1981.

Rendtorff, R., *The Old Testament: An Introduction*. London: SCM Press, 1985.

Roberts, J. J. M., *Nahum, Habakkuk and Nehemiah: A Commentary*, OTL. Louisville: Westminster John Knox Press, 1991.

Robinson, T. H., *Prophecy and Prophets in Ancient Israel*. London: Duckworth, 1980.

Rofe, Alexander., *Introduction to Prophetic Literature*. Sheffield: Sheffield Academic Press, 1997.

Rowley, H. H., *The OT and the Modern Study.* Oxford: Clarendon Press, 1951.

_________ (ed)., *Studies in O.T. Prophecy. Edinburgh:* T & T Clark, 1950.

Russell, Letty M., *Feminist Interpretation of the Bible*. Philadelphia: Westminster, 1985.

Sawyer, J. F. A., *Prophecy and the Prophets of the Old Testament.* Oxford: Oxford University Press, 1987.

Schmidt, W. H., *Old Testament Introduction*. Bombay: St. Paul's, 1992.

Schmithals, Walter., *The Apocalyptic Movement: Introduction & Interpretation.* Translated by John E. Steely. Nashville: Abingdon Press, 1975.

Soggin, J. Alberto., *Introduction to the Old Testament*. London: SCM Press, 1980. Revised Edition.

Thompson, Thomas L., *Early History of the Israelite People from the Written and Archaeological Sources*. Leiden: Brill, 1992.

Vaux, Roland de., *Ancient Israel: Its Life and Institutions*. Trans. John McHugh. London: Dalton, Longman & Todd, 1961. Reprint by Eerdmans in 1997.

von Rad, Gerhard., *Old Testament Theology.* Vol. I & II. Trans. D. M. G. Stalker. London: SCM Press and Oliver & Boyd, 1962-1965.

von Rad, Gerhard., *Wisdom in Israel*, London: SCM Press, 1972.

Wallace, Ronald S., *Readings in 1 Kings.* Grand Rapids: Wm. B. Eerdmans, 1995.

Westermann, Claus; *Genesis 1-11: A Commentary*. SPCK: London, 1984.

Westermann, Claus., *Basic Forms of Prophetic Speech.* Louisville: Westminster John Knox Press, 1991. Reprint Edition.

Westermann, Claus., *Praise and Lament in the Psalms*. Atlanta. John Knox Press 1981.

_________, *Isaiah 40-55: Old Testament Library.* London: SCM Press, 1978.

_________, *Roots of Wisdom: The Oldest Proverbs of Israel and other Peoples.* Trans. J. Daryl Charles Louisville: Westminster John Knox Press, 1995.

Whitelam, K. W., *The Invention of Ancient Israel: The Silencing of Palestinian History*. London: Routledge, 1996.

Whybray, R. N., *Isaiah 40-66: New Century Bible.* Grand Rapids: Eerdmans 1981.

_________, *Ecclesiastes: The New Century Bible Commentary*. Grand Rapids: Eerdmans, 1989.

Widengren, Geo., "The Persian Period." In *Israelite and Judean History.* Edited by John H. Hayes and Maxwell Miller. London: SCM Press, 1990. Reprint Edition.

Wielanga, B., *It is a Long Road to Freedom*. Madurai: Tamilnadu Theological Seminary, 1981.

Williamson, H. G. M., *Word Bible Commentary: Ezra, Nehemiah* Vol. 16. Waco, Texas: Word Books, 1985.

Wilson, Robert R., *Prophecy and Society and Ancient Israel.* Philadelphia: Fortress Press, 1980.

Wolf, Herbert., *An Introduction to the Old Testament Pentateuch.* Chicago: Moody Press, 1991.

Wright, Christopher., *Living as the People of God: The Relevance of the Old Testament.* London: InterVarsity Press, 1983.

Young, E. J., *My Servants, the Prophets,* Eerdmans, 1952.

_________, *An Introduction to the Old Testament.* London: The Tyndale Press, 1960. Revised Edition.

Zevit, Ziony., *The Religions of Ancient Israel: A Synthesis of Parallelactic Approaches.* New York: Continuum, 2001.